Sex ratio patterns in the Indian population

Sex ratio patterns in the Indian population

A fresh exploration

Satish Balram Agnihotri

Sage Publications
New Delhi • Thousand Oaks • London

First published in 2000 by

Sage Publications India Pvt Ltd
M–32 Market, Greater Kailash Part–I
New Delhi–110 048

Sage Publications Inc
2455 Teller Road
Thousand Oaks, California 91320

Sage Publications Ltd
6 Bonhill Street
London EC2A 4PU

Published by Tejeshwar Singh for Sage Publications India Pvt Ltd, lasertypeset by Accurate Graphics, Pondicherry, and printed at Chaman Enterprises, Delhi.

Library of Congress Cataloging-in-Publication Data

Agnihotri, Satish Balram, 1955–
    Sex ratio patterns in the Indian population: a fresh exploration / Satish Balram Agnihotri.
        p.   cm.
    Includes bibliographical references (p.   ) and index.
    1. Sex distribution (Demography)—India.   I. Title.
HB1889.A35   305.3'0954—dc21   1999   99–37984

ISBN: 0–7619–9392–4 (US–hb)   81–7036–867–7 (India–hb)

Sage Production Team: Abantika Chatterji, M.S.V. Namboodiri and Santosh Rawat

To Anita

who nudged me into this adventure;
gently yet firmly.

Contents

List of tables

List of figures

List of maps

List of abbreviations

*	significant at 10 per cent level
**	significant at 5 per cent level
***	significant at 1 per cent level
Adj. R. Sq.	adjusted R-square
AMPCE	average monthly per capita expenditure
Ann.	Annexure
AP	Andhra Pradesh
CMR	child mortality rates (1–4 year age group)
FFLP	family female labour participation
FLP	female labour participation
FMR	female–male ratio
FMR04	FMR in the 0–4 year age group
FMR09	FMR in the 0–9 year age group
FMR59	FMR in the 5–9 year age group
ICSSR	Indian Council of Social Science Research
IIPS	International Institute of Population Science
IMR	infant mortality rate (0–1 year age group)
JFMR	juvenile female to male ratio
MP	Madhya Pradesh
MW	main workers
MWW	main women workers
NFHS	National Family Health Survey
NSSO	National Sample Survey Organisation
PCE	per capita expenditure
SC	Scheduled Castes
ST	Scheduled Tribes
TN	Tamil Nadu
TW	total workers
TWW	total working women (main + marginal)
UP	Uttar Pradesh

Foreword

I agreed to write this foreword with full knowledge of my lack of competence. My familiarity with Satish Agnihotri's work and personality extends over some years, even if I am not in a position to comment on the quality of the tools that he has used for his analysis. It has been my fortunate (or unfortunate) role during the last quarter of a century to challenge many eminent specialists in quantitative analysis to 'check their own data' and methods in order to identify where and how they made women invisible by discarding the data available on them for any critical analysis. This of course applies particularly to economists but it also applie to many eminent demographers (with some honourable exceptions).

Dr Agnihotri's case is, however, very different. One cannot pin him down as a product of any single discipline—he seems to have acquired so many. A scientist, with a social conscience strong enough to familarise himself with considerable knowledge of many social sciences, a researcher with the purpose and mentality of an activist, and a man who has not allowed his bureaucratic profession to blunt either his intellectual curiosity or his sense of fairplay and justice: these are the qualities which make him exceptional. He appears to have avoided the spreading cynicism among successful members of his generation and profession.

In the course of his work on this volume, he visited many scholars in India and abroad, not only to discuss his project but also to show them his respect for the questions raised by them (possibly a decade ago) on the meaning of India's declining sex ratio. At least three of them called me to say how impressed they had been by the quality of his mind and the earnestness of his purpose. And all this was before he arrived in Delhi with the specific purpose of meeting me. His bubbling enthusiasm and excitement was infectious. In spite of the gaps of age and discipline between us, we had no problem in communicating.

With the increasing disappearance of male members of what I used to call the 'freedom generation' (whose members had became adults between 1927 and 1947) who became allies and ardent supporters of the women's studies movement that followed the Report of the Committee on the Status of Women in India, some of us were beginning to worry with the indifference and even occasional hostility amongst the younger generation, men in particular. Here was a representative who did not fit that stereotype. As he talked, it was easy to see that it was not only intellectual ambition that had driven him into this study. Something much more was involved. His actions since the study was completed confirmed all my expectations. My guru, J.P. Naik, had he been around, would have been equally happy to find a young person who believed that research can also be a tool for action.

Readers of this volume will find strong evidence for this assessment scattered through the book. His strategy of closing many 'favourite escape hatches' of other quantitative analysis was not used to score points but to challenge all those who are guilty of trying to explain away uncomfortable secular trends in data instead of asking the basic questions—why and how.

The fact that the author has been driven to ask an activist with no background of quantitative analysis to write this foreword is a proof of this rather harsh statement. Since raising questions is the *raison d'etre* of women's studies, I have already extended a warm welcome to this new entrant into our ranks. The new skills and methodology that he has brought to this area, and the combination of an interdisciplinary approach and innovative rigour visible in his use of theories, data, hypotheses and conclusions from many fields—economics, demography, development studies, and cultural studies—would have delighted many of the old friends and allies whom we have lost recently.

It is a pity that we could not get the book out before the demise of Asok Mitra, the first Indian to highlight and question the declining sex ratio, or of M.N. Srinivasan who always looked for the 'worm's eye view' being used in the process of developing a 'bird's eye view'—one of the reasons for his appreciation of the approach developed by the Committee on the Status of Women in India CSWI and Women's Studies.

He would have also enjoyed the way the author has used maps and tables to project the dynamics of cultural change apparent through the use of data at different points in time. The expanding black regions in Agnihotri's maps ought to convince anyone with an open mind (and some conscience) that female foeticide and female infanticide are two faces of the same phenomenon where tradition and modernity are not in opposition but in strong alliance—destined to lead to what Ashish Bose calls 'social turbulence'. It should make such readers look for the common factor which explains both, and should urge them to join us in influencing the discourse on population policy.

Even from its very beginning, women's studies in India discovered that the source of women's oppression does not lie only in poverty, illiteracy, malnutrition and the like, but also in prosperity. All of us would thank Agnihotri for the way in which he questions the 'prosperity effect'. I have always admired a scholar bold enough to challenge dominant theories and authorities. The CSWI's exercise was, to a great extent, a very risky gamble—inferring conclusions to give meaning to the oral evidence that it had gathered, and challenging wide ranging dominant understandings of the structure and dynamics of Indian society and its development. It is very heartening to find some of the inferences and hypotheses developed over the last quarter of a century being substantiated so skillfully by a young scholar.

Lastly, I thank the author for providing us with a very powerful tool to question the advocates of measurable indices for human development, human rights, gender empowerment and social development. Over the last 20 years, my sisters and teachers from the peasant communities of India have convinced me that if the Indian nation is ever to acquire a really just social order, the leaders of that revolution have to come from those whom we were taught to view as the least civilised and the most backward. I asked the late Professor Mahbub ul Huq if in the light of Agnihotri's analysis he would accept the validity of my question: In the Indian subcontinent who is more socially developed? The Adivasis, who do not dispose off their daughters by one method or another, or the rest of us? He noted the question but did not live to provide the answer. Fortunately, at my age I can afford to indulge in emotive language, risking my identity as a social scientist. I was brought up to believe that I must always weigh the consequences of my action—right or wrong—in my own lifetime. But just in case I have to be reborn may I wish to be an Adivasi woman in India.

Thank you, Satish!

Vina Mazumdar
Chairperson
Centre for Women's Development Studies
New Delhi, 25th December 1999

Preface

This book examines an issue of long standing concern: the low and declining proportion of women in India's population. The concern is not new. The high masculine sex ratios of the Indian population had been noted with concern nearly a century ago. It is not only the low female to male ratio (FMR henceforth), but also its steady and continuous decline, the regional variations in it and its likely correlates that have attracted considerable attention throughout this century. The attention covers both academic and policy discourse and has increased our understanding of the problem considerably. These analyses have more or less established that the high masculine sex ratios are a result of discrimination against the female members of society, giving rise to excess female over male mortality.

Why another attempt then? A number of reasons could be cited. First, the conventional analyses had reached a plateau of sorts and fresh grounds for discussion and further research were not being broken. One reason for this, it is felt, was that most of the analyses were not adequately sensitive to the diversities in the sex ratio patterns. These diversities occur along different dimensions, such as social, regional, cultural and even age group dimensions. The analysis presented here disaggregates sex ratio data along these dimensions and that is its chief feature.

The other major reason for making a fresh exploration was that the 1981 Census data had not been analysed in adequate detail. The two landmark contributions in the past, Visaria (1971) and Miller (1981), were based on the analysis of the 1961 Census data. A similar analysis of the 1981 data was not forthcoming. Perhaps the marginal increase in the female to male ratio in the 1981 Census, against the backdrop of a steady decline throughout the century, had created false a sense of complaisance. In fact, during the mid-eighties and before the final results of the 1991 Census were out, there appears to have been a 'lull' in the analysis of this problem. The decline in the ratio from 934 females per 1,000 males in 1981 to 927 females per 1,000 males in 1991 has given fresh impetus to discussions on this issue. The present analysis presents one such attempt.

This book is a result of about five year's obsession with the topic, first pursued as part of my MA dissertation followed by my doctoral thesis. The obsession began with a simple curiosity regarding the sex ratio figure at the all-India level. Since the tribal groups are known to be more equitable towards their female folk, it was plausible to expect less masculine sex ratios among them than among the non-tribals. In other words, the all-India average overstated the extent of the problem for one group, i.e., the tribals, and understated it for other group i.e., the non-tribals. It emerged, and surprisingly so, that the sex ratios of the tribal and the non-tribal segments of the population, and among the latter, the Scheduled Castes and the non-Scheduled Castes had not been systematically analysed in the received literature separately. Such analysis, using the state-level population data from the 1961 to the 1991 Census was first presented by me at the IASP (Indian Association for the Study of Population) annual conference at Bhubaneswar in 1992. This later appeared in the *Economic and Political Weekly* (Agnihotri, 1995a) and was titled 'Missing females: A disaggregated analysis'. It sowed the seeds of most of the disaggregated analysis done subsequently and brought home the need for a separate analysis of the sex ratio data for the three social segments of the Indian society and the seriousness of the problem among the Scheduled Caste population in the northern states of the country.

In my subsequent research, I used the sex ratio data for the juvenile age group population (0–9 year age group) instead of the overall population sex ratios. This turned out to be an appropriate strategy for more than one reason. Foremost among these is that the juvenile age group is not affected by sex-selective migration, a major 'noise' affecting the sex ratio data.

But the use of juvenile sex ratio (JSR) data offered further advantages. The major among these was the revelation that it is the sex differentials in juvenile mortality in South Asia that renders the overall sex ratios so masculine. This is one feature which sets contemporary South Asia apart from many other societies of the past, for example, pre-industrial Europe, 19th century USA or Meiji-era Japan. These societies also discriminated against the girl child. But such discrimination rarely affected the survival of female children below the age of 10 years as adversely as it does in South Asia today. Mortality levels in the juvenile age group being quite high compared to later decades, sex differentials in them have a much stronger impact on the sex ratios than the sex differentials in mortality in later years can have.

Attempts to link the sex differentials in juvenile mortality with their demographic consequence, that is, the sex ratio patterns, opened up another fascinating research area. This has been discussed in details in Chapter 3, the first substantive chapter. It also paved the way for separate analysis of the sex ratios in the two 5-year age groups that is, the 0–4 and 5–9 age groups. Of these, the latter emerges as the most effective indicator of the discrimination effect against the girl child.

Separate analysis of the sex ratio patterns in the 0–4 and the 5–9 year age groups helped to close certain escape hatches which recur in the literature and in policy debates. Under-enumeration of female children and the biological propensity of the Indian women to give birth to male children are the two among them. The tendency to use these two escape hatches to explain away or deny the problem of low FMRs is surprisingly strong within the demographic circles. This analysis counters such tendency and suggests steps that can be taken in the 2001 Census to confront these escape hatches once and for all.

A more enlightening use of the separate analysis of the 0–4 and the 5–9 year age group sex ratio has been made through the district-level mapping of the sex ratios. These maps reveal an amazing spatial contiguity in the FMR values and provide useful insights into the regional aspects of the sex ratio patterns (Chapters 4 and 5) highlighting various 'contours' of low and high sex ratios. Regional studies have a strong tradition in India. But these have not taken the gender dimensions of survival on board. The approach above can provide a suitable scope for doing so.

Spatial effects are a combination of both ecology and culture. The maps mentioned above also provide valuable insights into the cultural aspects of gender disparities. The traditional 'north–south' divide characterising the Indian space in many contexts, is modified through the identification of two different kinship systems, the Indo-Aryan and the 'rest' (Chapter 5). The close association between the Indo-Aryan kinship system, the culture of female subordination and the adverse female vis-à-vis male survival, revealed in the analysis (Chapters 5, 7 and 8) calls for a more detailed debate.

The factors used for disaggregation of the sex ratio patterns are also useful when it comes to examining the correlates of these patterns. This is effectively demonstrated in Chapter 7 which examines the role of female work force participation in female survival. This role has been examined before but the disaggregated approach sharpens the analysis considerably. It also quantifies the interaction between cultural factors and female work force participation. Such quantification has, in my opinion, not been attempted so far and has important policy implications.

Another important dimension of the sex ratio patterns which has been overlooked so far, has been the prosperity dimension. Increasingly, adverse survival conditions for females among the more prosperous regions/groups have been reported in sociological and anthropological literature. Economic literature, however, considers this to be counter-intuitive and has of late been arguing in terms of an inverse-U or a Kuznets curve-like pattern: the gender-based inequality would first increase with prosperity and will eventually decrease beyond a 'turning point'. An attempt is made to resolve this debate (Chapter 8) by examining the role of female contribution to prosperity rather than prosperity per se. Needless to say, the female contribution to prosperity turns out to be more relevant for her survival than prosperity itself. A disturbing trend emerges during the analysis of the recent NSSO (National Sample Survey Organisation) data which reveals unusually masculine sex ratios among the more prosperous groups even in the more female-friendly regions of southern India. The results are tentative but constitute an important and urgent research agenda.

The theoretical backdrop of the analysis presented draws heavily on Amartya Sen's three seminal contributions: his entitlements framework, the cooperative–conflict model of the allocational behaviour within a household and the capabilities approach to wellbeing. In doing so, certain important modifications have been made to these approaches (Chapter 6). The attempts to put the overall gender disparities in a coherent theoretical framework have much to gain from the approach I have taken. This is an exciting area for further work although it is beyond the scope of this study.

The study opens up a number of avenues for further research. But it also generates an agenda for policy. The disaggregated approach, in fact, allows the policy interventions to be planned for smaller manageable segments whether regional or social. It facilitates as well as demands plurality in policy planning. This is discussed in the final chapter 'Bringing it all together'. Many of the assertions there, in fact, support the intuitive and qualitative concerns raised by various sociological and anthropological studies.

This is one feature of the analysis that needs emphasis. The analysis is interdisciplinary and has built bridges among different approaches to the problem. This is partly a result of my being an 'outsider' in a disciplinary sense given my original background in physics at the master's level followed by masters degrees in environmental science, engineering and rural development. This perhaps helped me in not getting held down by the prejudices which had currency within different disciplines or feel deterred by the barriers that existed across these disciplines. A majority of the new grounds that have been broken in this analysis, listed in the concluding chapter, are a result of this. Some of these look quite straightforward, even trivial, with hindsight, but only with hindsight.

While the interdisciplinarity of the approach was useful in the long run, in the short run it created its own anxious moments—some funny, some agonizing and some others frustrating. For an anthropologist what I was doing was 'interesting' but not 'proper' anthropology. For an economist what I was doing was 'interesting' but not 'proper' economics. You can substitute demography, or sociology for the discipline, the results were similar. This was further compounded by my not 'belonging' to any of these disciplines and yet having the 'audacity' to advocate and put forth new approaches and methods.

A similar difficulty presented itself regarding the level of rigour to be used in the analysis. To me different analytical techniques were not an end in themselves, these were useful tools to examine a point and establish it or reject it. These were used to the extent that they were necessary but without going to the other extreme like Jerome's *Three (prudent) men in a boat* who decided to carry with them only such baggage that they could not do without rather than all the baggage that they could do with! But then the so-called 'softer' sciences would consider my analysis to be too 'techy' and trying to establish the 'obvious'. I have actually run into anthropologists who have said to me, 'But have we not been saying this all along?' On the other hand so-called 'hard' science circles showed disdain for my analysis for it was not rigorous enough or at least did not use the standard techniques they had been used to. Engaging with both these groups was useful for it sharpened my skills in presenting an argument. But there were times when I wished for a more sympathetic attitude.

It is in this context, that I owe a great debt to people like Ashish Bose, Jean Drèze, Barbara Harriss-White, Amartya Sen, Basia Zaba and my supervisors Richard Palmer-Jones and Cecile Jackson. They went beyond the narrow confines of discipline and rigour encouraged the good arguments and sifted out the silly ones without being derisive. This kept my spirits and research going. As far as the outcome is concerned I leave it to the reader, for, the proof of the pudding lies in its eating.

Where does this place the reader of this book? Given the wide range of readers who would find this analysis useful or interesting, I have essentially followed a 'twin track' approach. Those readers who can trust me with the technical parts of the analysis can skim through them paying more detailed attention to the interpretation. To facilitate their task, each chapter has a detailed outline in the beginning. It presents a gist of what the chapter elaborates and indicates the sequence in which different sections unfold. Those readers who have an inclination for engaging with the algebra or the statistics are welcome to wade through it and form their own conclusion and suggest additions, modifications or improvements. I will be thankful for these suggestions.

Most of my analysis has used the data from the 1961 and 1981 Censuses, National Family Health Survey (NFHS) 1992–93 and the NSSO data from the 43rd and the 50th rounds but not the 1991 Census data. The reader may be surprised to know that certain important parts of the 1991 Census data, for example, the 5-year age group data, were not available even until the middle of 1997 (when I finished my doctoral programme). It is likely to be another year before some other relevant details, for example, the ones related to the Scheduled Caste and Scheduled Tribe population become available. However, important lessons for the Census of 2001 can be drawn from the data available up to 1981 and these have been outlined. In addition, the available details from the 1991 data have been analysed in Chapter 9. These not only corroborate the overall results of the earlier analysis but open up some more exciting areas of analysis of child mortality data and its gender dimensions. The analysis presented in Chapter 9 essentially takes my doctoral research a step further.

The rest of the book is more or less an unabridged version of my Ph.D. thesis. I have kept it so on purpose and have instead incorporated the analysis of the 1991 Census data in an individual chapter. This is because I wanted the reader to share with me some of the flavour of this journey which is still unfinished. The scope for further research is quite large and any reader interested in pursuing it will benefit by seeing the trajectory I have traversed. The general reader too will find these details useful. These portray the process as it evolved rather than an ex post facto pretension of a 'neat', classical, scientific sequence of a well thought out hypothesis, experiment, data and the testing of the hypothesis. But real life processes never follow such a 'neat' route. They are messy, clumsy and tentative and data and theory interact iteratively. Yet they can be equally challenging intellectually, or more perhaps, and certainly more rewarding when discernible patterns are revealed.

The analytical chapter has been retained in toto on purpose. Application of Sen's different approaches to the field of gender inequalities is relatively new but has a very vast potential. Sen has himself elaborated on it at different places. To extend this application further, certain modification to these approaches are needed especially to integrate his capabilities approach to wellbeing and the entitlements approach. The analytical chapter elaborates these. But since some of these aspects have been developed for the first time here these are not available in published literature. It is important therefore, that it reaches the wider audience interested in the questions of gender-based inequalities which are critically linked to the issues of entitlements, wellbeing and the intra-household allocational behaviour. These two fields have much to gain from each other and the interested reader can then take the analysis further in that direction.

A word of apology would be in order at this juncture. While this analysis has been based on district-wise all-India data, it does not analyse the data for the north-eastern states in adequate details. First, this happened due to the limitations imposed by the form in which the data were available. Second, the focus of this analysis was more on the central Indian tribal belt, which constitutes about 70 per cent of the country's tribal population. I intend making amends for this 'gap' at a future date through a separate analysis of the sex ratio patterns in the north-eastern region.

Finally, let me admit that prior to 1991, if there were any suggestions that I would be doing any research in the field of gender inequalities I would have dismissed these with a hearty laugh. In fact, when Cecile Jackson asked why I had not taken any modules on gender while doing my MA in rural development, I had replied that it was better to do on ounce of practice than a ton of theory, only to eat my words rather rapidly. I ended up doing half a ton or so of theory! But it was a rewarding and fulfilling experience. I am sure that the readers will be able to share some of this sense of fulfilment with me.

Acknowledgements

First of all, I would like to thank my supervisors, Dr Richard Palmer-Jones and Dr Cecile (Sam) Jackson for their patience, support and guidance during my doctoral studies. While Professor Dereyke Belshaw, who earlier supervised my MA dissertation (1991–92), had taught me how to maintain the 'line and length' of a narration, Richard showed me how to handle its pace, the swing and occasionally, the spin. From Sam, I learnt to follow the spirit of the game. All three of them actively encouraged me to publish papers independently, a trend I have continued to follow.

In an interdisciplinary inquiry of this nature, support from sympathetic experts in individual disciplines is invaluable. This is particularly so if the researcher is an 'outsider' in terms of discipline, which I was given my original background in physics and environmental science. I, therefore, owe a great deal of debt to Ashish Bose, Tony Burton, Jean Drèze, Nancy Folbre, Barbara Harriss-White, P.D. Joshi, Amartya Sen, Bob Sugden and Basia Zaba for their support and encouragement. Amartya Sen and Jean Drèze in particular, have given me constant encouragement since 1991 even though they had to put up with many of my 'leaps of faith' and ideas in their raw form.

Taking this narration from a doctoral thesis to a book could not have been easy without the support from LEAD (Leadership in Environment and Development) International, New York, Professor Amartya Sen, Vina Mazumdar of CWDS (Centre for Women's Development Studies), who kindly agreed to write the foreword and Omita Goyal of Sage. The Fellowship programme support from LEAD allowed me the space to write the doctoral thesis in a form which could be quickly converted into a book. Vina*di*'s persuasion (read threats!) made me approach Sage. Omita Goyal's response was positive and prompt once the anonymous referee recommended the manuscript. She and Abantika Chatterji have gone about editing the manuscript painstakingly. I am grateful to all of them.

The patience showed by Anita and my children, Anushtubh and Srishti, enabled me to pursue this research with a free mind. I owe a special debt to Anita for handling the burden of double parenthood admirably and uncomplainingly. Anushtubh's interest in helping me with preparation of certain tables and maps and Srishti's enthusiastic 'supervision' of the two of us were a sheer source of joy. My parents were enthusiastic and supportive as ever.

Pursuing this research would have been difficult without suitable financial support. I must thank the University of East Anglia and the School of Development Studies for the award of scholarship and the Government of Orissa for granting me the necessary study leave.

There are many friends and well wishers to whom I am thankful for their support. It is difficult to name all of them. But I must thank both my sisters, Leena Mehendale and Chhaya Korde, Gaurang and Ila Dave, Helen Derbyshire, Liz Gibson, Laxmi and Mark Holsrom, M. Kutralingam, Ajay Mittal, Steph Simpson, Ajanta Sarkar, K.N. Unni and Francis and John Wilson, in particular.

If, after all this help, I have made any errors or mistakes, I have only myself to blame!

Chapter 1

Introduction

I

The story in a nutshell

The proportion of women in the Indian population, 927 women per 1,000 men, is strikingly below the world average of about 990 women per 1,000 men (Sen, 1987b). This ratio, FMR henceforth,[1] has steadily declined from 972 in 1901 to 927 in 1991 (Bose, 1991). There is adequate evidence to show that (*a*) the low FMRs mainly arise out of higher female over male mortality (Visaria, 1971) and (*b*) the sex differentials in mortality are in turn a result of discrimination against women which operates through their unequal access to life sustaining inputs, like food, nutrition and health care (Miller, 1981). *It is the 'lowness' and the decline of the FMR that is the main concern of this study.*

Neither the 'lowness' nor the decline in the FMRs is, however, uniform across the country. These vary by region, by social group, age group and levels of prosperity (see e.g., Agnihotri, 1995a; Dyson and Moore, 1983; Miller, 1981, 1984; Sopher, 1980). Among some of these, the problem of low FMRs are *far more serious than the averages reveal* while in some others FMRs are *unusually high*. The main *focus* of this study is on

---

[1] Conventionally, the term sex ratio is used in India to denote female to male ratio, while internationally it is the other way around. To avoid any confusion therefore *the term sex ratio will be used to mean male per 1,000 female population while FMR will mean number of females per 1,000 male population.*

mapping the *diverse and complex pattern of the FMRs* along different relevant dimensions.

It is contended here that most analyses of the problem of low FMRs have not been *adequately sensitive* to the above diversity. As a result, the current understanding of the problem has remained hazy even after a century of concern and debate (Bardhan, 1986; Dasgupta, 1993: 324; Kanitkar, 1991; Nath, 1991). Analyses which have shown the necessary sensitivity have improved the understanding of the problem considerably (e.g., Dyson and Moore, 1983; Kishor, 1993; Miller, 1981; Visaria, 1971) but the task is far from complete. As this study shows, sensitivity to diversity improves our understanding of the problem significantly *even at rudimentary levels of analysis.*

The *main features* of this analysis include the use of sex ratio data in the juvenile age group population at the district level. Within this popula-tion, FMRs in the 0–4 and 5–9 age groups (FMR04 and FMR59 hence-forth) are separately analysed. These FMRs are further disaggregated for three major social groups: the Scheduled Castes, the Scheduled Tribes and the remaining or the 'general' population. This disaggregation is followed by a cultural disaggregation using a dichotomous cultural variable: kinship, categorised as 'male-centred' versus 'female-friendly'. Finally, the sex ratio data are also analysed separately by levels of prosperity. Most of this disaggregation has not been seriously pursued in the literature so far.

Unveiling different masks

Disaggregation of sex ratio data on these lines remove various 'veils' of averaging which have masked the diversity of the FMR patterns. What does this unveiling reveal?

First and foremost, it shifts the focus of analysis from the state level to the district level. State-level data conceal considerable social, ecological and cultural diversity (see, e.g., Bose, 1994; Government of India, 1972). Second, it shifts the focus from the use of all-age group FMRs to juvenile age group FMRs,[2] thereby removing the problem of sex-selective migra-tion (Miller, 1981, 1989; Sopher, 1980). More importantly, it draws one's attention to patterns of excess female mortality in the juvenile age group, especially below the age of 5 years. This is a distinct feature of present

---

[2] The term juvenile is taken to mean 0–9-year age group throughout the text.

day India and, in fact, South Asia as a whole, (e.g., Chen, 1982; Government of India, 1988; Harriss, 1989: 62; Miller, 1984) compared to pre-industrial Europe, 19th century United States or Japan under Meiji rule, all of which were societies where discrimination against female children usually resulted in excess female mortality in the 10–19 age group.[3]

Preoccupation with excess female mortality has, however, blurred the focus on excess male mortality during infancy and its demographic consequences. One such consequence is the difference in the FMR patterns in the 0–4 and 5–9 age group. It emerges that:

- FMRs in the 0–4 age group are significantly higher than in the 5–9 age group.
- FMR59 is the most appropriate indicator of excess female child mortality.
- Unusually high FMRs in the 0–4 age group indicate excess male infant mortality.
- Unusually low FMRs in the 0–4 age group indicate excess female mortality during infancy itself.
- High FMRs are not the same thing as 'balanced' FMRs.[4]

Disaggregation of these FMRs among the three social groups reveal the seriousness of the problem among Scheduled Caste female children in the north-western part of the country. But it also identifies excess male infant mortality in some of the underdeveloped regions and groups, especially among the Scheduled Tribes in central India (Chapter 4).

District-level maps of FMRs in the 5–9 age group reveal two broad kinship regions: 'male-centred' and 'female-friendly'. The survival chances of female children in the former region, mainly in northern India, are adverse and worsening. The female-friendly regions in rest of the country are holding out against such an 'aberration' but there may be a need to consolidate the present social environment of non-discrimination against the girl child (Chapter 5).

A separate focus on levels of prosperity reveals increasingly adverse survival conditions of women among the non-poor in both kinship regions. This has important implications in the realm of both policy and analysis.

---

[3] See Johansson (1984, 1996) for England and Wales, Europe and Japan; Kennedy (1973) for Ireland; Ginsberg and Swedlund (1986) for the US; Klassen (1994) for Germany.

[4] In principle, if infant and child mortality is reduced to zero, FMRs in the 0–4, 5–9 or 0–9 group will be close to FMRs at birth or 940–970 (Also see Harriss, 1990: 367).

These findings are tentative and need urgent further research and collection of sex ratio data by prosperity levels (Chapter 8).

Theoretical framework

The theoretical framework for this study (Chapter 6) draws substantially upon Sen's entitlements framework (1981), capabilities approach (1985) and the cooperative–conflict model (1987a) of intra-household allocation of resources. It integrates the role of economic and cultural factors in determining women's relative access to resources within the household. It is also able to link the inequality in access to resources to the inequality in survival. This link between what is formally termed as the commodity space and the space of 'functionings', is plausible but not straightforward and requires one to incorporate the fact of human diversity. This is done by using the capabilities approach. However, a considerable extension of both the entitlements framework and the capabilities approach is needed for this purpose which has not been pursued in the literature before. This is an exciting, even though incidental, by-product of this study and promises to put various aspects of gender disparities in a coherent theoretical framework.

Economic correlates of FMRs

The framework enables one to look at two important economic correlates of the variations in FMR: female labour participation or FLP and levels of prosperity. A significant advance is made over the traditional analyses of the association between FMR and FLP. First, the use of FMR59 improves the association substantially. Separate analysis for the Scheduled Castes, Scheduled Tribes and the 'general' category sharpens the picture further while incorporation of the kinship variable provides further insights into the relationship. High FLP emerges as a sufficient condition for better FMRs but not a necessary condition. Where kinship ensures survival, the relevance of FLP is marginal; where it does not, FLP is crucial. The analysis once again draws attention to the seriousness of the situation for Scheduled Caste female children in the north (Chapter 7).

Current analyses of the role of FLP have overlooked an important point. Overall population data are heavily weighed in favour of the poorer groups both in terms of FMR and FLP. The poor are more numerous in the population and women from Scheduled Castes, Scheduled Tribes and landless households account for a large proportion of the female workforce (Bennet, 1991; Desai and Jain, 1994; Mathur, 1994; Visaria, 1994). The FMR patterns and the FMR-FLP relationship among the non-poor can be studied by analysing sex ratio data for rural cultivating households by landholding size groups (1961 Census) and of rural and urban households by per capita expenditure class (National Sample Survey Organisation; NSSO henceforth). Such an analysis provides important clues to the prosperity effect (Chapter 8).

Data sources

The analysis mainly uses the 1961 and 1981 Population Census data at the district level. Data for the 0–4 and 5–9-year age groups were not available for the Scheduled Caste and Scheduled Tribe segments prior to the 1981 Census. District-wise estimates of infant and under-5 mortality available for the first time in 1988 and the regional estimates of these mortalities available in 1995 have been used. The analysis has been carried out at a fairly rudimentary level. Yet, it generates a number of new insights and increases the current understanding of the problem considerably. What is of immediate interest is the implication for policy in terms of women and child welfare measures and the tabulation plan of the 2001 Population Census. A rich agenda for focussed micro-level research and analysis is also generated.

Organisation of the introduction

The detailed introduction is organised as follows. Section II provides a brief overview of the problem. Section III outlines the sequence of different chapters. Section IV discusses different methodological issues that an interdisciplinary and disaggregated analysis of this nature faces. The outline concludes by indicating the style of the narration to follow.

II

A brief overview

The high masculine sex ratios in India have attracted attention right since systematic census operations began in the country.[5] The decline in the FMRs has been continuous during this century except for a brief reversal between 1971 and 1981.[6] The downward trend in the FMR continued in 1991 as shown in Table 1.1a.

Table 1.1a
FMRs (females per 1,000 males) at the all-India level

Year	1901	1911	1921	1931	1941	1951	1961	1971	1981	1991
FMR	972	964	955	950	945	946	941	930	934	927

Source: Bose, 1991.

These FMRs need to be seen against the figures for the world and some of its regions (Table 1.1b). The world average of 990 is itself weighed down by India and China, the two most populous countries in the world, both of which have low FMRs. In the industrialised north and the economically less developed Africa, FMRs are well above 1,000; a pattern which triggered Sen's rather dramatic observation about the 68 million '*missing females*' in India and China (1987b: 25–26). These women would have been present in the population of the two countries if their sex ratios were close to those in Africa.

The incidence of low FMRs is disturbing because it arises due to sex differentials in mortality (Visaria, 1971). It cannot be attributed, except marginally, to factors like errors in enumeration, migration or any biological propensity of Indian women to give birth to more male children (Sen, 1987b: Chapter 2). A steady decline in FMRs signifies a widening gap in male and female mortality while an increase in it usually signifies

---

[5] Since the first census of 1881, the issue of female 'deficit' has been discussed in every decennial census report (Visaria, 1971; Natarajan 1972). One of the women scholars (Saraswathi, 1888) does, in fact, consider the deficit to be about 5 million and speculates upon its causes.

[6] Doubts have been raised about this 'reversal', for example by Dyson (1994). It is suggested that there was substantial undercounting of females in the 1971 Census.

Table 1.1b
FMRs in different parts of the world: 1980

Region	FMR	Region	FMR	Region	FMR
World	990	Western Europe	1,064	Western Asia	940
Africa	1,015	Eastern Europe	1,056	India	931
Northern Africa	986	USA	1,054	Pakistan	929
Non-N. African	1,024	Asia	953	Bangladesh	939
Latin America	999	Eastern & Southeast Asia	1,008	China	941

Source: Sen, 1987b; T-3.1.

closing of the gap. Understandably therefore, a marginal increase in FMR from 931 in 1971 to 934 in 1981 at the all-India level, generated a considerable amount of euphoria (e.g., Chhabra, 1981; Padmanabha, 1981). But it turned out to be short-lived as the FMRs again declined in the 1991 Census to 927, lower by 7 points than the 1981 figure.

While Visaria identified sex differentials in mortality as the main cause of the low FMRs, Miller (1981) traced the roots of these differentials to discrimination against women. This discrimination resulted in an unequal access for women to life sustaining inputs like food, nutrition and health care leading to higher female over male mortality. This was particularly so for female children in the juvenile age group. The neglect of daughters, according to Miller, amounted to 'extended infanticide'. Miller then analyses the causes underlying this discrimination and identifies female participation in the workforce as an important parameter affecting the FMRs. But there are two more features that are pointed out by her, the 'north–south sex ratio divide'[7] and the differences in FMRs among the rich and the poor.

The north–south divide

The north–south divide in sex ratios has also been highlighted by Sopher (1980). But the most influential exposition of this divide on the basis of cultural factors has been done by Dyson and Moore (1983). They consider the status of women[8] to be influenced by cultural factors, especially the

---

[7] This refers to the highly masculine sex ratios in the north-western region of the country and the higher female to male ratios in its south-eastern parts.

[8] Actually they prefer the term autonomy which indicates the decision-making ability with regard to personal affairs (Dyson and Moore, 1983: 45).

kinship system. They draw a contrast between the *kinship systems of the north and the south*. The northern kinship system with its strong emphasis of patrilocal exogamy, status asymmetry between bride-givers and bride-takers and curtailment of ties which a married woman can have with her natal kin, subordinates women quite strongly. The southern kinship system with its emphasis on cross-cousin marriage, spatially endogamous marriages and acceptance of close ties between a married women and her natal kin, is more 'female-friendly'. These differences are reflected in the sex ratio patterns in the two regions: one harsh on females and the other favourable to them. Map 1.1 (Miller, 1984: 10), presents the sex ratios in the juvenile age group in the Indian subcontinent.[9] A preponderance of male children in its north-western part is quite marked. Analysis in Chapter 3 indicates that the sex ratios have since become more masculine throughout the country; quite sharply in the north-west and less so in the south-east.

Economic correlates of sex ratios

Among the economic correlates the role of FLP has been extensively examined. There is a unanimity of opinion in the literature that high FLP ratios are associated with high FMRs although the converse is not necessarily true (see, e.g., Kishor, 1993, Murthi et al., 1995). High FLP increases the value of the females at the societal level and of the female child in the household. Bardhan (1974) hypothesises a link between low FLP, wheat growing regions in the north-west and the low sex ratios observed therein. In the rice growing south-east, female participation in agriculture is higher and females are valued more as a consequence. This 'work' as a determinant of 'worth' line has been advocated by Miller (1981), Rosenzweig and Schultz (1982) and recently Murthi et al. (1995).[10]

Recent literature has also started looking at the role of economic factors other than FLP. Agarwal (1994) makes a strong case for recognising the role of women's property rights as a determinant of their status. She argues that cultural factors are a reflection of the property right regime. The other line of inquiry pursued by Heyer (1992), and Subramaniam (1996) examines the role of dowry in the emergence and aggravation of an anti-female bias even in the south. Kanbur and Haddad (1994) have examined

[9] Sopher (1980) and Miller (1981) are the two usually cited maps in this context. But the map in Miller (1984) is more useful as it gives a picture of the north–south divide across the subcontinent.

[10] For useful up-to-date review, see Sargent et al. (1996) and Murthi et al.(1995).

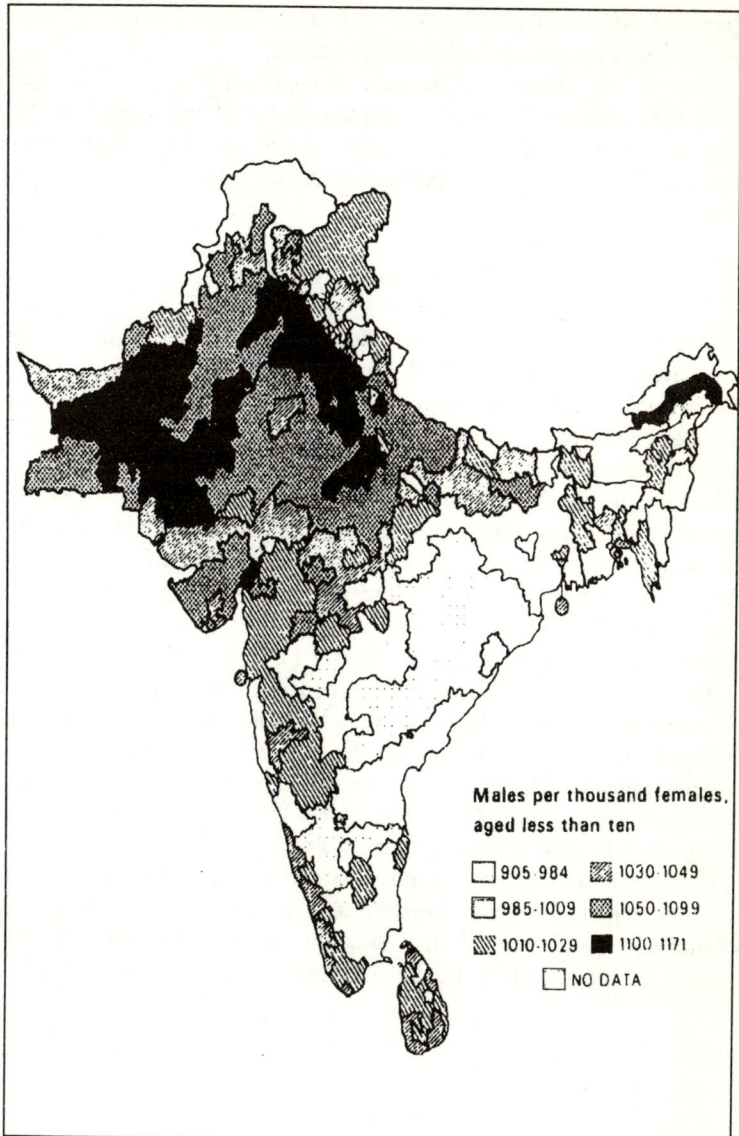

Map 1.1: Juvenile sex ratio map: Indian subcontinent.
Source: Miller, 1984.
Note: Juvenile sex ratios by district (urban and rural populations combined), India (1961), Pakistan (1961), Bangladesh (1961), and Sri Lanka (1971). Juveniles are children under 10 years of age; sex ratio refers to the number of males per 1,000 females.

the role of the overall prosperity of the household on the inequality in the distribution of resources within the household.

Until recently, the cultural and the economic lines of argument assumed competing postures. The need to integrate the two strands of analysis has now been recognised (Bardhan, 1986) and followed up (Basu, 1992; Kishor, 1993). The present analysis draws from both the streams and attempts to integrates them.

An entitlements view

Although the economic and cultural view points differ on what determines the status of women, they both see status as the determinant of sex differentials in access to resources. While status is a phenomenon at the societal level, access to resources like food, nutrition or health care is mainly decided within the domain of the household. It is necessary, therefore, to link the analysis of sex ratio variations with the issue of allocative behaviour within the household. Higher female mortality due to unequal access to resources can be seen as a case of 'entitlements failure'. Application of the entitlements framework to gender relations has gained currency recently (Aslanbeigui and Summerfield, 1993; Kabeer, 1991, 1995; Sen, 1987a, 1990).

The relation between access to resources and mortality, though plausible is not straightforward. How relative welfare is translated into relative longevity is complex and context dependent (Johansson, 1991) and depends considerably upon human diversity, an issue explored through the capabilities approach (Sen, 1985, 1990). However, application of this approach to gender disparities is still at a preliminary stage.

The present study takes these analyses further by drawing upon different strands of inquiry pursued within different disciplines. This raises a number of methodological issues. Before discussing these it is useful to briefly outline the structure of the discussions. This is done in the next section.

III

A brief outline of the analysis

The analysis is presented in five broad parts: a review of the literature (Chapter 2), elaboration of the disaggregated patterns (Chapters 3–5), development of an analytical framework (Chapter 6), some of the correlates of FMRs (Chapters 7 and 8) and the concluding chapter. These are briefly outlined below.

Review of literature (Chapter 2)

Chapter 2 reviews the current state of the debate. The interdisciplinary nature of the analysis has a bearing on the review given the vastness of the literature within individual disciplines and the rapid evolution of literature related to some of the topics. This has necessitated certain 'coping strategies' such as the use of up-to-date and authoritative reviews and exclusion of some of the dated material.

The review covers the debates on sex ratio at birth, sex-selective migration, and sex-selective enumeration errors. These three factors continue to be favourite 'escape hatches' in explaining away the problem of low FMRs even though these have a marginal impact, if any, on the lowness and decline of FMRs. This paves the way for focussing upon the main concern, i.e., discrimination driven excess female mortality and its demographic consequence: low FMR. The review then follows the chapter-wise sequence of arguments.

The disaggregated patterns (Chapters 3–5)

FMRs in the juvenile age group

A major feature of this analysis is the use of FMR data in the juvenile age group and within it the 0–4 and 5–9 age groups separately. The use of juvenile sex ratios offers several advantages. These are free from sex-selective migration (Miller 1981; Sopher, 1980 and more recently Murthi et al. 1995). These reflect the decennial changes in demographic variables like fertility, mortality and its sex differentials more readily compared to the all-age group sex ratio data. More importantly, these reflect the pattern of excess girl child mortality in the 0–5 age group which is a distinct feature of the sex ratio imbalances in contemporary South Asia. This results in very low FMRs, since the death rate in the juvenile age group is very high compared to the death rates in subsequent years. Within the juvenile age group again, deaths are highly skewed towards younger ages with 90 per cent of these deaths taking place within the age of 5 (Government of India, 1988; IIPS, 1995). As a result, it is the under-5 mortality patterns that really determine the juvenile sex ratios.

A 'fault line' in the under-5 mortality (Chapter 3)

Under-5 mortality again, has an internal structure which has a bearing on the sex ratio patterns in the 0–4 and 5–9 age groups. Briefly stated, these are also highly skewed towards younger ages[11] and are marked by a reversal in sex differentials in mortality beyond infancy. There is excess male mortality during infancy which is mainly a biological phenomenon[12] and excess girl child mortality in later years (1–4 age group) which is a socio-cultural or 'behavioural' phenomenon. Juvenile age group FMRs represent the net resultant of these mortality patterns but, within these, FMRs in the 0–4 and 5–9 age groups differ significantly from each other. While the use of juvenile sex ratios (Miller, 1981; Sopher, 1980) and more recently under-5 mortality figures (Kishor, 1993; Murthi et al., 1995) have gained currency, there has been an astonishing absence of analysis of the demographic consequences of this 'fault line'. Such an analysis is necessary given the composite nature of under-5 mortality.

A ten-lap race

While Chapter 3 presents this analysis in some detail, its flavour can be effectively captured through an analogy of a ten-lap race of life or its first ten years. A certain number of male and female children join (at birth) this race. In the first lap, there is a large drop out rate for both the sexes with more male infants dropping out compared to female infants. More female children begin dropping out in the next four laps while the male drop out rate comes down. The female drop out remains pronounced until the fifth lap. In the sixth to tenth lap, the drop out rate is insignificant for *both the sexes*.

The average of the *first five laps* shows a large number of female participants due to their preponderance in the first lap. The average in the *last five laps* will, however, show a higher proportion of male participants. It will primarily reflect the proportion of male and female children who *entered the sixth lap*.

What if the female drop out rate is high right in the first lap? Fewer females will reach the second lap. As their drop out rate is high in the

---

[11] 60 per cent of juvenile deaths take place during infancy in the first year of life (Government of India, 1988; IIPS, 1995).

[12] It is 'biological' in the limited sense of greater vulnerability of the male foetus and infant compared to its female counterpart in similar health environment (Waldron, 1983). As against this, the excess female child mortality in the 1–4 age group is 'behavioural' or driven by discrimination against the girl child.

second to fourth laps, their numbers will continue to decline. The ratio of female to male children in the first five laps (FMR04) will be low. It can even go below the initial ratio one began with, that is, FMR at birth, if there is a net excess number of female children dropping out. Even the starting ratio can become low if many of the female children are *prevented from joining the race* through sex-selective removal (prenatal selection or infanticide!) in the 'qualifying round', that is, the foetal stage.

What if the race takes place in a harsher environment with male infants being more prone to exhaustion? The harsher the environment, the higher will be the male drop out in the first lap. This would give a high FMR in the first five laps. If the girl child drop out rate is comparable to that of the boys in the subsequent laps (that is, there is no discrimination against them), the number of girl children will remain high even in the sixth to the tenth lap. *Unusually high FMRs in the 0–4 age group would therefore indicate excess male infant mortality.* If FMR continues to be high in the 5–9 age group it would indicate continuing poor performance of male children in an adverse health environment.

The *gap between FMR04 and FMR59 will indicate excess girl child mortality*. The more severe the proportion of girls dropping out during the second to the fifth lap, the lower will be the proportion of those entering the sixth lap and hence FMR59 will be lower than FMR04.

Similarly, the gap between FMR04 and the FMR at birth (FMR_0) will indicate the extent of the excess male infant mortality. As infant and child mortality declines substantially, FMR04 values will come closer to FMR at birth. It is only when excess girl child mortality is very high that the FMR04 values go below FMR_0. *Unusually low FMR04 values therefore indicate excess female infant mortality and unusually high FMR04 values signify unusually high male infant mortality.*

The importance of these distinctions will become clearer in the course of this analysis. Suffice to say here that *high FMRs are not the same as balanced FMRs*. Similarly, a decline in the FMRs from a very high levels to a balanced 'range' does not mean the same thing as deterioration in FMRs from a balanced range to very low values.

Disaggregating the data (Chapter 4)

The analytically anticipated differences between the two components of juvenile age group FMRs, are examined using data from the 1981 Census. This is followed by disaggregation of FMRs on the basis of three social groups: the Scheduled Tribes, the Scheduled Castes and the 'general' category. These differences are discernible even at the state level (Table 1.2). FMRs among the Scheduled Tribes are usually higher than the FMRs among non-Scheduled Tribes. Among the latter, the Scheduled Castes have lower FMRs compared to the 'general' category in the northern states.

Analysis of juvenile sex ratios at the district level confirms these differences further. Adverse survival conditions for Scheduled Caste female children in certain regions of the north are revealed through *unusually masculine sex ratios*. At the same time, the analysis also draws attention to certain *regions with unusually high FMR values*. It emerges that the 0–4 and 5–9 age group FMR data can be fruitfully used to infer sex differentials in infant and child mortality among different groups *even if the mortality data are not available*. This has important methodological implications.

Regions versus states (Chapter 5)

Another valuable insight is gained through the mapping of FMR values in the 5–9 age group. These maps reveal different clusters within which the FMR values are homogenously distributed. These clusters coincide with different *geophysical regions*[13] that cut across the boundaries of different states. These regions appear to be more appropriate units of spatial analysis of sex ratio patterns than states. They also recast the north–south divide in a new light. Several pockets in the geographical north reveal sex ratio patterns that resemble the 'south'. The north–south kinship dichotomy is re-examined using Berreman's classification (1993) of regions dominated by the 'core Hindu ethos' and the regions and groups peripheral to it. This classification is further informed through an analysis of the sex ratio patterns among different linguistic groups. A combination of Bereman's core–periphery classification and the classification of linguistic regions in terms of 'core' Indo-Aryan languages and other languages, leads to a regrouping of districts. The regrouping categorises different districts on the basis of the dominant kinship type—'male-centred' versus 'female-friendly'.

The meso-level analysis of FMRs thus shifts the focus from the use of state-level data aggregated over all age groups and social groups to data disaggregated at the district level, by social groups, kinship type and age group. The next step is to analyse the correlates of FMRs disaggregated in the above manner.

---

[13] Identified in different regional studies and in 1961 and 1981 Censuses (Bose, 1994).

Table 1.2

Statewise FMRs by social groups: 1961–91 (females per 1,000 male population)

State	Year	Total Population	Scheduled Castes	Scheduled Tribes	General Category	State	Year	Total Population	Scheduled Castes	Scheduled Tribes	General Category
India	1961	941	957	987	934	Maharashtra	1961	936	962	978	932
	1971	930	935	982	924		1971	930	947	973	926
	1981	934	932	983	930		1981	937	948	974	932
	1991	927	922	972	923		1991	934	944	968	928
Andhra Pradesh	1961	981	980	976	982	Manipur	1961	1,015	942	1,022	1,014
	1971	977	973	973	977		1971	980	914	1,009	969
	1981	975	971	962	977		1981	971	956	975	969
	1991	972	969	960	974		1991	958	973	959	957
Arunachal Pradesh	1961	894	–	1,013	299	Meghalaya	1961	937	796	1,001	670
	1971	861	904	1,007	460		1971	942	898	996	743
	1981	862	592	1,005	599		1981	954	790	1,002	776
	1991	859	627	998	658		1991	955	821	997	739
Assam	1961	869	883	918	862	Mizoram	1961	1,009	–	1,026	390
	1971	896	917	960	886		1971	946	38	1,021	208
	1981	–	–	–	–		1981	919	125	997	227
	1991	923	919	967	916		1991	921	157	982	243

Table 1.2 continued

Table 1.2 continued

State	Year	Total Population	Scheduled Castes	Scheduled Tribes	General Category
Bihar	1961	994	1,031	1,014	985
	1971	954	981	1,003	943
	1981	946	966	993	937
	1991	911	914	971	905
Goa	1961	1,066	–	–	'
	1971	981	936	742	982
	1981	975	956	845	976
	1991	967	967	889	967
Gujarat	1961	940	972	970	933
	1971	934	950	968	927
	1981	942	942	976	936
	1991	934	925	967	929
Haryana	1961	868	894	–	853 ⌐
	1971	867	871	–	866
	1981	870	864	–	872
	1991	865	860	–	866
Himachal Pradesh	1961	938	934	983	937
	1971	958	950	1,000	959
	1981	973	959	978	977
	1991	976	967	981	978

State	Year	Total Population	Scheduled Castes	Scheduled Tribes	General Category
Nagaland	1961	933	575	1,007	287
	1971	871	–	973	332
	1981	863	–	955	495
	1991	888	–	946	558
Orissa	1961	1,001	1,015	1,016	991
	1971	988	993	1,007	979
	1981	981	988	1,012	969
	1991	971	975	1,002	959
Punjab	1961	954	858	–	852
	1971	865	856	–	868
	1981	879	868	–	883
	1991	882	873	–	885
Rajasthan	1961	908	923	926	902
	1971	911	914	930	907
	1981	919	913	945	916
	1991	910	899	930	909
Sikkim	1961	904	–	–	904
	1971	863	842	–	864
	1981	835	913	927	801
	1991	878	939	914	862

State	Year				
J & K	1961	878	890	–	876
	1971	878	924	–	874
	1981	892	922	–	889
	1991	–	–	–	–
Karnataka	1961	959	965	953	958
	1971	957	957	957	957
	1981	963	968	971	961
	1991	960	962	961	959
Kerala	1961	1,022	1,013	1,006	1,022
	1971	1,016	1,012	995	1,017
	1981	1,032	1,022	992	1,033
	1991	1,036	1,029	996	1,038
MP	1961	953	973	1,003	934
	1971	941	941	998	925
	1981	943	932	997	926
	1991	931	915	985	916
Tamil Nadu	1961	992	993	951	992
	1971	978	984	951	977
	1981	977	980	968	976
	1991	974	978	960	973
Tripura	1961	932	921	955	921
	1971	943	940	954	938
	1981	946	942	962	940
	1991	945	949	965	931
UP	1961	909	941	–	901
	1971	879	896	880	874
	1981	885	892	919	883
	1991	879	877	914	879
West Bengal	1961	878	916	969	861
	1971	891	927	955	877
	1981	911	926	969	902
	1991	917	931	964	844

Source: Agnihotri, 1995a.

Note: Census operation could not be conducted in Assam in 1981 and in J & K in 1991.

– Indicates data not available or no population in that category.

An analytical framework (Chapter 6)

The entitlements framework

An analytical framework is introduced at this stage. To start with it looks upon low FMRs as a reflection of entitlements failure. The application of the entitlements framework to gender issues has gained currency in recent years along with the bargain theoretic view of the allocative behaviour within a household. This view departs from the neoclassical, unitary view of the household where the self-interests of its members uniquely converge and where there are no conflicts. In the bargaining models, the divergence of self-interests of different members and the existence of conflict is recognised and incorporated. It will suffice to say here that analytically the 'converging self-interest, conflict free' model of the household is but a special case of the more general, diverging self-interest, conflict aware models (McElroy, 1990).

Application of the entitlements framework to gender issues has modified and enriched the framework itself. The concept of *entitlements or a person's potential command over resources*, was earlier quite legalistic and oriented towards explicit economic or exchange processes. It now incorporates the concept of legitimacy and recognises the influence of exchange-independent processes, like culture, on a person's access to resources. However, the increased application of the entitlements framework to different issues has been accompanied by what Gasper (1993) describes as the 'decline of the formal apparatus'. The present analysis uses the 'formal apparatus' by elaborating an *entitlement-endowment*[14] relationship in the context of intra-household bargaining. This elaboration provides a number of useful insights into the intra-household dynamics including those obtained through the more discursive applications of the framework.

The entitlement-endowment relationship mentioned above takes into account the exchange-independent components of entitlements and satisfactorily integrates the role of cultural and economic variables. It is then used to extend the analysis of inequality within a stylised two-member household drawing upon the approach taken by Kanbur and Haddad (1994). In such a household, the two members cooperate to increase the prosperity or the 'size of the cake' but there is conflict over how to

---

[14] While entitlements represent the potential command over resources, endowments represent the means for generating such command.

distribute the increment in it. The distribution suggested by Kanbur and Haddad (1994) using a Nash bargaining approach is questioned, and alternative possibilities are introduced. It is argued that Sen's emphasis on the role of perceptions in determining allocational behaviour is closer to reality. This is used in a later chapter (Chapter 8) to examine the association between prosperity and sex ratios. It is shown that the *female contribution to prosperity is a more crucial determinant of her entitlements than the overall prosperity of the household.*

Sex ratios as functioning

The analytical framework is further extended using Sen's capabilities approach to wellbeing of which longevity is one aspect. Given the human diversity, entitlements do not tell the full story of outcomes. What people are able to do with their entitlements also depends upon their personal circumstances. Together, the two, i.e., entitlements and personal circumstances, determine the outcomes or what Sen calls the 'functioning'. Sex ratios as functioning thus provides a more complete view compared to sex ratios as a reflection of entitlement asymmetries.

This approach necessitates a linkage between the capabilities approach and the entitlements framework. So far, these two have been pursued independently. Use of the 'formal apparatus' makes this linkage straightforward and provides exciting insights into the question of survival disparities and the question of wellbeing and entitlements. The latter is beyond the scope of present discussion and is discussed only to a limited extent. The view of sex ratios as functioning is consistent with Johansson's (1987, 1991) framework which recognises the *complex and context dependent nature of sex differentials in mortality.* It also supports the analysis of sex differentials in infant and child mortality and their demographic consequences in terms of FMRs (Chapter 3).

Correlates of FMRs

'Work' as determinant of 'worth' (Chapter 7)

Female labour participation (FLP) has been identified as the most significant economic correlate of sex ratios. Chapter 7 examines the FMR-FLP relationship afresh. It analyses the 1961 and 1981 Census data on JFMRs and FLP, first without and then with disaggregation. The disaggregated analysis generates a number of new insights. Briefly, it is seen that high FLP provides a sufficient condition for survival but not a necessary one. Wherever culture takes care of survival, FLP is less critical. In female-friendly kinship regions it is nearly insignificant. The FMR59-FLP relationship emerges as a good indicator of the survival adversities for female children. Separate analysis of the FMR59-FLP relationship highlights the adverse conditions faced by the female children of the Scheduled Castes and the 'general' category in the 'core' Indo-Aryan kinship region. Further, it turns out that the FMR04-FLP relationship can act as an *early warning signal* for the deteriorating survival chances of the girl child even when mortality data among different groups are not available.

In the analysis so far, sex ratio data have not been disaggregated by levels of prosperity. Given the preponderance of the poor in the population and the higher incidence of female work force participation among them, FMR and FLP figures are weighed in their favour. This masks the patterns among the non-poor. It is, therefore, necessary to segregate sex ratio data by prosperity levels if its effects are to be studied.

The prosperity effect (Chapter 8)

How prosperity affects FMRs is intuitively not obvious. In the absence of any gender bias, high prosperity should bring down the mortality levels and sex differentials in mortality. This would maintain the JFMRs close to FMR values at birth.

Two diverging trends mark the literature on the effects of prosperity. One points towards the worsening condition of women in the wake of prosperity.[15] The other, a more optimistic one, expects an eventual reversal of fortunes for them. Kanbur and Haddad's hypothesised Kuznets curve or an inverse-U type relationship between the inequality at the household level and its overall prosperity falls in the latter category. They stipulate that the *inequality increases initially* as prosperity increases and then begins to decrease beyond a '*turning point*', that is, a certain level of the overall household prosperity. This is critiqued on analytical grounds in Chapter 8. It is suggested that even if a Kuznets curve did exist its shape will be crucially affected by the female contribution to prosperity.

The tension between these two diverging views on the effects of prosperity needs to be resolved for each has very different implications. This task is made difficult by the absence of suitable data. It is possible,

---

[15] This is discussed in detail in Chapter 8. Goody (1990), Heyer (1992), Rao (1993), Kapadia (1994) and Subramanian (1996) come in this category.

however, to use data from the 1961 Census and from the NSSO survey rounds. The 1961 Census data provides the household composition for rural cultivator families by size of the landholding. The NSSO rounds provide the household composition by per capita expenditure (PCE) classes. Both landholding and PCE can be taken as reasonable indicators of prosperity.

While the analysis of the 1961 data provide support for the Kuznets curve, the NSSO data reveal a steady decline in the FMRs at higher prosperity levels. Even in the analysis of the 1961 Census data it becomes clear that the *effects of prosperity cannot be studied independent of the female contribution to prosperity.* Where FLP is low and kinship male-centred, the inequality in survival aggravates with increase in prosperity and the 'turning point' occurs at unrealistically high levels of prosperity. Where kinship is female-friendly, the survival inequality at the turning point is not very severe. But these findings are tentative since the data are not free from sex-selective migration. There is, however, a strong case for repeating this enumeration for the 2001 Census[16] with the provision for computing the juvenile sex ratios.

The negative association between FMRs and prosperity revealed even in the southern region raises some disturbing questions about the links between prosperity, female subordination and the emerging trends of sex-selective abortions and female infanticide. These are discussed in some details and the need to generate suitable data is emphasised.

Evidence from the 1991 Census (Chapter 9)

Census data from the 1991 Population Census are not available in adequate details yet. But the analysis of the limited data available corroborates most of the findings above and confirms the trend of growing masculinisation of the sex ratios in various regions. Analysis of the estimates of the infant and child mortality at the district level in the 1991 Census further supports the analysis done in Chapter 3 about the gender bias in mortality. More importantly it opens up very exciting possibilities of inferring gender bias from the available mortality data.

Conclusions (Chapter 10)

The concluding chapter recapitulates different insights gained through this analysis and the directions to which they lead. The scope for further

---

[16] This enumeration has unfortunately been discontinued after the 1961 Census.

research and the policy implications are discussed along with the limitations of the study. These are not repeated here. Two important findings, however, need to be highlighted. First, infant mortality and child mortality (in the 1–4 age group) emerge as appropriate indicators of development and discrimination respectively. The objective of any social or policy intervention must be to ensure development without discrimination. Second, male children seem to face survival hurdle only once—during the neonatal period or the first month of life. Female children appear to face a number of them. Sex-selective abortion is one, infanticide is another, neonatal mortality is the third and childhood mortality the fourth. Each has to be addressed separately and simultaneously and lack of success in one cannot justify lack of effort in another. Otherwise female children in India will lose the race in the 21st century even before it begins.

IV

Methodological issues

The analysis presented in this study makes a number of departures from the conventional analyses of the sex ratio problem. These departures are necessary to improve the current understanding of the problem. As stated earlier, concern over low FMRs in India is as old as census taking and has generated a vast amount of literature. Yet, the official paper on the results of the 1991 Census observes that 'it is ... difficult to pinpoint any particular reason for the declining sex ratios which require a detailed analysis ... ' (Nath, 1991: 2149) and sums up the official position thus, 'the reasons for the decline have to be investigated in much greater details than has been done so far' (ibid.).

The situation regarding the regional variations in the sex ratios is not very different. The chapter on 'Sex' in the 1891 Census begins thus:

> Of the many problems that come to light in the course of reviewing the results of the Census ... none is more perplexing than that of having to account for the varying proportion of the two sexes in different parts of the country.

Regional diversity remains perplexing even after a 100 years (Kanitkar, 1991: 19). Bardhan describes it as a complex subject:

in which historical, demographic, cultural, ecological, economic and sociological factors interact.... In our present state of knowledge ... it is, in fact, quite unlikely that anyone can provide a fully *convincing and comprehensive* explanation. At this stage if each of us, from our own particular standpoint, make an admittedly partial blind man's probing of the elephant and compare notes with others, there is *some hope that we may some day have a better idea of the shape of the animal* (Bardhan, 1986: 1, emphasis added).

Such a situation is surprising and raises questions about why it is so. A major reason, as contended before, is inadequate sensitivity to the diversities in the sex ratio patterns. To get a 'better idea of the shape of the animal' it is necessary to use a level of resolution appropriate to the problem. This is one of the main features of this study and, as later chapters show, it yields rich dividends.

Appropriate resolution

The issue of appropriate level can be aptly described through an analogy of examining a landscape from different heights. A macro picture from a great height can show the large landscape and locate its broad features, its valleys, streams and plains. Very close to the surface, at a micro level, specific features of a stream, a hill or a crater can be examined in detail. But from that one cannot make generalisations about the larger picture. From an intermediate or a 'meso' level, one can see the larger picture and also the features hidden at the macro level. One can notice which stream has a strong vortex, which crater is very deep or which gorge is negotiable. It is this 'meso' level at which the present study is carried out. It does not negate the macro picture, but sharpens and enriches it. At the same time, it beings together different micro pictures, studies them and sometimes suggests a more focussed analysis at the micro level.

Unit of analysis

The first issue concerns the choice of a suitable level of aggregation. Micro-level studies provide useful insights into the processes that lead to the pattern of low FMRs (Bardhan, 1986: 7, Harriss, 1989: 61). But it is difficult to obtain patterns that emerge at the aggregate levels through these studies. Such patterns or what can be called the 'central tendencies' (Dasgupta, 1993: 324) emerge at larger levels of aggregation. In smaller populations (below 10,000), the magnitude of random errors in sex ratios becomes *comparable* with the variations that are being studied (Visaria, 1971: Table 6.1). The sex ratio estimates in these samples suffer from large variability. Moreover, the micro studies can sometimes diverge from the aggregate patterns (e.g., Harriss, 1989: 34). But this could be on account of locality specific factors and different 'initial conditions' and cannot be taken as 'counter examples' negating the broader picture (Dasgupta, 1993: 323–24).

While micro-level processes generate discernible patterns only beyond certain levels of aggregation, there is a danger of over-aggregating these patterns. Use of state-level sex ratio data provides one such example. Most analyses of regional variations in sex ratios continue to use state-level data[17] in spite of the large size[18] and substantial ecological, cultural and social[19] diversity which mark the Indian states. This is surprising given a well developed tradition of regional studies in India (Bose, 1994) and the insights provided by the district-level analysis of sex ratio patterns (Miller, 1981; Sopher, 1980).

Use of data at the district level provides a suitable level of aggregation for the analysis of FMRs. Districts constitute an administrative unit below the state level. On an average these have a population of about 2 million (Kishor, 1993) and most of the census data are available at these levels.

Beyond demography

While the present study uses a demographic variable, namely FMR, it is not a demographic inquiry. It is interdisciplinary in nature and closer in its approach to Miller (1981, 1984, 1989), Basu (1992) and Kishor (1993). One cannot, however, overlook the demographic viewpoint, especially the debate regarding the role of female under-enumeration, age misreporting and the high masculine sex ratios at birth (Chapter 2: Section III). The relevant literature reviewed in Chapter 2, and its further analysis in Chapters 4, 5 and 7 shows the marginal role of these factors in explaining the observed patterns of low FMRs. Some of this literature is well within mainstream demography and is by and large undisputed. The argument about sex-selective under-enumeration and age misreporting loses much of its teeth once direct estimates of child mortality at the district level are

[17] Some recent examples in authoritative texts are Agarwal (1994), Dasgupta (1993) and even Raju (1991) who looks at the gender bias from a 'geographical perspective'.

[18] Many of the Indian states are larger than most nation states in the world.

[19] Broad examples will include south and north Bihar, Uttarakhand region and western and eastern Uttar Pradesh.

available and when the FMRs in the 0–4 and 5–9 age groups are examined separately. It is legitimate therefore to shift one's focus beyond these recurring escape hatches and towards the real issue of concern, that is, excess female child mortality.

Appropriate rigour

The analysis of low FMRs is informed by a number of disciplines, from anthropology to demography. Each of these disciplines has its own level and tradition of analysis, some qualitative, some discursive and some oriented towards elaborate statistical techniques. Choice of an appropriate level of rigour becomes important in such a situation. In this study, different statistical and other techniques have been used at a fairly basic level. The temptation to wander into the by-lanes of sophisticated technical analysis has been avoided. Such techniques are more appropriate for the follow-up studies. As commented earlier, considerable insight is generated even at this rudimentary level once the analysis incorporates the diversity in the sex ratio patterns.

In certain instances, however, it was necessary to use certain techniques beyond a basic level. One has not shied away from use of such techniques. But the use of different techniques have been made mostly for broad substantiation of different insights. Use of more elaborate techniques to look at finer details in different fields would hopefully follow this analysis. The cart of more elaborate 'fine-tuning' should follow the horses of 'tuning' rather than preceeding these.

The tuning versus fine-tuning issue can be elaborated through one example. A number of analyses which use district-level data, use the dummy variable for the 'north' and include the districts of south Bihar, Uttarakhand region in Uttar Pradesh and southern Madhya Pradesh (Kishor, 1993; Mathur, 1994; Murthi et al., 1995). This is, as will be seen later, quite inappropriate in the context of gender analysis. It represents a case of emphasis on fine-tuning, for instance, the use of dummy variable in regression, before getting the tuning that is, which regions to include, right.

Finally, a considerable amount of empirical analysis has been done in this study (in five out of the nine chapters). In most instances, the results of this analysis support the views and insights generated by the more qualitative analyses of the problem which often generate ideas that are conceptually clear but problematic from the point of view of measurement. Papanek (1990) talks of the emerging convergence between data-intensive literature and concept-based literature in the field of gender-based inequalities. The approach here is to push this convergence pro-actively. For this, one had to look at the existing data in innovative ways sympathetic to the conceptual insights rather than leaving the burden of locating or generating the data on those who provide the insights. Such an approach has given fruitful results as the concerned chapters will show.

Use of data

The study mainly uses the 1961 and 1981 Census data. Data from 1931 Census, NSSO survey rounds and the recently conducted national family health survey (NFHS, IIPS, 1995) have also been used where required. Estimates of infant and child mortality at district levels are based on the 1981 Census data.

The reasons for not using the 1971 and 1991 Census data need to be explained. Both the 1961 and 1981 Census operations have been generally considered to be of quite good quality. Doubts have, on the other hand, been raised about the quality of the 1971 Census (e.g., Dyson, 1981, 1994; Visaria and Visaria, 1981). Second, the definition of women's workforce participation in 1971 does not permit a comparison with the 1961 data (Vannemann and Barnes, 1992). The third, and more important reason is that the 1971 data do not provide the 5-year age group break-up by the three social groups. Once the analysis moves to the disaggregation of the 5-year age group FMRs by social groups, even the 1961 data are no longer useful. But the 1961 Census has some other unique data like composition by sex of different language speaking groups and family composition among different land holding size groups.

As regards the 1991 data, it is unfortunate that these could not be used. The 5-year age group break-up for the Scheduled Caste (SC), Scheduled Tribe (SC) and general category is still not available. Even the district-level data for the total population by 5-year age group were not available until recently. Given these limitations, detailed analysis of the 1991 data could not be done.

Developing new links

Another aspect of the present analysis deserves mention. Some of the connections across different sub-topics have been made for the first time, for example, linking the entitlements framework and the capabilities approach or under-5 mortality patterns and FMRs. The final argument rests on developing some of the linkages in detail even though these may not be within the immediate scope of the analysis. A trade-off between developing these links fully and the scope of this analysis was necessary. In all such cases the links have been pursued only to the necessary extent and the scope for further work has been briefly mentioned. Such possibilities are also listed in the concluding chapter.

And finally, the benefit of hindsight

The narration that follows has considerably benefited from hindsight. The actual route was more tortuous and triggered by the observed patterns from the data. Differences in the 0–4 and 5–9 age group FMRs provides one example of this. The entire theoretical apparatus in Chapter 3 on the demographic consequence of sex differentials in infant and under-5 mortality actually followed the analysis of the FMR patterns did not precede it. Given that much of the disaggregations and connections across topics were developed for the first time, the tortuous route I followed is understandable. The final route that became obvious with the benefit of hindsight is, however, much shorter. In the interest of brevity *it is the shorter route that will be followed in the narration.*

Chapter 2

A review of literature

I

Introduction

Certain features of the present analysis have a bearing on the review of literature. The interdisciplinary nature of the study and the synthesis of different strands of inquiry being pursued within these disciplines is one such feature. Most of these strands are marked by vast literature of their own and contending schools of thought.[1] Weaving them together has improved the current understanding of the problem and has generated new insights.

In some of the topics concerned, for example, intra-household allocational behaviour, the literature has evolved quite rapidly. In some others, the avilability of recent data has rendered much of the earlier debate obsolete. Direct availability of district-level child mortality data (Government of India, 1988), for example, has convincingly established the fact of excess girl child mortality in certain regions and decisively weakened the argument that low FMRs in these regions can be attributed to enumeration errors.

Some of the approaches pursued in the present study have received little or no attention in the literature. Demographic consequences of the composite nature of under-5 mortality, separate analysis of the FMRs for

---

[1] For example, differentials in mortality, entitlements, gender stratification, intra-household resource distribution, regional diversities in India and kinship systems.

Scheduled Castes and Scheduled Tribe population, integration of the entitlements and the capabilities approach, are a few examples. Much of the mainstream literature on these topics, therefore, becomes marginal to this analysis though it is of considerable importance on its own.

Finally, the vast literature on certain aspects of the problem[2] is not matched by comprehensive and analytical work of a high quality.[3] There are certain milestones in the debate no doubt. But between these milestones, there are numerous analyses which merely repeat the established aspects of the debate.[4]

The scope of the literature review

The features mentioned and the constraints of space necessitate certain 'coping strategies'. Literature on individual sub-topics, for example, entitlements, kinship or child mortality, is not exhaustively reported but instead selected authoritative text and comprehensive review articles are referred to.[5] These are treated as essential readings and marked with an asterisk in the Bibliography. These again, are not summarised. Arguments relevant for this study are briefly indicated and quoted specifically where necessary. Similarly, literature rendered dated on account of new developments, is mentioned very briefly, if at all.

Literature proximately connected with developing an arguments is reviewed within the relevant chapter, for example, literature on sex differentials in infant and childhood mortality is reviewed in Chapter 3. The less proximately connected yet essential literature, for example, literature on sex ratios at birth or kinship patterns, is reviewed in some details in the present chapter. Gaps in the literature and the departure made in the course of analysis from the main currents in the literature, are briefly indicated.

---

[2] See, for example, Papanek (1984) on the subject of women in India. Similarly, the review by Harriss (1989) on sex differentials in mortality in South Asia has about 950 references.

[3] A view expressed by Miller (1981: 89), Papanek (1984: 127–33 and Clark (1987).

[4] The north–south divide in sex ratio patterns is a good example. This pattern was established convincingly by 1985. Since then it has not made much headway.

[5] See, for example, Trautmann (1981), Karve (1965) on Kinship systems; Goody (1976, 1990), Sen (1981), Visaria (1969) as texts; Bose (1994) on regional classification in India; Waldron (1983) on infant mortality; Gasper (1993) on entitlements; Doss (1996) on intrahousehold models; and Harriss (1989) on sex differentials in mortality as reviews.

Organisation of the discussion

Section II briefly lists different milestones that have marked the debate on sex ratio variations and low values of FMRs over the years. Section III to VIII follows the chapter-wise sequence of arguments. The final section briefly reviews some specific themes not covered above.

II

A brief overview

Visaria's analysis, 'Sex ratios of the population of India' (1971) is acclaimed as the first landmark in this debate.[6] Earlier analyses, especially in different census reports (reviewed in Natarajan, 1972) lacked Visaria's depth and rigour. Visaria clearly established that the low FMRs in India arise mainly due to the sex differentials in mortality. Effect of factors like migration, under-enumeration of females or sex ratios at birth was only marginal.

This analysis enabled the debate to turn towards the causes and correlates of these mortality differentials and low FMRs. Miller's in-depth analysis (1981) followed a decade later. It highlighted the socio-cultural discrimination against female children, pronounced in certain regions in India, as the primary reason for higher girl child mortality. Such discrimination resulted in unequal access for the girl child to life sustaining inputs like food, nutrition, health care and parental care, vis-à-vis male children in the family. Miller termed this 'extended infanticide' (1981).

Female labour participation

Miller's work opened up many important lines of inquiry, well beyond the domain of demography. The role of economic factors in determining the intra-household distribution of resources is one among them. Miller

---

[6] For example, Miller (1981: 70), Caldwell and Caldwell (1990: 5). Coale in his foreword (Visaria, 1971: ix) observes that the analysis 'is an excellent example of dispassionate sifting of evidence to arrive at a better understanding of circumstances that had long been erroneously interpreted' (by others including Coale himself, who is large hearted enough to concede this in the same foreword).

emphasised upon the effect of female labour participation (FLP) on sex ratios. This 'work'-as-determinant-of-'worth' line of inquiry has been followed by many others, notably Rosenzweig and Schultz (1982), and recently by Murthi et al. (1995). The FMR-FLP relation is further analysed using the overall population figures at the district level. However, the FMR and FLP data, based on the overall population, are strongly weighed in favour of the poorer population. This has rarely been explicitly recognised in the literature except by Desai and Jain (1994). Chapter 8 takes this into account and studies the 'prosperity effect'[7] in the context of FMR-FLP relationship.

The importance of FLP had earlier been highlighted by Bardhan (1974: 1304) in his 'wildly conjectured' wheat–rice divide in sex ratio patterns. Briefly, the argument suggested that the predominantly wheat growing regions in north-western India required much less female labour participation compared to the predominantly rice growing south-east. As a consequence, women were valued less in the former, leading to a lower status and higher discrimination against them. In the south-east, they are valued more on account of their high participation in agricultural activities, and therefore face less discrimination. This was the main underlying cause of the north–south divide observed in the sex ratio patterns across the country. This divide was later highlighted by Sopher (1980) through the district-level map of juvenile sex ratios (JSR) and Miller through her analysis of the relation between FMRs and FLP (1981: chapter 4) and the JSR map (1981, 1984).

The north–south divide

However, the north–south divide was brought to the centre stage of discussions by Dyson and Moore (1983) who highlighted the role of cultural factors in determining the status of women. The north and south are characterised by two different cultural and kinship systems. The 'male-centred' kinship system (a term used by Kishor, 1993) in the north undervalues and subordinates females while the southern kinship system values them more and allows them to retain their ties with their natal kin. The difference in their status, which is culturally mediated, plays an important role in determining their access to resources both within the

---

[7] I am thankful to S.R. Osmani for pointing this out during his discussion of my paper on 'Intra-household Kuznets curve' at the IEA (International Economic Association) 1995.

household and at the level of the society. The culture-as-determinant-of-status argument has been followed, among others, by Basu (1992), Berreman (1993), Dasgupta, M. (1987, 1995) Madan (1993) and Papanek (1990).

A *phase of consolidation*

The cultural and economic explanations of variations in sex ratios had assumed competing posture for some time. The need to integrate these two was explicity recognised by Bardhan (1986). He felt that the dispute about the primacy of one set of factors over the other was 'tiresomely pointless' (1986: 7). However, in-depth attempts to integrate the two sets of factors took place only recently (Basu, 1992; Kishor, 1993).

Different aspects of the debate have been reviewed by Harriss, first in an exhaustive review of sex differentials in mortality and health care among children in South Asia (1987) followed by a review of intra-family distribution of hunger (1990). Caldwell and Caldwell (1990) and Chatterjee (1991) are two other useful reviews. In much of the late eighties, however, there was a lull in research on the sex ratio 'problem' at the macro level with some exceptions like Miller (1989). Using the 1961 and the 1971 Census data, she drew attention to the increasingly masculine juvenile sex ratios across the north–south divide. The Caldwells too, draw attention towards the process of 'northernisation' (1990: 11) of gender relations in southern India.

The concern renewed

A probable reason for the lull was the improvement in the 1981 FMR figures[8] over the previous census figures. This had happened for the first time since 1901. Even though the increase was marginal, the euphoria generated was understandable. There were cautioning voices (e.g., Dyson, 1981, 1994; Karkal, 1987; Visaria and Visaria, 1981) but it was mostly assumed that the turn around had begun (Chhabra 1981: 28; Padmanabha, 1981: 6) and that FMRs would henceforth move up steadily even if in

---

[8] 934 on an all-India level compared to the FMR of 931 in 1971.

small steps. Not surprisingly, Miller's analysis was never followed up using 1981 data.[9]

Against this background, the provisional FMR figure of the 1991 Census (930 at all-India level) must have been an unwelcome surprise and the final figure (927) a rude shock. Declining FMRs again attracted notice. In the meantime, district-level estimates of infant and under-5 mortality by sex became available in 1988. These have been utilised recently by Kishor (1993) and Murthi et al. (1995). These two analyses are likely to emerge as important and in-depth contributions to this debate. Both use district-level data, examine sex differentials in child mortality directly and use multi-variate analysis techniques.

Role of property

Another important development in recent years relates to the role of economic factors other than FLP. Miller incorporated the role of prosperity in her analysis through a distinction between the 'propertied' and 'unpropertied' classes, highlighting the pattern of low FMRs among the propertied groups in the north. She identified dowry as one of the major culprits which creates the perception of the girl child as a liability. While the ill effects of dowry in the north have been discussed for quite some time (Sharma, 1993), the role of dowry in the south has also come under scrutiny in recent years. Notable among these are Heyer (1992), Kapadia (1994) Rao (1993) and Subramaniam (1996).[10]

Dowry is one manifestation of the role of capital, inheritance is another. The role of inheritance has been emphasised by Agarwal (1994). She traces the roots of status to property rights and the inheritance system. The north–south divide according to her is closely related to the issue of property rights. The northern social structure denies women any significant property rights which lowers their status and consequently their access to resources. In the southern or the eastern system, women have significant property rights and therefore enjoy a better status than their northern

[9] In 1989, When Miller's article was published, the 1981 JSR data were available in India. Even Miller who expressed an intention of analysing the 1981 data (1989: 1235) has not published the results of her analysis if any.

[10] For a detailed analysis of different aspects of dowry both in the north and the south see Goody (1990: Chapter 7 and Chapter 8) and for an interesting aspect of 'dowry evil' among the Christians in Madras see Caplan (1993).

counterparts. However, the question of why different property rights regimes or inheritance patterns prevail in different regions brings us back to issues of ecology and culture.

As mentioned earlier, sex ratio variations have not been studied across the prosperity dimension. The literature has mainly looked at the issue of the status of women in the wake of prosperity including their withdrawal from the labour force. Two contradictory trends are noticed in the literature on this. One, outlined here, expresses concern about increasing gender disparity in the wake of prosperity. The other is optimistic about the eventual gender equality at higher levels of prosperity (e.g., Kanbur and Haddad, 1994; Pissani and Zaba, Forthcoming). The two have quite different implications for policy. The tension between these two trends is analysed in Chapter 8 and resolved to some extent by incorporating the role of female work force participation.

The larger context

Analyses such as these, take the issue of survival disparities to a broader domain of gender disparities. Sen has made important contributions in this field by looking at the intra-household resource allocation as a process of cooperative conflict and low FMRs as a consequence of entitlements failure (Sen, 1987a, 1990). This is followed up further through the capabilities approach to wellbeing (Sen, 1985, 1990), viewing survival as a crucial aspect of wellbeing and FMRs as an expression of inequality in the space of survival. These are discussed in Chapter 6.

Literature on gender disparities or stratification has been pursued in three different disciplines, often independent of one another. Economic literature focusses on allocational behaviour within the household. Anthropological focusses on historical and cultural variables while sociological literature has concerned itself with organisational and social aspects. There is considerable scope of integrating these schools of thought. A pioneering inquiry towards building a 'general theory of gender stratification' has been made by Blumberg (1991), Collins (1991) and others. This is briefly reviewed in Section IX along with anthropological literature on the genesis of gender stratification. Finally, the line of analysis pursued by Johansson (1984, 1996) from the perspective of historical demography is briefly described. Johansson stresses the historical and context-specific nature of changes in mortality patterns and excess female mortality as opposed to the ahistorical and context-independent approach adopted by many. Her analysis covers patterns of excess female mortality across different cultures and times.

Micro studies and other specific themes

At the micro level, there are numerous studies (e.g., review in Harriss 1989: 29–39). The limitation of these studies has been mentioned in Chapter 1. These illuminate various processes but not patterns (Harriss, 1989: 61). These processes coalesce into discernible patterns, for example, sex ratios, only beyond a certain sample size.[11] Yet, many of these studies tend to make generalisations on a broader, often all-India level without suitably qualifying themselves.[12] In this analysis, micro-level studies are cited as possible instances of specific processes but not extrapolated further. However, the insights generated from the micro-level studies can be fruitfully pursued and substantiated through available data, a strategy that has been pursued in this study with some success.

The next few sections review the literature connected with the chapter-wise sequence of arguments. It prepares the background for the analysis to follow and also indicates major departures intended to be made from the main currents in the literature.

III

Three demographic factors

Before following the sequence of arguments in different chapters, it is necessary to review the debate about certain demographic factors frequently used as escape hatches in explaining away the problem of low FMRs. These are: (*a*) high masculine sex ratios at birth (*b*) sex-selective migration and (*c*) sex-selective enumeration errors (see, e.g., L.C. Chen, 1982; Coale 1971: ix; and, more recently, Srinivasan, 1994). Available literature on

---

[11] Visaria (1971). This is discussed in some detail in the following section.

[12] It is not unusual to come across titles referring to rural India or north-west India, while the study may be based on, say, 10 villages in Himachal Pradesh (Bhati and Singh, 1987) or few villages in Uttar Pradesh (Simmons et al., 1982). It is not the quality of these studies that is in question but their generalisation.

these factors is considered here to show that sex-selective enumeration errors and sex ratios at birth affect FMRs only marginally while the effects of sex-selective migration can be controlled using data for the juvenile age group.

Sex ratio at birth

Sex ratio at birth is one of the 'initial conditions' which determines the sex ratio of the overall population. It is nearly constant—within a range of 104–107 male live births per 100 female live births—in the absence of any sex-selective human intervention (McKee, 1984: 92; Visaria, 1971). Various biological, environmental and socio-economic factors affect sex ratio at birth. Important among these are birth order and the child-bearing conditions which are reflected in the proportion of stillbirths to live births.

It is widely believed that the '*primary*' sex ratio (sex ratio at conception) is much higher than the sex ratio at birth or the '*secondary*' sex ratio (Klasen, 1994: 1064–65; McKee 1984; Miller, 1981: chapter 2). Owing to higher biological vulnerability of male foetuses, 3–37 per cent more male foetal deaths take place over female foetal deaths (Ramchandran and Deshpande, 1964: 90).[13] The sex ratios of stillbirths decline as the proportion of stillbirths to live births decreases (ibid.). As a result, sex ratios at birth becomes more masculine as the conditions of childbearing become more optimum, health care improves and proportion of stillbirth come down, (Klassen, 1994). This is quite small in magnitude, however, since the ratio of stillbirths to live births is quite low, i.e., less than 50 stillbirths per 1,000 live births. The secondary sex ratio at birth increased in Sweden, for example, by less than three points over 200 years (1780–1980) and by less than four points in the UK between 1861 to 1980 (Ananthram, 1989: 93; Klassen, 1994). The improved health environment, as reflected in the life expectancy at birth, indicates an increase of one percentage point in the sex ratio at birth for every increase of 13 years in life expectancy (Klassen, 1994: 1066).

As regards birth order, there is clear evidence that the sex ratios at birth among the first born is universally higher than among the subsequently born children (Klassen, 1994: 1065; Pakrasi and Haldar, 1973: 41; Ramchandran and Deshpande, 1964: 90).

---

[13] This is based on a 26-country analysis for three decades between 1915 and 1944.

million live births recorded in hospitals and health centres during 1949–58 in different regions of India. It confirms that sex ratio at birth varies very little by regions and lies within the range of 104–108. The low value of 104 for the northern zone and the higher value of 108 for the central zone is attributed to the relatively small sample size (about 50,000 live births!). Pakrasi and Halder (1973) report unusually high secondary sex ratios (120) among the first born children. This sharply drop among subsequently born children closer to the 104–108 range. These estimates are required to be viewed with caution on account of the smaller sample sizes (around 20,000 at zonal level for all birth orders) and extraordinarily high sex ratios recorded in the villages of the north-western states (1973: 50). Ananthram (1989: Chapter 7) shows that a unit change in the sex ratio at birth changes the sex ratio of the population by about 9 points. This is very small compared to the lowness of the FMRs encountered. The question of sex ratios at birth is further examined in Chapter 4 using some indirect methods.

Enumeration errors

Since the census operations began enumeration errors, namely under-enumeration of females and age misstatements, continues to be invoked to explain the low FMRs in certain regions (Miller, 1984: 112; Natarajan, 1972). It is contended that the regions in the north-west, where consider-able gender bias exists, are marked by under-enumeration of daughters. This is attributed to the social circumstances under which the presence of nubile young daughters is not reported as they are considered sexually vulnerable and in need of protection (1984 ibid.).[16] Where they are not hidden, their age is wrongly stated. These errors are of two type, digital preference, i.e., preference for the years ending with 5 and 0, and constant age bias which results in shifting the age of particular age groups systematically up or down. Dyson (1975: 4–6) does not consider the digital preference as a significant factor in the 0–9 age group.

Visaria has examined the issue of under-enumeration in detail using the 1951 and the 1961 data from post-enumeration checks and direct comparison of the census population figures with direct observations from

---

[16] Meera Chatterjee had made this point about girls among the Scheduled Caste in the north. (in personal conversation [p.c here after], 1993). See also Mendelbaum (1988) in a broader context and Srinivasan who makes this claim even for the 1991 Census enumeration (1994).

the well known Khanna study.[17] The corrections in sex ratios from the post-enumeration checks are very small in magnitude and the results of the Khanna study do not show any significant differences in sex ratios from the census figures (Visaria, 1971: chapter IV). Visaria also looks at the indirect evidence (Visaria, 1969: chapter V) and finds that unlike earlier censuses of 1891–1931 which showed some signs of under-reporting of females in the 'never married' category, the 1961 Census shows 'no indication of any significant omission' (ibid.: 24). Ananthram (1989: 92) found that the gap between the female and the male in undercount had declined in the next two censuses while the sex ratio continued to become more masculine.

Visaria's analysis should have settled the issue of under-enumeration. But '... ink continues to be spilled over this issue' (Miller, 1984: 112) even in discussion of 1991 Census results (Srinivasan, 1994). Miller provides further arguments against the enumeration errors excuse. Since her analysis, as well as this analysis, focusses on the 0–9 age group sex ratios, the under-enumeration of nubile daughters can be ignored. Further, the longitudinal studies of the Khanna report and the Ludhiana Christian Medical College study, involving a large sample, confirm the high masculine sex ratios among children (ibid.: 113). Kelly's comparative analysis of children in Punjab and Kerala also confirms this (1984: 112). Miller's exasperation is understandable when she remarks:

> To say that the north Indian census data on the juvenile population are of poor quality because the sex ratio is unbalanced is to deny that the scarcity of the girls is a fact. To try to 'correct' the sex ratio through sophisticated demographic manipulations is to distort the truth (Miller 1984: 113).

Attempts at such 'correction' are problematic when the question of the choice of right life tables for the Indian population itself is far from settled with Clark even suggesting the use of different sets of life tables for Indian males and Indian females (Clark, 1989: 139–45).

Debate of this nature would remain inconclusive in the absence of good quality mortality data, a need noted by Miller (1984) and Visaria (1971). Luckily, child mortality levels for male and female children have been estimated at the district level from the 1981 Census data (Government of

---

[17] A detailed population study undertaken in 16 villages of the Ludhiana district (1956–60) by the Population Studies Unit of the School of Public Health, Harvard University.

India, 1988). These confirm the pattern of excess female level mortality in the low FMR districts of the north-west. Availability of this data has, in fact, shifted the focus of analysis from sex ratios to sex differentials in mortality (Kishor, 1993 and Murthi et al., 1995) as a direct indicator of the female disadvantage making much of the enumeration excuse inoperative.

The migration factor

Most analyses of sex ratio patterns in India use data not corrected for migration.[18] The reason perhaps lies in use of state-level data.[19] At the state level, effects of sex-selective migration are assumed to be insignificant, which may not necessarily be the case (Agnihotri, 1995a: 2083). While female migration in India mostly arises on account of marriage, most long distance migration is heavily male dominated and arises out of economic necessities (Desai, 1969: 206–207 and Chapter 7; Srivastava, 1979: 58–59, 71) High net male in-migration in metropolitan areas, net male out-migration from Kerala or male dominated in-migration among non-Scheduled Tribes in some of the north eastern states bear this out. This results in considerable variations in the FMRs. For instance FMR is 772 for Mumbai, 1032 for Kerala, 558 for non-tribal Nagaland (Agnihotri, 1996b).

To overcome the problem of sex-selective migration, both Sopher (1980) and Miller (1981) have used juvenile age group data.[20] The 'ingenuous' use of district-level JSR data (Papanek, 1984: 143) has provided considerable insights into the issue of regional variations in sex ratios. Yet the use of JSRs has not gained much currency. Some of the debate about sex ratio variations continues around the role played by migration.[21] However, once relative survival of females is recognised as the central issue and JFMRs are used for analysis, debate on migration becomes unnecessary.

---

[18] Except those using JSRs or under-5 mortality data (see footnote 19).

[19] For, example, Raju's analysis of (1991) gender issues with a 'geographical perspective' and Agarwal (1994) who traces 'cross-cultural diversities'.

[20] While both mention the absence of sex-selective migration in the JSR data they do not examine it in any detail.

[21] See, for example, Kundu and Sahu (1991: 2342), who claim that 'at the state or district level, migration is the single most important factor explaining the temporal and cross-sectional variations in sex ratio'.

reversal in sex differentials beyond infancy that is, the first year of life. Societies in which bias against the girl child or strong son preference is not reported, reveal higher male mortality during infancy. Beyond infancy, however, the pattern reverses. Mortality rates in the 1–4 age group (child mortality rates or CMRs[24] henceforth) for females are higher than for males. However, the difference is mostly marginal and levels of CMR are much smaller than levels of IMR (UN Demographic Yearbooks, 1966, 1988).

Excess male mortality during infancy is attributed to the relative biological advantage enjoyed by female infants compared to male infants in a health neutral environment (Klasen, 1994: 1064–65; Nathanson, 1984; Waldron, 1983: 323–25). As against this, excess female mortality invariably results from behavioural factors (Harriss, 1989; Johansson, 1991; Kishor, 1993; Miller, 1981; Waldron, 1983 among others).

The gender bias

Societies where gender bias against females operate, can experience large sex differentials in child mortality rates (Caldwell and Caldwell 1990: 661–71; Harriss 1989; Hill and Upchurch, 1995: 147). The 'access disadvantage' to life sustaining inputs, for example, mother's milk, nutrition, immunisation and health care, negates the biological advantage that the girl child has. Harriss describes excess female mortality in the 1–4 age group as (1987: 62) ' ... (at present) the *most sensitive and specific measure of female disadvantage*'.

Components of under-5 mortality

Three components of juvenile mortality are usually differentiated: *neonatal* (0–1 month) and *post-neonatal* (1–11 months) mortality which together constitute *infant mortality* (0–1 year) and *childhood mortality* (1–4 year). All the three components are affected by *endogenous, exogenous and behavioural* or discriminatory practices. There is general agreement in literature (Caldwell and Caldwell, 1990 UN, 1966; Visaria, L. 1988; Waldron, 1983; among others) that:

(*a*) Neonatal mortality is primarily affected by endogenous factors, for example, maternal or foetal physiology, prenatal circumstances or the process of birth.

---

[24] Throughout this text CMR will mean mortality rates in the 1–4 age group.

(b) Exogenous factors, mainly relating to physical environment and including risk of infectious, respiratory or parasitic diseases affect post-neonatal mortality.

(c) Behavioural factors related to discrimination, mainly affect childhood mortality.

These observations are based upon some *tacit assumptions*, like the assumption that behavioural factors do not operate significantly during infancy, or that the effect of exogenous factors is marginal at the neonatal stage. When these assumptions are violated, e.g., infanticide is a behavioural factor, neonatal tetanus operates through exogenous factors,[25] above patterns may not hold.

Where these assumptions generally hold, post-neonatal mortality declines more rapidly than neonatal mortality. As a result, neonatal deaths account for an increasingly larger share of infant deaths as infant mortality declines (UN, 1966: 2–3; Visaria, L. 1988; Waldron, 1983: 324). Child mortality rates also decline rapidly compared to infant mortality as mortality levels come down.

There is some debate about a physiologically irreducible minimum gap between male and female infant mortality[26] but what concerns the discussion here is that the gap is wider at higher levels of mortality. This widening of course cannot continue indefinitely as there must be some limits to the 'biological advantage' of the female infant.[27]

One of the worrying trends in India is of excess female mortality in post-neonatal stage (IIPS, 1995). As a result, excess *female* mortality can

---

[25] Waldron (1983), and also Smucker et al. (1980) have reported that up to 60 per cent of the neonatal deaths were due to tetanus in a sample study conducted in UP.

[26] i) At present the IMRs expressed per 1,000 live births show higher male IMRs even at IMRs levels of 5 or 6 (UN, 1992). As this level reduces, the comparison may shift to an IMR expressed per 10,000 live births and the debate may continue.

ii) It is normally believed that Waldron contests the concept of biological advantage. But a careful reading (Waldron, 1983: 324) clarifies the position. She accepts greater male infant vulnerability and even speculates upon its causes. Where she emphasises importance of environmental factors is in foetal mortality. There too the argument is that *as the health environment improves*, the risk of foetal mortality becomes approximately equal for both the sexes. [emphasis added]

[27] Data available for the US for the late 19th century (Ginsberg and Swedlund, 1986) suggest that the gap reduces beyond certain levels of mortality. Data on famine in India [Maharatna, 1996] also indicates a plateau in the gap. However, this is not a major issue, at least at levels of mortality prevailing today. It could be worth examining though in situations of high IMR levels, for example, when they are, above 400, as was the case of single room dwellers in Bombay in early part of this century (Dyson, T. 1992).

be noticed in certain regions even during infancy (IIPS,1995, for details see chapter 3).

Literature on infant and child mortality usually focusses more upon levels of mortality than on sex differentials in them. The analysis in Chapter 3 uses a completely new way of inferring the male or female disadvantage from the longitudinal data on mortality levels by sex. In the hypothetical event of male and female children being identical, male and female mortality levels would be equal. A plot of male versus female mortality rates over time would be a straight line passing through the origin with a slope of unity. In the event of a male or a female disadvantage, the slope will deviate from unity. Longitudinal data on mortality supports this approach.

The major departure from the current literature made in Chapter 3 is the analysis of the demographic consequences of sex differentials in infant and child mortality. This has not received any attention[28] in literature. I use a rudimentary model to show that the patterns of sex differentials give rise to significantly different patterns of FMR in 0–4 and 5–9 age groups. These differences are then analysed in Chapter 4 using the 1981 Census data. Another new feature of the analysis (see Chapter 4) is the disaggregation of the FMRs by social groups. This is briefly discussed next.

V

Disaggregation by social groups (Chapter 4)

Overall population in any given region is not homogenous and sex ratios among its different substrata differ not just by age but by socio-cultural factors like caste or class. Miller (1981) recognised this and opted for a caste-based analysis of sex ratios using the 1931 Census data. But caste-wise data are not available in subsequent censuses. Data are, however, available for the three broad segments of the population: the Scheduled

---

[28] Kishor (1993: 250), in fact, rejects Caldwells' suggestion (1990: 1) to exclude the first year of life while studying the gender differentials in childhood mortality arguing that 'available evidence suggests gender discrimination ... even in the first year of life'.

Tribes, the Scheduled Castes and the rest of the population (Agnihotri, 1996b).

Scheduled Caste and Scheduled Tribes

The Scheduled Castes and Scheduled Tribes constituting about 16 per cent and 8 per cent (respectively) of the country's population (Agnihotri, 1995a), represent historically disadvantaged sections of the society. The Scheduled Castes represent the socially isolated groups at the bottom of the caste hierarchy. In fact, they are outside the fourfold structure of castes and as practitioners of 'unclean' occupations were treated as untouchables by other caste groups (Dunn, 1993: 55).

The Scheduled Tribes, represent certain ethnic aboriginal groups inhabiting specific spatial clusters, by and large unsuited for settled agriculture (Raza and Ahmad, 1990: 38). It is believed that in the past, fertile river basins attracted early peasant communities which pushed the aboriginal groups to peripheral areas which were 'less attractive, or relatively isolated ... hilly, forested or dry (areas) and were away from the natural routes of communication within the country' (ibid.: 7). These isolated regions, which have sheltered the tribal segment of the population with their primitive economies, have 'remained as blind alleys in the history of India' (ibid.). In the course of time, some of these tribes have been integrated into the mainstream Hindu society among certain warrior castes and in some cases certain 'lower' castes (Karve, 1965: 15; Parkin, 1992: 7). By and large, however, those identified as tribals today are the unassimiltated people.[29]

Both Scheduled Castes and Scheduled Tribes share certain common economic features. They are both, for example, poor, have marginal land assets both qualitatively and quantitatively and are major suppliers of casual and agriculture labour (Boserup, 1970: 66–75; Dunn, 1993: 58; Miller, 1981: 74–80). But socially and culturally the two are quite different. Scheduled Castes are quite evenly spread across the country. There are 339 districts where their population accounts for more than 1 per cent the

---

[29] Traditionally, the study of tribal population has been regarded as a preserve of the anthropological domain while that of the Scheduled Castes has moved further into the domain of sociology and political science. There are very few demographic or economic studies concerning these communities. 'An atlas of tribal India' by Raza and Ahmad (1990) is perhaps the first serious non-ethnographic study. For Scheduled Castes any such effort is yet to be made.

district's population. (Chapter 4) Within the districts too, their population is quite evenly spread.

The Scheduled Tribe population is unevenly spread and confined to specific clusters. Nearly three-fourths of the country's STs are concentrated in central India along the north–south divide (Nanda, 1993: 7; NSSO, 1994). Along this belt that runs east to west, they also represent a sizeable proportion of the local population—a point often ignored under the argument that STs constitute only 8 per cent of the country's population. Further, STs in central India differ from the north-eastern STs in many respects (NSSO, 1994). Scheduled Tribes form the major population of most of the north-eastern states. In the analysis here the focus will be on the central Indian STs and not on the north-eastern STs.

Differences in sex ratio patterns among the ST, SC and the general category have not attracted serious attention in the literature. Generally, high FMRs among 'animist' population has been noted in old census reports from time to time (Natarajan, 1972). High FMRs among the STs in Madhya Pradesh is explicitly discussed by Dange (1972). But this has not been followed up further. Miller herself explicitly opts out of this line of analysis preferring to use older (1981) data on individual castes[30] rather than the data from more current census which used 'just three categories'. The usefulness of these 'just three categories' will become clear when the sex ratio data among these groups are analysed separately (Chapter 4).

VI

The north–south divide (Chapter 5)

The distinct sex ratio divide between the north-western and south -eastern region of the Indian subcontinent (Miller, 1984), is part of a wider cultural division recognised as the Indo-Aryan (north)–Dravidian (south) divide.[31]

---

[30] 'Given the choice between using the modern (census) data for just three categories ... (i.e., ST, SC and general)... or using somewhat old data (1931 Census) on castes, I opted for the latter'. Miller (1981: 74)

[31] There has been considerable academic debate over the issue of essential 'unity' of the Indian social structure vis-à-vis its essential diversity [See Parkin (1992: 2–15), Trautmann (1993: 62–108) and Karve (1965: 14–16)]. It has covered and affected some emotive issues like the Aryan–Dravidian divide and the distinct or otherwise 'identity' of tribals. At certain

This division is reflected in the kinship system, languages (Trautmann, 1981: 19–27) and crop patterns (Bardhan, 1974) to mention a few.

The kinship systems

One major respect in which the north and south differ is in terms of the kinship system.[32] The Indo-Aryan kinship is characterised by strong subordination of women. Relevant features of this kinship systems, identified by Dyson and Moore (1983: 43–45) are: spatially exogamous marriage rules; social cooperation between males based on descent; and exclusion of women from property inheritance chain. These contrast with the features of the southern kinship system, namely, spatially endogamous marriages, equal importance of affinity and descent in social cooperation among males and inclusion of women in the property inheritance processes. In India, as in most agrarian societies, kinship provides a major avenue of access to social resources and interaction, and hence determines the freedom or autonomy women can enjoy.

In the Indo-Aryan system, the consanguines, that is, the blood realtions, are strictly separated from the affine or the in-laws. There is a clear-cut distinction between the family of birth and the family of marriage. In the Dravidian system these are merged. The mother's brother, a relative within the family of birth, can be one's husband and for the person who marries his elder sister's daughter, his elder sister becomes his mother-in-law. Such overlap is disallowed in the Indo-Aryan system which divides the affine further into two separate categories, bride-givers and bride-takers. The bride-givers are accorded an inferior status compared to those who receive the bride. Reciprocal exchange of brides between two lineages is discouraged. In the Dravidian system, reciprocal exchange is not just permitted, it is preferred, even insisted upon. This exchange of brides between two lineages perpetuates affinity between the two. This is forbidden in the Indo-Aryan system.

The Dravidian system classifies blood relations into two groups: those whom a person can marry (cross) and those whom the person cannot

---

stages, the debate between the two approaches—one to atomise the social structre and the other to homogenize it—has turned rather polemical (Parkin 1992: 7). This analysis requires recognition of various relevant differences and a study of their effects on the sex ratios if any. To that extent it follows the accounts which establish significant differences between kinship systems and structure of languages across major geographical regions of India. For a recent overview see Goody (1990: Chapters 7 and 8).

[32] Discussion of different aspects of the kinship here mostly follow Karve (1965) and Trautmann (1993). For recent concise reviews, see Basu (1992) or Kishor (1993).

(Parallel). This grouping can change across a generation. The group of blood relatives which were 'cross' for the father may become 'parallel' for the son and vice versa.[33] This is ruled out in the Indo-Aryan system where one cannot marry one's blood relatives.[34]

The cultural consequences of these two patterns of bride exchange—'reciprocal' in the Dravidian system and 'extended' in the Indo-Aryan system—are far reaching. In the southern system, a bride does not enter a household as a stranger. She is not an 'outsider' whose behaviour is to be closely watched and whose freedom has to be restricted compared to that of the 'daughters'. Her communication with her natal kin after marriage remains considerable and so does her frequency of visit to her parents' house. In the northern system, the bride is an outsider and has to shift loyalties completely from the family of birth to the family of marriage. She gets assimilated into one at the cost of the other. Giving birth to a son facilitates this 'assimilation'.

Status inferiority of the bride-giving group in the Indo-Aryan system deserves further scrutiny. It is institutionalised even in marriage rituals like washing the feet of the groom's parents by certain person(s) from the bride's side making it clear as to who has a superior status. This asymmetry is also reflected within the languages.

Kinship and the language

Inferior status conferred upon the bride-givers is reflected in the Indo-Aryan languages in a number of ways. The most common among these is use of the term '*sala*' (wife's brother). *Sala* is a very common term of contempt and mild abuse (Karve, 1965: 113, Madan, 1993: 298). Calling somebody '*Sala*', when he is not one, is a definite insult insinuating that 'I have dominated your sister sexually'—an idea not stated explicitly. It is quite common to use the term to encourage a person to beat up his

[33] For example, mother's sisters will represent a 'cross' group for a person's father while for that person, mother's sister and her children will represent a 'parallel' group (unmarriageable) while mother's brother and his children will represent a 'cross' or marriageable group.

[34] One consequence of the Dravidian Kinship practice has been 'misunderstood' for a long time by anthropologists steeped in the Indo-Aryan tradition (Karve 1965: 247). It is possible in the Dravidian system for a person to marry a girl who can, in generational terms, be his granddaughter. Yet their age difference will not be large (Karve, 1965: 247) and the marriage is permissible according to the rules. Such a concept will be unheard of and unthinkable in the Indo-Aryan system although a marriage between an old man and an unrelated girl, young enough to be his granddaughter, is perfectly acceptable.

adversary by saying '*Maro sale ko*' (the correct flavour of which would be 'beat up that bastard!'). Even the term '*sasura*' meaning father-in-law is used as a less mild yet contemptuous term when applied to a stranger (Madan 1993: 298). Such usage is not found in the non-Indo-Aryan languages and the reason is not far to seek. The reciprocal exchange ensures that the wife's brother may also be the sister's husband or for that mater the mother's brother may be ones father-in-law. Who then 'insults' whom? Such 'insult' is only possible under the safe presumption of exclusion between the wife-giving and wife-taking group.

Another phrase used in Hindi, whose context is readily understood in all Indo-Aryan languages, is 'bride's father'. It is often used to express the weak, even pitiable, bargaining position of a man. It is a very common refrain that the bride's side always has to 'bow down' or swallow their pride ('*jhukna padta hai*') if it comes to any difference of opinion between the two side. One does not know if these usages reflect the process of 'bride capture' in the remote past when the Indo-Aryans came to the Indian subcontinent. If it does, the gradual establishment of '*sala*' or '*sasura*' as a classificatory term of insult make sense.

Creating a distance

The 'social distance' between bride-givers and bride-takers can be threatened by spatial proximity (Madan, 1993: 304–306). This necessitates furtherance of territorial exogamy, perhaps gradually, and of distinctions between bride-giving and bride-receiving lineages. Institutionalisation of consanguine exogamy through elaborate rules of exclusion, a well-recorded feature of the Indo-Aryan system, can be understood in this context. This can then extend to exclusion of villages (Karve, 1965: 57)[35] and can even harden into exclusion of villages in a particular direction, for example, receiving brides from the eastward villages and grooms from westward ones (ibid.: 125).

This exogamous pattern is corroborated by Libbee's analysis (1980: 93–98) of the spatial structure of marriage in India. The north–south divide again marks regional variations in 'marriage distances', that is, the distance between the bride's home of birth and home of marriage. There is a remarkable clustering of low village endogamy and high marriage distance in the the north-west. This region comprising of Rajasthan, Punjab, western

---

[35] It is quite usual in the north to refer to a person as the son-in-law of a particular village rather than a family.

Uttar Pradesh (UP) and western Madhya Pradesh (MP) is characterised by the most extensive taboos on cross-cousin marriages and the most rigorous prescription of territorial exogamy.[36] Kishor (1993) also uses exogamy as an effective indicator of female subordination.

What is the extent to which particular marriage rules or preferences translate into actual practices? Obviously all marriages in the Dravidian kinship region are not cross-cousin marriages. Nor is spatial endogamy practised completely in a given region. Data on this is very difficult to come by and different micro level studies estimate that cross-cousin marriages account for 10–30 per cent of the total marriages (IIPS, 1995; Trautmann, 1993: 279–86) but these figures do not cover distant cross-cousin marriages. These represent, however, the 'ideal stereotypes' in society. Complete adherence to these stereotypes is never expected but these represent the accepted norm in the society. Symmetry of status between bride-givers and bride-takers is an ideal stereotype in the Dravidian and Munda system. In the Indo-Aryan system it is the asymmetry which is the ideal stereotype. Both have their consequent effects on the attitudes and practices within the society.

The higher autonomy enjoyed by females in the south is a relative term, for, the FMRs in south India are low in an absolute global sense (Dyson and Moore, 1983: 46–47). Limitations to autonomy of women have been noted by different scholars, for example, the Caldwells (1990) for rural Karnataka. The description above is useful, however, in drawing out the two stereotypes and observe the extent to which the southern stereotype deviates in practice and shows the spread of the northern traits (Caldwell and Caldwell, 1990; Heyer, 1992; Kapadia, 1994).

The munda kinship system

It is necessary to recognise another kinship layer that covers the Indian landscape: the Munda kinship system. The Austro-Asiatic groups represented by Mundas of central India have a distinct linguistic and kinship system (Parkin, 1992). This had received very little attention until recently (1992: 12 and Chapter 8). Munda marriage practices are closer

---

[36] Libbee does acknowledge the role played by the distance friction which characterises low marriage distances in the hilly areas of the northern states (1980: 94). The lower marriage distances in eastern UP and Bihar according to him corresponds with 'an ecological transition from the primary wheat farming areas in the west to the wetter rice areas of the east' (1980: 94).

to the southern system permitting marriage between distant cross-cousins and symmetry between the bride exchanging groups (1992: 216).[37]

The linguistic regions

There is a broad agreement about the existence of four major language groups in India (Nigam 1964: CLXXIX)—the Indo Aryan, the Dravidian, Munda or the Austro-Asiatic and the Tibeto-Burman. Genetic relation among these four, even if it existed would be 'so remote in the past that it cannot be recovered' (Trautmann, 1981: 18). The Tibeto-Burman family is not considered in this analysis as it has little bearing on the issue of the north-west– south-east differences.

The linguistic map of India shows three clear regions (Map 2.1). Indo-Aryan language group covers most of the north-west. Munda group covers most of the tribal belt in eastern and central region. Dravidian languages mainly cover the south and the tribal languages in the south-west. Non-tribal Gujarat, Maharashtra and Orissa represent the confluence of the two linguistic streams where the Indo-Aryan languages have prevailed (Map 2.1). These have extended as far a Konkani in the south and Assammes in the east. These also cover tribal pockets of Bhilli-speaking tribes in the north-west. Some pockets of Dravidian languages have survived in central and even northern India among tribals.

There are strong grounds for believing that the Dravidian languages did prevail in the entire sub-continent along with the Austro-Asiatic ones prior to the spread of the Indo-Aryan languages and culture (Spate and Learmonth, 1967: 173–78; Trautmann, 1981: 11–16). It is also accepted that the incoming Indo-Aryan population assimilated the local population rather than displacing or 'pushing' them south of the dividing belt (Trautmann, 1981: 6–9). A certain amount of displacement of the tribal people from the fertile agricultural plains to the hilly terrain has taken place. This was done by both Dravidians and subsequently the Aryans and the process has continued even up to recent past (Raza and Ahmad 90: 7, 38).

The broad congruence between the linguistic regions and the kinship is discussed in more details in Chapter 5. Here, the focus is shifted to a

---

[37] Parkin (1992: Chapters 9 and 10) in his detailed study of the Munda kinship system has identified aspects, other than marriage rules, in which the Munda kinship concepts differ from the two system and may have influenced some of the concepts in both Indo-Aryans and Dravidian systems. But these, for example, the equivalence of alternate generation and reincarnation, do not concern us here.

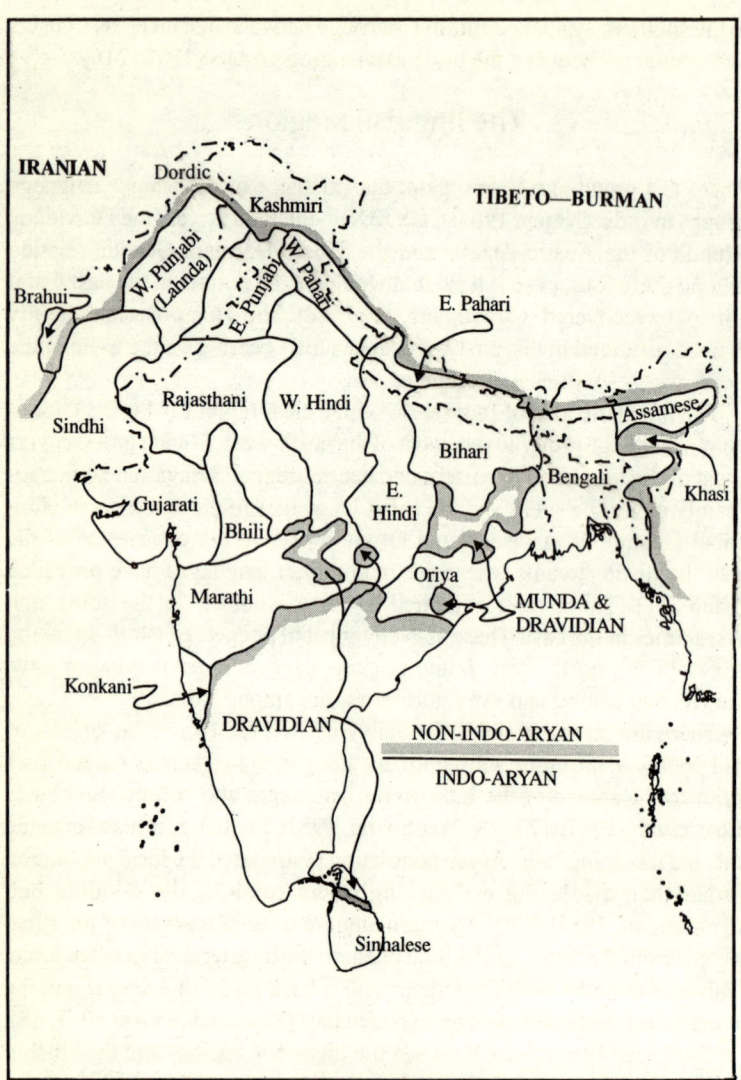

Map 2.1: Linguistic map of India.
Source: Trautmann, 1981.

different view of the cultural divide which questions the simple and static north–south dichotomy.

North–south or core–periphery?

The north-south divide has been critiqued by some scholars. The Caldwells consider the 'Aryan-Dravidian' contrast exaggerated (1990: 11). They consider the contrast to be really between the 'heartland of an ancient peasant civilisation and its periphery'. To them 'nearly all of what characterises north India, developed on the upper Gangetic plain' a heartland which bears resemblance with other 'old, closely settled peasant civilisations with sedentary farming and a closed frontier'. It is this heartland that is characterised by strong age and gender hierarchy.

A more pertinent point raised by the Caldwells is the spread of the 'dominant model' from the core into in the periphery especially with reference to differentiation by sex (1990: 11). As mentioned earlier, they explicitly refer to it as 'northernisation' in the Indian context and cite the 'recent rapid spread of dowry' as an example. Kapadia (1994) describes this shift in detail while Heyer's description about the position of the girl child among the Thottam farmers in Tamil Nadu reads as if it is from the north-west (1992).

The above view finds echo in the distinction made by Berreman (1993: 366) between regions and groups subjected to the dominant Hindu ethos; or the 'core' and the rest of the groups, a periphery. He identifies some of the peripheral groups among whom the subordination of women is less severe as:

1. Groups which are largely or entirely outside the purview of traditional Hindu beliefs, values and social organisation, e.g., tribal societies.
2. Hindus at the bottom of or low in the caste hierarchy e.g., the Scheduled Castes.
3. Hindus who are peripheral to the dominant society socio-culturally or geographically in ways that make them peculiar, suspect or attenuated adherents to the creed, e.g., Pahari Hindus, or Hindus with matrilineal or bilateral descent systems, unconventional marriage rules, atypical economies and the like (Berreman 1993: 367).

Berreman also refers to the process of adoption of the dominant model by the 'social' periphery. Some of the *features of female subordination practised within the dominant 'core'* listed by him are: patrilocal marriage; patrilineal descent and inheritance; dowry; prohibition of wife-initiated divorce; widow remarriage; female deference to males in the household of her husband; female economic dependence upon males, especially after marriage; strict prohibition of extra marital sexual activity for women with dire consequence if the man is lower in caste, while tolerating such activity for men, especially with low caste women (ibid. 368–69). Any caste which seeks to attain higher status must demonstrably adopt these features.

The adoption of the 'high culture' norms (Goody, 1990) by the low culture substratum in a society have been described by Goody not only between castes but within a given caste itself. The poorer members of a given caste start adopting the high culture norms associated with gender subordination as they become prosperous or as a status enhancement strategy (ibid.). The high culture norms summarised by Goody (1990: 182; Table 2.2 below), bring out the element of female subordination quite clearly.

Table 2.2
Attitude towards women in 'high' and 'low' cultures[38]

Culture	Divorce	Money-flow	Widow Remarriage	Household Forms	Age at Marriage	Position of Women
High	None	Dowry	Condemned	Complex	Lower	Restraint
Low	Some	Bride Price	Allowed	Nuclear	Higher	Freedom

This view puts the north-south divide in a different perspective. According to this view, relatively female-friendly cultural norms once prevailed in the subcontinent. These were gradually replaced in the current 'core' region through the spread of Indo-Aryan culture, its kinship system and its ethos of female subordination.[39] Such spread has admittedly been uneven and incomplete as evidenced by the existence of different

[38] Goody (1990: 180) also characterises the 'high' culture with (a) vegetarianism (b) offering of cooked food to Gods who are scriptural, ancestral, male and married, and (c) the hold of written orthodoxy in these cultures. In contrast, the 'low' culture are (a) omnivorous, (b) have local, female Gods to whom blood sacrifice is offered and (c) there is no mediation through written orthodoxy in communicating with these Gods.

[39] Why the ethos of strong female subordination might have prevailed in this 'core' is briefly speculated upon in the concluding chapter.

'peripheries'—social, cultural and geographical. But the process of spread still continues. The groups which adopt the norms of the 'dominant system' do so by adopting the aspects of female subordination listed here (Berreman, 1993). Within a given region, the ethos spreads through the process of status acquisition by the upwardly mobile segments of the substratum while across different regions it spreads through diffusion among the social upper strata of the 'peripheral' regions.

The spreading ethos

This view contrasts with the rather static view of the north–south divide and has important consequences for this analysis. The first relates to an uncritical import of the 'core–periphery' description in the sex ratio context and the second relates to the spread of the process of female subordination à la the 'dominant' system. This is discussed in Chapters 5 and 8. Briefly stated, the uncritical acceptance of the 'core–periphery' description creates an unstated link between core patterns as 'norms' and the peripheral patterns as exceptions. It is argued that the political core need not be the social or cultural core nor a numerical core. The pattern of female subordination in the political 'core' should on the other hand be considered a deviation[40] and the 'core–periphery' description should be turned on its head into a 'norm versus aberration' description. This has important consequences for both policy and social action for it opens up a space for questioning the ethos of female subordination in the north–west rather than looking upon its spread as somewhat inevitable.

As regards the spread of the ethos of female subordination in the 'periphery', two loci are involved. In physical terms such locus will match with the route of cultural circulation between the north and the south. In social terms, it will spread among the prospering groups in the north (Berreman, 1993; Goody, 1990) and prosperous groups in the south (Caldwell and Caldwell, 1990; Heyer, 1992; Kapadia, 1994). Such prospect necessitates an analysis of the 'prosperity effect', a subject matter of Chapter 8.

---

[40] Raju (1991: 2877) is the only one who has used this term so far.

VII

Survival, entitlements and capabilities (Chapter 6)

The debate on the north–south divide centres around women's status which, in turn, is looked upon as a major determinant of her access to available resources. This access determines a person's wellbeing; longevity being its most basic, though not the only, manifestation. The link between access to resources and well being is plausible though hazy. These are elaborated in Chapter 6 through the entitlements framework (Sen, 1981).

The entitlements framework

Originally developed to examine the questions of famine and hunger (Sen 1981), the scope of the entitlements framework has been widened in recent years to look at the questions of distribution of resources in general (Gasper, 1993). It has been used in the field of gender analysis by Sen himself (1982, 1990), Papanek (1990) and, most notably by Kabeer (1991, 1995) among others.

Entitlements essentially represent the potential command a person has over resources while endowments refer to the means through which such a command can be established. One's own labour, skill, land or capital are examples of one's endowments. Through this use, a person is able to effect a command over a bundle of commodities.

While endowments may represent a necessary condition for one's entitlements, the link between the two is established through what is formally called the exchange entitlement mapping or E-mapping or simply E(.). It contains the rules and conditions of exchange, availability of goods and commodities, legal framework and so on. Sen uses a very wide definition of the E-mapping which, according to him, depends upon the 'legal, political, economic and social characteristics of the society in question and the person's position in it' (1981: 46).

A major argument in Sen's analysis was that *availability does not guarantee access*. Starvation and resultant deaths, at least a large number of these, could and did occur due to access failure and not, from food availability decline as many would tend to believe from a 'common sense' perspective. These deaths occurred because of a decline in *access to available food*. Similar entitlements failure could very well operate within a society or the household resulting in avoidable excess female deaths whether through infanticide or 'extended infanticide'. While analysing the relative survival of male and female children at different levels development, Kishor echoes this argument: 'Clearly gender-based discrimination in the allocation of resources persists and even increases, even when availability of resources is not a constraint' (1993: 262).

Originally, 'entitlements had strong legal overtones (Sen, 1990: 140) and emphasised exclusively upon exchange. But these later evolved into 'extended entitlements' to include possibilities like use of public goods or transfer entitlement, for example, through social security network (Drèze and Sen, 1991). The concept of legality has also been broadened to include notions of legitimacy. This is especially relevant for the distribution of resources within the household.

Within the household the rules of allocative behaviour are not explicitly codified. Nor are they static. They are influenced significantly by the extra household environment and practices (Kabeer, 1995: 4–5). These form components of E-mapping which translates a member's endowments into his or her entitlements. These decide who gets how much of what be it food, nutrition, access to health care and the like.

The capabilities approach

Entitlements do not tell, however, the entire story of one's wellbeing. What a person is able to do with his or her entitlements is equally important. The outcome of given entitlements crucially depends upon human diversity and the circumstances under which one is placed. An identical entitlement set for two different individuals can, therefore, produce two quite different outcomes.

The capabilities approach (Sen, 1985) deals with the issue of eventual outcomes and the freedom enjoyed by a person to achieve certain sets of outcomes given his entitlements. The space of outcomes is formally termed as the space of functionings and is linked to the space of entitlements through another mapping involving one's personal characteristics.

Chronologically, the capabilities approach has followed the entitlements framework. It links the outcomes with entitlements while entitlements framework links entitlements and endowments. It appears quite logical that the two approaches be integrated to link these three factors: functionings, entitlements and endowments. Somehow, the two approaches have remained unconnected and have been pursued independently of each other. This gap in the literature has been bridged in Chapter 6.

Application of entitlements framework to gender relations inside the household has been done through the cooperative–conflict approach to the process of allocation within the household (Sen, 1987). Briefly, such approach recognises that (*a*) different members of the household may have diverging preferences and (*b*) while these members may cooperate in augmenting the overall resource level of the household there could be considerable amount of conflict in distribution of these resources within the household.

The subsequent developments of the cooperative–conflict approach to intra-household bargaining have been qualitative and discursive in nature. In fact, most of the applications of the entitlements analysis into different domains[41] have been of this nature making very little use of the 'formal' conceptual apparatus (Gasper, 1993). As a result, a number of useful extensions of this approach have either been overlooked or not developed fully. Chapter 6 uses the 'formal apparatus' to elaborate one possible form of E-mapping taking into account the exchange-independent component of a person's entitlements explicitly. Such explicit recognition of the exchange-independent components of entitlements allows one to integrate the role of cultural factors and economic factors, two separate and competing strands in the literature. This also enables one to identify situations where economic factors are critical and where they are not and advances the understanding of the allocational behaviour within the household.

Unpacking the household

The household as an economic unit has been the subject of a great deal of analysis in the past. Two major and competing view points have engaged themselves over the nature of allocational behaviour within household. These can be broadly categorised as the 'common preference' models and the 'diverging preference' models. The former, based largely on the neo-classical economic approach draws upon Becker (1981). It presume commonality, if not identity of preferences of the members within a household articulated adequately by the head of the household, usually male. The household then pursues maximisation of a 'joint utility function' thus articulated.

[41] For a comprehensive review see Gasper (1993). It has summed up other aspects of the debate which are not of immediate relevance to the analysis in Chapter 6.

The second group does not presume any communality of preferences and analyses the allocative behaviour on game theoretic lines, mostly using Nash bargaining model. The distribution of resources takes place on the basis of bargaining between different members of the household and depends upon their threat points or fall back options in the event of non-cooperation.

Details of this ongoing debate are outside the scope of this discussion. Suffices to say that analytically the common preference model can be shown to be a special case of the diverging preference model (McElroy, 1990). Empirically, more and more evidence is becoming available to validate the bargain theoretic approach (Schultz, 1990; Thomas, 1990). The common preference approach can also result in substantial margins of error in the estimates of overall inequality (Haddad and Kanbur, 1990). A recent and thorough review of various models has been made by Doss (1996).

Entitlements analysis begins with an emphasis on the economic factors in determining the access to resources and then goes on to incorporate the exchange-independent components. It is equally possible to begin with the concept of 'status' of women and speculate upon how economic factors might affect it. The next section explores the impact of one important economic factor, female labour participation on women's status.

VIII

Status, work-force participation and prosperity

The concept of 'status' of women is frequently used in literature on gender inequalities. Basu (1992: Chapter 3) identifies three separate but inter-dependent components of women's status viz:

(*a*) the extent of exposure to the outside world,
(*b*) the extent of interaction, especially the economic interaction with the outside world, and,
(*c*) the level of autonomy in decision-making within and outside the household.

The emphasis placed on women's interaction with the outside world has to be understood in the context of the gendering of space. The association of men with the 'external' or 'public' sphere and women with the 'domestic' or private 'sphere' is commonplace in literature on gender hierarchies.[42] Why women's association becomes a determinant of their status can be understood through the concept of 'capabilities'. As mentioned above, capabilities represent the freedom that an individual has to achieve certain outcomes. When it comes to the public versus domestic sphere, this freedom makes an important distinction. Men choose not to be in the 'domestic' sphere. They can move into it at will except in the case of childbearing. Women on the other hand cannot move into the 'public' sphere at will. Their exclusion from it is not a matter of their choice but a matter of restriction placed upon them by the larger structures of family, kin-group, cultural group and the state.

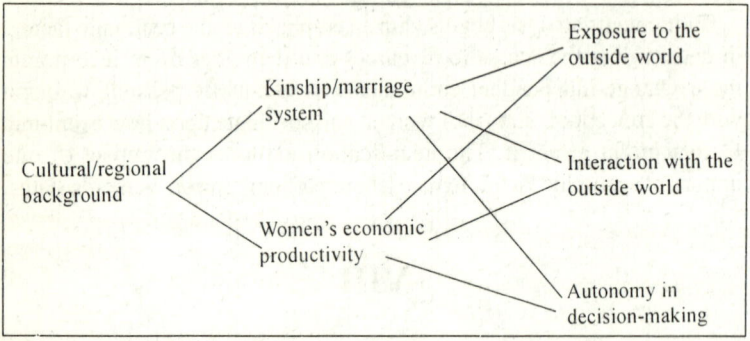

Figure 2.1: Factors affecting the status of women.
Note: Adopted from Basu (1992).

Hence, the extent to which this choice is available is a good indicator of the status of women in that society. Basu's description ' ... probably, the best placed mother is one who does not work herself but knows that there are no restrictions on her finding work ... *should the need arise*' (Basu, 1992: 222, emphasis added), highlights the element of choice, a basic feature of one's capability.

The kinship practices described in Section VI along with the practice of seclusion (described in detail by Mendelbaum, 1988) influence both exposure to the outside world and the economic participation within it. At the same time, the labour market may be influenced by other factors

---

[42] Bennet (1991: Chapter 2) for an excellent representation in the context of work.

like ecology, crop regime, level and choice of technology. This will also affect the exposure and the interaction with the outside world. The autonomy in decision-making is also affected by the two factors together. This is schematically represented in Basu (1992: 69).

Discussion of the interaction between the cultural and economic aspects of FLP have by and large been qualitative in nature except Kishor (1993) who explicitly examines the interaction between the two factors. Chapters 7 and 8 also analyse this interaction quantitatively.

Positive association between higher FLP among adult women and reduced female mortality disadvantage in childhood has been confirmed by Rosenzweig and Schultz (1982), Kishor (1993) and Murthi et al. (1995). All three are large-scale empirical studies. As to the mechanism underlying the association, Murthi et al. list out a number of alternative possibilities. Some or all of these can hold at a given time. It is argued that a higher FLP could (a) raise the returns on investment made on the girl child, (b) lower dowry levels and the cost or raising a girl child, (c) lower women's (parents!) dependence on sons in old age (d) increase women's status in society and through it the value of the girl child and, finally, (e) raise the bargaining power of women in allocational decision within the household.

Apart from the effect of higher FLP on status enhancement, Basu (1992: 222) also mentions the possibility of reduced son preference. She makes another important distinction by considering the potential for participation as the relevant variable rather than actual participation at the household level. It is not necessary for a women to actually participate in the work force: availability of such choice is adequate to enhance her survival chances. The importance of aggregate level FLP figures has also been highlighted by Desai and Jain (1994). This point is important in the context of seclusion, for, high participation at the aggregate level will also mean a high level of 'exposure' which goes against the spirit of seclusion and its enforcement. This issue is taken up further in Chapter 8.

There has been a considerable amount of discussion on the measurement of FLP, especially through the census operations. It is often argued that the work done by women is not 'recognised' by the census enumerators. Further, the definition of workers, main workers and marginal workers keeps undergoing change in the census operations and inter-censal comparisons are not valid.

Different aspects of this debate have been summed up in Vannemann and Barnes (1992) and will not be gone into here. It suffices to say that the measure of FLP in the census represents the 'recognised' part of women's work. It is recognised not just by the state but also by the social and kinship structure. As far as the unwaged household maintenance work is concerned, that is common to all household and would not 'add' to the economic worth of the female (Kishor, 1993). The more real issue relates to the unpaid productive work when additional income generating activity, such as dairying, is taken up by the household. Case studies reveal (Sharma and Vanjani, 1993) that such an activity adds a burden on the women without commensurate enhancement in her status and at the cost of her leisure. Sen (1990) and Basu (1992) also emphasises the importance of explicitly recognised wage earning activity.[43]

Higher FLP among the poor, however, has mixed consequence. It is associated with high child mortality levels in absolute terms (Basu, 1992; Desai and Jain, 1994; Kishor, 1993; Murthi et al. 1995). The suggested mechanism behind this association is the conflict between the task of child-rearing and work-force participation. Desai and Jain (1994), however, argue that it is the burden of unwaged work of household reproduction and not the labour-force participation that affects child care. If this be the case the intervention should more appropriately take place to reduce the avoidable drudgery and time consumed in unwaged work rather than reducing FLP.

While unwaged economic activity creates one kind of problem for women, their withdrawal from wage earning activity in the wake of prosperity poses a different type of problem. Such withdrawal is usually done for the purpose of status enhancement (Gulati, 1978) or what Papanek terms 'status production' activity (1989). But this creates a dilemma for the women as this higher status within the community entails a loss of status within the household as the perceived contribution to the household prosperity declines (Desai and Jain, 1994; Papanek, 1989). As time goes by, the ability to get back in the labour market also declines resulting in a loss of autonomy which solidifies with time. This aspect of prosperity and status is discussed in further details in Chapter 8.

Concerns expressed in literature on the worsening relative position of the females in the wake of prosperity (Kishor 1993; Murthi et al. 1995) need to be examined in this context. The uneven distribution of the gains of development among the male and the female children can operate in two ways: The actual decrease in the survival chances of the female child in the wake of relatively high levels of agricultural development (Kishor 1993: 262) or, an increase in the survival chances for boys more than those for girls in other cases, for example, due urbanisation (ibid.).

---

[43] For a thorough review on women's work-force participation, see Bennet (1991).

A contradictory trend in the literature is reported in the context of prospertiy. This trend of 'prosperity optimism' expects the eventual turning point in the lot of the female members of society with increasing prosperity (Kanbur and Haddad, 1994; Lentican et al. 1996). Alternatively, it is argued that the girl children will become more valued as they get more scarce (Pisani and Zaba, Forthcoming).

The tension between these two contradictory trends is needed to be resolved. This is done in Chapter 8. It is shown both by an analytical and empirical basis that it is the female contribution to prosperity that is the crucial variable in deciding the turning point rather than prosperity itself.

Both Murthi et al. (1995) and Kishor (1993) take the district-level development as an indicator of prosperity. It is more appropriate to take population sub-samples by prosperity and analyse the sex ratios within these. Such disaggregation has not been done before except Krishnaji (1987). Chapter 8 fills this gap by using a less direct set of data.

IX

Some broader issues

As this analysis move ahead, the focus gradually shifts from the patterns to the processes, and from the static aspects of sex ratio imbalances to the dynamic aspects. The larger demographic behaviour reflected in the sex ratios has its origins in the gender inequalities that operate at the micro and the macro level. Considerable work has been done in investigating the genesis and the patterns of gender inequality at these levels.

Gender stratification

A pioneering line of inquiry relevant to the present analysis has been taken up by Blumberg (1991) and others. It attempts to examine the 'triple overlap' between gender stratification, economic variables and the household domain. Details of this cross-cultural, data-backed analysis which aspires at some future date to come up with a 'megatheory' of gender stratification (ibid.: 21) are not within the scope of this study. However, a brief description of the main findings is given next.

The analysis considers women's economic power relative to men as the 'most important and achievable (though not the sole)' independent variable affecting gender stratification at a variety of nested micro and macro levels ranging from the family to the state (Blumberg 1991: 23). However, it proposes that a woman may not 'get a dollar's worth of economic power for every dollar she brings into the household' on account of various 'discount rates' which operate through the cultural, ideological, political, economic and legal systems operating at different levels (ibid.: 23). (A striking similarity with Sen's E-mapping). Such discount rates at the household levels are affected, among other factors, by (*a*) 'women's socialisation to bargain less hard to realise economic leverage', (*b*) relative commitment of the two partners to the household, (*c*) relative local 'market value' of each partner and, (*d*) the man's felt economic dependence on the woman's income.

Two more observations are of crucial importance. First, the contribution to subsistence is less valued than the contribution to the surplus (ibid.: 101), and women contribute more to the subsistence (a point usually made in a large number of micro studies). Second, women who lose income, lose domestic power more quickly and sharply than gain it when income rises (ibid.: 101).

Another useful observation about the socialisation (Collins, 1991) is that men usually form an order-giving class and women an order-receiving class. The giving and receiving of order forms an important characteristic of power within a group whether household or a firm. This is illustrated in an organisational context where women mostly perform 'Goffmanian labour' presenting the organisational frontstage, for example, as receptionists, waitresses, salespersons or secretaries. In the context of the household this parallels women's engagement in status production activities.

The tension between the increase in family status and loss of individual autonomy of women withdrawn from the labour market for the purpose of status enhancement and production can be understood in the context of the observations above. Status production can very conveniently be relegated to the 'subsistence' sector through socialisation. As a result, the woman concerned loses on two counts, loss of direct earnings and loss of power as she now contributes to subsistence activity and not surplus generation.

The sociological approach followed by Blumberg and others has much to gain from and contribute to the entitlements approach to the allocational behaviour within the household. Curiously, there is hardly any dialogue between the two streams of inquiry.[44] The interface between the two approaches is explored further in Chapter 6.

The genesis

The genesis of gender hierarchies is briefly explored by Huber (1991). Such inquiry has been pursued in the anthropological literature in detail. In certain ways all of these are connected with the issue of social reproduction as societies became more complex and differentiated in the contents of their production. The role women have played during this transition have been analysed by Goody (1976, 1990), Harris (1993) and Meillassoux (1981) from three different angles.

Goody's work deals with the emergence of control over female sexuality in the context of transition from subsistence to surplus agriculture. It attributes the rise of gender hierarchies to the pattern of control over means of production and distribution. Meillassoux considers the control over the means of reproduction and therefore women as the key factor. Harris considers the role played by the biological differences between men and women in the exercise of the controls mentioned above.

The broad picture that emerges from the above three analyses is as follows. Gender hierarchies are insignificant in classless societies or in societies where the mode of production is communal. Accumulation of surplus and exchange are at a very primitive level if at all. Essential biological differences between men and women do exist but these are inconsequential. Big game hunting is one area where men develop specialisation as it is incompatible with childbearing. But they also engage in it on account of their being expendable. That is also the reason why they participate in wars. This incidental specialisation has in it the seeds of the 'public/domestic' pattern which separates men and women in stratified societies. It also becomes useful in wars yet at a primitive level. These techniques are utilised in an institutional way when the capture of women of reproductive age group from another band is necessitated. These are also used when territory or surplus is acquired from another group through wars.

Generation of surplus through intensive agriculture is another factor where the control over female sexuality becomes necessary. Their role as

---

[44] None of the contributions in *Gender, family and economy* (Blumberg [ed.], 1991) refer to Sen's work and Sen's usually exhaustive references list (1990) does not cover the work of any of the main contributors in Blumberg's book. All the scholars work in North America.

producers is accorded secondary status resulting in their withdrawal from productive labour. With the process of class formation women's role as reproducers becomes important and restrictions are placed on their interaction with men. This necessitates their seclusion from the 'public' domain during the critical years and protection as daughters and wives. Their access to sex is restricted through creation of ideological constructs and physical power. This physical power is used to 'protect' women from men of other groups. But it is also invoked to 'discipline' women within given group. Both 'protection' and 'discipline' are relevant in the context of biological reproduction giving rise to various restrictive practices. The status of women becomes that of an object that could be acquired along with other property in the event of a conquest.

Societies facing frequent warfare are always alive to the possibility of defeat and the consequent vulnerability of their women. The constant need for 'protection' of their women and coveting those of the adversary leads to devaluation of women's status and their exclusion from the external or the public domain.

While agreeing with this broad picture, Huber (1991) makes two pertinent observations. First, she distinguishes between childbearing and child-rearing and suggests that the external versus domestic separation between men and women mainly arises on account of child-rearing tasks rather than childbearing (Huber 1991: 41–43). Second, there is nothing unique about the pathways a society follows in its patterns of female subordination. It could take the form of foot binding in one, female circumcision in another and bride burning in a third (ibid.: 45–46). Finally, technological changes can have unexpected consequences. The invention of sterilisation techniques, for example, have resulted in safe bottle feeding and removed a big constraint on married women's participation in the formal labour force (ibid.: 47) in the West.

A cross-cultural, historical view

Johansson's observations (1984, 1996) about the changing pattern of excess female mortality (EFM) with development may be relevant in this context. From an analysis of historical data in Europe and Japan she finds that the EFM had been low during traditional agriculture. With development of surplus and commercial agriculture it worsened. With eventual urban and industrial development EFM tended to disappear. The key to the improved female survival chances can plausibly be attributed to the labour force participation opportunities that become available to women.

Johansson's analyses look at the historical aspects of mortality in general and female mortality in particular. She analyses the excess female mortality patterns in Europe (1984), Japan (1986, 1987, 1996) England and the US (1991) and makes a convincing case for looking at the EFM in its historical context rather than in any ahistorical, timeless fashion (1991). This is discussed in more details in Chapter 6. Interestingly, she finds the incidence of excess female mortality (EFM) to be pronounced in the 5–19 age group in all these societies. This is in sharp contrast with the pattern of EFM both in infancy and under-5 mortality in contemporary South Asia (Chapter 3).

To sum up

The overview admittedly provides a very brief outline of the literature relevant to the analysis that follows. It is brief given the large number of topics involved. However, it provides adequate background information about the synthesis of different strands attempted in different chapters. Further details are discussed in the relevant chapters where necessary.

The next three chapters are concerned with disaggregation of sex ratio across different regions and social groups. Before attempting this, the nature and pattern of juvenile mortality itself needs to be scrutinised in greater detail. This is done in the next chapter. It provides some new exciting insights into the sex ratio patterns which completely change the nature of the debate. Subsequent chapters build further on these insights.

Chapter 3

Childhood mortality patterns and juvenile sex ratios

I

An outline

Sex differentials in under-5 mortality have important demographic consequences reflected in the sex ratios in the juvenile age group. As described in the 'ten-lap race', the highly skewed nature of juvenile mortality towards younger ages and the reversal in sex differentials in mortality beyond infancy gives rise to significantly different patterns of FMRs in the 0–4 and 5–9 age groups.

FMRs at birth, usually between 930–960, universally favours male children. Excess male infant mortality reduces this surplus of male children bringing FMRs closer to parity (Chatterjee, 1990: 3; Miller, 1989; Government of India, 1988: Chapter III. If child mortality levels are low and their sex differentials marginal, FMRs would not vary significantly in the subsequent years. But, if child mortality levels are high with an excess of female child mortality, the proportion of female children would decline considerably in the 1–4 age cohort. The decline 'stabilises', however, by the 5th birthday as few deaths occur in the 5–9 age group. But its effect is reflected in the lower proportion of female children in the 5–9 age group. The extent of this low FMR depends upon the extent of excess female child mortality. Sex ratios in the juvenile, that is, 0–9 age group, are a composite of these two FMRs, that is, FMR04 and FMR59.

Mortality and FMRs

This composite nature of juvenile age group FMRs has not been analysed in the literature on sex ratios before. In the present study, it first came to notice during the empirical examination of the 5-year age group data (Agnihotri, 1996b) which revealed significant differences in the FMRs in 0–4 and 5–9 age groups. These differences arise, as mentioned above, as a result of the differences in the levels of infant and child mortality and sex differentials within these. It is possible, as shown below, to estimate the FMR04 and FMR59 from the mortality data. Such an exercise is clearly called for, given the distinct patterns of juvenile sex ratios and childhood mortality in India and well-documented effect of gender bias on both. Curiously, this has remained a neglected area of research.

A preliminary simulation of FMR04 and FMR59 is done here (Section IV) using certain simplifying assumptions. Relative influence of infant and child mortality levels and sex differentials on FMRs in the 0–4 and 5–9 age groups is assessed. A possible range of these ratios is simulated from the observed range of sex differentials in infant and child mortality.

These calculations show that FMRs are more strongly affected by *sex differentials* in mortality than by mortality *levels*. Further, FMR04 are affected more strongly by sex differentials in infant mortality than sex differentials in child mortality while both terms affect the FMR59 equally. As excess female mortality in 1–4 age group is significant in most regions, it pushes FMR59 appreciably below FMR04. FMRs in the 5–9 age group are therefore a more effective indicator of the gender bias than the composite FMRs in the 0–9 age group, a point substantiated in Chapters 4 and 7.

Different possible combinations of FMR04 and FMR59

Different levels of the excess male infant mortality and excess female child (1–4 years) mortality can result in different combinations of FMRs in 0–4 and 5–9 age groups. Nine possible combinations emerge if we assign three levels each to the sex differentials in infant and child mortality: *high, moderate* and *low*. Analysis of these combinations provides new insights into the discussion on sex ratios. The positive effect of high infant mortality levels on FMRs in the 0–4 age group is one of these insights. Factors like poverty, which are known to be positively associated with high infant mortality rates (Government of India, 1988; Jain and Visaria, 1988; Khan, 1993) will also show positive association with FMRs. The *traditional explanations of the high FMRs observed among the poorer groups do not take this effect into account.* Further, high levels of male infant mortality can also mask the gender bias in later years in analyses which use composite variables like under-5 mortality.

The gap between FMR04 and FMR59 provides another insight. This drop indicates the extent of excess female child mortality: the sharper the excess female mortality the greater the drop. Similarly, the gap between FMR04 and FMR at birth emerges as an indicator of adverse survival conditions for the male or female infant.

The possibility of inferring the nature of sex differentials in mortality from observed patterns of sex ratios in the 0–4 and 5–9 age groups has important policy implications. Mortality data at disaggregated levels are hard to come by. But disaggregated sex ratio data are available. Inferring mortality patterns from such data opens up interesting possibilities for policy purposes and for planning focussed micro-level research. This is discussed in some detail.

Organisation of the discussion

Section II substantiates the 'received' assumption that juvenile age group FMRs are free from the problem of sex-selective migration. Section III suggests a useful method of examining the patterns of sex differentials in mortality by examining the linear relationship between male and female mortality. Longitudinal data on the decline in IMRs in certain countries are then compared with the trend in India. Patterns of mortality levels and sex differentials in India are examined next using two recent data sets. The relation between FMRs and mortality levels and sex differentials is elaborated in Section IV, and the range of FMRs in the 0–4 and 5–9 age groups is estimated. The relative impact of sex differentials in infant and child mortality on female to male ratios is discussed next. Effect of factors associated with high IMR (infant mortality rates), like poverty, are discussed briefly in the final section together with the possibility of making inferences about mortality patterns from FMR data. Other implications of these findings are also discussed. Subsequent chapters examine the actual sex ratio data from the 1981 Census figures and compare these with the analytically anticipated patterns.

II

The migration factor

As mentioned in Chapter 2 (Section III), juvenile age group FMRs are free from sex-selective migration. This can be verified by comparing the variance in the FMRs for the juvenile age group and the all-age group. The all-age group FMRs are subject to considerable variation on account of sex-selective migration. If juvenile age groups are free from sex-selective migration, such variation should be significantly less in the juvenile age group FMRs.

Table 3.1a provides the data for six metropolitan cities in India. These cities are known for net male in-migration as a result the all-age group FMRs should be considerably less compared to the FMRs in the 0–9 age group. This is indeed the case. Low FMRs for the all-age group are quite pronounced in Mumbai, Calcutta and Delhi.

Table 3.1a
Comparing all-age group FMRs with juvenile age group FMRs
(six metropolitan cities—1981 Census)

City	Mumbai	Calcutta	Delhi	Chennai	Bangalore	Hyderabad
All-age FMR	772	712	808	934	916	920
Juvenile FMR	934	933	917	973	996	991

Source: IDDD, Vannemann and Barnes, 1992.

A reverse pattern should be found in the areas with net male out-migration. Districts of Kerala known for net male out-migration provide such an instance. FMRs for all-age population are generally higher and fluctuate over a wider range compared to the JFMRs in these districts as shown in Table 3.1b.

Comparison of variance in JFMRs and all-age group FMRs confirms this pattern further. Table 3.2 presents results for 366 districts at all-India level and for 12 districts of Kerala. *The variance in JFMRs is considerably less* than the all-age group FMRs especially in Kerala.

The difference between the all-age FMR (mean 936.1) and juvenile FMRs (mean 957.8) is highly significant (T = 7.93***) at the all-India level, as revealed by T-test for paired samples.

Table 3.1b
Comparing all-age group FMRs with juvenile age group FMRs
(districts of Kerala)

District	All-age FMR	JFMR
Kannanore	1,034	974
Wayanad	949	979
Kozhikode	1,020	976
Malappuram	1,052	964
Palghat	1,056	986
Trichur	1,100	971
Ernakulam	998	967
Idukki	963	991
Kottayam	1,001	969
Alleppey	1,050	977
Quilon	1,026	971
Trivandrum	1,030	977

Source: IDDD, Vannemann and Barnes, 1992.

Table 3.2
Comparing variances in FMRs

Unit	FMRs	Mean FMR	Variance	Std. Dev.
All India	All-age FMRs	936	4,095	64
	JFMRs	958	1,678	41
Kerala	All-age FMRs	1,023	1,730	42
	JFMRs	975	59	8

Source: IDDD, Vannemann and Barnes, 1992.

Rural–urban differences

The absence of sex-selective migration in 0–9 age group can also be inferred by analysing the urban and the rural FMRs. The low mean for the all-age group FMRs in urban areas, 895 females per 1,000 males, compared to a mean of 946 in rural areas is consistent with *net excess male in-migration into urban areas*. The difference between urban and rural sex ratios, is highly significant (T = 16.3***). However, rural and urban JFMRs do not differ significantly. Their mean value for the overall population in rural area (955) and in urban areas (958), are close to each other and the difference between them is not significant at a 5 per cent level (T= 1.76). This confirms that the sex-selective migration in the 0–9 age group is insignificant.

Migration data from the Indian censuses do not provide composition of migrant population by social groups. A comparison of all-age FMRs and the JFMRs among these groups, like for example, the Scheduled Tribes the Scheduled Castes, can throw interesting light on the nature of migration among them. This could be of considerable policy interest. But this merits a separate investigation and is not pursued here further.

This analysis confirms that the use of JFMR data eliminates the problem of 'migration noise' and paves the way for analysing the effects of sex differentials in juvenile mortality.

III

Declining trends in child mortality

Reduced levels of mortality

Levels of infant and child mortality have declined dramatically in most countries during this century (see, e.g., Hill and Pebley, 1989: 661–71; Shapiro et al., 1968; UN Demographic Yearbook, 1969:66 [Chapter 1]). Infant mortality rates (measured as deaths per 1,000 live births) of 200 were not unusual towards the end of 19th century even in some of today's developed countries. Infant mortality rates below 20 are not uncommon today in Sri Lanka, Kerala or Costa Rica (see Government of India, 1988; Preston et al., 1972; Preston and Haines, 1991: Chapter 2; UN Demographic Yearbook, 1988). This considerable decline has come about through improvements in health environment, nutrition and in quality and availability of medical care.

Does this decline differ by sex? It would not if male and female children were identical in all respects. Formally stated, female and male mortality decline will be linearly related: the line passing through origin with a 45 degree slope.

Differential decline

But male and female children are not 'identical in all respects'. They are differentiated both socially and physiologically, and mortality rates are associated with both physiological and social factors. These factors affect different components of childhood mortality differently. Given these differences, the relationship between female and male mortality rate, if linear, well be given by:

$$MRf = a + b* MRm \qquad\qquad 3.1$$

Where MRf and MRm stand for female and male mortality rates expressed per 1,000 live births of the concerned sex.[1] The slope of the line b indicates the nature of sex differentials. If b < 1, it indicates excess male mortality at high mortality levels. If b > 1, it indicates higher female mortality rate at high mortality levels. The constant term should ideally be close to zero. If it is positive, it indicates residual excess female mortality even when the male mortality reduces to zero. If it is negative it would indicate that the girl child mortality, for example, in infancy, will decline to zero faster than the male mortality.

Trends in declining IMRs in some countries

Figures 3.1a and 3.1b show the trend in decline in male and female IMRs in Sri Lanka, USA, UK, and Italy. The linear relationship is striking. The slope is less than unity, being 0.81 for USA, 0.82 for UK, 0.91 for Italy and 0.85 for Sri Lanka. The slope values are consistent with the inference that male infant mortality is higher at high mortality levels and indicates the extent these decline faster than the female IMRs. The data are presented in Tables 3.3a to 3.3c.

Infant mortality in India

Mortality patterns in India, however, show a different trend. Sex differentials in infant mortality are smaller compared to the countries referred to above and these narrow down faster as mortality levels decline. A comparison between Table 3.3c and the Tables 3.3a and 3.3b reveals that the male–female gap in infant mortality rates has narrowed down to less

---

[1] It turns out, as seen later, that the relationship is linear at least in the range of observed mortality rates.

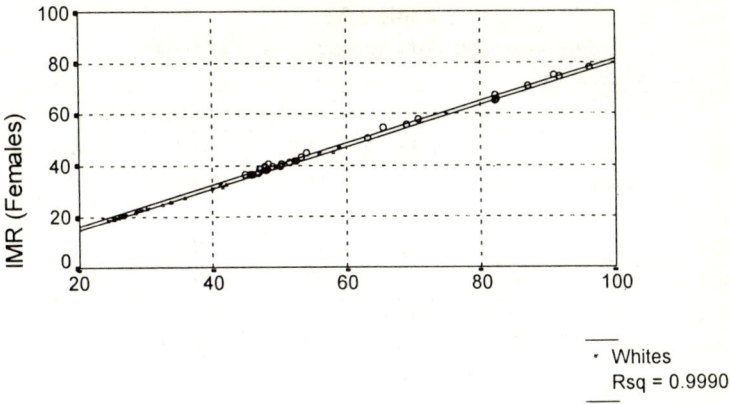

IMR (Male)
IMRf = -1.3 + 0.81* IMRm (White)   R.Sq. = 0.99
IMRf = -0.3 + 0.81* IMRm (Non - White)   R.Sq. = 0.99

Figure 3.1a: Declining IMRs by sex: USA (1935–64).
Source: Shapiro et al., 1968.

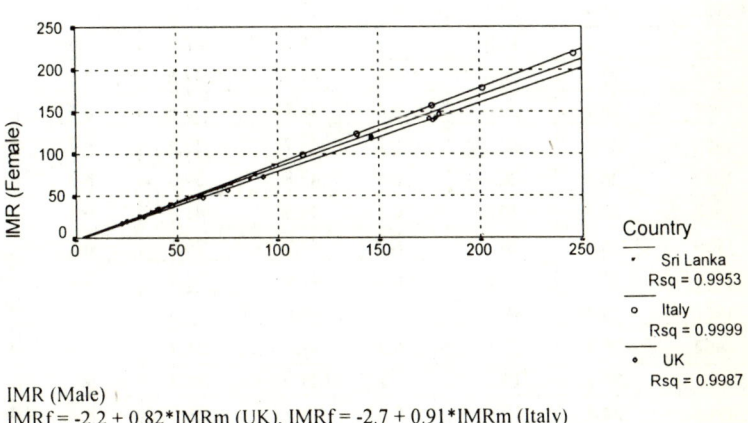

IMR (Male)
IMRf = -2.2 + 0.82*IMRm (UK), IMRf = -2.7 + 0.91*IMRm (Italy)
IMRf = -0.3 + 0.85*IMRm (Sri Lanka)

Figure 3.1b: Declining IMRs by sex: Sri Lanka, UK and Italy.
Source: Preston et al., 1972; UN Demographic Yearbooks, different years.

Table 3.3a
Infant mortality data by sex: USA (1935–64)

Year	White Population			Non-White Population		
	IMR (Male)	IMR (Female)	Differnce (m–f)	IMR (Male)	IMR (Female)	Difference (m–f)
1935	58.1	45.2	12.9	91.7	74.6	17.1
1936	58.9	46.5	12.4	96.3	78.6	17.1
1937	56	44.4	11.6	91	75.2	15.8
1938	52.5	41.4	11.1	87	70.9	16.1
1939	49.2	39.1	10.1	82.3	66	16.3
1940	48.3	37.8	10.5	82.2	65.2	17
1941	46	36.1	9.9	82.1	67.3	14.8
1942	41.6	31.3	10.3	70.7	58.3	12.4
1943	42	32.7	9.3	68.9	55.9	13
1944	41.2	32.4	8.8	65.5	55	10.5
1945	39.9	31.1	8.8	63.2	50.8	12.4
1946	35.8	27.5	8.3	54	44.8	9.2
1947	33.9	26	7.9	53.2	43.7	9.5
1948	33.7	25.9	7.8	51.4	41.4	10
1949	32.5	25	7.5	52.5	42	10.5
1950	30.2	23.1	7.1	48.9	39.9	9
1951	29.2	22.4	6.8	50	39.6	10.4
1952	28.7	22.1	6.6	52.3	41.7	10.6
1953	28.4	21.5	6.9	48.4	40.8	7.6
1954	27	20.6	6.4	47.1	38.6	8.5
1955	26.7	20.3	6.4	46.9	38.6	8.3
1956	26.2	20	6.2	46.7	37.3	9.4
1957	26.4	20.1	6.3	47.8	39.6	8.2
1958	26.7	20.6	6.1	50.3	41	9.3
1959	26.3	20	6.3	47.8	39.5	8.3
1960	26	19.6	6.4	47.9	38.5	9.4
1961	25.4	19.3	6.1	44.8	36.5	8.3
1962	25.4	19.1	6.3	45.7	36.9	8.8
1963	25.1	19	6.1	46	36.9	9.1
1964	24.4	18.6	5.8	45.5	36.6	8.9

Source: Shapiro et al., 1968.

Table 3.3b
Infant mortality data by sex: UK, Italy and Sri Lanka

| Year | UK | | |
	IMR (Male)	IMR (Female)	Difference (m–f)
1861	178	142	36
1871	180	148	32
1881	146	118	28
1891	177	140	37
1901	175	142	33
1911	146	120	26
1921	93	72	21
1931	75	57	18
1940	63	48	15
1951	34	26	8
1960	25	20	6
1964	23	18	5
	Italy		
1881	246	220	26
1891	201	179	22
1901	176	158	18
1910	139	124	15
1921	139	124	15
1931	112	100	13
1960	47	40	8
1964	41	34	7
	Sri Lanka		
1950	89	74	14
1951	89	75	14
1952	86	71	15
1953	77	65	12
1956	72	61	12
1957	73	62	11
1958	70	59	10
1959	62	53	10

Table 3.3b continued.

Table 3.3b continued

Year	Sri Lanka		
	IMR (Male)	IMR (Female)	Difference (m–f)
1960	62	52	10
1961	56	48	8
1962	57	48	9
1963	61	51	10
1965	58	49	9
1968	55	46	9
1976	47	41	6
1977	46	39	7
1978	40	34	6
1979	41	35	6
1980	37	31	6
1981	32	27	4

Sources: Preston et al., 1972; UN Demographic Yearbooks.

Table 3.3c
Infant mortality data by sex: India

Year*	IMR (Male)	IMR (Female)	Difference (m–f)
1905	231	218	13
1906	228	218	10
1907	222	209	13
1908	250	241	9
1909	261	227	34
1910	217	201	16
1911	214	196	18
1912	216	199	17
1913	193	197	–4
1914	219	204	15
1915	208	195	13
1916	209	195	14
1917	212	198	14

Table 3.3c continued.

Table 3.3c continued.

Year*	IMR (Male)	IMR (Female)	Difference (m–f)
1918	274	260	14
1919	228	220	8
1920	210	188	22
1921	205	190	15
1922	183	166	17
1923	183	168	15
1924	197	180	17
1925	181	167	14
1926	197	180	17
1927	174	159	15
1928	151	164	–13
1929	185	169	16
1930	189	172	17
1931	187	170	17
1932	177	160	17
1933	177	163	14
1934	195	178	17
1935	171	176	–5
1937	170	153	17
1938	176	158	18
1939	163	147	16
1942	170	156	14
1943	175	162	13
1944	175	164	11
1948	152	140	12
1949	128	117	11
1950	132	122	10
1951	123	114	9
1952	115	106	9
1953	116	108	8
1954	110	102	8
1955	99	91	8
1956	92	88	4
1957	98	94	4

Table 3.3c continued.

Table 3.3c continued

Year*	IMR (Male)	IMR (Female)	Difference (m–f)
1958	99	96	3
1959	90	83	7
1960	89	85	4
1961	85	81	4
1962	101	100	1
1963	78	73	5
1964	76	72	4
1965	67	64	3
1972**	132	148	–16
1974	132	135	–3
1976	124	134	–10
1979	119	121	–2
1980	113	115	–2
1981	110	111	–1
1982	106	104	2
1983	105	105	0
1984	104	104	0
1985	96	98	–2
1986	96	97	–1
1987	95	96	–1
1988	94	93	1
1989	91	90	1
1990	78	81	–3
1991	81	80	1
1992	79	80	–1

* **Source** (1905–65): Chandrasekhar, 1959: T-18 and 1972: T-36.
** **Source** (1972–92): Tinker, 1996: 115.

than 5 at mortality rates of 60 to 70 deaths per 1,000 live births. At these mortality levels, the corresponding gap in the other 4 countries was two to three times higher. Clearly, the male infants are gaining more rapidly from the reduced levels of infant mortality in India.

[2] Source: Chandrasekhar. S (1959) Table 18 and (1972) Table 36. These IMR refer to registered births only. But that is the best one can get in terms of continuous longitudinal data.

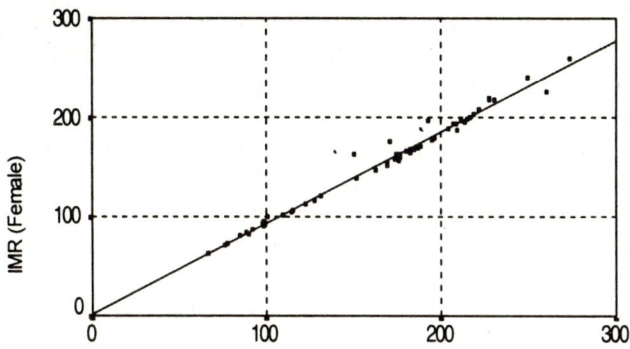

IMR (Male)
IMRf + 2.2 + 0.92*IMRm   R. Sq. 0.96

Figure 3.1c: Declining IMRs by sex: India (1905–65).
Source: Chandrasekhar, 1959, 1972.

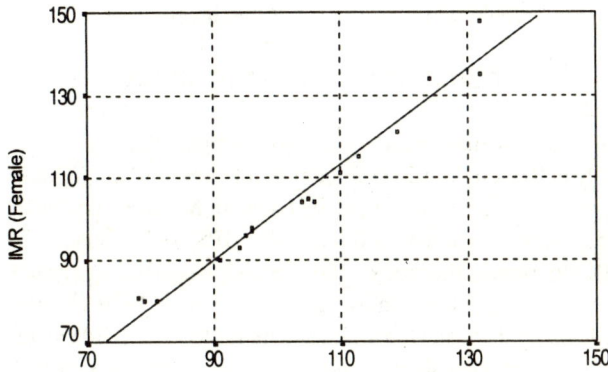

IMR (Male)
IMRf = -13.9 + 1.16*IMRm   R.Sq. = 0.97

Figure 3.1d: Declining IMRs by sex: India (1972–92).
Source: Tinker, 1996.

Figure 3.1c, based on the infant mortality rates between 1905 and 1965[2] shows that the male and female IMRs are linearly related. The slope of the IMRF–IMRm line is signigicant and less than unity (0.92) indicating excess male infant mortality at the all-India level.

However, a more recent set of data on IMRs between 1972–92 (Tinker, 1996) reveals a different trend. It indicates excess female mortality rates (Table 3.3c). The association between male and female IMRs is linear and significant (R.Sq. = 0.97) but the slope (1.15) is significantly higher than unity (T = 21.3***). The high and negative constant term–14, is somewhat unusual[3] but it is not significant at a 1 per cent level. If the unusually high values of the excess female mortality in 1972 and 1976 are ignored, the IMRf–IMRm relation is given by:

$$IMRf = -2 + 1.03 * IMRm \quad [R.\ Sq. = 0.99;\ F\ ratio\ and\ slope\ significant\ at\ 1\ per\ cent\ level]$$

This relationship indicates that the male disadvantage during infancy has disappeared. But as the mortality levels are still high, it is reasonable to suspect that it is the female advantage that has disappeared. Such a trend of excess female mortality during infancy has been revealed in some of the regions in the country known for their gender bias against the girl child (IIPS, 1995). This is an area where further research is called for. As subsequent analysis will show, it will be necessary to examine the IMRf–IMRm relationship at regional rather than all-India level.

Level of child mortality rates in India

Two features of child mortality in India need to be emphasised. First, these rates are typically half to one-third of infant mortality rates in India. This is quite high compared to a fifth to a sixth in Sri Lanka or Mauritius and even less in the US or UK (Government of India, 1988; IIPS, 1995; Shapiro et al., 1968; UN Demographic Yearbook 1966) Second, it is in this age group that significant excess of female mortality occurs (Chatterjee, 1990; Harriss, 1989;). It is quite likely then, that the high child mortality rates (CMRs) are primarily a result of excess female mortality, a point that is analysed here.

---

[2] Source: Chandrasekhar. S (1959) Table 18 and (1972) Table 36. These IMR refer to registered births only. But that is the best one can get in terms of continuous longitudinal data.

[3] It would mean that female IMR will reach near zero values while the male IMR is around 12. But this extrapolation to values if IMR below 75 may not be valid as seen from the changing value of the slope. The two sets of data are not analysed together as these have a non-comparable origin.

Regional variations in infant and child mortality

Sources of data

There are two recent data sets on under-5 mortality. The first, based on the 1981 Census data (Government of India, 1988), provides mortality estimates at the district level. The second, based on the National Family Health Survey[4] (IIPS, 1995), provides estimates of mortality rates at the regional level. These regions are spatial units below the state level and above the district level. While the data are cross-sectional and cannot strictly be used to indicate the time trends, these provide valuable information about the levels of mortality and sex differentials in mortality. These figures are then used in simulating the female to male ratios, the primary purpose of the analysis.

NFHS data

Figure 3.2a and 3.2b provide the distribution of male and female IMRs for the 27 NFHS regions. A list of these regions and the mortality data are provided in Table 3.3d.The male and female IMRs are highly correlated even though the range of mortality levels is quite wide. They vary from a low of nearly 30 per 1,000 live births for the west coast to a high of about 150 in the UP Uplands. The IMRf–IMRm regression line[5] (Figure 3.2d) is given by:

$$\text{IMRf} = 7.1 + 0.83 * \text{IMRm} \qquad\qquad 3.2.1$$

The constant term is not significant. The slope is highly significant and is less than one indicating excess male IMR. The gap between male and female IMR (Figure 3.2c) ranges from −14.9 in the upper Ganga region, indicating excess female infant mortality, to 27.5 in the Orissa uplands with a mean value of 5.0 across 26 regions (excluding one outlier + 54.2, Tamil Nadu Upland).

The situation reverses in the 1–4 age group marked by excess female mortality (Figure 3.3c). It covers a range of 29.2 in Uttar Pradesh Uplands

---

[4] A large-scale, detailed, nationwide survey covering about 90,000 female respondents.

[5] The significance of the IMRf–IMRm line will not be the same for the cross-sectional data as it is for the longitudinal data. The argument that the slope indicates excess male or the female mortality at the high mortality end, will remain however.

Table 3.3d
Infant and child mortality data by sex: NFHS regions

Region Number	Region Name	IMR (male)	IMR (female)	Difference (m-f)	CMRm	CMRf	Difference (m-f)
1.	J&K Himalaya	44.9	53.6	-8.7	14.5	24.5	-10
2.	Himachal Himalaya	67.2	62.9	4.3	17.6	25.3	-7.7
3.	UP Himalaya	75.9	70.5	5.4	26.5	52.3	-25.8
4.	N-E Himalaya	60.4	58.8	1.6	26.8	43.4	-16.6
5.	Eastern Hills	68.9	63.3	5.6	33	46.8	-13.8
6.	Punjab	55.6	49.1	6.5	12.7	23	-10.3
7.	Haryana	70.7	77.1	-6.4	16.7	35.7	-19
8.	Arid Rajasthan	58.4	66	-7.6	18.2	28.6	-10.4
9.	Upper Gangetic Plains	104.9	119.8	-14.9	36.7	65.9	-29.2
10.	Middle Gangetic Plains	115.3	120.9	-5.6	39.1	66.3	-27.2
11.	Lower Gangetic Plains	97.6	90.4	7.2	29.8	47	-17.2
12.	Brahmaputra Valley	102	80.4	21.6	51.2	51.5	-0.3
13.	Semi-Arid Rajasthan	84.3	88.8	-4.5	32.7	52.4	-19.7
14.	UP Uplands	146.4	140.4	6	51.1	66.3	-15.2
15.	Northern MP Uplands	113	110.2	2.8	56.9	72.7	-15.8
16.	Central MP Uplands	99.3	109.6	-10.3	41	68.3	-27.3
17.	Southern MP Uplands	91.2	68.8	22.4	45.2	39.2	6

Table 3.3d continued

18.	Bihar WB Plains	83	64.3	18.7	27.9	40.2	−12.3
19.	Orissa Uplands	120.1	92.6	27.5	20	21.8	−1.8
20.	Northern Maharashtra	67.5	63.5	4	24.4	27.5	−3.1
21.	Maharashtra Plateau	68.4	47.2	21.2	19	24	−5
22.	Karnataka Plateau	84.7	73	11.7	26.6	32	−5.4
23.	Tamil Nadu Uplands	119.2	65	54.2	55.1	47.5	7.6
24.	Andhra Plateau	68.1	58.1	10	21	24.9	−3.9
25.	Gujarat Plains	72.3	74.8	−2.5	27.1	38.6	−11.5
26.	West Coast	38.8	32.6	6.2	11.2	12.4	−1.2
27.	East Coast	90.5	82.7	7.8	20.7	25.3	−4.6

Source: IIPS, 1995.

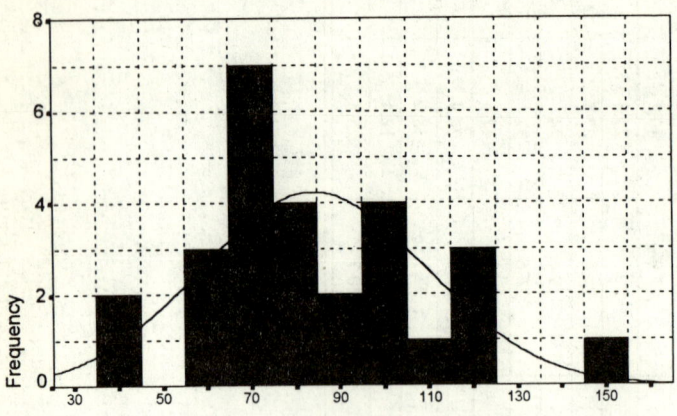

IMR (Male)
Mean IMR = 84   Std. Deviation = 25.4
Figure 3.2a: Histogram of male IMR: NFHS data (27 regions).

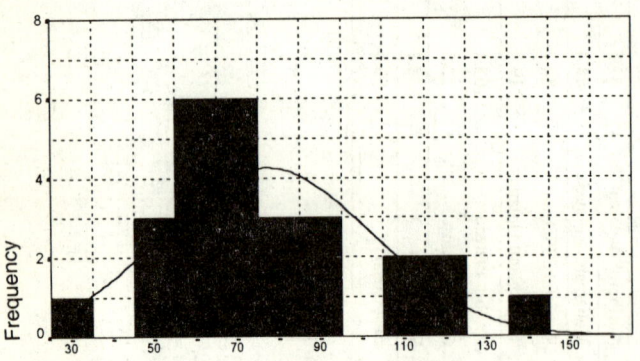

IMR (Female)
Mean IMR = 77   Std. Deviation = 25.2
Figure 3.2b: Histogram of female IMR: NFHS data (27 regions).

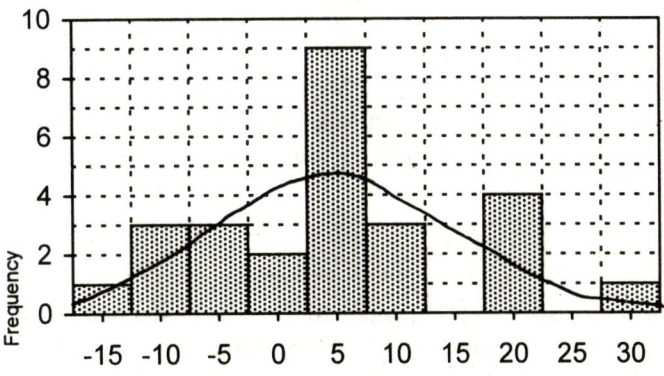

Number of regions = 26
Mean excess male IMR = 5   Std. Deviation = 11
Figure 3.2c: Histogram of excess male IMR: NFHS data (27 regions).

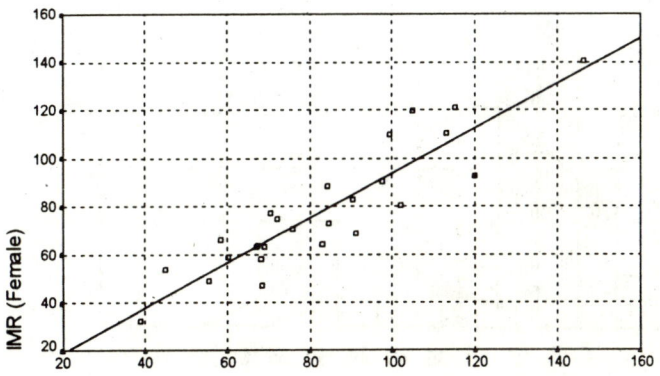

IMRf = 7.1 + 0.83* IMRm
R. Sq. = 0.70; F = 59***   T (Slope) = 7.7***
Figure 3.2d: Plot of IMR (male)–IMR (female): NFHS data (27 regions).

to –7.6 (i.e., excess male mortality) in Tamil Nadu Uplands. The mean value of the gap is 11.1 indicating excess female mortality.

The CMRf–CMRm relation is shown in Figure 3.3d through a LOWESS curve. The linear regression line for all the 27 regions is described by:

$$\text{CMRf} = 10 + 1.04* \text{CMRm} \qquad\qquad 3.2.2$$

However, if we take the range of CMR below 50, the slope is much steeper. This can be noticed from the curve itself. The regression line is described by:

$$\text{CMRf} = 1.8 + 1.4* \text{CMRm} \qquad\qquad 3.2.3$$

The trend of excess female child mortality at high mortality levels is also borne out by the distribution of male and female child mortality (Figures 3.3a and 3.3b). Mean mortality rate by gender, 40.9 (female) and 29.7 (male), differ significantly at 1 per cent.

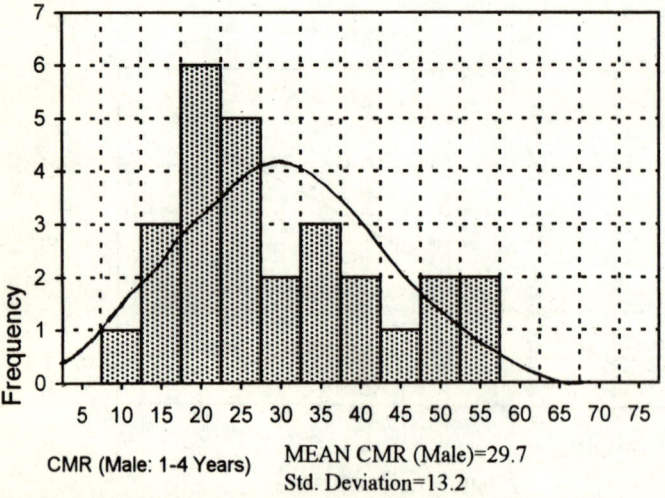

CMR (Male: 1-4 Years) MEAN CMR (Male)=29.7
Std. Deviation=13.2

Figure 3.3a: Histogram of male CMR: NFHS data (27 regions).

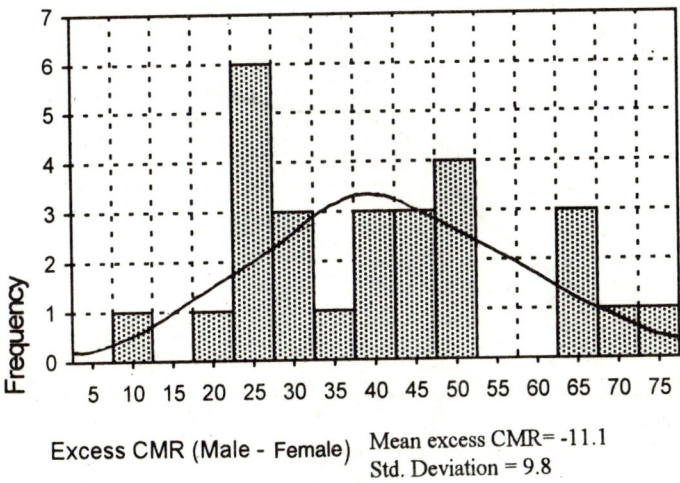

Excess CMR (Male - Female)   Mean excess CMR= -11.1
                              Std. Deviation = 9.8

Figure 3.3b: Histogram of female CMR: NFHS data (27 regions).

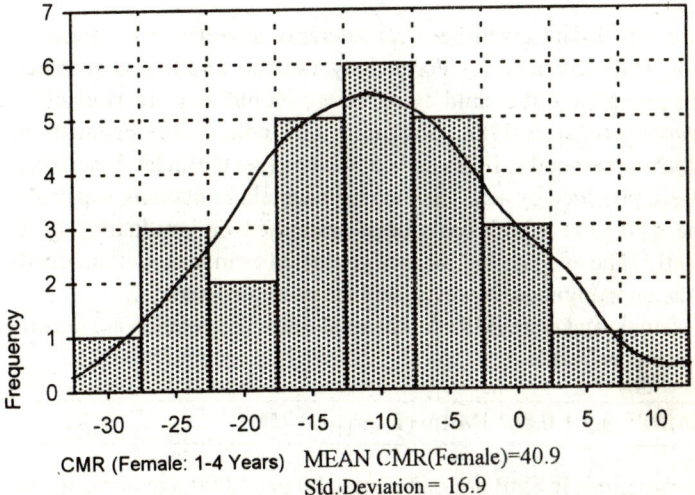

CMR (Female: 1-4 Years)   MEAN CMR(Female)=40.9
                           Std. Deviation = 16.9

Figure 3.3c: Histogram of excess male CMR: NFHS data (27 regions).

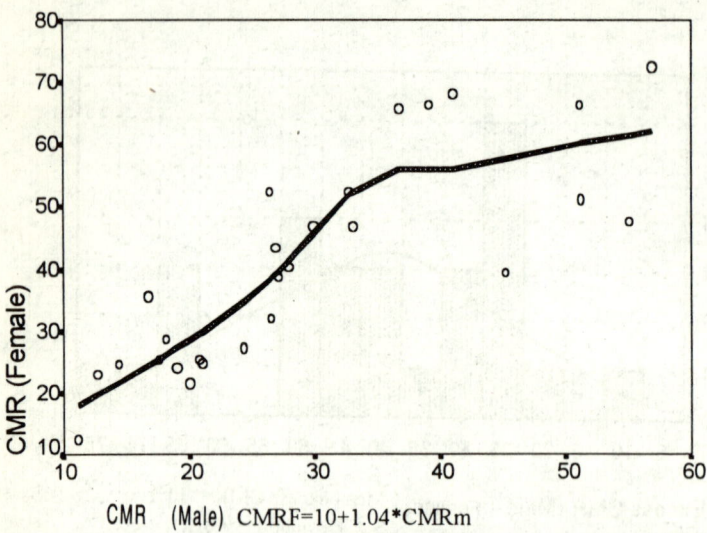

Figure 3.3d: Plot of CMR (male)–CMR (female): NFHS data (27 regions).

District–level estimates—1981 Census

Regional-level data given here considerably aggregates variations in mortality at the district level. Fortunately, estimate of different qi values, i.e., the probability of a child dying before ith birthday are available at the district level since 1988 (Government of India, 1988). Estimates of q1, which correspond to IMRs and q5, which gives the under-5 mortality, have been provided by sex. The data have certain limitations, especially for the q1 figure which have been smoothed or 'graduated' quite frequently. The analysis below uses graduated estimates. Certain trends are quite unambiguous, however, and are presented here.

The female and male IMRs for the total district population are linearly related (Figure 3.4d):

$$IMRf = 9.9 + 0.86* IMRm \ (R. \ Sq. = 0.75) \qquad 3.3.1$$

The variations in IMR are quite large: 20 per 1,000 live births to 200 per 1,000 live births (Figures 3.4a and 3.4b). The sex differentials in

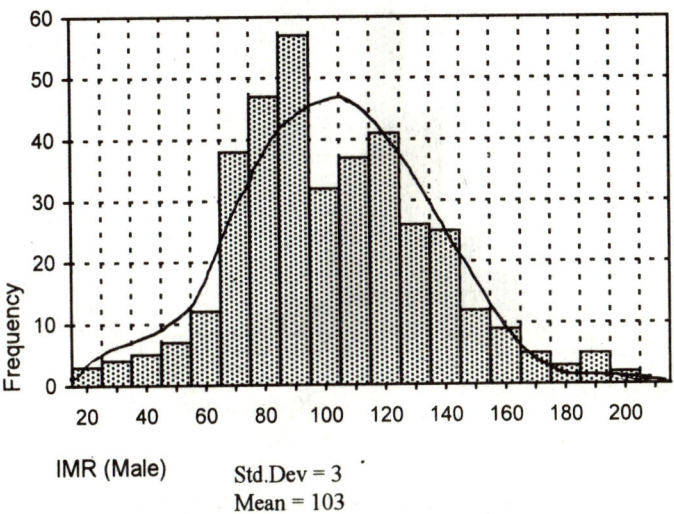

IMR (Male) Std.Dev = 3
Mean = 103

Figure 3.4a: Histogram of male IMR: 1981 Census (366 districts).

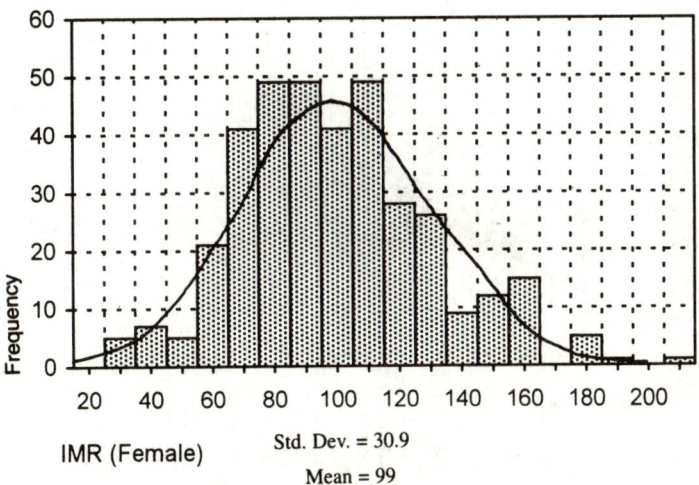

IMR (Female) Std. Dev. = 30.9
Mean = 99

Figure 3.4b: Histogram of female IMR: 1981 Census (366 districts).

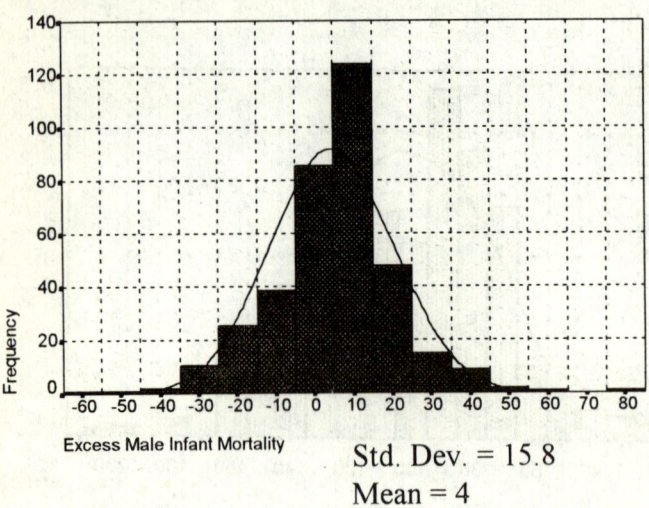

Std. Dev. = 15.8

Mean = 4

Figure 3.4c: Histogram of excess male IMR: 1981 Census (366 districts).

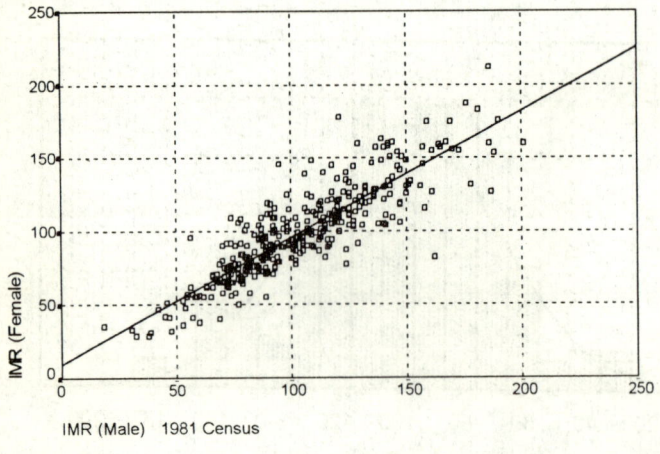

IMRf = 9.9+0.86IMRm; (R.Sq. = 0.76)

Figure 3.4d: Plot of IMR (male)–IMR (female): 1981 Census (366 districts).

IMR (male–female) go from +60 to –40 (excess female infant mortality) with a mean of 4 (Figure 3.4c).

Estimates of under-5 mortality are considered more robust and have hardly required any 'graduation'. These reveal a higher female mortality (Figure 3.5b).

$$\text{U5MRf} = -4.7 + 1.1*\text{U5MRm} \quad (\text{R. Sq.} = 0.84) \qquad 3.4.1$$

Excess female child mortality (1–4 age group) varies over a wide range (Figure 3.5a): between –20 (excess male child mortality) to +80 with a mean of +14. These are indicative figures especially since these CMRs have been derived as the difference between q5 and q1 values. Errors in q1 values will reflect in the errors in CMR values. The errors would be further magnified when the differences in male and female CMRs are analysed. However, for the purpose of the present discussion this issue is not critical. In the analysis that follows one requires only the *extent of sex differentials* in IMR, CMR or U5MR (under-5 mortality rate) values. The other purpose, to show that the variations at the district level is large compared to the regional or the national level, is adequately served by the distributions shown.

Sex Differentials in Child Mortality

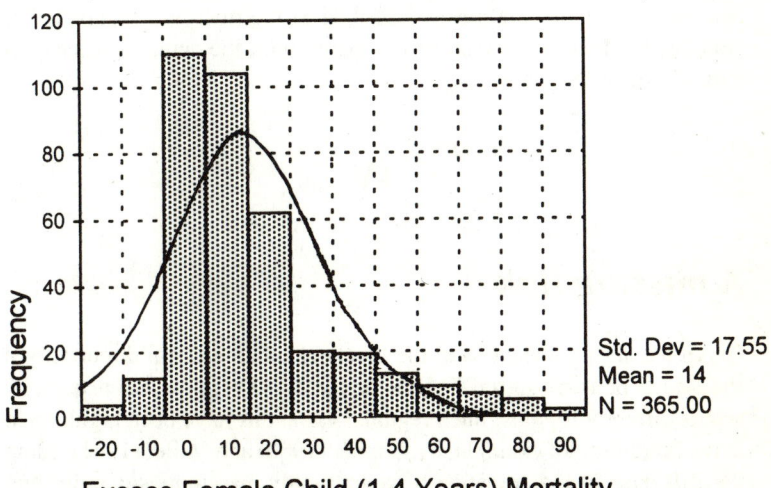

Std. Dev = 17.55
Mean = 14
N = 365.00

Figure 3.5a: Histogram of excess female CMR: 1981 Census (366 districts).

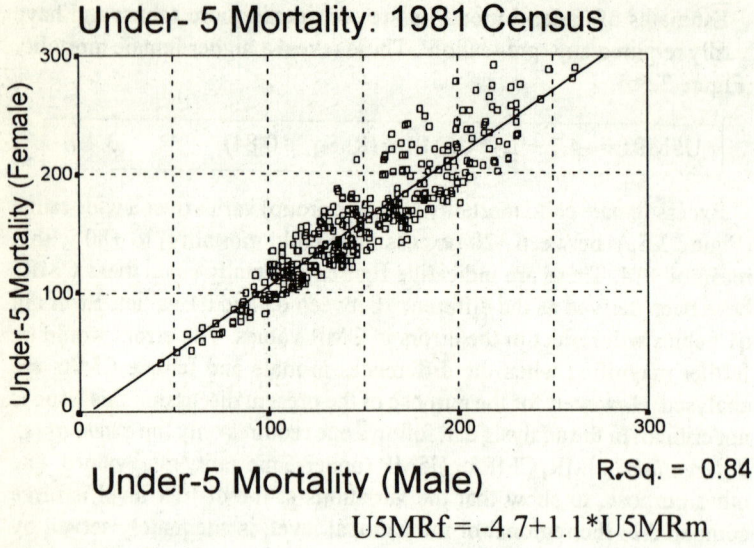

$$U5MRf = -4.7 + 1.1*U5MRm$$

R.Sq. = 0.84

Figure 3.5b: Under-5 male and female mortality: 1981 Census (366 districts).

With this information it is possible to simulate FMRs in the juvenile age group. This simulation is described in the next two sections. The simulated values could then be compared with the actual district-level data (Chapter 4).

IV

A missing link

Given the above variations in the levels of infant and child mortality it should not be surprising if FMR04 and FMR59 vary quite substantially across different regions. Such regional variations have been highlighted in the literature, for example, by, Sopher (1980) and Miller (1981), using the JSR data. The association between highly masculine sex ratios and high female child mortality have also been recognised. Nevertheless, the links between sex differentials in mortality and sex ratios in juvenile age group have remained a neglected area of study.

This neglect is surprising as infant and child mortality as well as declining female to male ratios have been topics of extensive research in India often within similar academic circles and institutional settings.[6]That the two are linked is intuitively obvious even to a casual student of the subject and the need to study this has been emphasised.[7] Yet, the quantitative impact of the actual pattern of mortality on sex ratios has not been investigated seriously.[8]The analysis given here fills this gap to some extent and speculates on one plausible reason of this neglect.

Different combinations of FMRs

FMRs in the 0–4 and 5–9 age groups can have different combinations. Nine combinations are possible if we assign three levels for each of the FMRs: *high, moderate* and *low*. Implication of each of these combinations will be different. From the 'ten-lap race' description these implications can be qualitatively described as done in the Table 3.4.

Table 3.4
Possible combinations of FMR04 and FMR59

FMR levels	*Very Low FMR04*	*Moderate FMR04*	*High FMR04*
Very Low FMR59	Alarming (Female)	Adverse (Female)	Serious (Female)
Moderate FMR59	Unusual	Frequent	Frequent
High FMR59	Check Data	Infrequent	Alarming (Male)

The combination of moderate to high FMR04 and moderate FMR59 will be frequently encountered in the absence of gender bias. When the FMR04 values are moderate or high and the FMR59 values very low,

[6] It is not unusual to find both these topics covered in, say, the annual conferences of the IASP (Indian Association for the Study of Population). Even the edited volume by Jain and Visaria (1988) on infant mortality contains contributions from researchers working in the field of sex ratios. Visaria himself has made a seminal contribution in both the fields.

[7] Harriss, emphasises the need to analyse sex ratio data by age group (1989: 49), specifically suggesting that 'the infant and child mortality rates mask countervailing trends' so that 'age group 1–5' needs disaggregation into: under 1 month, ... 6–12 months and then by every Year'(1989: 61). But this has not been followed up seriously.

[8] Except briefly by Murthi et al. (1995), Chatterjee (1990), Sargent et al. 1996 and Dyson (1992). Chatterjee, in fact, observes (1990: 4) that 'A point ... which bears emphasis is that the gender gap in survival is the greatest during the first five years of life when mortality is the highest; about 20 times higher than in any other 5-year age group'. Murthi et al. (1995) look at the association of juvenile sex ratio and under-5 mortality. As this chapter shows, it is sex ratio in 5–9 age group which correlates with under-5 mortality *not* the sex ratio in 0–4 age group.

adverse survival conditions are indicated. These conditions are alarming when both the FMR04 and FMR59 are very low.

It is unusual to have very low FMR04 and moderate FMR59 and where FMR04 are very low but FMR59 are very high, it is worthwhile to check for enumeration errors. It is more fruitful to systematically search for such 'enumeration error' districts than invoke these errors in a blanket manner.

It should also be appreciated that the situation of very high FMR04 *and* very high FMR59 indicates adverse survival conditions for the male child not just during infancy but beyond it. Such regions need attention to ascertain the causes of male vulnerability. As we will see later in Chapter 4, harsh health environment, low levels of health infrastructure and general malnutrition may be the possible causes for such a pattern of FMRs.

It is thus possible to identify *regions of excess mortality* for female children, male infants and female infants *from the FMR data*. The extent of the excess mortality can be judged through the drop between FMR04 and FMR59 and between FMR at birth and FMR04.

While Table 3.4 indicates the mortality implication of different combinations of FMRs, it is similarly possible to combine sex differentials in mortality and examine their implications for the FMRs. Taking three levels again for these sex differentials, *high, moderate* and *low*, nine combinations are possible. Corresponding FMRs in juvenile age group are described below.

Table 3.5
***Possible combinations of sex differentials in
infant and child mortality***

Excess Mortality	Girl Child (High)	Girl Child (Moderate)	Girl Child (Low)
Male infant (High)	Balanced(?)	High	Very High
Male infant (Moderate)	Low	High/Balanced	High
Male infant (Low)	Very Low	High	Balanced

The balanced(?) female to male ratios in the top left hand corner shows that high male mortality during infancy can mask the excess female mortality in subsequent years. Similarly, unacceptably high levels of male mortality can create very high levels of female to male ratios and it is necessary to make a *distinction between balanced female to male ratios and high female to male ratios*. So far such distinction has not been reported in the literature.

Modelling a relationship

A stylised juvenile population

It is useful to simulate the FMR pattern in more quantitative terms. One can start with a stylised juvenile population characterised by F(0)—FMR at birth—and a constant fertility and mortality over a 10-year span.[9] One can begin with a very simple model using some formal notation given below:

i) let IMRm and IMRf denote infant mortality rate for male and female children. Similarly let CMRm and CMRf denote the child mortality rates in 1–4 age group

ii) let there be F_j girls and M_j boys left at the jth birthday

iii) let FMR04 and FMR59 denote FMRs in the 0–4 and 5–9 age groups and F(04) and M(04) the number of female and male children in the 0–4 age group. F(04) and M(04) can be approximated as:

$$
\begin{aligned}
F(04) &= (F0 + F1)/2 + (F1 + F2)/2 \ldots (F4 + F5)/2 \\
&= [F0 + F5 + 2(F1 + F2 + F3 + F4)]/2 \quad\quad 3.5.1a \\
\\
M(04) &= [M0 + M5 + 2(M1 + M2 + M3 + M4)]/2 \quad\quad 3.5.1b \\
\\
FMR04 &= 1{,}000* F(04)/M(04) \quad\quad\quad\quad\quad\quad 3.5.1c
\end{aligned}
$$

The implicit assumptions here is that death rates are not skewed but are distributed uniformly over the five-year span. One can make another simplifying assumption that no deaths takes place between age 5–9[10] so that FMR59 can be approximated as FMR59 = 1,000* F5/M5. Later this assumption can be dropped to examine the extent to which FMR59 changes even if all deaths in the 5–9 age group are only female or male. Different Fi and Mi can be expressed in terms of mortality rates as:

---

[9] Gradual decline in fertility does not affect the arguments here significantly.

[10] These simplifying assumptions are rather strong. But most of these 'err on the safer side'. More realistic assumptions, e.g., skewness towards early ages, will make the FMRs even more feminine. *The main purpose here is to get a feel of the FMR04 and FMR59 range* from the simulation. The overall argument is, therefore, not vitiated by making these assumptions.

F1 = F0* (1 – IMRf/1,000); M1 = M0* (1 – IMRm/1,000)   3.5.2a
F2 = F1* (1 – CMRf/4,000); M2 = M1* (1 – CMRm/4,000) 3.5.2b
and so on until.
F5 = F4* (1 – CMRf/4,000); M5 = M4* (1 – CMRm/4,000) 3.5.2c

One can select a realistic range of IMR and CMR levels and sex differentials in these. Based on the analysis above a range of excess male IMR of +40 to –40 and excess female CMR of +80 to –20 is selected.

The differential impact

Table 3.6 shows the FMR values in 0–4 and 5–9 age groups for three male IMR levels of 200, 100 and 50. CMR are taken at half these values and the female to male ratio at birth is taken to be 960. The pattern is consistent with Tables 3.3 a–d and 3.4. In specific terms:

- *FMRs in 0–4 age group are much higher than those in 5–9 age group* except where there is excess male mortality in 1–4 age group, i.e., CMRm ≥ CMRf.
- *Differentials in infant mortality rates affect FMR04 more strongly than those in the 1–4 age group.*[11] *Similarly, mortality gap has a much sharper effect on FMRs than mortality levels.* A reduction in infant mortality level from 200 to 100 changes FMRs by 3 to 5 points. The same change can be brought about through a reduction in the sex differentials by less than 10 per cent.
- *Excess girl child mortality is reflected in FMR59 more sharply than in FMR04.* In the worst case scenario of excess female mortality of 40 in infancy and 80 in childhood, FMR04 drops to its lowest value of 890, while FMR59 drops to 839. If we chose a still higher value of 60 for excess female infant mortality, FMR04 and FMR59 drop further to 870 and 817 (not shown in the Table).
- High FMR values of 1,000 and above are encountered where *excess male infant mortality is quite high* and there is either marginal difference in child mortality or excess male child mortality. These are also the circumstances under which FMR59 values are quite high and exceed the FMR04 values. It is useful in fact to flag the range IMRm–IMRf > 20 and CMRf > CMRm as the range where the FMR04 and 5–9 values typically exceed 980.

[11] If the skewness of deaths towards earlier age group is taken into account, the effects of sex differentials in infant mortality will be even more pronounced.

• When mortality differentials in 1–4 age group are negligible, sex ratios do not drop below 910 *even if there is appreciably high excess female mortality (IMRf–IMRm = 40) in infancy.*

Table 3.6
FMR values for different levels of sex differentials in infant and child mortality

Excess Female CMR	Excess Male IMR	Male IMR = 200		Male IMR = 100		Male IMR = 50	
		FMR04	FMR59	FMR04	FMR59	FMR04	FMR59
80	40	971	928	967	924	965	922
	20	951	906	948	904	947	904
	0	931	884	930	885	930	885
	−20	910	862	912	865	913	866
	−40	890	839	894	845	895	848
40	40	986	967	982	963	980	961
	20	966	944	964	942	963	941
	0	945	921	945	922	945	922
	−20	925	898	926	901	927	903
	−40	904	875	908	881	909	883
0	40	1,002	1,008	998	1,003	996	1,000
	20	981	984	979	981	978	980
	0	960	960	960	960	960	960
	−20	939	936	941	939	942	940
	−40	918	912	922	917	924	920
−20	40	1,010	1,029	1,006	1,023	1,004	1,021
	20	989	1,004	987	1,001	986	1,000
	0	967	980	968	980	968	979
	−20	946	95	949	958	949	959
	−40	925	931	929	936	931	938

Notes: i) FMR at birth = 960,
    ii) Child Mortality Rate = Infant Mortality Rate/2.

The reasons for these trends are not far to seek. Annexure 3A elaborates calculation of these female to male ratios in terms of mortality differentials and mortality levels. FMR01 is determined by sex differentials in infant mortality rates. FMR14 is a resultant between the sex differentials in infant and child mortality rates although the former have a stronger influence. The expression for FMR59 is determined by the FMR at the fifth birthday by which time the mortality pattern has stabilised. Sex differentials in infant and child mortality have similar influence on it. But as sex differentials in child mortality are larger they push the FMR59 values down considerably. Even if we assume that only female children or only male children die, change in FMR59 will not be more than 8–10 points, comparable to the magnitude of deaths during the 5–9 are group. This is much smaller compared to the range over which these female to male ratios fluctuate.

An overlooked link

The above calculations are quite preliminary. But to the extent that this researcher is aware this line of inquiry has not been pursued before, *even the differences between 0–4 and 5–9 age group FMRs have not been analysed in details so far*. Why have these links between childhood mortality patterns and JSRs remained a neglected area of scholarship in India? FMRs corresponding to excess male infant mortality rates of 0–20 and negligible excess female child mortality provide *some clues* to this neglect. This is the range that would obtain in most of the developed countries and countries not reporting any gender bias against female children. As a result, FMR04 as well as FMR59 would remain within a range of 960 to 1,000 (Natarajan 1972: 32–33), a 'balanced' sex ratio range and there would hardly be any need to go into the details of the algebra in Annexure 3A. This range of FMRs obtains even at high levels of mortality, for example 200, which prevailed in some parts of Latin American countries or, say, England and Wales in the earlier part of this century (Preston et al., 1972). It was thus a 'normal' if not 'natural' range to encounter across different regions at different times and stages of development.

This dominant world view has escaped critical scrutiny in India even when FMR values occur well below and well above this 'normal' range. The links between patterns of infant and childhood mortality and the sex ratios in the juvenile age groups were not seriously explored even as an academic exercise in 'reinventing the wheel'. As a result, a number of important implications of the sex ratio patterns have been overlooked. Some of these are briefly discussed next before moving on to the exploration of actual FMR data in the next chapter.

V

High levels of infant mortality rates

An important implication of above analysis pertains to very high FMR values: typically above 1,000. While lower FMR values are attributed to discrimination against the girl child and justifiably so, high FMR values have been viewed as necessarily better, a view even this author entertained initially. That these could be an indicator of 'underdevelopment' in terms of high IMRs has not received any attention.

The poverty connection

The issue of high infant mortality rates is quite significant in the poverty context. Poverty is a clear indicator of underdevelopment and is known to be positively associated with high IMRs (Dyson, 1992; Jain and Visaria, 1988; Khan, 1993). At the same time, FMRs among the poor are known to be high (Miller, 1981 to Murthi et al., 1995). There are two popular explanations of generally higher FMRs among the poor. The first relates to the higher female labour participation (FLP) which increases their 'worth'. As such there is less discrimination against the girl child among the poorer households which is reflected in high FMRs. The relatively egalitarian character of the poorer households in general and of the Scheduled Tribe and Scheduled Castes in particular and has been stressed quite often in the literature[12] including my own analysis earlier (1995a).

The second popular explanation relates to migration: higher male migration among the poor resulting in higher FMRs (Krishnaji 1987, Kundu and Sahu 1991). But this has been questioned by some, for example, Krishnaji (1987) and is not very pertinent when we are talking of juvenile sex ratios.

But as shown above, there is excess male mortality at high levels of IMR. The positive effect of poverty on IMR would clearly translate into

---

[12] Egalitarianism among SC is referred to by (Murthi et al., 1995). They also indicate that the proportion of Scheduled Tribes in the population has significant effect in reducing the extent of anti-female bias 'even after controlling for female labour participation' and go on to suggest that tribal society may have other features that 'enhance the relative survival chances of female children' (Drèze et al., 1996: 1740). *Higher male infant mortality may be one such factor*!

high level of FMR04. If the discrimination against the girl child is marginal even FMR59 will be high. As seen in Table 3.6 FMR04 remains reasonably high when excess male infant mortality is high. This remains the case even for an excess female CMR of 80. If, for example, the excess male infant mortality rate is 40, the FMR04 and FMR59 assume values of 971 and 928. If excess female child mortality level is lower, these values increase substantially. High male infant mortality may therefore contribute significantly to the high FMRs among the poor.

Poverty and FLP

This is not to detract from the importance of female labour participation among the poor. The point simply is that poverty may be making a significant contribution to high FMRs through excess male infant mortality along with, *and in some cases rather than*, FLP. This effect will not be captured in the analyses that use FLP alone if the IMR gaps are not incorporated explicitly.[13] In fact, four combinations of FLP and IMR gap can emerge:

i) Poverty resulting in excess male infant mortality IMR and high FLP resulting in low excess female mortality: Very high FMRs in 0–4 and 5–9 age group or FMR59 ≥ FMR04.

ii) Poverty with moderate excess male IMR and high FLP with low excess female CMR: balanced FMRs, e.g., 960–990.

iii) Poverty with low excess male IMR and low FLP with excess female FMRs: low FMRs, e.g., 920–950.

iv) Poverty with higher female IMRs, low FLP with very high excess female FMRs: FMRs approaching 800.
None of these are hypothetical scenarios: Each can be located in India and calls for different policy interventions.

---

[13] Caldwell and Caldwell (1990) suggest that infant mortality figures should be excluded from analyses of gender bias. Kishor (1993) refers to this but considers this as unimportant: 'although maternal health and nutritional status probably cause "noise" in the data on infant mortality this does not justify excluding mortalitly in the first year from analysis' (1993: 250). But these two factors can make significant difference as their effects are non-linear. Further Kishor's reasoning that substantial gender bias exists in the post-neonatal stage is based on a study in UP which is not representative of the all-India pattern. While gender bias in post-neonatal stage is important in some regions, child mortality differentials are definitely a better guide to gender bias.

The masking effect

Another consequence of the 'purdah' of scholarship on the differences in the FMR04 and FMR59 concerns regions with 'intermediate' FMR values. Here high infant mortality can mask the effects of severe discrimination against the girl child in later years. If excess male IMR is between 20–40 and excess of female CMR is severe, i.e., 80, FMR04 will still remain in an 'acceptable' range of 948–971 and FMR59 in the range of 904–928 giving rise to a 'reasonable' juvenile FMR between 920–960. ·Excess male IMR in such circumstances, will mask the effect of discrimination against female children among the poor quite well *while in terms of intervention both require urgent attention*!

Differences in IMRs between poor and non-poor groups can be quite substantial (Government of India, 1988). Estimates of infant mortality by mother's occupation (ibid.), reveals high mortality levels among the children of rural manual workers and agricultural labourers. IMR levels among children of urban non-working mothers who are less poor, are quite low. To quote one example, in Madhya Pradesh, the IMRs among rural manual workers are 211 (male) and 178 (females). Among agricultural labourers these are 200 (males) and 175 (females). Compared to this, non-working urban mothers reported IMRs of 81 (male) and 76 (female). Similarly, NFHS data indicates high IMR values for the Scheduled Castes and the tribal population compared to the 'general' category (IIPS, 1995).

Though this discussion relates to the poverty context, it applies equally for other factors associated with high infant mortality rates. Mother's age at marriage is one such factor.[14]

Inferring mortality patterns from FMR data

The possibility of using FMR04 and FMR59 to identify priority intervention areas has obvious methodological advantage from the policy point

---

[14] Mother's age at marriage has significant association with infant mortality rate of a U-shaped nature (e.g., Khan, 1993). At low ages of marriage IMR is high. As such, if one finds 'balanced' female to male ratios in 'low age at marriage' groups, the likelihood of excess female deaths in post neonatal or post infancy stage is quite strong.

point of view. Data on infant mortality, child mortality or under-5 mortality is often not available at a very disaggregated level. District-level IMR figures were unavailable until 1988. Even today, these are not available in respect of the SC and ST population. The IMR data also has problems of accuracy at smaller sample sizes. But FMR figures do not suffer from these limitations. These are available for the total population samples and at more disaggregated levels like sub-district levels. It is possible to examine these and draw inferences about sex differentials in mortality and set agenda for further research at the micro level. In fact, motivation for the present inquiry itself arose from analysis of FMR04 and FMR59 for the ST, SC and general population at the district level. This is described in detail in the next chapter. Similarly, very low FMRs in 0–6 age group in the 1991 Census have been used to shortlist a number of districts to investigate likely incidence of infanticide.[15] On the same lines, one can identify a number of districts corresponding to possibilities (i) and (iv) above and assess the need for intervention. This may amount to some kind of 'reverse engineering'. But that is preferable to inaction for want of data. Even in methodological terms, what has been suggested is not a 'quick and dirty' method against 'long and clean' methods. It is a 'quick and clean' method, to use the metaphor further.

VI

Conclusion

Debate on sex ratio patterns in India has a long and distinguished history. Yet it has missed out the demographic significance of the internal structure of under-5 mortality. This aspect has been examined here elaborating the need to unpack the juvenile age group FMRs into the 0–4 and 5–9 age groups. The need can be further substantiated by examining actual FMR data from the 1981 Census. This is the aspect to which we turn now.

---

[15] Former Registrar General and Census Commissioner of India, A.R. Nanda, in p.c.

Chapter 4

Disaggregation of juvenile sex ratios

I

An outline

The theoretically anticipated distribution of the FMRs in the 0–4 and 5–9 age groups can be examined with the help of the district-level JSR (juvenile sex ratio) data. The 1981 Census provides 5-year age group data by different social groups. These are analysed here. First, the overall population data for the 0–4 and 5–9 age groups are analysed and compared with the patterns anticipated in Chapter 3. For this purpose, the range and distribution of the FMRs in the 0–4, 5–9 and 0–9 age groups are examined. Sixteen different combinations of 0–4 and 5–9 FMRs are examined using four levels for each of the FMRs: low, moderate, high and very high. This is analogous to the ninefold classification elaborated in the previous chapter.

This classification enables one to identify *regions of excess mortality* for male infants, female infants and the girl child. Districts where high values of FMR04 combine with low FMR59 values to give a misleading impression of balanced juvenile sex ratios can also be identified.

The effect of sex differentials in mortality on FMRs, hypothesised in Chapter 3, is analysed by regressing the FMR values on the sex differentials. The association is strong in the case of FMR59 but weak in the case of FMR04. It also provides an interesting possibility of inferring FMRs at birth from the data on mortality differentials and the FMRs. This is used to investigate if the low FMRs in the northern region can really be attributed to low FMRs at birth. It appears that low FMRs at birth cannot account for the extent of low FMRs in the 0–4 and 5–9 age groups except marginally.

Patterns among the three social groups

Disaggregation of the data among the three social groups is taken up next. As mentioned previously, the differences in sex ratios among the Scheduled Tribes, Scheduled Castes and the 'general' category, have rarely received attention from policy-makers or the academic circles. This gap is briefly reviewed and is followed by an analysis of the FMR data. Within each social group FMR04 and FMR59 differ significantly from each other. Differences among different social groups for each of the two FMRs are also examined.

Different combinations of FMR04 and FMR59 levels for the Scheduled Caste and Scheduled Tribes and their implications are examined. The FMR data indicate that the Scheduled Tribe population in certain regions may be experiencing excess male infant *and* male child mortality. Among the Scheduled Castes there appears to be an unusually high rate of girl child mortality. This strongly suggests the need for separate estimation of mortality rates for these two groups.

Spatial mapping

Districts corresponding to different combinations of FMR04 and FMR59 levels form distinct regional patterns. This merits a closer look at the spatial distributions of the 0–4 and 5–9 FMRs. This is done through maps of FMR04 and FMR59 at the district level. These highlight the differences between the FMR04 and FMR59 patterns and bring the *regional diversities in FMRs* into sharper focus.

The spatial mapping also highlights the differences in FMRs among the three social groups. Differences between the Scheduled Tribe and the non-Scheduled Tribe population are particularly striking. Separate analysis of the juvenile sex ratio data for these three groups has not been attempted so far even though the 5-year age group data for the Scheduled Castes and the Scheduled Tribes did become available in the 1981 Census.[1]

The FMR patterns display a remarkable spatial clustering in the four broad ranges of FMRs: below 910, between 911 and 960, between 961 and 1,010, and above 1,010. The maps clearly indicate clusters where the anti-female bias is sharp. But they also identify clusters where there is excess male infant mortality.

Spatial contiguity of FMRs is particularly pronounced for the non-Scheduled Tribe population. This provides an unexpected insight into the regional variations in sex ratios: *the importance of geophysical regions vis-à-vis states as units of spatial analysis.* Administrative boundaries of the states contain within them varied geophysical regions. On the other hand, many geophysical regions cut across the boundaries of different states. Within a state, district-level FMR59 vary significantly. Within the geophysical regions, however, FMR59 are quite homogenously distributed.

The patterns described above redefine the 'north–south' divide. This forms the subject matter of Chapter 5. Analysis of sex ratios by geophysical regions and kinship systems suggests that the dichotomous north–south classification needs modification. A new classification is suggested, which, although dichotomous, is more representative, in terms of the status of women. It groups the districts in terms of 'male-centred' versus 'female-friendly' kinship systems. This is elaborated upon in the next chapter. This classification fruitfully informs all subsequent analysis.

A comparison of the results with the analysis done by Murthi et al. (1995) provides an unexpected corroboration of the conclusion that FMR59 are able to identify more effectively regions where there is discrimination against the girl child.

Organisation of the discussion

Section II analyses the FMR04 and FMR59 data for the overall population. Section III carries this analysis further for the three social groups. The spatial distribution of the FMRs is described in the next section. Different implications of the result are discussed in the concluding section including policy and research issues that emerge.

---

[1] Earlier census operations provide data for the broad age groups of 0–14, 15–44 and 45+.

II

FMRs for the 0–4 and 5–9 Age Groups (Overall population)

The data analysed here pertain to the overall population at the district level. The 1981 Census provides dàta for 402 districts in the country (excluding Assam where census operation could not be conducted). The data used here are, however, taken from the Indian District Development Database (IDDD) (Vannemann and Barnes, 1992) and the special tables for the Scheduled Castes and Scheduled Tribes have been taken from 1981 Census. The IDDD uses 366 district units, combining some of the districts from smaller states into a single unit, and provides compatibility between census data from three different decades, that is, 1961 to 1981.

Range and distribution of FMRs

Figures 4.1a–c provide the distribution of FMR04, FMR59 and JFMRs. As expected, the mean of FMR04 is much higher than that of FMR59. FMR04 values are less dispersed, close to a normal distribution and rarely fall below 875. FMR59 are quite dispersed, relatively skewed and can assume very low values. T-test for paired samples shows *significant differences between FMR04 and FMR59* (T = 15.23***). FMR09 are a combination of the two.

Different levels of FMRs and their combinations

More useful light is thrown on the distribution of these FMRs by assigning each of them four different levels: *low* (below 910), *moderate* (910–960), *high* (960–1,000) and *very high* (above 1,000).[2] This gives 16 possible combinations, analogous to the ninefold combination discussed in the previous chapter. The number of districts in each combination and the mean of the FMR value in these districts are presented in Table 4.1a.

[2] The cut off values for these levels do not have any 'analytical' justification except for 960 which is close to the FMR at birth. These were basically chosen by examining the spatial distribution of FMRs which reveal contiguous district clusters with these FMRs as cut off points.

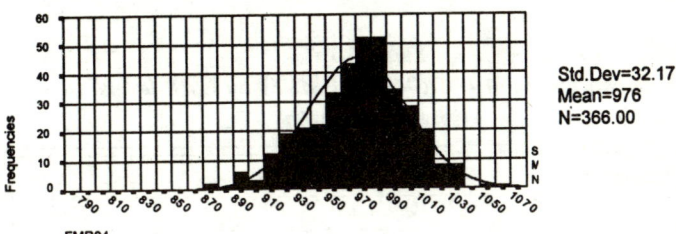

Figure 4.1a: Distribution of FMR04: 1981 Census (366 districts—total population).

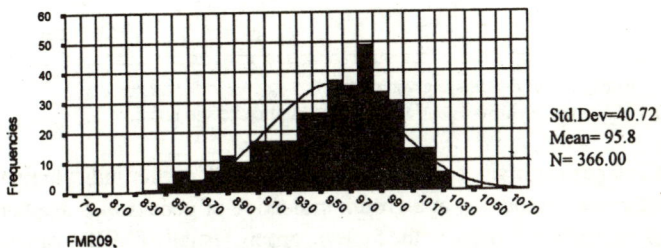

Figure 4.1b: Distribution of FMR09: 1981 Census (366 districts—total population).

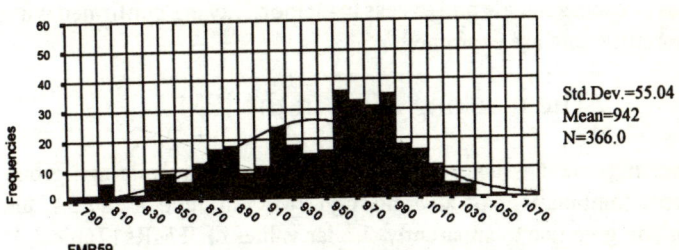

Figure 4.1c: Distribution of FMR59: 1981 Census (366 districts—total population).

Mean values of FMR04 and FMR59 for these districts are indicated in each of the cell. Together these give an idea of the extent of drop in FMR between the 0–4 and 5–9-year age groups; an indicator of excess girl child mortality.

Table 4.1a
Mean values of FMR04 and FMR59 by FMR levels
(total population)

FMR59 Range	FMR04 Range			
	Low	*Moderate*	*High*	*Very High*
Low	10 (897/863)	54 (937/863)	27 (977/879)	6 (1,012/894)
Moderate	1	26 (945/930)	55 (979/940)	18 (1,018/939)
High	0	12 950/971	83 (983/978)	28 (1,018/983)
Very high	0	1	15 983/1,011	30 (1,017/1,020)

Notes: 1) The number of districts is given in line 1.
2) FMR04 and FMR59 values are given within brackets in line 2.

The blank or near blank columns at the bottom left corner indicate that low FMR values in the 0–4 age group, indicative of gender bias against the girl child, *rarely increase* in the 5–9 age group. Usually FMR04 values drop further down in the 5–9 age group depending upon the extent of excess female child mortality. All districts in the first row and the 18 districts in the second row (last cell) come in this category. The negative drop between FMR04 and FMR59 on the other hand signifies excess male child mortality in 27 districts left of the major diagonal. These aspects of excess female and excess male mortality are confirmed when the mortality data are examined.

The masking effect in the JFMRs

Another important issues relates to FMRs in the juvenile age group. Different combinations of low and high FMRs in the 0–4 and 5–9 age groups can give rise to apparently similar values of JFMRs (Table 3.4). Table 4.1b substantiates this.

Table 4.1b

Mean values of JFMRs by different FMR ranges
(total population)

FMR59 Range	FMR04 Range			
	Low	*Moderate*	*High*	*Very High*
Low	10 (866)	54 (897)	27 (925)	6 (947)
Moderate	1	26 (937)	55 (958)	18 (976)
High	0	12 (961)	83 (980)	28 (999)
Very high	0	1	15 (997)	30 (1,019)

Notes: Number of districts given in each cell with mean of FMR values in brackets.

The masking effect, is quite pronounced in districts where FMR59 is low while FMR04 is moderate to high. The JFMR values appear 'balanced' and hide the adverse condition for the survival of the girl child reflected in very low FMR59 values and sharp drop between FMR04 and FMR59. The number of such districts, 105, is quite large (JFMR values underlined).

District-level maps

The discussion so far has not taken the location of the districts into consideration. It is useful to take this into account through the district-level maps of the three FMRs, i.e., FMR04, FMR59 and FMR09. This is essentially a logical extension of the maps presented by Sopher (1980) and Miller (1981) using the juvenile age group data of the 1961 Census. Maps 4.1a–c give the spatial distribution of the three for the overall district population.[3]

The maps vividly show the differences between the FMRs in the 0–4 and the 5–9 age groups. The high values of FMR04 and low values of FMR59 are clear. The 'masking effect' of FMR04 is also clear when the maps for FMR59 and FMR09 are compared. Both these maps use identical FMR ranges. The contiguous belt with FMR59 < 850 in the north, is masked in the FMR09 map. A similar effect is seen in eastern UP and northern Bihar. The north–south divide is also quite vivid, especially in the FMR59 map (Map 4.1b). These maps are useful in the discussion

---

[3] To facilitate quick reference against the FMR maps, an administrative map of India with district boundaries (Map I) is provided at the end.

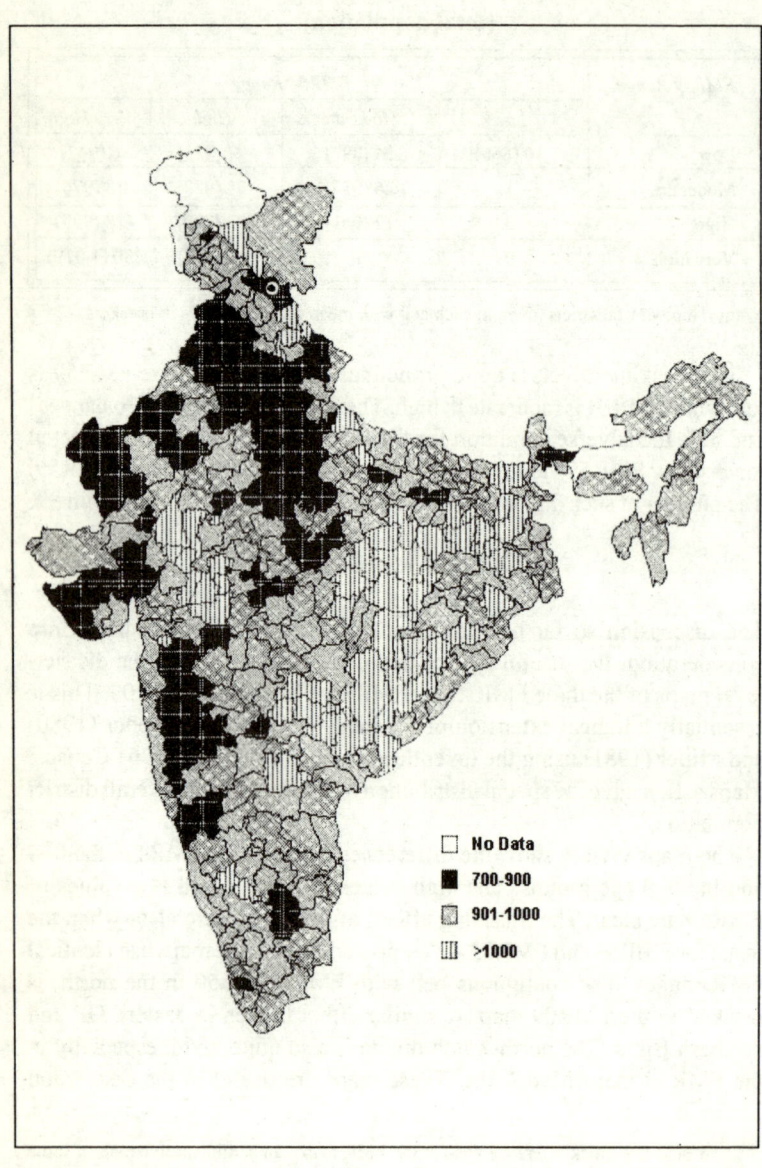

Map 4.1a: District-level map of FMR04: 1981 Census (total population).

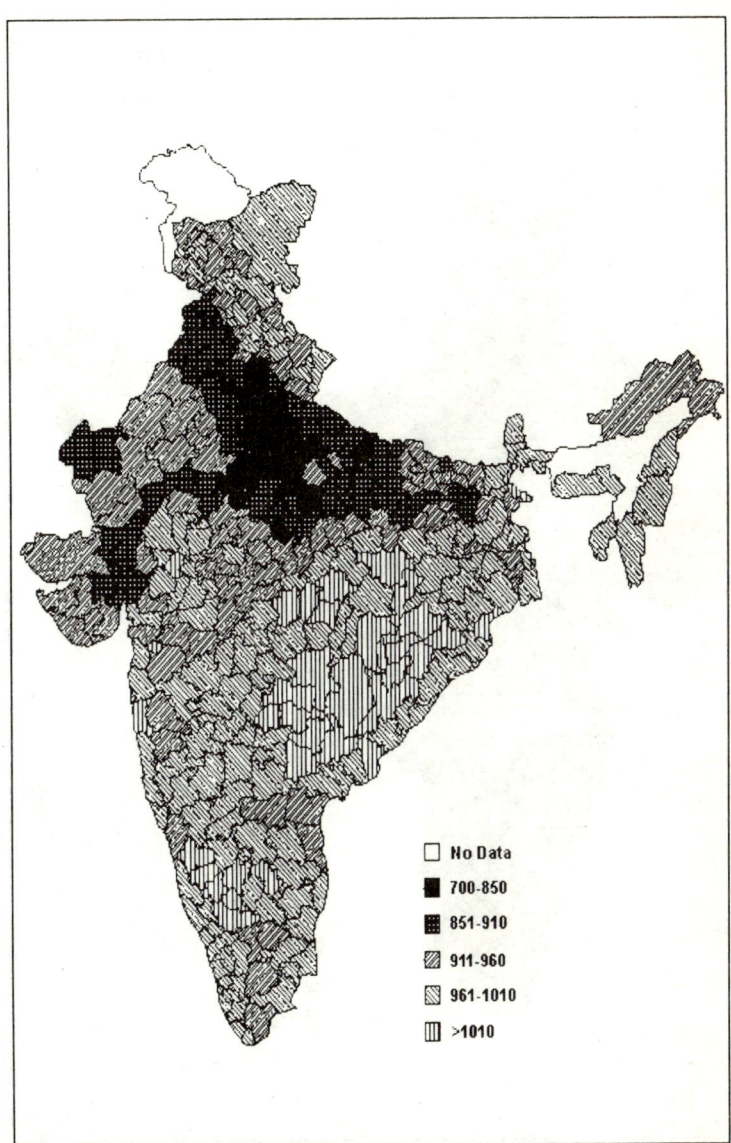

Map 4.1b: District-level map of FMR59: 1981 Census (total population).

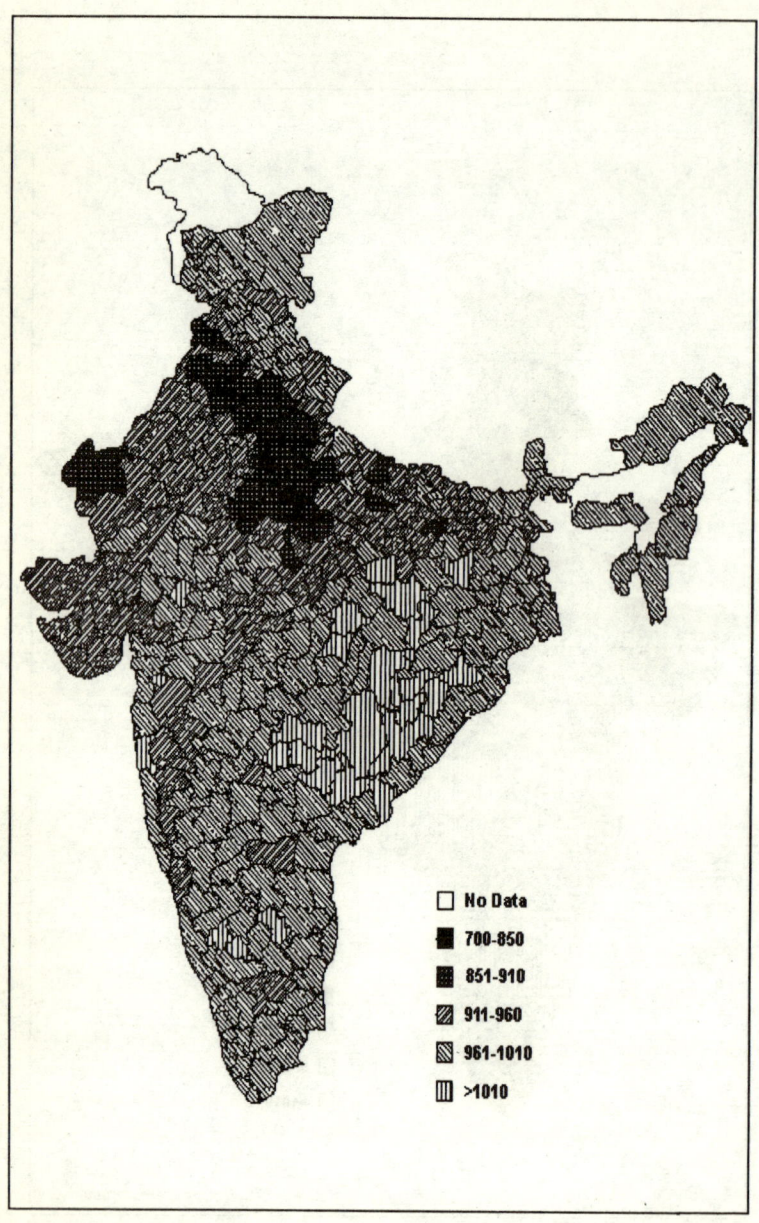

Map 4.1c: District-level map of FMR09: 1981 Census (total population).

presented here and are analysed in further details in Section V after disaggregating the FMR data for the three social groups.

Excess male and female mortality by FMR ranges

The positive association between excess male infant deaths and high FMRs in 0–4 and in 5–9 age groups and the negative association between excess female deaths and FMRs is revealed through the correlation coefficients given here:

Table 4.2

Correlation between sex differentials in mortality and FMRs

	Excess male infant mortality	Excess under-5 female mortality
FMR04	0.39***	−0.53***
FMR59	0.51***	−0.86***

Box plots of the sex differentials in mortality for the four FMR ranges also confirm the above association. Figure 4.2a provides the box plots of the sex differentials in infant and under-5 mortality for the four ranges of FMR04. Excess female under-5 mortality in the low FMR range is quite pronounced. It is less at high FMRs. Similarly, excess male infant mortality is quite high in the high FMR range. It is low, even negative, in the low FMR range. A similar pattern is revealed in Figure 4.2b which provides similar box plots for the four ranges of the FMR59. As anticipated *there is excessive male under-5 mortality when FMR59 is very high.*

The mortality data

The nature of this association is demonstrated even more starkly when one looks at the actual mortality figures for two sets of districts; one set where both FMR04 and FMR59 are very low (below 910) and the other where both are very high (above 1,000). As seen in Table 4.1a, there are 10 districts in the first category and 30 in the second.

Table 4.3a gives the values of FMR04, FMR59, excess male infant mortality and excess female under-5 mortality in the 10 districts with low FMR04 and FMR59. All these districts, except Gandhinagar (the capital of the state of Gujarat), show *excess female mortality during infancy* and are parts of the contiguous region of Punjab, Haryana and western UP, known for its anti-female bias.

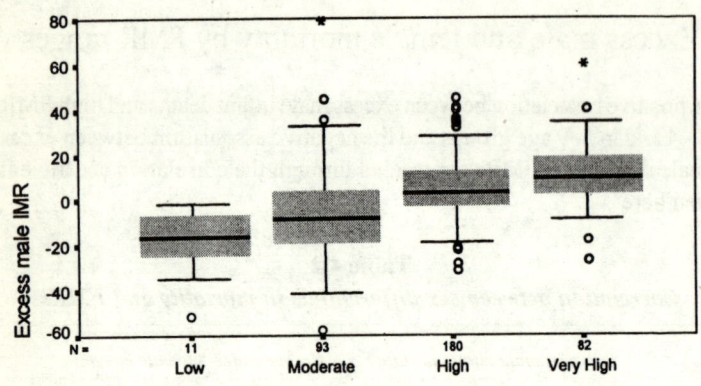

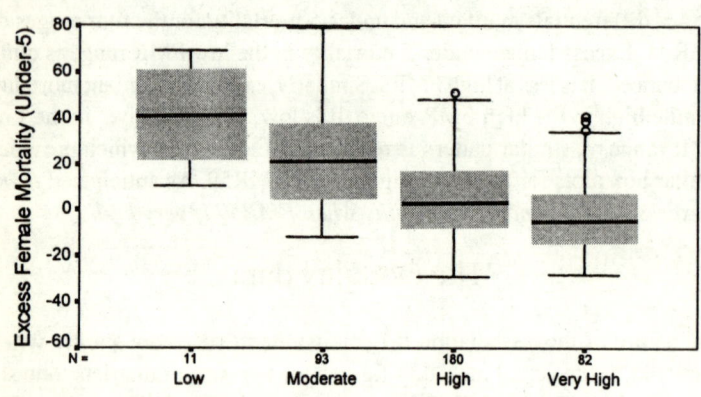

DIFFERENT LEVELS OF FMR04
(N = Number of Districts: 1981 Census)

Figure 4.2a: Box plot of sex differentials in infant and under-5 mortality by FMR04 ranges.

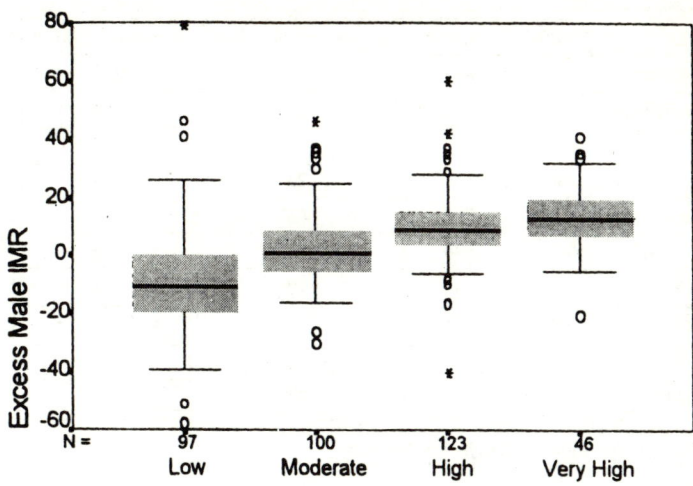

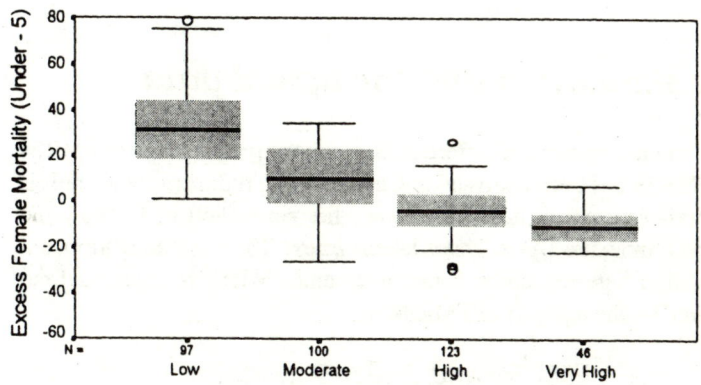

DIFFERENT LEVELS OF FMR59
(N = Number of Districts: 1981 Census)

Figure 4.2b: Box plot of sex differentials in infant and under-5 mortality by FMR59 ranges.

Table 4.3a

Sex differentials in mortality in low FMR districts

District	FMR04	FMR59	Excess female U5MR	Excess male IMR*
Gandhinagar	898	881	15	0.00
Kurukshetra	880	867	37	–14
Jind	879	837	51	–51
Sonepat	890	829	23	–9
Bhind	909	791	68	–11
Kapurthala	903	880	32	–29
Patiala	901	888	10	–2
Bulandshahar	900	812	51	–16
Mathura	908	788	68	–33
Mainpuri	904	813	69	–1

Note: * a –ve sign shows excess *female* mortality.

In striking contrast, the 30 districts which have very high values of both FMR04 and FMR59 (above 1,000) show *excess male infant mortality and excess male under-5 mortality* (Table 4.3b).

The simulation and the actual data

Association between sex differentials in mortality and levels of FMR04 and FMR59 has been analysed in Chapter 3 at a rudimentary level. It is appropriate to check how satisfactory the simulation of FMR04 and FMR59 (Annexure 3A) is. This is taken up next. The more straightforward association between under-5 mortality and FMR59 is explored first, followed by the analysis of FMR04.

FMR59 and under-5 mortality

The relationship between FMRs in the 5–9 age group and *survivorship ratio* $S5 = (1-Q5f)/(1-Q5m)$, stipulated in Annexure 3A, turns out to be linear and highly significant. It can be described as:

Table 4.3b
Sex differentials in mortality in high FMR districts

District	FMR04	FMR59	Excess Female U5MR	Excess Male IMR
East Godavari	1,020	1,012	−15	15
Medak	1,008	1,008	−16	17
Nizamabad	1,023	1,014	−6	24
Adilabad	1,030	1,020	−13	15
Karimnagar	1,011	1,017	−7	21
Warangal	1,024	1,012	−9	32
Khammam	1,021	1,017	−16	16
Nalgonda	1,003	1,012	−11	24
The Dangs	1,013	1,020	−16	4
Mandla	1,021	1,040	−15	41
Balaghat	1,012	1,027	−18	14
Surguja	1,024	1,014	−9	23
Bilaspur	1,018	1,001	−9	11
Raigarh (MP)	1,022	1,032	−16	12
Raipur	1,013	1,019	−11	19
Bastar	1,024	1,039	−15	27
Raigarh (Mah.)	1,005	1,017	−15	12
Parbhani	1,007	1,000	−10	10
Hassan	1,010	1,034	−22	34
Kolar	1,001	1,033	−10	5
Mandya	1,019	1,014	−6	18
Kendujhar	1,000	1,006	−14	13
Baleshwar	1,005	1,011	−1	9
Dhenkanal	1,018	1,015	−2	7
Phulbani	1,012	1,041	−19	18
Balangir	1,017	1,038	−17	14
Kalahandi	1,037	1,060	−14	14
Koraput	1,031	1,015	−7	29
Banswara	1,045	1,021	−11	8
Cooch Bihar	1,001	1,003	−5	35

FMR59 = –971 + 1936* S5		4.1a
T: (–16***) (31***)		
F: 115*** Adj. R. Sq. = 0.73		

At Q5f = Q5m, the survivorship ratio is unity and FMR59 equals 965 which is quite close to FMR at birth. This is consistent with the expectation that in the absence of any gender bias, reflected in equal Q5 value for both male and female children, FMR59 will be close to FMR at birth or FMR_0.

This can be corroborated independently by regressing FMR59 on the *sex differentials in mortality* (the alternative expression in Annexure 3a). The regression results are given below:

FMR59 = 962 + 0.3* SDIMR(MF) – 2.2* SDU5MR(FM)		4.1b
T: 515*** 2.7*** –26***		
F: 520*** Adj. R. Sq. = 0.74		

If sex differentials in both infant and under-5 mortality are set to zero, FMR59 is given by the constant term 962.

This indirect estimation of FMR_0 can be quite useful in discussions about regional variations in FMR_0. This is discussed further after analysing the association between sex differentials in mortality and FMR04.

Determinants of FMR04

Unlike FMR59, FMR04 depends upon a number of parameters (see Annexure 3A). It is therefore affected more strongly by the different simplifying assumption about absence of skewness in mortality, constant fertility, homogeneity of the population in respect of the infant mortality rates and so on. Not surprisingly, regression of FMR04 on the F(0. 4)/ M(0, 4) ratio yields a less satisfactory result:

FMR04 = 4.6 +972* F(0, 4)/M(0, 4)		4.2c
T: 0.05 10.6***		
F: 112*** Adj. R. Sq. = 0.23		

The constant term is not significant but the coefficient is. The value of F is high but that of R. Sq. is low.

The expression for FMR04 in terms of sex differentials in mortality gives following result:

FMR04 = 980 + 0.4* SDIMR(MF) – 0.58* SDU5MR(FM)   4.1d
T: 528***   3.7***   –6.9***
F: 61*** Adj. R. Sq. = <u>0.25</u>

Once again, if the sex differentials in mortality are set to zero, the FMR04 value turns out to be 980, corresponding to a high FMR at birth.

Sex ratio at birth

Low FMRs in some of the regions are quite often attributed to highly masculine sex ratios at birth (Chapter 2: Section III). This is done in spite of the compelling evidence, based on reliable data from large samples, that the regional variations in FMRs at birth are only marginal. In the absence of any break up of juvenile age group FMRs, the low FMR at birth argument continues to carry weight.[4] But once FMR04 and FMR59 are examined separately, the *drop between FMR04 and FMR59, an indicator of the extent of excess female mortality can no longer be attributed to low FMRs at birth.* A low FMR at birth, say, 910 cannot explain why the FMR59 values drop below 850, or as in the case of the SC population, below 800 in many districts.

The possibility of indirectly assessing the FMR at birth is used here to examine the likely extent to which FMR at birth can be low. In addition, the drop between FMR04 and FMR59 is also examined for districts with low FMRs.

A regression of FMR59 on the sex differentials in mortality for districts with low FMR59 values (< 960) yields:

FMR59 = 940 + 0.13* SDIMR(MF) – 1.7* SDU5MR(FM)   4.1e
T: 319***   1.0   –16***
F: 156*** Adj. R. Sq. = 0.61 (Number of Districts = 196)

---

[4] The argument that FMRs at birth and under-5 mortality together determine JFMR and hence low FMRs at birth can cause low JFMRs, is quite compelling and difficult to disprove until the JFMRs are unpacked.

If the sex differentials in mortality are set to zero, the constant term, an indirect estimate of FMR_0 is 940. Even if the regression is carried out for the districts with low FMR59 (< 910), the constant term does not drop below 909.[5]

More direct evidence against the low FMR at birth argument is provided by the set of 28 districts (Table 4.4) where FMR59 goes below 850. In all these districts, except Jind and Sonepat, the *FMR04 values are above 920*. It will take an extraordinary amount of ingenuity and obstinacy to argue that in these districts the FMR at birth is actually low but increases to 920 and above because of high male infant mortality. But such argument can still be advanced. It, however, flies in the face of *the observed excess female mortality during infancy 23 out of these 28 districts*.

Table 4.4
List of 28 districts with low FMRs **(1981 Census)**

Name of the district	FMR04	FMR59	Excess male IMR	Excess female U-5 MR
Jind	879	837	−51	51
Sonepat	890	829	−9	23
Faridabad	921	845	−29	38
Morena	922	813	−16	30
Bhind	909	791	−11	68
Datia	926	835	−17	60
Bharatpur	929	808	−31	79
Sawai Madhopur	975	845	−12	51
Jaisalmer	929	850	−14	27
Saharanpur	927	844	−22	28
Muzaffarnagar	941	847	−27	37
Meerut	951	847	−23	39
Ghaziabad	918	837	5	48
Bulandshahar	900	812	−16	51
Moradabad	930	832	−27	48
Budaun	930	800	−17	73
Aligarh	925	801	−8	54
Mathura	908	788	−33	68

Table 4.4 continued

[5] This result should, however, he handled cautiously. In the low FMR59 range, the effects of excess female mortality in the 5–9 age group will also start becoming significant.

Table 4.4 continued

Name of the district	FMR04	FMR59	Excess male IMR	Excess female U-5 MR
Agra	929	809	16	65
Etah	945	808	–57	75
Mainpuri	904	813	–1	69
Farrukhabad	959	848	–26	43
Etawah	940	823	20	56
Jalaun	941	848	7	53
Lalitpur	936	838	8	48
Hamirpur	931	817	11	65
Hardoi	962	837	26	45
Gonda	975	844	0	48

Note: FMR04 = Female–Male Ratio in the 0–4 age group (Females per 1,000 Males)
IMR = Infant Mortality Rate; U-5 MR = Under-5 Mortality Rate.

Clearly, the low FMRs in the north-west cannot be attributed to the low FMRs at birth except marginally. Unless its effect is conclusively quantified by its protagonists, policy must give the benefit of doubt to the female children and *initiate measures to reduce excess female mortality.*

An argument can, in fact, be made in favour of *shifting the concern* to the regions of high FMRs at birth. As late foetal mortality and neonatal mortality arises from similar causes (Waldron, 1983), it is possible that regions of high neonatal mortality will also have incidence of high levels of late foetal mortality. This will result in higher FMR at birth than usual as such underdevelopment could *subject the males to the twin disadvantage of high foetal wastage and high neonatal death rate.*

As far as higher FMRs at birth are concerned, regression of FMR04 on sex differentials in mortality in the 168 districts with FMR59 > 960 does actually yield a constant term, 982, which is significant, even though the R.Sq. value is low (0.29).

One can thus conclude that low FMRs at birth can explain low FMR04 only to a small extent and cannot detract one from the seriousness of the problem of excess female child mortality. The concern about FMRs at birth should, in fact, shift towards the regions or groups with high FMR at birth as indicator of less than desirable health environment for childbirth.

III

Disaggregation by social groups

This section focusses on the differences in the sex ratio patterns among the Scheduled Tribes and the Scheduled Castes and the rest or the general category. It was also indicated (Chapter 2: Section V) that the differences in sex ratio patterns among these three groups have not attracted serious attention in the literature.

This lack of attention cannot be attributed to an absence of data. Given the constitutional position of the Scheduled population, the task of collection of data in their respect is done quite routinely and regularly. But beyond this it is not put to much use. Not surprisingly, therefore, state-level sex ratio figures for the ST, SC and the general categories for the four census decades, 1961 to 1991 (Table 1.2), compiled together by this author (1995: 2075) happens to be available for the first time[6] in this form.

Absence of such a compilation has masked some of the sharp declines in FMRs which had occurred for the SC and ST population in some of the states. The FMR among the SC have declined almost everywhere and at a faster rate than the decline in the FMR of the overall population[7] since 1961. Similarly, while the FMRs for the ST population remain at a high level, in certain states, for example, Rajasthan, these declined significantly. Yet this did not attract the attention of policy-makers or academics.[8]

This preliminary analysis (Agnihotri, 1995a) using state-level data clearly indicates a need to study the sex ratio patterns among the SC and

[6] Agnihotri, 1995: 2075. This table was first compiled in December 1992 without the data for 1991. Figures for 1991 were incorporated in 1993. Surprisingly such a compilation was not readily available in any of the census publications or any academic publication (Jean Drèze—p.c.).

[7] All-India level FMRs declined between 1961 and 1971 by 11 points (941 to 930) for the total population and 22 points for the SC population (957 to 935). In 1981, when the all-India FMR figure went up to 934 from the level of 930 in 1971. But for the SC population it had actually declined by 3 points (935 in 1971 to 932 in 1981). The trend has continued in 1991: overall FMR declined by 6 points and for the SC population by 10 points (Table 1.2).

[8] Though this may be on a personal note, I was surprised to find that even the persons associated with census operations, the National Commission for Women, and the Welfare Ministry dealing with the SC/ST welfare schemes, appeared somewhat surprised when the decline in SC FMRs were pointed out to them by me during personal discussions.

the ST population separately form those for the general population. It shows that these two groups cannot be clubbed together under the shared features of poverty, for example, coming from weaker sections,[9] or under-development, that is, being 'scheduled' in the constitutional sense. Differences in the sex ratio patterns between these two groups and their implications are analysed here with the help of the district-level data.

FMR04 and FMR59 for the three categories

As indicated earlier, these data became available for the first time in the 1981 Census but have not been put to any use. However, while using these, the non-uniform distribution of the SCs and STs across the country has to be taken into account. The SCs are more evenly spread across the country; there are 342 districts with a SC population of more than 1 per cent. The STs are spread more unevenly. There are only 198 districts with a ST population of more than 1 per cent. It is only in 189 out of the 366 districts that the SC and ST population is above 1 per cent of the district population. Within these districts the concentration of these two populations is inversely correlated (Pearson's coefficient = 0.45***).

It is useful therefore, to differentiate the districts by the levels of SC and ST population concentration. Four levels will be used in this analysis: **negligible** (less than 1 per cent), **low** (1–10 per cent), **significant** (10–20 per cent) and **high** (above 20 per cent).

Tables 4.5a and 4.5b give the number of districts in these categories and the mean of the FMR values.

Table 4.5a
Mean FMRs by levels of ST population percentage

ST Percentage	Low (1–10 per cent)	Significant (10–20 per cent)	High (above 20 per cent)
Number of Districts	102	39	57
ST FMR04	1,005	1,004	1,015
ST FMR59	959	974	986

---

[9] 'Weaker sections' is a very commonplace label in official parlance and records for SC, ST and women!

Table 4.5b
Mean FMRs by levels of SC population percentage

SC Percentage	Low (1–10 per cent)	Significant (10–20 per cent)	High (above 20 per cent)
Number of Districts	68	180	94
SC FMR04	977	986	962
SC FMR59	957	931	890

Increasing FMRs among the STs as their concentration increases contrast with the declining FMRs among the SC population as the concentration of the SC population increases. This is more pronounced in the 5–9 age group.

T-tests for paired samples confirm *significant differences between FMR04 and FMR59 among the SC and the ST population.* (Table 4.6) All the differences are significant at the 1 per cent level.

Table 4.6
Differences between FMR04 and FMR59 (Scheduled Caste and Scheduled Tribe population)

Population Percentage	Scheduled Caste		Scheduled Tribe	
	Districts	T-value	Districts	T-value
Low	68	3.7***	102	9.9***
Significant	180	12.9***	39	4.2***
High	94	12.9***	57	7.2***

The differences in the FMR04 and FMR59 are significant for the general category as well (T-value 11.3***).

Differences in FMRs between the social groups

The next important question is whether the FMRs differ significantly between different social groups. This is analysed first between the ST and the non-ST FMRs and then between the SCs and the general category.

Differences in FMR04 between the ST and the non-ST population are significant with the FMR04 among the ST population always being higher than FMR04 among the non-ST population. This could signify higher male infant mortality among the STs. Separate estimates of infant and

Table 4.7a
***Differences in FMRs* (Scheduled Tribe and non-Scheduled Tribe population)**

Population Percentage (ST)	Number of Districts	T-value	
		FMR04	FMR59
Low	102	6.9***	0.3
Significant	39	2.1***	0.9
High	57	2.3***	0.9

child mortality rates are necessary for confirming this apprehension. In the 5–9 age group, however, FMRs do not differ significantly between the ST and the non-ST population.

Among the SC and the general category, the differences in the FMR04 are not very significant, except in the intermediate range of SC population levels. However, the differences in the FMR59 are highly significant (1 per cent level) in all the three sets of districts. These would signify differences in excess female mortality between the two groups. Once again, separate estimates of infant and child mortality for the SCs are necessary to confirm this.

Table 4.7b
***Differences in FMRs* (Scheduled Caste and general population)**

Population Percentage (SC)	Number of Districts	T-value	
		FMR04	FMR59
Low	68	0.5	2.9***
Significant	180	2.8**	6.3***
High	94	0.6	5.0***

In the 189 districts where both the SC and ST population are above 1 per cent of the total population, both FMR04 (T = 6.4***) and FMR59 (T = 4.7***) differ significantly between the two groups.

Different levels of FMR04 and FMR59

While the statistical significance of the differences in the FMRs are borne out above, it is useful to examine different possible combinations of FMR04 and FMR59. This is done on the same lines as the sixteen fold classification for the overall population above. However, for the

SC population, another level of FMR59, very low (below 850) has been added.

Table 4.8a
Different combinations of FMR04 and FMR59
(Scheduled Caste population)

FMR59 Range	FMR04 Range			
	Low	Moderate	High	Very High
Very Low	18 (883/770)	24 (933/802)	11 (979/841)	0
Low	2 (906/862)	34 (933/871)	31 (981/890)	9 (1,022/896)
Moderate	2 (903/970)	15 (947/938)	34 (980/935)	25 (1,026/930)
High	0	6 (951/980)	53 (984/980)	33 (1,025/980)
Very High	0	2 (950/1,008)	11 (985/1,008)	30 (1,014/1,010)

Introduction of the category 'very low' makes immediate sense. The 53 districts in the top row represent *unusually high levels of female mortality*. This effect is equally worrying in the 9 districts where the FMR04 are very high while FMR59 levels drop below 900. *There cannot be a more compelling evidence against the 'low FMR at birth' optimism.* More important than scoring this academic point, however, is the *urgency for social and policy intervention in these districts. Estimation of the actual levels of child mortality for the SC population in these districts becomes an immediate priority.* A list of districts where FMR04 is low and FMR59 is very low, is specifically given (Table 4.8b) to draw attention to the magnitude of the problem. These are all located in a belt that covers Haryana, western UP and the Gwalior division of MP.

These districts readily reveal the serious survival adversities faced by Scheduled Caste female children. FMRs in their case, particularly in the 5–9 age group are alarmingly low and lower than those for the general category.

There is another set of districts where high FMR04 values mask very low FMR59 *if juvenile FMRs are used.* These districts are mostly located in the eastern UP and northern Bihar region. This region has conveyed an

Table 4.8b
Districts with very low FMR values among the Scheduled Castes

District	FMR04(SC)	FMR59(SC)	FMR04(Gen)	FMR59(Gen)
Kurukshetra	904	828	873	878
Karnal	900	835	938	884
Jind	906	782	872	851
Faridabad	878	759	929	863
Gurgaon	908	795	965	905
Morena	870	731	930	826
Bhind	860	742	924	804
Datia	888	782	940	852
Shivpuri	910	809	948	890
Bharatpur	889	717	940	836
Saharanpur	868	790	945	861
Muzaffarnagar	849	749	958	867
Meerut	908	792	960	859
Ghaziabad	852	752	935	860
Bulandshahar	810	715	926	842
Jalaun	908	746	954	888
Jhansi	906	810	948	906
Hamirpur	876	728	950	847

impression of more balanced FMRs compared to the upper Gangetic region (Libbee, 1980 ; Miller 1981; Sopher, 1980). *Such 'balance' camouflages both high male infant mortality and high girl child mortality.*

Districts where FMR04 and FMR59 are both high are invariably located in the south-east. While the absence of bias against the girl child in these regions is not defined, the suspicion of higher infant male mortality cannot be avoided.

The pattern of different combinations of FMR04 and FMR59 levels suggests the need to examine the spatial distribution of these FMRs. This is a logical extension of the district-level mapping of JSRs (Miller 1981; Sopher 1980). This is taken up after completing the analysis of these combinations for the ST population in Table 4.8c.

The first striking feature of this Table is the high FMR04 values. There are only 3 districts where these values go below 910 and another 13 where these are below 960. This signifies absence of excess female mortality during infancy among STs.

Table 4.8c
Different combinations of FMR04 and FMR59
(Scheduled Tribe population)

FMR59 Range	FMR04 Range			
	Low	Moderate	High	Very High
Low	1	4 (930/842)	7 (982/885)	4 (1,009/896)
Moderate	2	6 (945/930)	25 (981/939)	28 (1,033/942)
High	0	2	27 (988/981)	52 (1,030/980)
Very High	0	1	8 (990/1,000)	36 (1,021/1,022)

FMR59 values are also high by and large. In fact, there are only 11 districts in Rajasthan where FMR59 for the STs go below 900. Even the 45 districts where FMR59 values are between 900–950, lie mainly in the plains of Rajasthan and northern Madhya Pradesh (MP). However, in about 16 out of these 56 districts (top row in Table 4.8c), there is a disturbing drop from high levels of FMR04 to low levels of FMR59. These FMR59 values are not high by the standards of ST FMRs even though these are higher compared to those of the non-ST population.[10]

But the point of more serious concern is, however, the *unusually high FMR values among the STs*. The set of 36 districts where both FMR04 and FMR59 assume very high values need special scrutiny. As previously mentioned, the absence of discrimination against the girl child may be one contributing factor for the high FMRs. However, *the possibility of excess male foetal wastage and infant mortality driven by poverty and underdeveloped health infrastructure cannot be ruled out*. The NFHS survey does reveal poorer antenatal care and immunisation coverage of the ST children and supports such a concern (IIPS, 1995).

[10] This drop cannot be explained away using the excuse of 'under-enumeration of girl children' work except by invoking under enumeration in the 5–9 age group and its absence in the 0–4 age group. That is quite unrealistic. Moreover, the ST groups are far less likely to practice under-reporting of female children given their social structure.

IV

Spatial distribution of the FMRs

District-level maps of FMR04 and FMR59

The analysis presented in Section III, though useful, does not do adequate justice to the diversity of the FMRs across the country. This diversity is physical, social, cultural and demographic. Some of it is revealed through the district-level FMR maps for the overall population. The spatial distribution of the FMRs disaggregated by the three social groups high-lights it further.

Map 4.2a–c present the spatial distribution of FMR04 for the general, SC and ST populations. Map 4.3a–c show the corresponding distribution for FMR59. The patterns are quite striking and do not need much elaboration. The generally high values of FMR04 compared to those of FMR59 are clearly brought out by comparing Maps 4.2a–c with 4.3a–c. Higher FMR values among STs are also vivid. However, districts with low FMR59 among the STs are also noticeable. The issue of low FMRs among STs has not been raised in the literature so far. It has important implications for ST welfare policies.

Spatial clusters

FMR04 values for the non-ST population display a remarkable spatial cluster below the cut-off level of 960, close to the FMR at birth. It descends from the northern plains of Punjab and Haryana, travels through the upper Gangetic plains in UP, the ravines of the Chambal river and goes down south across the river Narmada through the Khandesh region of Maharashtra. For the Scheduled Castes it does not go further south, while for the 'general' category it reaches as far south as Karnataka.[11] The pattern is similar for the overall population. Another branch of this belt encircles the hilly regions of Rajasthan and Gujarat in a continuous chain except the Nagaur and Sikar districts in Rajasthan.

A more elaborate clustering is seen in the case of FMR59 for the non-ST population. There is one clear cluster of very low FMR59 (below

---

[11] Except the districts of East Nimar (FMR04 = 969) and Bijapur (FMR04 = 965).

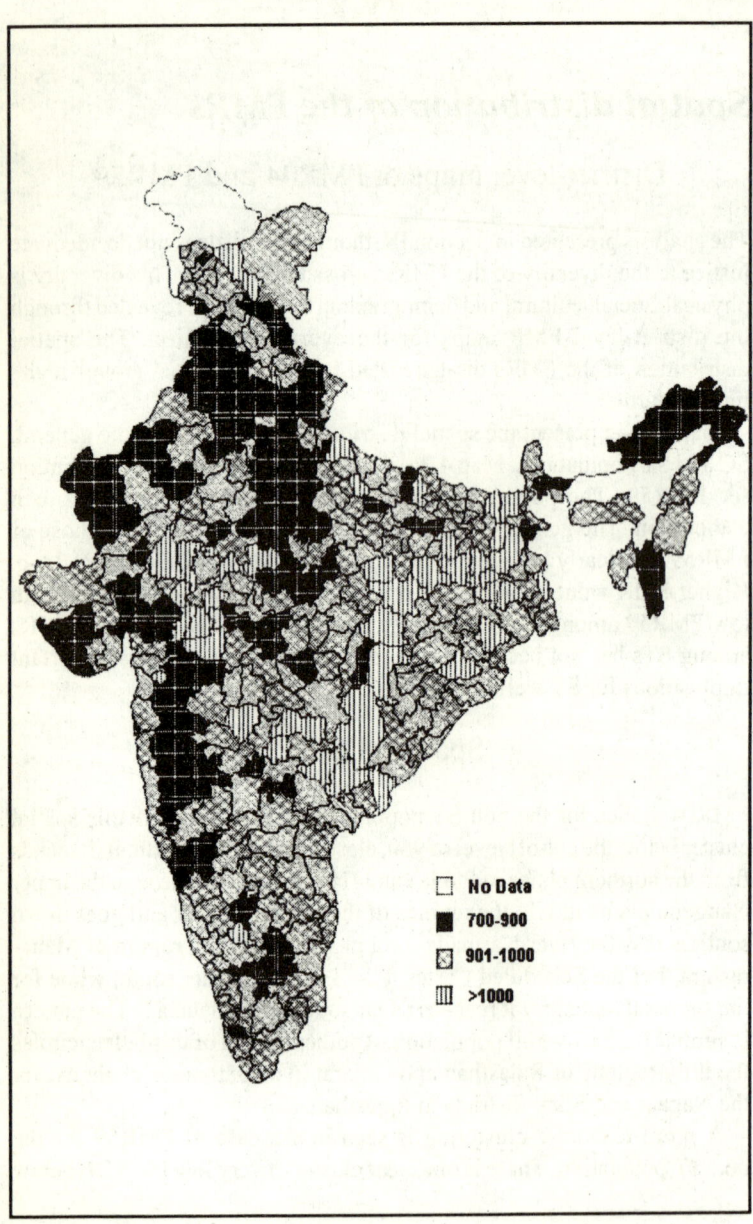

Map 4.2a: District-level map of FMR04: 1981 Census (general population).

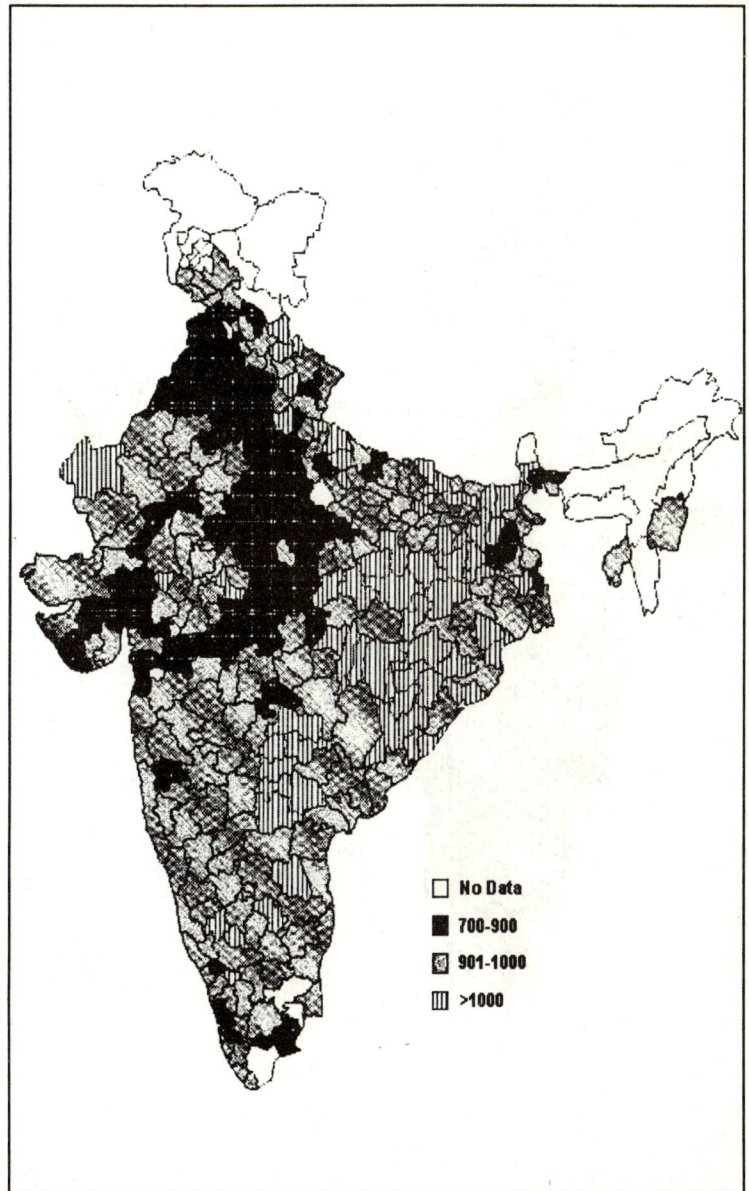

Map 4.2b: District-level map of FMR04: 1981 Census (SC population).

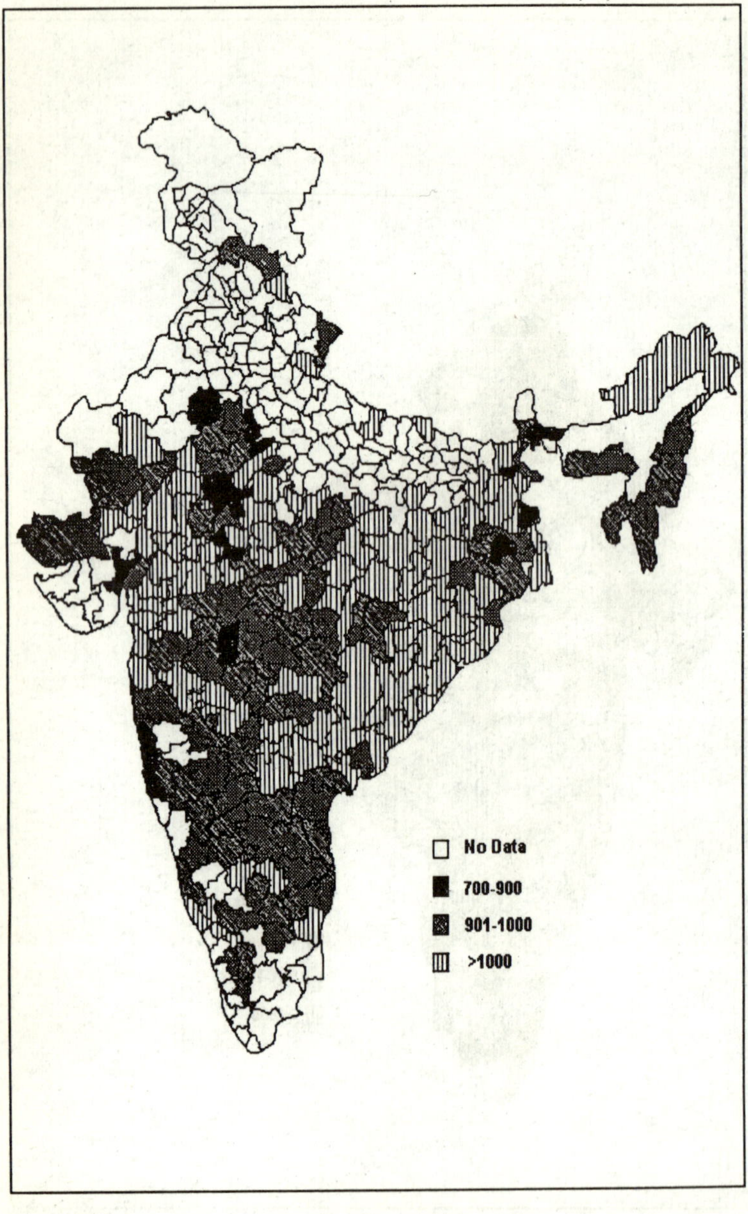

Map 4.2c: District-level map of FMR04: 1981 Census (ST population).

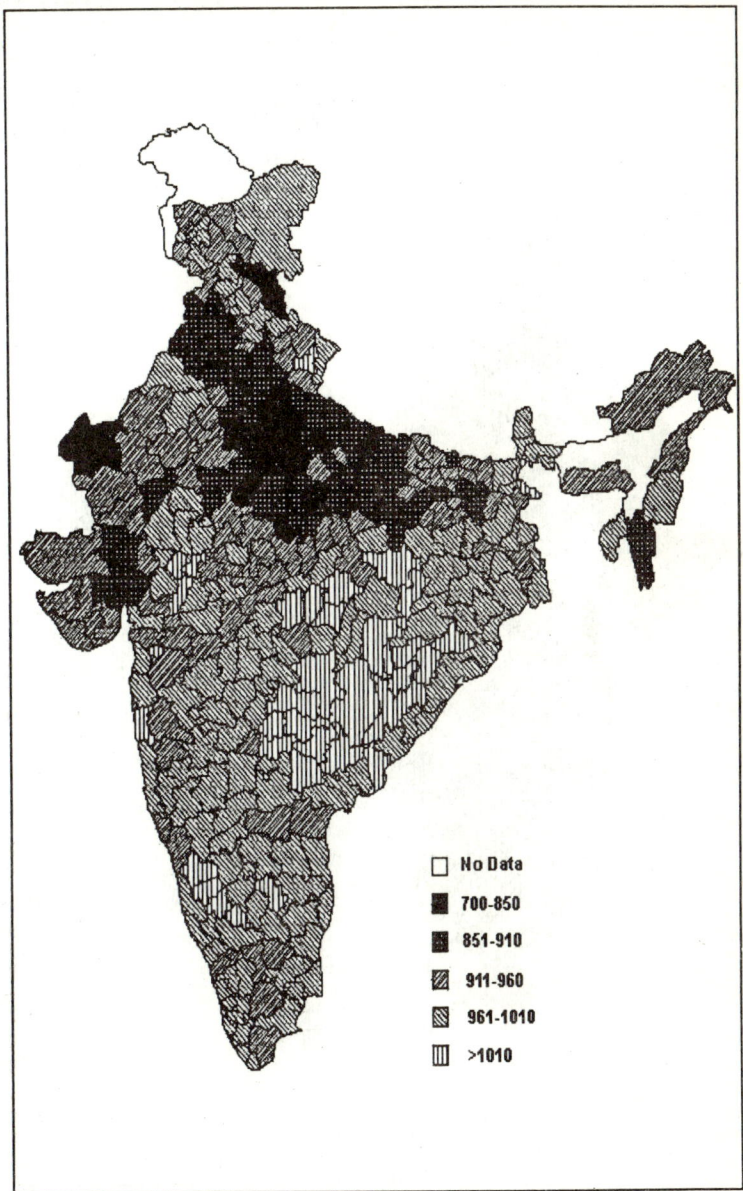

Map 4.3a: District-level map of FMR59: 1981 Census (general population).

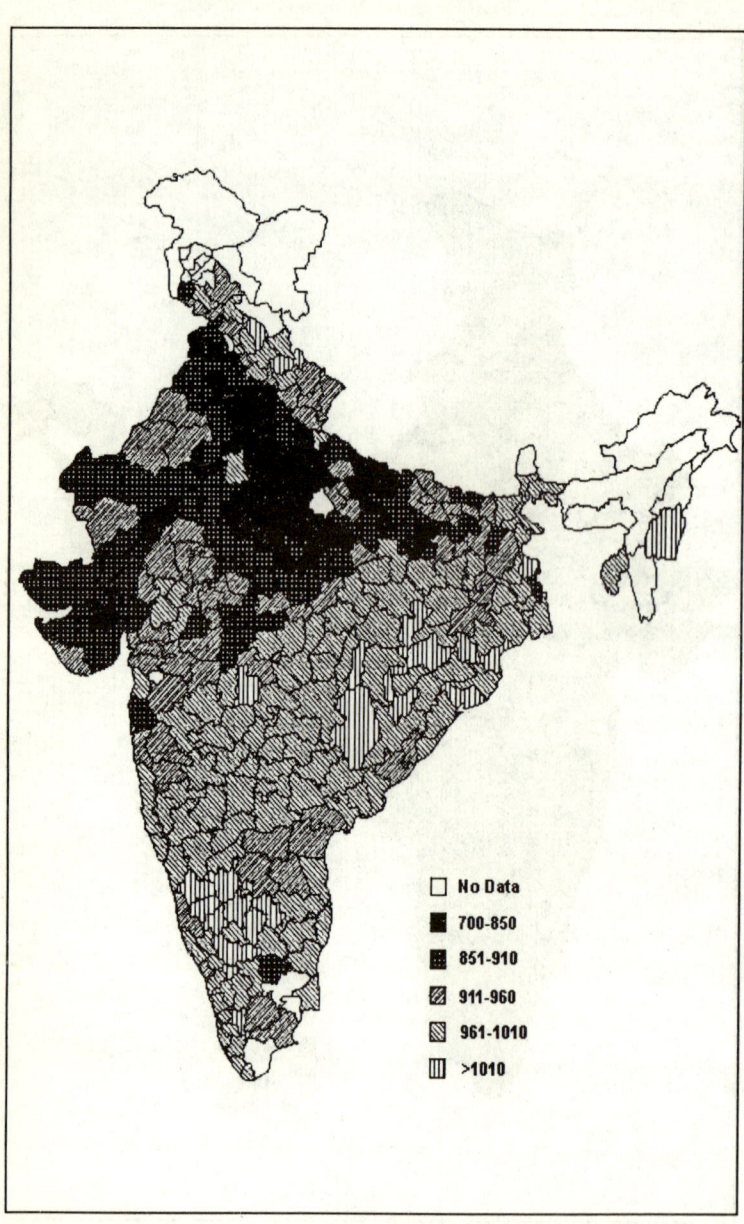

Map 4.3b: District-level map of FMR59: 1981 Census (SC population).

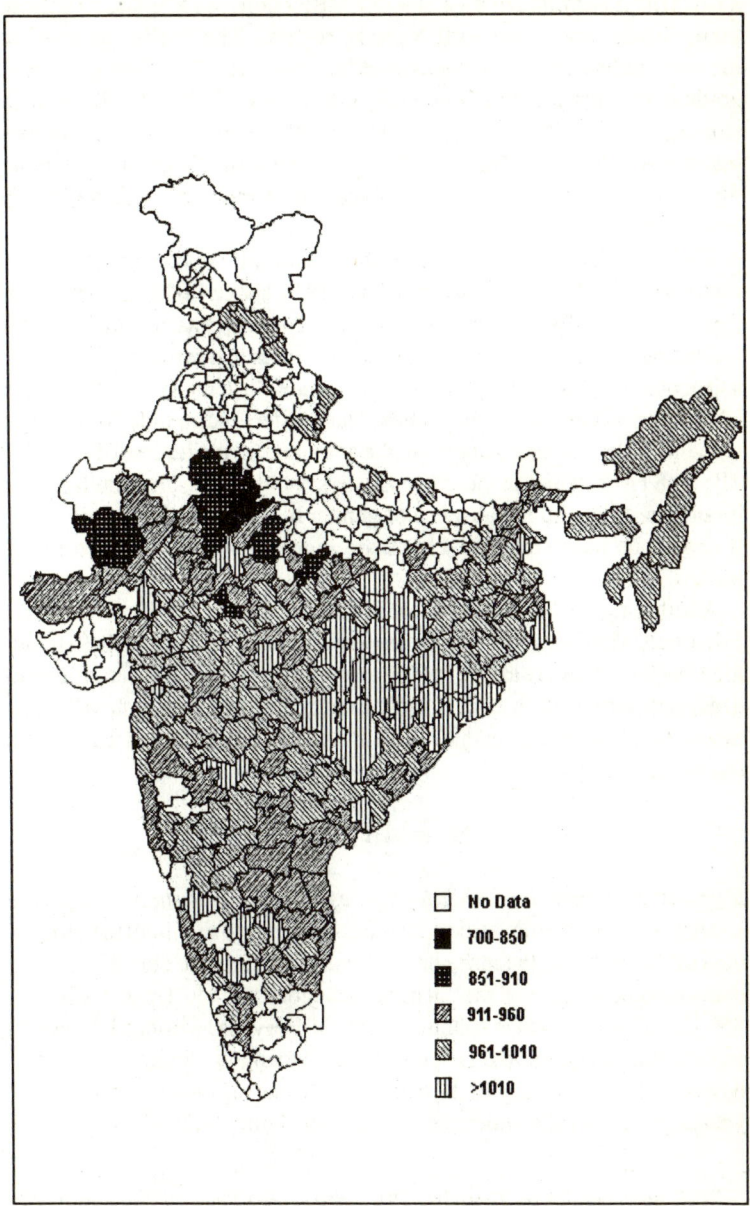

Map 4.3c: District-level map of FMR59: 1981 Census (ST population).

850). This is surrounded by a belt of FMR59 between 850 and 910. Both these clusters are in the north-western regions. The FMRs 'recover' in the surrounding cluster (values range between 910–960). This pattern of gradual recovery justifies Oldenberg's description (1992: 2658) 'pit with sloping sides'. Interestingly, this low FMR (below 960) track spreads into the 'south' across Narmada along a route which is also known to be the route of cultural circulation between the north and the south.[12] This point is discussed further in Chapter 5.

FMR59 values above 960 mark the rest of the regions, mostly in the south-east. However, two clusters with FMR59 above 1,000 need attention. One covers a set of districts in Orissa, Madhya Pradesh, Bihar and Maharashtra and is characterised by poverty and backwardness in terms of infrastructure and economy (Bose, 1994). A similar but small cluster in the 'north' covers hilly region of Gujarat and Rajasthan. This cluster is surrounded by districts with FMR04 < 960 and stands out like a 'mound'—the reverse of the 'pit'! The high FMR values in these two clusters could be a result of both excess infant mortality and the absence of gender bias against the female child. It should be noted that the FMRs are high among all the three social groups.

Another region in the north that needs attention is the eastern UP and Bihar belt. Here, FMR59 values are low, ranging between 850–910, but the FMR04 values are above 960. In terms of the sixteenfold classification described earlier, both excess male infant mortality **and** excess female mortality would be high in this region and appearance of 'balanced' JFMRs can be misleading.

Low FMR regions

Regions with very low FMR59 values deserve attention. While the sixteenfold classification used earlier has been able to highlight the seriousness of the problem, the maps draw attention to the close clustering of the concerned districts. For the 'general' category this cluster of FMR59 < 850 includes 21 districts spanning parts of Haryana, western UP, north-eastern Rajasthan and the ravines of MP. Among the Scheduled Castes, however, there is a cluster of 24 district in the same region *where the FMR59 values go below 800.* Oldenberg's use of the term *'Bermuda triangle for*

[12] See Bharadwaj (1973: Chapter II and V), Sopher (1980: Chapter 10), Spate et al.(1971, Chapter 6) and Schwartzberg (1992: IIIA and related maps) on the point of cultural circulation between the north and the south.

the girl children' (1992: 2658), even though sensational, aptly characterises this region.

Similarly, two isolated cases of low FMR04 deserve attention: Lahaul and Spiti and Kinnaur districts in Himachal Pradesh and Salem in Tamil Nadu. Lahaul and Spiti and Kinnaur districts have very low FMR04 as well as low FMR59. Being situated in a zone surrounded by districts with high FMRs, these present an anomaly that needs investigation.

Salem district has already been in the news for the practice of sex-selective infanticide (George S. et al. 1992: 1153–157). Such practice in large numbers will automatically show up in low 0–4 FMRs and this is precisely the case with Salem. It is the only district in the south where FMR04 value goes below 900 (876 for the non-ST/SCs[13]). *A focussed search for extremely low values of FMR04 among different regions and groups at the block level (for which the 1991 Census data would soon become available), may be a very useful method of detecting areas where female infanticide or foeticide may have assumed serious proportions.*

Districts where FMR59 are higher than FMR04 also deserve attention. This category will not usually be encountered as the pattern of excess female mortality that sets in early is unlikely to be reversed in later years of childhood. Such cases, if stray, probably indicate data error and, if persistent or systematic, call for detailed micro study.[14]

FMR59 as an indicator of the female disadvantage

The advantage of using FMR59 as an indicator of adverse survival conditions for the female children finds a *surprising corroboration from an independent quarter*. Murthi et al. (1995: 751) present a district-level map of female disadvantage (Map 4.4) defined as:

---

[13] This increases to 922 in the 5–9 age group signifying absence of excess female mortality beyond the neonatal period. It has been argued by Pisani and Zaba (forthcoming) that the mortality rates for female children will come down in the wake of prenatal sex selection (even though they do not have female infanticide in mind). Interestingly the FMR04 for the SC in Salem is 995 which indicates that infanticide may not be common place among the scheduled castes. Figures for 1991 are not yet available.

[14] There are seven such instances for ST groups, 16 for the SC and 31 for the general population. These are mostly stray cases except for one continuous belt of eight districts in Maharashtra and three in Karnataka for the general category which warrants scrutiny if the pattern repeats in 1991. Similarly for SC there is a contiguous belt of four districts in Kerala viz., Waynaad, Trichur, Ernakulam and Kottayam. Bilaspur (Himachal Pradesh), Betul (MP) and Jalpaiguri (West Bengal) show this trait for both SC and general category.

$$FD = (Q5f–Q5m)/Q5f \qquad\qquad 4.2a$$

The similarity between the map for FD and FMR59 maps for the overall and the non-tribal population is striking. The reasons for this similarity can be understood in light of the expression in Chapter 3:

$$(FMR59–FMR_0)/FMR_0 = (Q5m–Q5f)/Q5m \qquad\qquad 4.2b$$

In other words, (Q5f–Q5m) or the sex differentials in the under-5 mortality are capturing the pattern of FMR59 and not of FMR09 or FMR04; *an outcome neither intended by Murthi et al. nor anticipated in this study.* Murthi et al. (1995) go on to use juvenile sex ratio as a 'rough indicator of gender inequality' (1995: 34). FMR59 would, however, be a more appropriate indicator for this purpose.

Significance of geophysical regions

Unpacking the north–south divide

Several important points emerge from the maps above. The north–south divide gets elaborated much further. Pockets of 'southern' FMR patterns can be found in the geographic north. The route along which the northern patterns are making an ingress into the south can be identified. The masking of the low FMR59 signifying adverse survival condition, by high FMR04 on account of higher male infant mortality can be uncovered. The most important point, however, relates to the *diversity of the FMRs within individual states and their homogeneity within different geophysical regions.* State-level averages hide the diversity that differentiates eastern UP from western UP, Gwalior division from the rest of MP or south Bihar from north Bihar. These obscure the sex ratio patterns and the seriousness of the situation in certain regions. There is thus a strong case for moving the analysis of the sex ratio patterns below the state level to the level of regions.

Regionalisation of FMRs

Patterns seen in the maps show considerable variation in sex ratios within the boundaries of different states. The clusters within which the FMRs,

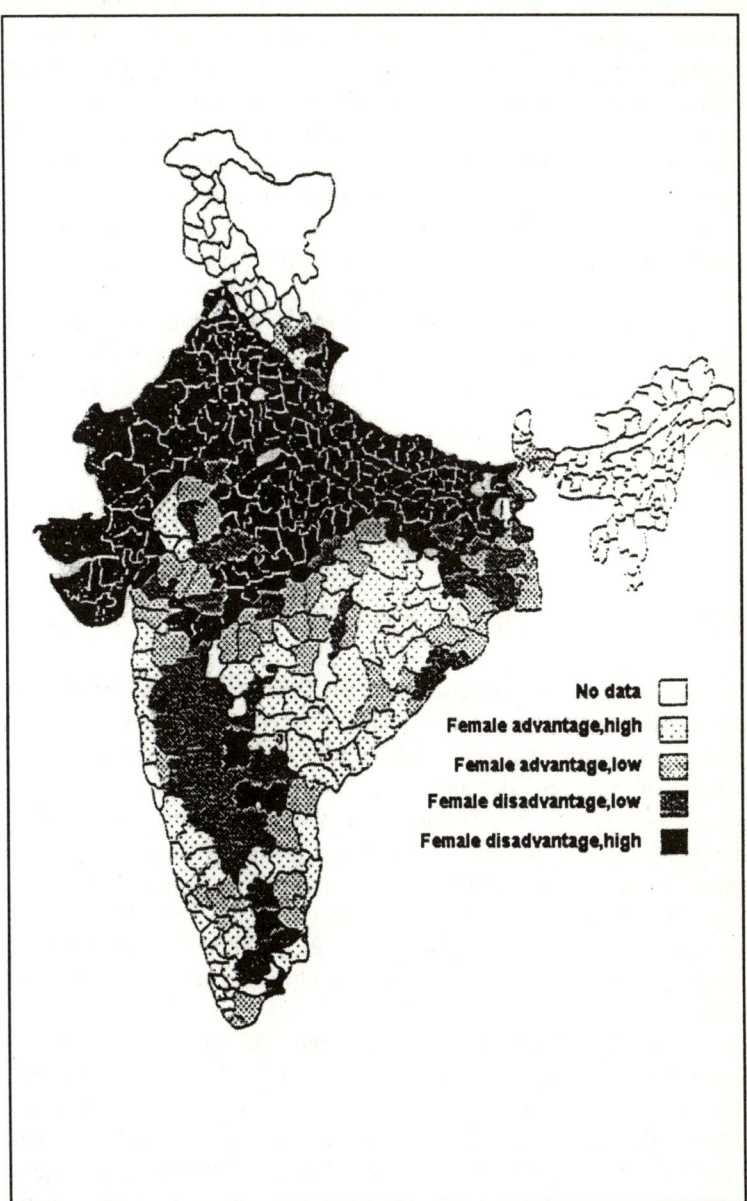

Map 4.4: District-level map of female survival disadvantage in childhood.

especially FMR59, are homogenously distributed cut across the boundaries of various states. Some of these clusters have been noted for discernible ecological or geophysical boundaries (Bardhan, 1974; Libbee, 1980). On the other hand, various states contain within them different and distinct geophysical regions. This calls for a regional analysis of the sex ratio patterns. Such an analysis has not been seriously pursued in the field of sex ratios and has remained confined to the north–south divide.

Do these geophysical regions have any bearing on sex ratio patterns and do these provide a more appropriate unit for spatial grouping of sex ratios than the state? While this appears to be the case prima facie, especially from Maps 4.3a and 4.3b (FMR59 maps for general and SC categories), a more detailed analysis is called for to answer this question. This is done in Chapter 5 where region and kinship systems are examined in greater detail.

V

Significance of the results

What does the analysis done so far signify in policy and academic terms? Several points emerge. First, analysis of sex ratio patterns has to move away from the use of all-age group data not corrected for migration, and the use of JSRs provides an appropriate solution to this problem. But JSRs themselves need unpacking in view of the difference in the infant and child mortality patterns. A 5-year age group classification is appropriate for this purpose even if fortuitously so. It is a happenstance that more than 90 per cent of the juvenile deaths do take place below the age of 5. As a result, FMR59 is virtually unaffected by the deaths in the age group of 5–9 and is able to reflect the gender bias in juvenile mortality effectively.

Recognition of the effects of excess male IMR in regions with very high FMR is a *new feature of this analysis*. It has shown that very high FMRs, say, above 1,000, should cause concern and indicate a need for improving health infrastructure in regions with such high FMRs. Where such infrastructure exists, access to it has to be ensured. The cogent message that 'availability does not guarantee access' has been brought out in Sen's entitlements analysis in general terms and in Kynch and Sen (1983) in the particular context of women's access to health care system.

Such an access will result in an *inevitable and desirable reduction in unusually high FMRs*. At the state or all-India level, the overall FMR will drop further once the districts with FMR > 1,000 no longer remain available to compensate for the districts with alarmingly low FMRs. But this should not be misread as an indicator of the increasingly adverse survival condition for the girl child. Currently both the academic and the policy mindset sees higher FMRs as necessarily a good thing and reduction in FMRs as necessary undesirable. *It is time that a distinction is made between high FMRs and balanced FMRs*. This analysis suggests a range of 960–980 as a balanced figure or 'norm'. Districts with FMRs below this level have to catch up with the 'norm', districts with FMRs above this need closer scrutiny.

While FMR59 is an appropriate indicator of the gender bias, FMR04 can serve as an *early warning system*. The spatial contiguity of FMR04 for the SCs and general category below a value of 960 can be understood in this context. It is no coincidence that the belt where FMR04 go below this level is known for gender bias in terms of excess female mortality in the early years of childhood. The earlier the incidence of excess female mortality, the lower the FMR04. It is likely that this threshold of 960 may decline as mortality levels drop and sex ratios at birth become more masculine. But such 'masculinisation' is slow and of a far smaller magnitude (Chapter 2: Section III) than what concerns us here.

Separate analysis of FMR04 and FMR59 for the three social groups is also needed given their significant differences. One immediate use of such segregation is to identify *regions with severe survival adversity for the SC female children*, a point other analyses have failed to unravel.[15] Likewise, the likelihood of unusually high male IMRs in regions with high ST concentration has also not been highlighted before.

Another point that merits urgent attention in this context is the incidence of very low FMRs among poorer groups among whom levels of IMR and the consequent excess male infant mortality are bound to be high. Low FMR04 or very low FMR59 that obtain in spite of this gap indicate *very strong discrimination against the girl child*.

Excessively high FMR04 and higher FMR59, particularly among Scheduled Tribes indicate *unacceptably high male mortality* primarily due to harsh health environment and bad health infrastructure.

The analysis decisively weakens the 'low-FMR-at-birth' optimism to explain away the low FMRs, especially in the 'Bermuda Triangle' region.

---

[15] Wadley (1993) talks about it in terms of a village or a region. But the analysis here can reveal the patterns systematically generating suitable agenda for micro research.

It also shows the implausibility of 'female under-enumeration' as the cause of such low FMRs. It also draws attention to regions of very high FMRs at birth as an *indicator of unsatisfactory health delivery system*.

The analysis in this and the previous chapter brings into sharper focus the role of excess female mortality in early years of childhood. More importantly, it offers a method of identifying survival disadvantage based on the FMR data *even in the absence of suitable disaggregated mortality estimates*.

Scope for further research

Based on this analysis, a number of macro and micro level studies can be launched quickly. Study of mortality patterns disaggregated by social groups, study of FMR at birth, special enumeration in some districts could be some of these.

Visaria had once suggested that sex ratios at birth may vary by ethnicity (Visaria 1971). This was based on his observations of the black population in different regions in the world with sex ratios at birth lower than other population groups. In the Indian context, the study of FMR at birth for the ST population vis-à-vis non-ST population may be of some interest. FMR at birth for the STs may turn out to be higher. But this may be due to the health environment and not due to 'ethnic' reasons. This can perhaps be verified through a comparison of the sex ratios at birth between the STs in the central and the north-eastern belt as the health environment and infrastructure for the latter is of a better quality (NSSO, 1994; Raza and Ahmad, 1990).

The spread of low FMR04 and FMR59 between 1961 and 1991 will provide useful insights into the trends in gender bias and the concerns raised by Miller (1989) about the southward spread of the low FMR pattern. Spatial distribution of FMR04 and FMR59 among the SCs, and STs both spatially and caste-wise and tribe-wise will be another important area. It will have considerable bearing on the issue of 'assimilation' of these groups within the 'mainstream' society. Of these, the districts with low FMR for STs may be of special interest.

To sum up

Age and social group emerge as important bases for disaggregation of juvenile age group sex ratio data. The disaggregation has immediate policy and research relevance, some of which has been listed. District-level mapping of FMR04 and FMR59 has thrown unexpected light on the issue of regionalisation of FMRs. Its detailed scrutiny forms the subject matter of Chapter 5. As will be seen there, geophysical regions turn out to be another important dimension for disaggregation of the sex ratio data.

Chapter 5

Regions, kinship and the status of women

I

An outline

So far, this analysis has examined the sex ratio data disaggregated by age and by social groups. The approach has provided some new and useful insights into the patterns of sex ratio imbalances in India. Such an approach is compatible with the diversities that mark the Indian society and its landscape.

The next step is to disaggregate the sex ratio data by geophysical regions. Spatial maps presented in Chapter 4 reveal a more homogenous distribution of FMRs within different geophysical regions than within different states. This is particularly so for the FMR59 among the non-Scheduled Tribe population. Socio-cultural discrimination against the girl child, to the extent that the FMR59s reflect it, appears to follow a distinct regional pattern.

The homogeneity of distribution of district-level FMRs grouped by different regions and states is compared using analysis of variance. Following the regional classification of the 1961 and 1981 Censuses, the districts are grouped into 19 regions, a number comparable to the number of states. Differences in the homogeneity of distribution are reflected in the differences in F-ratios. These differences turn out to be significant in the case of FMR59 for the non-Scheduled Tribe population while among the Scheduled Tribe and for the 0–4 age group these are not significant.

Modifying the 'north–south divide'

The regional classification described above goes beyond the conventional north–south divide. Pockets of 'southern' FMRs appear in the geographical north and vice versa. As reviewed in Chapter 2, the north and the south are characterised by different kinship systems which have a bearing on the status of women. This status, in turn, affects their access to life-sustaining resources the consequences of which are reflected in the FMR patterns at the societal level.

It is necessary therefore, to analyse the kinship patterns in the regions identified and look for a classification more detailed than that of the north–south divide. The classification suggested by Berreman (1993) (Chapter 2: Section V) is used for this purpose by examining the nature of different kinship systems: the 'core' Indo-Aryan kinship system corresponding to the 'dominant Hindu ethos', the peripheral Indo-Aryan system, representing incomplete assimilation within this ethos, the Dravidian system (both non-tribal and tribal) and, the exclusively tribal, Munda kinship system.

Kinship and language groups

Absence of suitable quantitative data often constrains the use of cultural variables in analyses of female subordination and its demographic consequences reflected in the FMRs. Kinship is no exception to this. However, census data on people speaking different mother tongues, inform the present analysis in an interesting way. There is a close congruence between languages and kinship systems in India. It is likely therefore, that the sex ratio pattern among the speakers of different linguistic groups are significantly different. Six linguistic groups are examined here: Three among the non-tribal—the 'core' Indo-Aryan, the 'peripheral' Indo-Aryan and the Dravidian; and three among the tribal—Aryan, Dravidian and the Munda.

Analysis of variance of FMRs by mother tongue reveals three significantly different groups: (*a*) speakers of the 'core' Indo-Aryan languages (*b*) speakers of Dravidian languages, 'peripheral' Indo-Aryan languages and the non-Munda tribal languages and (*c*) speakers of Munda languages. FMRs in the first category are significantly low while those in the Munda-language speaking groups are significantly high. This corroborates the classification suggested by Berreman. Analysis of FMRs by mother tongues had never been attempted in the literature before except Agni-hotri (1996a) although such data have been available since the 1961 Census.

Male-centred versus female-friendly kinship

Based on this analysis of regions and kinship practices, the districts are grouped into two kinship regions. The 'male-centred' kinship system dominates in about 164 districts in the 'core' north while the 'female-friendly' kinship practices cover 202 districts. This dichotomous classification is used for further analysis of the FMR and mortality data. FMR patterns, infant and under-5 mortality rates and sex differentials in mortality turn out to be significantly different in the two kinship regions. It becomes clear that excess female mortality during infancy and childhood prevails in the 'core' northern region and is the main cause of low FMRs there.

The 'core' and the 'periphery'

An important issue about the 'received' classification of the 'core' and the 'periphery' is discussed at this stage. As remarked earlier, an uncritical import of the 'core–periphery' description in the sex ratio debate creates an unstated link between the 'core' and the 'norm'. Such a linkage and indeed the 'core–periphery' description has to be questioned and, in fact, reversed. A 'core' in political sense is not necessarily a 'core' in either a cultural or numerical sense. Both these aspects, cultural and numerical, have a bearing on the sex ratio imbalances. Kinship practices within the 'periphery' differ. But these have one feature in common: these are 'female-friendly' as against the 'male-centred' kinship practices in the political 'core'. Further, these predate the advent of Indo-Aryan kinship system. Thus both culturally and numerically, the female-friendly kinship system and the consequent FMR patterns should be looked upon as the 'norm' and the system and the pattern obtaining in the political 'core' as a 'deviation' from this norm. *Such shift in description from core–periphery to norm versus deviation or indeed aberration has important consequences for policy and social action.*

Organisation of the discussion

Section II describes the 19 geophysical regions among which the FMRs
are homogenously distributed. Results of analysis of variance (ANOVA)
are presented next. Section III discusses the links between kinship and
linguistic configuration. All-India level FMR data by languages are
analysed in Section IV. Section V describes the dichotomous kinship
classification by which the districts are grouped and analyses the
differences in FMR and mortality patterns by kinship. Section VI questions
the 'core–periphery' description and argues in favour of a shift to 'norm'
versus 'aberration' description. The final section concludes the discussion.

II

Regional patterns in sex ratios

Geophysical regions

As seen in Chapter 4, sex ratios especially in the 5–9 age group, vary
considerably within the boundaries of a state. But within different regions,
these show remarkable contiguity. Some of these regions have been noted
for discernible ecological or geophysical boundaries.[1]

The 1981 Census has classified different geophysical regions and sub-
regions across the country (Government of India, 1988: 1981 Census
Atlas: 192–98). The 1961 Census had laid considerable emphasis on such
a classification and had initiated a number of studies related to their
significance (Bose, 1994). Apart from the census classification there
have also been other classifications, for example, the ones followed by
the NSSO or those followed in the NFHS (IIPS, 1995). A comprehensive compilation of different classifications has been done in Bose
(1994). The regions in different classifications overlap considerably.
While regional studies have not been a new phenomenon in India,

---

[1] For example, Libbee (1980: 94) on the ecological distinction between eastern and
western UP; Bardhan (1974) on the wheat and the rice divide; Dange (1972) on the regions
of Madhya Pradesh and sex ratios.

their application in the field of demography, at least sex ratio analysis, has not been frequent.[2]

A regional classification

The system of classification mentioned earlier is used here to identify 19 different geophysical regions within which FMR59 are homogenously distributed (Map 5.1). A list of districts in these regions and the corresponding census regions and sub-regions is given in Annexure 5A. Departure from the census scheme, when done, is indicated separately. Table 5.1 gives the mean of FMR04 and FMR59 values for the districts in these regions. It is useful to compare Map 5.1 against the physical map of India.

A brief outline of the regions

The north

The first region consists of the states of Himachal Pradesh, Jammu and Kashmir and the hilly region of UP, representing the 'southern' sex ratio patterns within the north. Mean district level FMR59 among the general category population in 32 out of 34 districts in this region is 961.[3] FMRs for the SCs are comparable (mean 957). This region, largely above 300 metres from the sea level, marks an important ecological boundary between the northern mountains and the plains in northern India.

Adjoining this region are the plains of Punjab and Haryana marked by highly masculine sex ratios: the mean district level FMR59 being 887 for the general category and 842 for the ST. There is *no ST population in this belt*.

Patterns in region 3 are more alarming. It comprises of the upper Gangetic plain of western UP, the three districts of Alwar, Bharatpur and Sawai Madhopur of Rajasthan, the ravines of Chambal in MP and Zansi Uplands of UP. These 32 districts have a mean FMR59 of 850 for the non-ST/SC population and 797 for the SC population.

---

[2] Even recent studies like Raju (1991) dealing with 'Gender and deprivation—a theme revisited with geographical perspectives' or Agarwal (1994: Chapter 8, 316–419) while 'tracing cross-cultural diversities' in respect of women's position have confined their attention to the state level. Murthi et al. (1995) is perhaps the first to take up regional classification systematically in the gender context.

[3] The districts of Lauhaul and Spiti and Kinnaur have low FMRs and merit separate scrutiny as noted in Chapter 4.

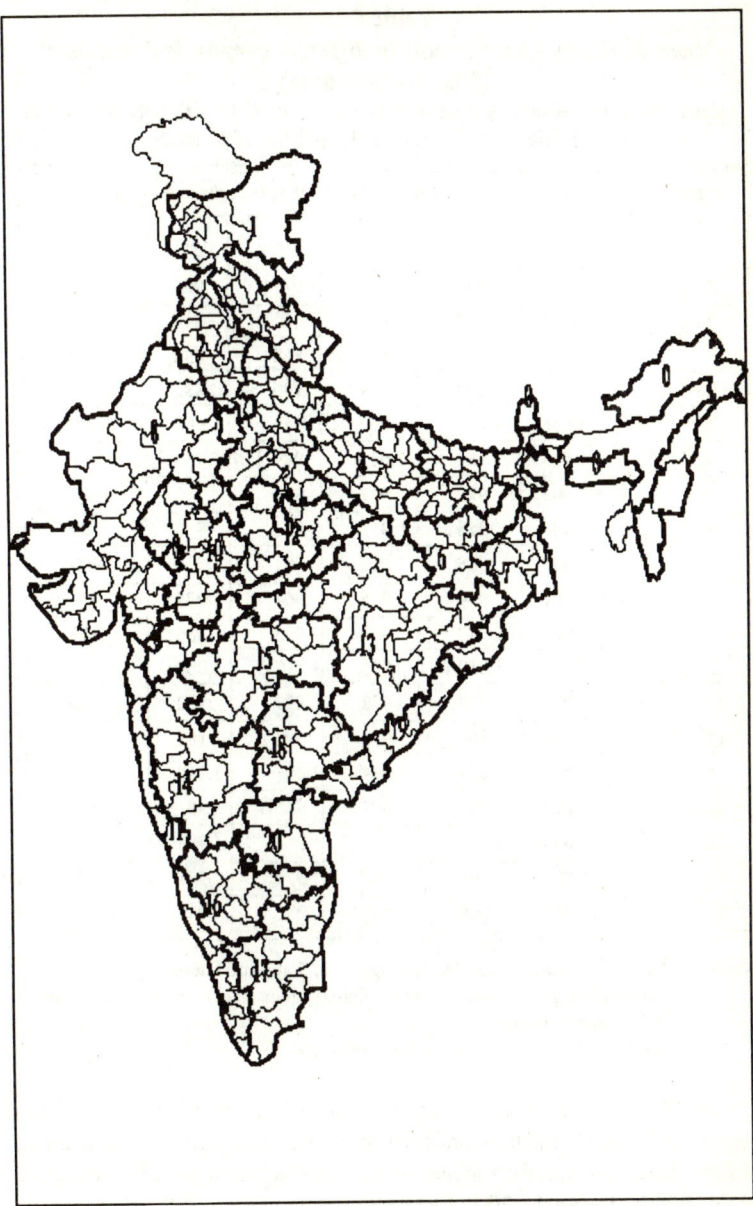

Map 5.1: Map of 19 geophysical regions.

Table 5.1
Mean FMRs by social groups in different geophysical regions
(1981 Census data)
(Mean FMR values here are the mean of FMR values for the districts in the regions and not the FMR value for the overall population of the region)

Region Number	FMRs in the 0–4 age group			FMRs in the 5–9 age group		
	ST	SC	Others	ST	SC	Others
1.	1,015	988	972	977	957	956
2.	Nil	921	924	Nil	842	887
3.	972	932	947	854	792	850
4.	1,028	992	979	996	882	892
5.	1,056	1,012	993	949	908	920
6.	1,033	989	1,022	989	956	972
7.	1,003	996	997	975	981	980
8.	988	958	958	937	886	920
10.	1,009	988	1,010	961	934	980
11.	1,001	974	975	964	975	979
12.	1,008	948	962	955	886	925
13.	1,030	1,019	995	1,017	1,000	1,019
14.	989	978	952	977	982	972
15.	998	980	975	992	983	982
16.	1,008	1,004	984	1,001	1,016	1,009
17.	1,004	991	971	945	981	973
18.	1,020	1,013	1,007	968	998	1,014
19.	1,027	1,001	995	979	971	993
20.	987	996	980	931	937	961

Notes: 1) Region 8 is to be further divided into 8 and 9 at some future date. To keep that exercise compatible with rest of the classification Region 9 is not incorporated in the current analysis.

2) Region 2 has no Scheduled Tribe population.

Low FMRs in regions 2 and 3, given that these are relatively prosperous regions of India, should be a matter of concern in both policy and academic realm. These also warrant a special coverage of at least some of the districts in this region during the 2001 Census to set at rest the optimistic speculation that under-enumeration of females, age misreporting or highly masculine sex ratios at birth may be the cause of low FMRs in them.

A gradual recovery

The 23 districts of the mid-Gangetic plain represent the eastern side of the slope around the 'pit' with mean FMR59 of 892 for the general category and 883 for the SC population. The FMRs increase in the lower Gangetic plains of north and south Bihar (region 5). Purnia and Katihar districts of Bihar show a closer pattern to the lower Gangetic plain districts of West Bengal and have been grouped with these as such. These districts have high FMR59 for all the three groups and a sizeable presence of ST population.

The southern Bihar hills and plateau mark an ecological transition from the plains to the hills and also mark one end of the north–south divide. These seven districts have a sizeable ST population, high and comparable FMR59 among the ST and the general population but relatively lower FMR59 for the SCs.

The semi-arid plains of Rajasthan and Gujarat, the Kachchh and Kathiawar peninsula and some areas of semi-arid Rajasthan, form a block of 34 districts. These adjoin the low FMR regions 2 and 3 on one side and the central belt dividing the north and the south on the other. The FMR59 values for the general category are marginally better (mean of 920) but continues to be low for the SC population (mean of 886). The FMR59 for the ST population in 21 of its districts are low by the overall standards of ST population (mean of 937). As a matter of fact, there is a low FMR track starting from Ajmer in Rajasthan, which descends down through the Pali and Sirohi districts to the Mehasana, Ahmedabad, Bhavnagar route in Gujarat. This track is flanked by districts with relatively high FMRs on its western and south-eastern side. But a further classification of this region on the basis of FMRs has not been done as this track cuts across different geophysical regions.[4]

The districts of Udaipur, Chittaurgarh, Dungarpur, Banswara and Bhilwara in the relatively difficult and hilly terrain of the Aravali range of Rajasthan form a contiguous block with districts of Malwa plateau in MP extending to the three districts of Narmada Valley viz., Jabalpur, Narsimhapur and Hoshangabad through West Nimar in the Satpura hills.

---

[4] The soil map of this region (Roy, 1972) reveals a fertile wheat growing plain tract within this region which can be linked with the spread of the Indo-Aryan culture along the Mathura-Dwarka route. But this 'fine-tuning', a separate analysis of this tract, is not taken up in the current analysis. At some future date, the region 8 is proposed to be classified into region 8 and 9. As such region 9 has been kept blank in this classification.

FMRs are high among the general and the ST population but low among the SC.

The other remaining region north of Narmada covers the northern Uplands of MP, the Sagar and Bhopal plateau and East Nimar, descends into the Khandesh region of Maharashtra and the Nasik Basin. It has mean FMR59 values of 925 for the non-ST/SC, 886 for the SC, and 955 for the ST population.

Transition to high FMR region

The transition to high FMR zones begins with the central and eastern Satpura hill range of MP, the Baghelkhand plateau, the Chhattisgarh region, Dandakaranya and Orissa highlands. This block of 23 districts also lies on the central tribal belt and joins the south Bihar hills and plateau region. The mean FMR59 here are 1,000 or above for all three social groups.

South of the dividing belt, the west coast region spreads from Valsad in Gujarat (the Dangs district included), to Kerala through the Konkan region which covers parts of Maharashtra, Goa and Karnataka. It has high FMRs for all three groups.

Inland of this coastal belt, the Western ghats of Maharashtra, north Karnataka plateau and the central *màidan* in Karnataka form one block of 13 districts. Similarly, the Vidarbha, Marathwada and Mahakoshal region of Maharashtra form another contiguous block of 13 districts with high FMRs for all three groups (mean FMR59 typically in the 975–990 range). The 17 districts of Tamil Nadu have similar FMRs, but the FMR59 among the STs are low.

Two contiguous blocks of very high FMRs (mean FMR59 above 1,000) need attention. One block covers 11 districts of the central south and the southern Karnataka plateau and Chittoor district of Andhra Pradesh. The other block covers 10 districts of the Telangana region in Andhra Pradesh. It adjoins the Dandakaranya region and the Chandrapur-Bastar-Koraput tribal belt known for its underdevelopment. Likewise, the eastern coastal region of Andhra including the district of Ganjam in Orissa also has uniformly high FMRs for all the three groups.

A group of 5 districts in the Rayalaseema region of Andhra Pradesh, stands out for its low FMRs by southern standards (mean FMR59 of 961 for non-ST/SC, 936 for the SC, and 931 for the ST population). It covers the districts of Prakasam, Nellore, Cuddappah, Anantapur and Kurnool.

Regions versus the states

One can now examine, through analysis of variance, if these 19 regions provide a more homogenous grouping for the FMRs compared to the 20 states involved. The variance within the group would be significantly less if a given grouping is more homogenous. The F-ratios would as a result be higher. The hypothesis here is that socio-cultural discrimination is associated more strongly with geophysical regions whereas the biological factors are spatially random. As such, the FMR04 patterns among all the three groups and FMR59 patterns among the STs will not be affected much whether we group these by states or geophysical regions. But the FMR59 patterns among the SC and the general category will be affected by the choice of grouping variable. For these the F-ratios will be higher when grouping is done by regions. Table 5.2 confirms this pattern.

The regions provide a much more homogenous grouping than the states do for the FMR59 for the general and the SC population. When grouped by states, the variance within the group accounts for nearly half of the total variance. Grouping by regions reduces it to less than one-fourth of the total variance. The corresponding jump in the F-ratios is also significant.[5]

While the grouping by regions appears quite appropriate for the spatial analysis of FMRs in the non-ST population, such is not the case with the ST population. This signifies absence of discrimination against female children among the ST unlike the discrimination seen among the non-ST. This is discussed further in the next sub-section.

Improvement in the F-ratios is not appreciable in the case of FMR04 even though the regions provide a more homogenous grouping compared to the states. But if prenatal selection, sex-selective infanticide and the post-neonatal mortality among female infants become more commonplace, the regional classification will become more and more significant even in the case of FMR04. It will be instructive to check the situation with the 1991 Census data once these become available.

Regional differences in FMR levels

Distribution of FMRs is homogenous within different geophysical regions but varies considerably across these. It will be useful therefore, to examine

---

[5] It is possible to further 'fine-tune' the regional grouping and improve the F-ratios. Such an exercise of cluster formation with minimum internal variance is not attempted here.

Table 5.2
Analysis of variance: FMRs grouped by states and geophysical regions

Variable	Region (DF = 18) Sum of squares (in '000)				States (DF = 19) Sum of squares (in '000)			
	Within	Between	Total	F-ratio	Within	Between	Total	F-ratio
FMR59 (General)	245	835	1080	62.5	526	554	1080	20.5
FMR59 (SC)	369	1422	1790	67.8	811	980	1790	22.5
FMR59 (ST)	187	166	326	8.9	219	134	326	8.9
FMR04 (General)	242	186	428	14.0	297	131	428	8.6
FMR04 (SC)	422	284	705	11.8	528	177	705	6.3
FMR04 (ST)	66	179	245	3.7	205	41	245	2.9

the distribution of these regions corresponding to different combinations of FMR04 and FMR59 levels. In terms of the sexteenfold classification used in Chapter 4, the following distribution is obtained for the general (Table 5.3a) and the Scheduled Caste category (Table 5.3b)

Table 5.3a
Distribution of regions by different levels of FMR04 and FMR59
(General category)

FMR59 Range	FMR04 Range			
	Low	Moderate	High	Very High
Low		2, 3	4	
Moderate		8, 12	1, 5, 20	
High		14	7, 11, 15, 17, 19	6, 10
Very High			13, 16	18

Table 5.3b
Distribution of regions by different levels of FMR04 and FMR59
(Scheduled castes)

FMR59 Range	FMR04 Range			
	Low	Moderate	High	Very High
Low		2, 3, 8, 12	4	
Moderate			1, 6, 10	5, 20
High			7, 11, 14, 15, 17	18, 19
Very High				13, 16

Among both the categories, regions 2, 3, 4, 8 and 12 represent one end of the sixteenfold classification while regions 13 and 16 represent the other end. Regions 2, 3, 4, 8 and 12, it may be noted, essentially cover the FMR04 < 960 belt (Chapter 4: Map 4.2a and 4.2b). Regions 13, 16 and 18 form a nearly contiguous tract of backward and underdeveloped districts. Even among the STs, regions 13 and 16 form a distinct group (Table 5.3c). The general pattern of high FMRs among the STs is clear from the clustering of districts in the bottom right hand corner.

Test of significant difference in FMR04 and FMR59 between different regions can be examined using analysis of variance. Such an analysis

Table 5.3c
Distribution of regions by different levels of FMR04 and FMR59
(Scheduled Tribes)

FMR59 Range	FMR04 Range			
	Low	Moderate	High	Very High
Low			3	
Moderate			8, 20	5, 10, 12, 17
High			14, 15	1, 4, 6, 7, 11, 18, 19
Very High				13, 16

reveals that region 3, covering western UP, the ravines of the Chambal and the Zansi Uplands, has significantly low FMRs among all the three social groups compared to the rest of the regions. Similarly, the Rayala-seema region (region 20) also displays an anomalous position compared to rest of the southern region. FMR59 values in this region are low for both the SC and ST population. On the other hand, regions 13 and 18 covering tribal MP, Orissa and the Telangana region of Andhra Pradesh stand out for very high FMRs, an effect very likely arising out of higher male infant mortality.

Regions 1, 6 and 10 or the hilly regions in the 'north' and eastern regions of Bihar and Bengal, although situated in the geographical 'north' display less masculine patterns than the 'core' northern region. This calls for a closer look at the north–south classification.

III

The kinship system in the north and the south

As reviewed in Chapter 2, the north–south divide in the sex ratio patterns is basically linked to differences in the kinship systems in the two regions. The southern kinship structure allows greater autonomy to women and hence a 'better decision-making ability with regard to personal affairs' (Dyson and Moore 1983: 45). The northern societal system does not allow this autonomy.

The 'northern' kinship characteristics identified by Dyson and Moore are not uniformly followed in the geographical north. These are the features of the social superstrata within the geographical 'core'.

In Berremann's scheme, STs are outside the purview of the 'dominant Hindu ethos' while the SCs are at the 'bottom' of the hierarchy. For the 'general' category, regions 2, 3, 4, 8 and 12 represent the regions where the 'ethos' prevails. Regions south of the Narmada represent the geographic periphery as well as 'peculiar adherence to the creed' in terms of the marriage practices discussed in details below. The eastern region of Bihar, Bengal and Orissa represent attenuated adherence to the ethos (Karve, 1965: 106–107 and Chapter 2 in this volume) regions 1, 10 and 6 represent the hilly social periphery (Goody, 1990: 251).

This classification goes a step further than a simple north–south classification. An interesting corroboration of this classification comes from the sex ratio data by different linguistic groups from the census data. Before analysing this, it is useful to further highlight the strong association between kinship practices and linguistic groups.

Kinship and linguistic configuration

Even though the Indo-Aryan culture has spread and taken roots in north-western India, the nature and pace of this spread has been uneven (Chapter 2). This unevenness is still reflected in myriad cultural layers in India. Two of these, the linguistic configuration and the kinship systems related to marriage practices, are relevant to the discussion here. The latter are important as these relate to the process of a woman's assimilation into the family of marriage where she spends nearly three-fourths of her life span. Kinship systems have an important and explicit bearing on this.

A close congruity between the languages and the kinship pattern can be seen by combining the maps of linguistic and kinship regions of India as shown in Map 5.2. The broad configuration of the linguistic as well as the kinship zone has been discussed in Chapter 2. The Indo-Aryan language zone in the north-west follows the Indo-Aryan kinship practices. The Dravidian-language speaking groups in the southern region practice the Dravidian kinship system. In the intermediate zone extending from Gujarat in the west to Orissa in the east, both the systems coexist in different degrees. The Mundas in the central region follow a kinship system closer to the Dravidian one as far as marriage rules are concerned.

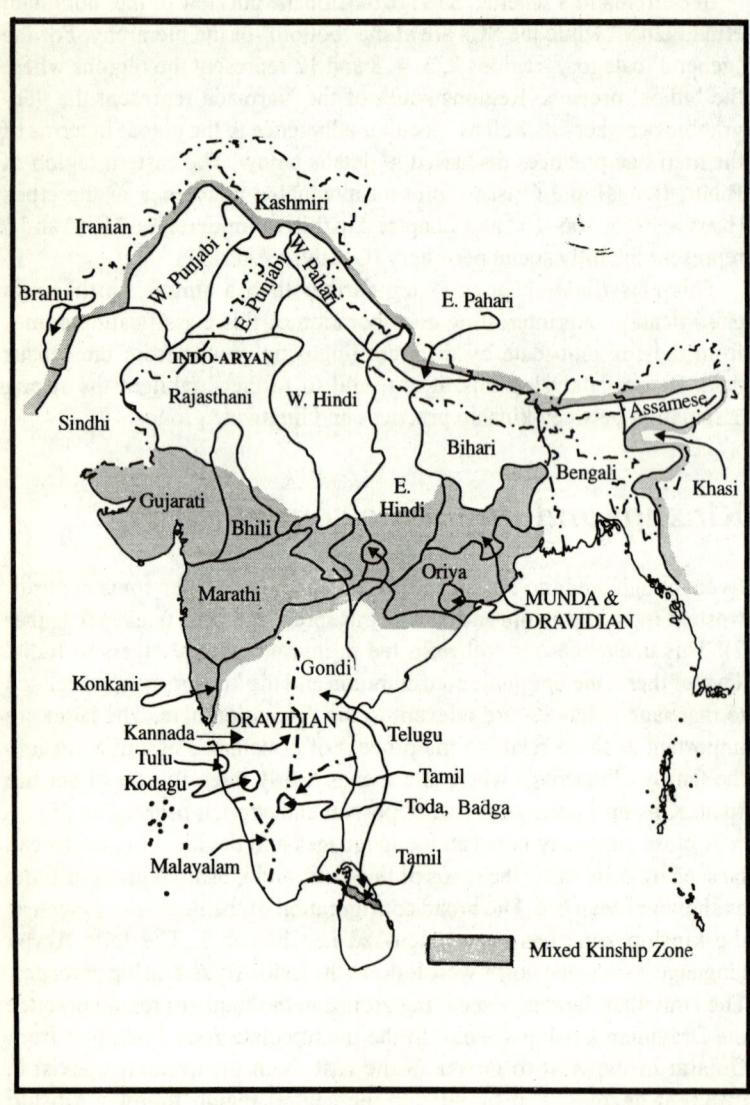

Map 5.2: Language and kinship map of India.
Source: Trautmann, 1981 and 1993.

In the hilly regions of the north, the kinship practices differ from the Indo-Aryan practices (Berreman, 1993: 372–75; Trautmann, 1981: 110). There is greater incidence of sibling exchange, less spatial exogamy, more equality between wife-givers and wife-takers and even hypogamy. This indicates that while Dravidian marriage rules and practices facilitate symmetry between bride-givers and bride-takers, it is not the only manner in which such symmetry can be achieved.

The language and kinship patterns in the intermediate zone provides a mixed picture. Gujarati, Marathi, Konkani and Oriya are Indo-Aryan languages lying on the outer southern and south-eastern fringes of the language zone (Nigam: 1964). But sizeable segments of population speaking these languages follow Dravidian kinship practices (Karve, 1965; Trautmann, 1981). Some of the groups also retain a distinct mother tongue, line Khandeshi, while some do not. Some others belong to particular social groups, for example, the Kunbis in Maharashtra, usually 'lower' in the caste hierarchy (Karve, 1965). One finds that the linguistic and social 'substrata' in these regions have retained the Dravidian kinship practices. Further south it is no longer the substrata alone but also the superstrata or the higher castes who practice and defend the Dravidian kinship system. While Maharashtra is an example from the mixed zone where cross-cousin marriage is permitted among some of the Brahmins (Goody, 1990; Karve, 1965), all the Pancha Dravidas—the five important Brahmin clans of the south practice and defend cross-cousin marriage (Sopher, 1981: 293). In addition, there is Konkani, an Indo-Aryan language whose speakers follow Dravidian kinship practices (see, however, Karve, 1965: 25 endnote 3). Among the STs, Bhils represent a Dravidian group whose language has been Aryanised but who practice 'cross-cousin marriage (Karve, 1965: 174).

A gradient

There is thus a gradient across the north-west–south-east axis in terms of the spread of languages and kinship patterns. It starts with the region where both Indo-Aryan languages and kinship prevail. This is followed by an intermediate zone where the languages, particularly of the non-ST population, have been largely 'Aryanised' but the kinship system has retained the Dravidian pattern to various degrees. In the tribal belt, where Austro-Asiatic languages prevail the kinship structure has been influenced only marginally depending upon the extent of contact with the Indo-Aryan group. There is exclusion of marriage with first cross-cousins in some cases and with any cross-cousins in some others. South of the dividing belt, Dravidian languages and kinship structure both hold sway even though considerable influence of Sanskrit is seen on some of the Dravidian languages—particularly Telugu, Kannada and Malayalam. There is hardly any Dravidian language speaking group practising marriage rules of the Indo-Aryan variety.[6]

The eastward spread of the Indo-Aryan culture shows, however, a relatively different pattern. Here the languages in the Bihari group, Bengali and Assamese have been Aryanised and so have the kinship practices (Fruzzeti, 1990). But the adherence to the ethos is attenuated with the ancient provinces of Anga (Bihar) and Vanga (Bengal) being regarded as outside the pale of the 'core' Aryan territory (Goody, 1990: Chapter 7; Karve, 1965: 106–107). The low culture norms in the religious context (Goody, 1990: 180–82) and the cult of the mother Goddess still prevail in these regions. Further, Bihar also represents a zone of 'ecological transition' from a dry, wheat cultivation belt to a wet, rice cultivation belt (Libbee 1980: 94) which extends all the way to the north-east.

The dynamics of assimilation

The above pattern hints at the dynamics of cultural assimilation. As the Indo-Aryan culture spread in the southern and eastern direction, it assimilated the local languages and cultural practices to various degrees. The languages were modified more easily while cultural practices, particularly those pertaining to marriage were not. This is understandable as the élite group among the 'assimilated' people would need to pick up the language of the dominating group for communication, recognition, co-option and other exchanges. They would go 'bilingual' first before losing their language eventually. The other groups in the social substrata would gradually follow suit. Cultural practices, particularly those relating to marriage practices would be far more resistant to such assimilation. Strict norms of caste endogamy in marriage would enable such 'insulation' of these practices.[7]

---

[6] Except the isolated pocket of Brahui-speaking people in Pakistan (Trautmann, 1981) which is not analysed here.

[7] The relatively slow nature of the change in marriage practices can be seen among, say, the people of Indian origin staying in the UK.

It is plausible to conclude therefore, that assimilation of the pre-Aryan population operated first in the realm of languages followed much more slowly by the kinship practices related to marriages. Given the ethos of strong subordination of women in the Indo-Aryan culture and its association with low FMRs, one should be able to find an FMR pattern corresponding to the degree of assimilation into the 'dominant Hindu ethos'. The more complete the assimilation in the Indo-Aryan system, the more masculine will be the FMRs in the given population group. The FMRs should increase as one moves southwards and across the dividing belt. The ST groups should also exhibit high FMRs, particularly those among the Dravidian and Munda language groups. While the classification by geophysical regions shows these patterns, the corroboration based on the FMR data by linguistic groups is more striking.

IV

FMRs by linguistic groups

Sources of data

Absence of suitable quantitative data often constrains the incorporation of cultural or non-economic factors in the analysis of regional variations in sex ratios. FMR data by cultural indicators covering large segments of the population are hard to come by. Data from ethnographic accounts cover too small a sample of the population. Census data on population by mother tongue do not face the problem of small sample size. In India, there are 14 constitutionally recognised languages. Besides these, there are over a hundred languages and dialects spoken in different parts of the country by sizeable population groups. Census operations cover all these languages across different states and districts.

This analysis first uses data from the 1981 Census followed by the data from the 1961 Census. The language survey in the 1961 Census was very comprehensive and included 1,549 languages/dialects (Nigam 1964: CLXXIX). Subsequent census operations have tended to merge different dialects into one major language group (Padmanabha 1981: 4–5). The trend is most obvious in the case of Hindi *which has subsumed as many as 47 dialects between 1961 and 1981*. Some of these dialects, for example, Chhattisgarhi and Marwari, are spoken by well over a million people. As against the 1,549 languages included in the 1961 Census, the 1981 Census provides information on about 110 different languages.[8]

To avoid small sample sizes, the analysis only includes languages spoken by 20,000 or more people. Language groups like Nepali and Sindhi which have a substantial presence outside the borders of India have also been excluded as these may be affected by migration across national borders. The language groups of the north-east have also been excluded as these have no bearing on the issue of the north–south divide.[9]

Analysis of the data

Table 5.4 provides FMRs by language groups on the basis of the 1981 Census. It classifies the languages into Indo-Aryan, Dravidian (both ST and non-ST) and Munda. The FMRs are calculated both at the all-India level and at the level of the major states where the language is spoken.

FMRs among the speakers of Indo-Aryan language groups are consistently low, ranging from 880–940. This includes Hindi, Punjabi, Kashmiri, Rajasthani, Urdu and Dogri speaking groups. Gujarati (950), Marathi (960), Oriya (970) and Konkani (1,039) group of languages has higher FMRs. Dravidian language groups have still higher FMRs whether we consider the main southern languages like Tamil, Malayalam, Kannada or Telugu, dialects like Coorgi and Tulu spoken by the non-tribals or Gondi and Kondh, spoken by the tribals. FMRs among speakers of the tribal languages is much higher than the non-tribal ones. High FMRs also characterize the two isolated pockets of Dravidian language in the north: Malto in Bihar and Kurukh (Oraon) in MP, Orissa and Bihar.

Interestingly, FMRs among the speakers of Bhilli, an Indo-Aryan language, are high even in Rajasthan a state known for low FMR. This is the only region where tribals speak an Indo-Aryan language. Of these the Bhils, Kolis, Warlis, Dhodias and Dhubas are all from the Proto-Australoid racial group while the Minas are the only Proto-Nordic group (Raza and Ahmad, 1990: 40–42). While the Bhils (1,006), Warlis (961), Kolis (974) and Dhodias (1,040) identified with the Mundas and Gonds have high FMRs, *the Minas who are closely integrated into the Indo-Aryan system have a low FMR (904).*

Another significant instance is provided by the Khandeshi-speaking non-tribal substratum in Gujarat, Maharashtra and MP. All the three groups

---

[8] The analysis here uses the series-1 tables which provides information only at the state levels and not below it, i.e., at the district level.

[9] Assamese has not been included as census could not be conducted in Assam in 1981.

Table 5.4
FMR by linguistic groups: 1981 data (women per 1,000 men)

Language	Region	FMR 81	Language	Region	FMR 81
Indo-Aryan Core Group:			Dravidian Group:		
Hindi	India	899	Telugu	All-India	976
Hindi	UP	884	Telugu	AP	979
Hindi	Rajasthan	915	Telugu	REST	948
Hindi	MP	935	Kannada	All-India	960
Hindi	Bihar	940	Kannada	Karnataka	963
Hindi	REST	827	Kannada	REST	912
Punjabi	All-India	892	Coorgi	Karnataka	1,053
Punjabi	Punjab	890	Tulu	All-India	1,041
Punjabi	REST	897	Tulu	Karnataka	1,062
Kashmiri	Kashmir	883	Tulu	REST	890
Dogri	All-India	915	Malayalam	All-India	1,020
Dogri	Kashmir	926	Malayalam	Kerala	1,006
Dogri	REST	719	Malayalam	REST	759
Urdu	All-India	922	Tamil	TN	998
Bengali	All-India	938			
Bengali	WB	939	Dravidian (Tribal)		
Bengali	REST	927	Gondi	All-India	1,019
Assamese	Assam	892	Gondi	AP	1,006
Gujarati	All-India	948	Gondi	MP	1,026
Gujarati	Gujarat	950	Gondi	Maharashtra	1,004
Gujarati	REST	925	Gondi	Orissa	996
Marathi	All-India	959	Gondi	REST	838
Marathi	Maharashtra	960	Gadba	All-India	1,012
Marathi	REST	951	Gadba	AP	1,030
Khandeshi	All-India	986	Gadba	Orissa	1,000
Khandeshi	Gujarat	992	Jatapu	AP	943
Khandeshi	MP	1,028	Korwa	MP	990
Khandeshi	Maharashtra	985	Korwa	Maharashtra	952
Oriya	All-India	974	Kurukh	All-India	1,011
Oriya	Orissa	981	Kurukh	Bihar	1,019
Oriya	REST	872	Kurukh	MP	1,032

Table 5.4 continued

Table 5.4 continued

Language	Region	FMR 81	Language	Region	FMR 81
Konkani	All-India	1,039	Kurukh	Orissa	1,012
Konkani	Karnataka	1,042	Kurukh	WB	977
Konkani	Maharashtra	979	Kui	Orissa	1,106
Konkani	Goa	1,073	Koya	All-India	1,001
Halbi	All-India	1,004	Koya	AP	997
Halbi	MP	1,015	Juang	Orissa	1,106
Halbi	Maharashtra	964	Kondh	Orissa	1,016
Halbi	Orissa	1,043	Kisan	Orissa	1,002
			Savara	Orissa	1,058
Indo-Aryan (Tribal):			Malto	Bihar	979
Bhilli	All-India	1,006			
Bhilli	Gujarat	996	Munda		
Bhilli	MP	994	Group:		
Bhilli	Maharashtra	996	Mundari	All-India	1,020
Bhilli	Rajasthan	1,028	Mundari	Bihar	1,029
Bhilli	REST	1,021	Mundari	Orissa	1,010
			Mundari	WB	1,011
Munda Group:			Mundari	REST	400
Munda	All-India	955	Santali	All-India	985
Munda	Bihar	960	Santali	Bihar	987
Munda	Orissa	966	Santali	Orissa	999
Munda	WB	957	Santali	WB	984
Munda	REST	711	Santali	REST	341
Bhumij	All-India	1,022	Kharia	All-India	1,018
Bhumij	Orissa	1,029	Kharia	Bihar	1,050
Bhumij	REST	1,007	Kharia	Orissa	1,024
Kora	WB	975	Kharia	REST	884
Korku	MP	983			
Korku	Maharashtra	984			

Source: Government of India, 1983 (Table C-7).

show a high FMR. It must be noted here that Khandesh is one region where the Brahmins permit cross-cousin marriage (Karve, 1965: 181–82). Similarly the Mers of the Saurashtra region of Gujarat also practice cross-cousin marriage (Trautmann, 1981: 230–32). It will be interesting to see if FMR pattern among the Mers differs from the mainstream Gujarati-speaking population. Such data are, however, not readily available.

The 1981 Census data do not provide adequate number of observations, particularly in the Hindi group of languages for a satisfactory statistical analysis. The 1961 Census data (Table 5.5) however, provide much more elaborate data permitting such an analysis.

1961 Census data

There are in all 63 languages/dialects in the Indo-Aryan category. These readily lend themselves into the classification of 'core' group (Group 1) and 'peripheral' group (Group 2). The core group consists of the north-western states, while the peripheral group consists of eastern Hindi and central Hindi and southern group of Indo-Aryan languages, like Marathi, Konkani and Oriya. The eastern Hindi languages are mainly spoken in Bihar while the central Hindi group covers the zone of intermixing viz., Madhya Pradesh, Maharashtra and Orissa.[10]

Sex ratios among the speakers of Indo-Aryan languages in the 'core' group are highly masculine (Table 5.5). Indo-Aryan languages and kinship system completely prevail in this region. This contrasts with the high FMRs among the Munda and Dravidian groups and even with the Indo-Aryan tribal group where, as observed before, cross-cousin marriages prevail.

The eastern Hindi group of dialects viz., Magadhi, Bhojpuri, Sadri, Khortha and Maithili have high FMRs. Similarly, FMRs among speakers of the Indo-Aryan languages from Baghelkhand and Chattisgarh region of MP are high. This pattern continues southwards across Narmada through Maharashtra. When it comes to Konkani, spoken in the states of south, the FMR pattern merges with that observed for the Dravidian language groups (Group 4).[11] Within the Indo-Aryan language groups, the STs (Group 3) have higher FMRs than those among the non-STs.

Given the presence of a large number of speakers of the four major south Indian languages, namely, Tamil, Telugu, Kannada and Malayalam in all the four south Indian states, FMRs for these languages in each of

---

[10] These FMR figures are not corrected for migration. However, the migration effects are insignificant at the all-India basis (Agnihotri, 1995a). However, in this analysis the Pahari group of Hindi languages are not included in view of known problem of male out-migration to plain areas.

[11] As a matter of fact the Konkani-speaking groups of Kerala, Karnataka and Goa should belong to the Dravidian group as against those in Maharashtra (Karve 1965: 25, endnote 3).

Table 5.5

FMR by linguistic groups: 1961 data (women per 1,000 men)

Language	Region	FMR 61	Group	Language	Region	FMR 61	Group
Indo-Aryan Core Group:				**Indo-Aryan (Tribal):**			
Hindi	India	898	1	Bhilli	All-India	981	3
Hindi	UP	902	1	Bhilli	Gujarat	1,026	3
Hindi	Rajasthan	875	1	Bhilli	MP	964	3
Hindi	Himachal	817	1	Bhilli	Maharashtra	972	3
Khari Boli	Rajasthan	868	1	Bhilli	Rajasthan	1,106	3
Awadhi	UP	860	1	Barel	MP	977	3
Braj Bhasha	UP	866	1	Bhilali	MP	951	3
Kashmiri	Kashmir	851	1	Bhilodi	Gujarati	1,015	3
Dogri	All-India	906	1	Chodhari	Gujarati	980	3
Gojri	Kashmir	876	1	Dhodia	Gujarat	1,011	3
Punjabi	All-India	854	1	Gamti	Gujarat	959	3
Bhateali	Himachal	885	1	Kokna	Guj + Mah	1,002	3
Bilaspuri	Himachal	1,017	1	Mawchi	Maharashtra	956	3
Urdu	All-India	931	1	Pawri	Maharashtra	981	3
Rajasthani	Rajasthan	906	1	Wagdi	Rajasthan	988	3
Bagri	Rajasthan	877	1				
Dhundhari	Rajasthan	912	1				

					Dravidian Group:			
Harauti	Rajasthan		927	1	Telugu	AP	985	4
Jaipuri	Rajasthan		1,044	1	Telugu	TN	998	4
Khairari	Rajasthan		903	1	Telugu	Karnataga	957	4
Marwari	Rajasthan		922	1	Telugu	Kerala	981	4
Mewari	Rajasthan		951	1	Telugu	Orissa	987	4
Mewati	Rajasthan		934	1	Kannada	Karnataka	962	4
Nagarchal	Rajasthan		931	1	Kannada	Kerala	975	4
Shekhawat	Rajasthan		909	1	Kannada	AP	986	4
Sondwari	Rajasthan		926	1	Kannada	TN	987	4
					Tulu	Karnataka	1,080	4
Central Rajasthani Group:								
Banjari	Rajasthan		949	1	Tulu	Kerala	1,012	4
Lambadi	Rajasthan		946	1	Malayalam	(India)	1,001	4
Malwi	Rajasthan		954	1	Tamil	TN	998	4
Nimadi	MP		966	1	Tamil	AP	989	4
Gujarati	Gujarat		940	1	Tamil	Kerala	964	4
Gujaru	Maharashtra		932	1	Tamil	Karnataka	907	4
Bengali	WB		924	1	Tamil	Pondi.	1,006	4
					Dravidian (Tribal):			
Pahari Hindi Group:								
Kumauni	UP		1,049	2	Badaga	Karnataka	985	5
Garhwali	UP		1,196	2	Vadari	Maharashtra	978	5

Table 5.5 continued

Table 5.5 continued

Language	Region	FMR 61	Group	Language	Region	FMR 61	Group
W.Pahari	Himachal	1,095	2	Yerukala	AP	992	5
U.Pahari	Punjab	1,086	2	Dorli	MP	1,087	5
U.Pahari	Himachal	965	2	Maria	MP + Maharashtra	968	5
				Gondi	AP	946	5
Eastern Hindi Group:				Gondi	MP	1,039	5
Bhojpuri	Bihar	1,037	2	Gondi	Maharashtra	1,012	5
Khortha	Bihar	996	2	Gondi	Orissa	1,009	5
Magadhi	Bihar	1,000	2	Kurukh	Assam	1,036	5
Maithili	Bihar	1,017	2	Kurukh	Bihar	1,040	5
E.Magadhi	Bihar	933		Kurukh	MP	995	5
Sadri	Bihar	1,014	2	Kurukh	Orissa	1,034	5
P.Pargani	Bihar	930	2	Kurukh	WB	895	7
				Kui	Orissa	1,016	5
Central Hindi Group:				Koya	AP	1,007	5
Bagheli	MP	1,018	2	Koya	Orissa	994	5
Ch.Garhi	MP	1,063	2	Dhurva	MP	1,035	5
Lodhi	MP	1,025	2	Parji	Orissa	1,001	5
Marari	MP & Maharashtra	1,055	2	Kolami	Maharashtra	995	5
Pardesi	Maharashtra	960	2	Malto	Bihar	995	5
Powari	Maharashtra	1,002	2				
Laria	Orissa	1,084	2				

Southern Indo-Aryan:

Saurashtra	TN	2	990
Kachchi	Gujarat	2	1,078
Marathi	Maharashtra	2	965
Halabi	MP	2	931
Parwari	MP	2	1,006
K.Marathi	Maharashtra	2	992
Varli	Maharashtra	2	998
Ahirani	Maharashtra	2	1,016
Dangi	Maharashtra	2	937
Oriya	Orissa	2	982
Bhatri	MP	2	1,024
Konkani	Maharashtra	2	855
Konkani	Karnataka	2	1,027
Konkani	Kerala	2	1,001
Konjani	Goa	2	1,082

Munda Group:

Kol	Orissa	1,016	6
Mundari	Bihar	999	6
Mundari	Orissa	1,069	6
Mundari	WB	1,010	6
Karmali	Bihar	978	6
Santali	Bihar	981	6
Santali	Orissa	1,018	6
Santali	WB	964	6
Ho	Bihar	1,075	6
Ho	Orissa	996	6
Kharia	MP	1,087	6
Kharia	Orissa	1,100	6
Bhumij	Bihar	969	6
Bhumij	Orissa	1,018	6
Korku	MP	1,001	6
Korku	Maharashtra	980	6
Munda	Orissa	1,041	6
Munda	WB	884	6

Source: Nigam, 1964.

these four states have been separately included. However, in the case of Malayalam, only the all-India level figures have been included in view of the consistent and well documented male out-migration from Kerala.

One can discern marginally, yet consistently, higher FMR among the tribals in the Dravidian kinship region (Group 5). The FMRs are still higher for the speakers of the Munda group of languages (Group 6). This is consistent with the results about the FMRs among the tribals as seen in Chapters 3 and 4.

Analysis of variance

Table 5.6 gives the results of the analysis of variance and the descriptive statistics for FMRs in the 6 different language groups: core and peripheral Indo-Aryan, Indo-Aryan tribal, Dravidian non-tribal and tribal and Munda.

Table 5.6
Results of ANOVA: FMR by language categories

Group	Number	Mean	S.D.	95%CI	Diff. (LSD)
Indo-Aryan Core	29	906	37	892–920	
Indo-Aryan Peripheral	28	1,006	44	989–1,023	*
Indo-Aryan Tribal	13	983	24	969–998	*
Dravidian	15	986	16	977–995	*
Dravidian (Tribal)	19	1,004	26	991–1,016	*
Munda	16	1,012	38	992–1,032	**

Notes: 1) F ratio 34.8***.
    2) Homogeneity of Variance (Levenne's test): T = 2.9**.
    3) Significant differences shown by LSD test (Last column).

Three distinct groups emerge: the Indo-Aryan 'core' with lowest FMRs; groups 2 to 5 which are not significantly different among themselves; and the 'Munda' language group. FMRs among the 'core' Indo-Aryan group are significantly low, while those among the Munda group are significantly high. FMRs among the 'peripheral' Indo-Aryan, Dravidian and tribal Aryan and Dravidian groups do not vary significantly.

The 'periphery'

This classification matches Berreman's scheme. The groups identified by Berreman as being outside the pale of the dominant Hindu ethos match closely with groups 2 to 6. Groups 3, 5 and 6 are the tribal groups. The Dravidian group or group 4 is the peripheral group having 'unconventional' marriage rules as they do no follow the Indo-Aryan marriage rules.

It is the Indo-Aryan 'peripheral' group or group 2 which provides interesting support to Berreman's classification. This represents a socio-political periphery and a geographical fringe. Pahari or the hill people identified by Berreman, regions of Baghelkhand and Chhattisgarh in Madhya Pradesh, Magadhi (in recent times at least) and the Sadri-speaking regions of Bihar are in the first category while Marathi, Konkani and Oriya fall in the second category. The more peripheral a region is geographically, the more prevalent are the Dravidian (or Munda as the case may be) kinship practices.

Regions geographically proximate to the 'core' Indo-Aryan areas and yet peripheral to it, have two characteristics. They either have a high concentration of tribal population indicative of their incomplete 'integration' into the Indo-Aryan system or, like Magadh, they have been clear challengers to the Indo-Aryan expansion. It is only the Mithila region of north Bihar, and Bhojpuri-speaking group of Bihar that are difficult to fit into any of the above groups. They have high FMRs but are also confirmed adherents of the Indo-Aryan kinship ethos. Hence fitting these into the above categories poses a problem.

The difficulty of classifying the eastern states of Bihar, Bengal and Orissa has also figured in the analysis done by Dyson and Moore (1983: 47). Orissa does not pose a major problem and can be grouped under the Dravidian/Munda kinship system. The problem of classifying Bihar basically arises due to the problem of its tribal and non-tribal groups. The language based FMR analysis provides for such a separation and narrows down the problem of classification to northern Bihar. The southern part of Bihar fits into the tribal or 'peripheral' category. Areas of northern Bihar need further scrutiny and identification of other factors which may result in higher FMRs. As indicated in Chapter 4, higher infant mortality may be one such factor.

Bengal emerges as somewhat of an anomaly. It is a 'peripheral' Indo-Aryan region and cannot be 'tentatively' grouped with the 'southern' system on the ground of 'short marriage distances and high rates of village endogamy' (ibid.:47). This is especially so given that the marriage rules and practices in Bengal are completely Indo-Aryan (Fruzzetti, 1990). However, this is the case in the social upper stratum while on the whole the adherence to the 'high culture' norms is fragile (Goody, 1990: Chapter 7). Further, the low FMR of the all-age group population (924) does not match with fairly high juvenile age group FMRs in Bengal in 1961. A probable reason for this contradiction is the fact of the partition of Bengal and the consequent demographic upheavals through migration. In the analysis above Bengali has therefore been left out. The anomaly represented by Bengal calls for a more detailed research.

V

The modified kinship classification

The regional patterns analysed above suggest a modification of the conventional north–south classification. This modification is also based on kinship practices but is a more layered one. The tribal layer marked by 'female–friendly' kinship system is separated out in this analysis as FMRs among the tribals are studied separately. Among the non-tribals, the districts in the 'core' region are put in one category and the rest of the districts in another category (Map 5.3; see Annexure 5A for the list of districts in the two categories). It is possible to further classify the 'rest' of the districts into 'Dravidian' and 'mixed'. But as seen before these differences are not significant (Table 5.6).[12] It could also be argued that the population within a given district will itself need to be separated into groups which may differ by kinship practices. A separate analysis for the SC population achieves this separation to some extent. Beyond this, however, limitations are imposed by the availability of data. Disaggregation of FMRs by levels of prosperity can inform this debate further but that is the subject matter of a later chapter (Chapter 8).

The classification suggested here is an attempt to improve the 'resolution' of the analysis and does not rule out fine tuning. As it will be seen here and in Chapter 7, it provides useful insights into the variations in FMR patterns. A rudimentary analysis of the differences in mortality patterns by kinship variable is done here. This is followed in Chapter 7 by use of the kinship variable in the FMR-FLP analysis.

---

[12] In Chapter 7, the association between the FMRs and female labour participation (FLP) has been analysed by kinship variable. There too the differences within the 'rest' category do not turn out to be significant.

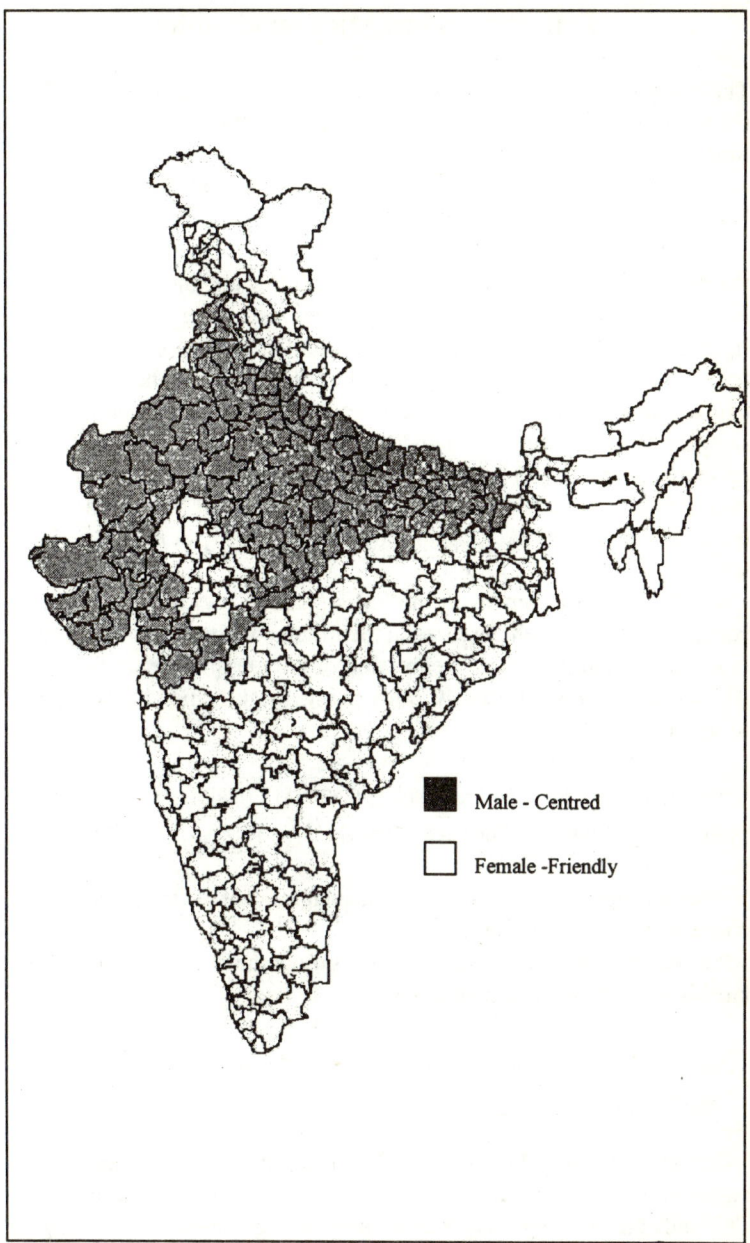

Map 5.3: Districts classified by 'male-centred' and 'female-friendly' kinship systems.

Differences in FMRs by kinship

The grouping of districts by kinship variable itself suggests that FMRs in the 'core' north-west will be lower compared to the rest of the regions. Still, it is useful to see how the districts in the two kinship regions are distributed in terms of the 16 possible combinations of FMR04 and FMR59 levels. This is shown in Table 5.7.

The 164 districts in the 'core' northern region, are mainly clustered in the range of moderate and high FMR04 and low and moderate FMR59. Among the 202 districts in the rest of the regions, clustering in the bottom right hand corner can be noticed. This signifies high to very high FMR for both the 0–4 and 5–9 age groups. The differences in the FMR in the two kinship regions can also be tested using T-test for independent samples. These indicate that both FMR04 and FMR59 differ significantly (at the 1 per cent level) by the kinship group for each of the social group except for the tribal population in the 0-4 age group. FMR04 among the tribals differ by the two kinship groups significantly at the 10 per cent level.

Given these differences in the FMR patterns by kinship, it will be useful to analyse the differences in the infant and the under-5 mortality in the two kinship regions. Regression of female infant mortality rates on the male infant mortality rates using the kinship dummy gives following result:

IMR (female) = 6.2 + 16.1* Kinship + 0.82* IMR (male)	5.1
Adj. R. Sq. = 0.82 T-Stat. 3.1*** 11*** 36*** F = 935***	

The kinship variable turns out to be insignificant as far as the slope is concerned.

For the child mortality in the 1–4 age group, the differences in the two kinship systems are much stronger:

CMRf = 21.6 - 34* Kin. + (0.72 + 0.67* Kin.)* CMRm	5.2
Adj. R. Sq. = 0.84 T-Stat. 12*** -14*** 20*** 22*** F = 539***	

The slope of the CMRf–CMRm line is less than 1 in the kinship = 0 region while it is considerably steep (1.4) in the 'core' northern region. This indicates that the discrimination against girl children resulting in excess female mortality in the 1–4 age group is the main feature of the

Table 5.7
Combination of FMR levels in the two kinship regions

FMR59	Kinship = 0 FMR04				Kinship = 1 FMR04			
	Low	Moderate	High	Very High	Low	Moderate	High	Very High
Low	0	0	0	0	10 (897, 839)	54 (937, 863)	31 (977, 880)	6 (1,012, 894)
Moderate	1	8 (946, 937)	21 (975, 953)	8 1,018, 946)	0	18 (944, 927)	34 (981, 931)	10 (1,019, 933)
High	0	12 (950, 971)	79 (982, 978)	43 1,018, 983)	0	0.00	4 (990, 968)	1
Very High	0	1	15 (983, 1,011)	44 (1,016, 1,015)	0	0	0	0

'core' northern regions and also the main mechanism for lowering the FMRs.[13]

This feature is shown more sharply in the patterns of excess male infant and excess female under-5 mortality. Figures 5.1a and 5.1b give the distribution of the sex differentials for the infant and the under-5 mortality for the districts in the two kinship regions separately. Distribution for the 366 districts taken together is also given. The scales are kept similar to facilitate comparison. Excess female mortality even in infancy characterises the 'core' north. In the 'rest' of the regions, sex differentials in under-5 mortality are not very sharp and are spread over a narrow band. In the north-western region, these are significantly high and spread over a large range (–5 to +80).

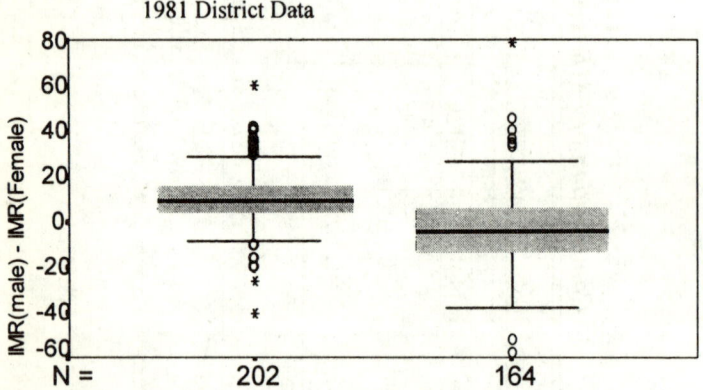

Excess Male Infant Mortality

1981 District Data

KINSHIP (Rest = 0; 'Core' North = 1): N = No. of Districts

Figure 5.1a: Box plot of excess male infant mortality rates by kinship group.

[13] As pointed out by Dasgupta and Bhatt (1995) excess mortality of girl children in the post-neonatal period remains the main cause of the lower FMRs notwithstanding the increase in the incidence of prenatal selection.

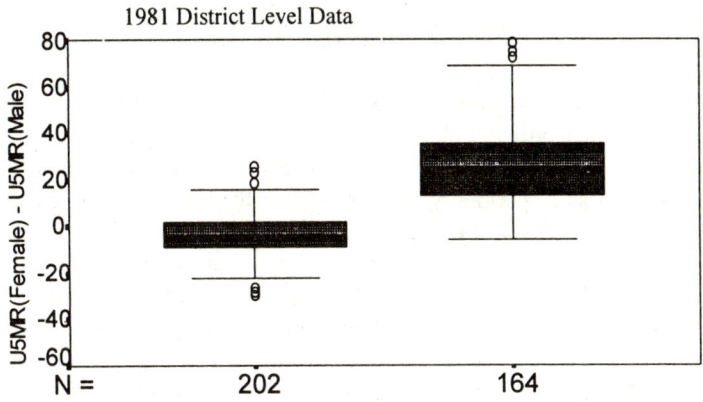

Figure 5.1b: Box plot of excess female under-5 mortality rates by kinship group.

VI

The core–periphery paradigm

The grouping of 202 districts within the 'rest' category has been justified on the ground that the different kinship systems there share the feature of being female-friendly and that the differences between FMRs in these are not statistically significant. But a feeling of uneasiness could still persist about the classification 'rest'. It is indeed a combination of three or four different systems: the Dravidian; the 'peripheral Indo-Aryan'; and different tribal kinship systems. During a personal discussion, a colleague described this as 'a ragtag combination of groups lumped together on the basis of 'what they are not' (i.e., not being similar to the 'core' north Indian kinship system), rather than what they are'.[14] Merely labelling these as 'female-friendly' was not enough. This criticism

---

[14] I am, in retrospect, thankful to Dr Jim Sumberg for this candid criticism.

appeared legitimate until I realised that it was tied up with the issue of 'core' and 'periphery'.

The 'core' and the 'norm'

The 'core' northern region described above has historically been the dominant political core in India. In the context of the sex ratio debate too its description as a 'core' continues with the rest of the regions and social groups treated as a 'periphery' of one type or the other (Caldwell and Caldwell, 1990; Goody, 1990; Harriss, 1989; Sopher, 1980). This has two subtle consequences. First, the political core is also treated as a core in the social and cultural context and therefore tacitly treated as a 'norm'. So the 'norm' here becomes one that is defined in terms 'power' or 'hegemony' and not in 'numerical' terms. Hence the FMR patterns in the 'core' north comes to be regarded as the 'norm' and there is a *tinge of inevitability* about their spread into rest of the regions (e.g., Miller, 1989). Such a spread may be looked upon or even rationalised as the 'price' of economic progress, presumably achieved in the north especially in Punjab, Haryana and western UP. Alternatively, it could be regarded as the price required to be paid for the establishment of a 'superior' cultural pattern. When emulation of this pattern in the periphery creates adverse consequences for females, the society finds out ways of rationalising or obscuring these. Both these attitudes need to be challenged explicitly.

Such a challenge is not difficult to support through concrete examples from regions like Kerala, Himachal Pradesh, Manipur and Goa, where development has been achieved without adverse consequences for women. However, such examples will always be discounted as 'exceptions', unachievable in the core political region. Once the 'norm' mind set operates, even the hope for change (and despair about its absence) gets focussed excessively on the 'core' region. The wrong notion that progress and a better status of women are mutually exclusive, does prevail and the declining FMRs in the north-west continue to be considered as inevitable. The concern then becomes so one sided that the unusually high FMRs in many regions and among many a groups escape analysis; a situation adequately highlighted in the previous two chapters. In fact, the maps by Sopher (1980), Miller (1981, 1984) should have automatically raised the issue of excess male mortality in the pockets with very high FMRs. In reality such a question was never raised seriously.

Questioning the dominant 'core'

As it happens, the dominant political 'core' is neither the socio-cultural core nor certainly the numerical core in India. Further, as far as the status of women is concerned, it is the 'female-friendly' kinship system that represents the 'norm' rather than the female-adverse' kinship system prevalent in the political 'core'. The lower status of women in the political 'core' represents a 'deviation' from this norm or more appropriately, an aberration, and should be looked upon as such.[15]

Such an explicit shift from the 'core–periphery' description to the 'aberration versus norm' description is necessary. The current attitude of looking at the masculine sex ratio patterns in the north-west as a norm spreading in other regions will continue unless these low FMRs are explicitly highlighted as an aberration.[16] Such explicit recognition has several advantages. First, it puts the gender insensitive promotion of 'development' on the defensive. Second, it allows one to look at the 'decline' in FMR in different regions differently and appreciate the distinction between high FMRs and balanced FMRs. The 'declining' FMRs from 1,000 to say, 965, in tribal Madhya Pradesh would not mean the same thing as the decline from, say, 910 to 890 in Haryana. Third, it brings home the need to consolidate the 'norm' of balanced FMRs against the deviant FMR patterns emanating from the political 'core'. This is qualitatively different from defending a 'periphery' against the spread of a 'normative', even if unacceptable, pattern of FMRs. Fourth and most importantly is the recognition of the patterns in Kerala, Manipur or Himachal Pradesh as both 'achievable' and 'desirable' *to be emulated in the 'core' region*. This is diametrically opposite to regarding these as 'exceptions' not achievable in the north.

It is possible that some read in this approach a threat to the 'Indo-Aryan' culture. More charitably this will be described as impractical.[17] Surely one cannot expect the 'core' north to change its kinship system or marriage practices! Such views are unwarranted. The simple point being made here is that the bath water of female subordination impinging on

[15] As mentioned earlier, only Raju (1991: 2877) explicitly uses the term 'deviant' for the FMR patterns in north.

[16] These concerns are not hypothetical. The 1991 Census data shows a further and steep decline in the FMRs in some of the districts in north and as some micro studies show, the practice of female infanticide is emerging among communities where it was not practised earlier [in p.c with ADITHI, an NGO working in Bihar].

[17] You cannot legislate cultural change, is one common refrain.

their survival itself, need not be retained along with the baby of the Indo-Aryan culture. This is especially so because the above subordination does not have mandatory cultural sanctions. Impression of such sanctions arise out of the convenient interpretation of culture suitable to the strongly patriarchal order in the political 'core'.[18] To that extent it is essentially a political exercise. Precisely therefore, it is open to questioning, challenge and modification.

Two points need to be explicitly stated here before closing this discussion. First, the low FMR patterns in the 'core Indo-Aryan kinship region' do not represent the 'norm' but a deviation. Regarding these implicitly as the norm dilutes the understanding of the problem and the urgency and design of policy interventions. A shift from 'core–periphery' mode of description to an 'aberration–norm' mode of description is therefore necessary. This issue requires a further and fuller debate which is outside the scope of this discussion. But it is *crucial enough* to be expressed in this rather preliminary form.

Conclusion

This analysis of the regional variations in FMR highlights the role of cultural factors. Culture is a significant determinant of the position of women in the soicety. Where the culture is female-friendly, survival chances of the girl children are better. The analysis also reveals different cultural layers covering the Indian landscape and the need to take these into account while analysing the problem.

The importance of geophysical regions as units of analysis has important implications for regional studies, data collection and policy planning. Study of regional patterns of FMRs need to be pursued more seriously. The census data can be significantly supplemented by the NSSO survey results which can now be tabulated at levels of NSS regions which quite closely correspond with the census regions. There is considerable data already available which can allow incorporation of cultural variables in the analysis of sex ratio variations. Language-based population data available since 1961 illustrates this point. On the policy side, region-specific planning of some of the welflare policies merit serious thought; a point already highlighted in Chapter 4.

---

[18] This tempting debate is outside the scope of present analysis but it may be necessary to engage into it elsewhere.

The analysis here has led to a modification of the conventional north–south classification. This has given useful results and also raised very important questions regarding the notion of 'core', 'periphery' and 'norms' which need to be debated seriously. The kinship classification developed here is followed up further in Chapter 7 while examining the role of female work force participation.

Disaggregation of sex ratio data by age groups, social groups and finally by kinship regions has been highly useful. These elaborate the diversity in sex ratio patterns far more than any previous analysis does. This elaboration is useful for policy and further research. But the analysis now has to move from the pattern of diversity to its underlying causes. An important distinction has been made here between two different mechanisms for sex differentials in mortality: biological and behavioural. Excess female child mortality is an outcome of discrimination or the behavioural processes. Overall mortality levels and excess male child mortality on the other hand are a result of biological and environmental factors. Available literature has concentrated much more on the former than on the latter. It is necessary to look at the consequences of both these processes; sex ratios are a summary indicator of these.

It is possible to take both biological and behavioural aspects into account in a coherent theoretical framework. The next part of the analysis does that. It draws upon Sen's entitlements framework (1981) to highlight the behavioural aspects. The inequality of access to life sustaining resources is looked upon as an 'entitlements failure'. This is then linked to the capabilities approach (Sen, 1985) which takes the biological and environmental factors into account through what is called the 'personal features'. The two approaches are then integrated to reveal the outcomes of different possible combinations of behavioural and biological aspects. These correspond to the variations in the FMR patterns analysed here. Having outlined the framework, the threads of data analysis are picked up once again to examine some of the correlates of the observed sex ratio patterns.

Chapter 6

Sex ratio imbalance and entitlements failure

I

An outline

Sex ratio imbalance reflects an asymmetry of survival. This asymmetry can be viewed as a case of entitlements failure. To do so one has to draw upon the entitlements framework (Sen, 1981), the cooperative–conflict approach to intra-household resource allocation (Sen, 1990) and the bargain theoretic analysis of inequality within a stylised two-member household (Kanbur and Haddad, 1994). However, the issue of survival inequalities goes well beyond the realm of entitlements and must incorporate the role of human diversity which affects survival outcomes. The capabilities approach (Sen, 1985) enables us to do so. It also provides an organising framework and a rationale for a disaggregated approach to the analysis of sex ratio patterns.

The case for entitlements failure is fairly clear-cut. Low FMRs in the juvenile age group are primarily driven by excess female mortality in the 1–4 age group and, in many cases, during infancy. This excess female mortality is a result of the inequalities faced by female children in access to life-sustaining resources.

It is worth noting that excess male mortality is never attributed to discrimination against men vis-à-vis women. Even the most explicit accusation of discrimination is levelled against nature which 'arbitrarily denies this legitimate aspiration (for survival) and continues to discriminate against the stronger sex' (Gbenyon and Locoh, 1992). Factors like biological vulnerability of the male infant (Waldron, 1983), or misuse of various freedoms by men themselves (Johansson, 1991), have been invoked to explain such an excess. The case for excess female mortality is different. It is almost always attributed to resource allocation inequality: the girl child may be given less food, breastfed for a smaller time span, female member of the household may have to make do with less and delayed health care. This may happen for a variety or reasons. For our immediate purpose these reasons are not as important as the denial of access is. Papanek (1990) describes this entitlement failure in graphic terms: 'To each less than she needs, from each more than she can do'.

Access inequality within the household

Such 'access inequality' represents a special and strong case of entitlements failure. This failure mainly operates at the household level though there are structural constraints to women's access to resources at the societal level as well. The constraints at these two levels influence each other (Blumberg, 1991).

It is necessary therefore, to look at intra-household allocational behaviour in order to understand the nature of access inequalities faced by the female members and its impact on survival inequalities. This is done by bringing together three separate strands of inquiry namely, entitlements framework, cooperative–conflict model and the Nash bargaining model in a two-member household.

The entitlements approach

As mentioned in Chapter 2 (Section VII), the entitlements approach deals with the links between a person's entitlements or effective command over resources, and endowments or the wherewithals for creating such a command. This link is created through the 'exchange entitlement mapping' which reflects the social organisation in which a person is situated.

Such social organisation affects the entitlements within the household resulting in differential, often unequal, access to resources for its members. This unequal access can be a matter of life and death in certain societies;

in others it may manifest itself less severely. At the societal level, the cumulative pattern of mortality differentials is reflected in the sex ratios.

Intra-household models

Until recently, the household used to be treated as an individual unit where preferences of different members uniquely converged and were adequately articulated through the head of the household, usually male. This view has been increasingly and effectively challenged in recent years (Chapter 2, Section VII). The alternative approach recognises the divergence of preferences within the household and looks at the intra-household dynamics in a bargain theoretic framework. This approach has been used here along with Sen's cooperative–conflict model of the household.

Elaborating the E-mapping

The analysis here elaborates one possible form of E-mapping recognising the exchange-independent component of a person's entitlements explicitly. Such recognition allows one to integrate the role of cultural factors and economic factors, two separate and competing strands in the literature. Through this integration one is able to identify situations where economic factors are critical and where they are not. The E-mapping formally elaborated here analyses the links between the commodity vector and the endowment vector. The vector form emphasises the possibility that different elements of entitlements are affected differently within the same household. This has important implications for the pattern of survival inequalities and design of policy interventions.

The inequality vector

The entitlement-endowment relationship developed thus is then used to analyse the inequality within a stylised two-member household. The scalar, one dimensional expression for inequality developed by Kanbur and Haddad (1994) is extended to its vector counterpart. The inequality vector has different elements, like inequality in respect of food, nutrition or health care. These correspond to different elements of the entitlement vector.

Inequalities in respect of these elements can significantly differ from each other, a fact not readily recognised in the single element analysis. Moreover, these different inequalities have a combined and interdependent impact in the space of outcomes. The nature of this interdependence is highlighted.

Incorporating human diversity

The issue of outcomes logically takes the analysis to the question of wellbeing, longevity being an important component of it. This shift of focus to the space of wellbeing is important for two reasons. First, there is a many to one relation between inequalities in the space of entitlements and the space of outcomes.[1] Certain inequality in the space of outcomes can arise out of many possible combinations of inequalities in the space of entitlements. The second reason is the fact of human diversity. It can generate two different outcomes for two different individuals even if they have identical entitlements.

The capabilities approach (Sen, 1985) takes human diversity into account explicitly. It links the space of outcomes, formally termed the space of 'functionings', with the space of entitlements through human diversity. This is analysed in some detail.

Linking the two approaches

Entitlements provides a common link between the capabilities approach and the entitlements framework. Yet the two approaches have been pursued independent of each other so far. Bringing them together immediately connects the spaces of functionings, entitlements and endowments and makes dynamic the linkages between the three. This is developed in the second part of this chapter.

---

[1] In the context of mortality, Harriss (1989: 50) uses the term 'multifactoral mutual causation' to describe the many to one relationship between the factors that give rise to mortality and the effect, i.e., mortality.

Organisation of the discussion

The discussion is organised as follows: Section II briefly reviews the literature on entitlements and its application to gender relations. It develops one possible form of E-mapping and contours of an 'anti-women' policy that logically follow from it. The next section briefly reviews the debate on household models and describes the cooperative–conflict model. Section IV examines the concept of resource distribution suggested by Kanbur and Haddad and suggests possible modifications. Finally, the need to go beyond entitlements into the space of functionings is outlined leading to the next part of this chapter.

II

Entitlements framework

In this framework, every person possesses a set or 'bundle' of resources including his or her own labour power which are termed as the 'endowments' of that person. Skill, land, capital or other means of production are other examples of endowments. Through their use the person is able to have a command over a bundle of commodities. The set of such commodity bundles is called the person's entitlements. The space of commodities and space of endowments are linked through the exchange entitlement mapping or E-mapping or simply E(.). The terms used by Sen have been elaborated by Gasper (1993) as described in Table 6.1.

An entitlement–endowment relationship

The transformation of endowments into entitlements can be captured in a simple form given below. In what follows the term entitlement is used both as a set and as a vector[2] while endowment is treated as a vector with different components. One can begin with a single element of the endowment vector, say, unskilled labour. Its conversion into net exchange value will depend upon the corresponding component of a 'value vector'

---

[2] Very strictly, entitlement set is a set of commodity vectors and the term 'space of commodities' is more appropriate than the term 'space of entitlements'.

Table 6.1
Terms in entitlements framework and their referents

Sen's terms	Referents
Endowments	Labour power, skills, information, land, Produced means of production, locatioon
Entitlement Relations, e.g.: Trade-based etc., Production-based etc. Own labour etc. Inheritance and transfer etc. (Rest of the determinants of) E-mapping	Rules of entitlement from: trade, production, labour, inheritance, transfer, including: − civil rights and obligation − non-legal rights and obligations Production and trade conditions Availability of public goods Social security and taxation schedule Another formulation is to include within endowments a measure of effective access to public goods
Exchange entitlements/entitlements Entitlement failures: -direct failures -trade failures	Legitimate effective command: − via own production − via trade − after transfers to and from government
Extended entitlements	Potential command via non-legal as well as legal rights and obligations

Source: Gasper, 1993: 684.

v. In the present case it will be the wage rate. For an endowment vector **d** with k components, the net exchange value or the contribution c will be given by the dot product d.v.

$$c = d.v = S\,(d_k * v_k)\ k = 1\ \text{to}\ k \qquad\qquad 6.1$$

Entitlement vector x_i of the person i will depend upon this exchange value d.v. Quantity of rice, quantity of fish and purchase of medicine can be combined in different ways depending upon this exchange value which is equivalent of a budget constraint. It is possible to introduce a distortion parameter b ranging from 0 to 1, representing some type of discount, for example, a tax resulting in a 'net exchange value' c = b(d.v) and

$$x_i = x_i\,\{b(d.v)\} \qquad\qquad 6.2a$$

There is a difference between the actual commodity vector that a person has and and the set of such vectors over which he could have a command. In an n-dimensional space of commodities (and services etc.), any commodity vector will be represented by a point. The outer boundary of such feasible points that a given vector can occupy will be governed by the condition of corealisability given certain exchange value $c = b(d.v)$. It will be a $n - 1$ dimensional surface representing the 'best case' commodity vectors. The volume bound within it will be the entitlement set or simply the entitlements of the concerned person. In other words, the entitlement set is the set $X(i)$ of all possible $x(i)/X(i)$.

Until recently, literature on entitlements has mainly focussed on exchange. Yet, non-market entitlements (Kabeer, 1995: 6) or exchange-independent bundle of commodities very much exist. Any element of the entitlement vector will, therefore, have two components: an *exchange-dependent component* and an *exchange-independent component* or a 'core' component. Exchange-independent entitlements are highly relevant to this analysis. Resources like air to breath, water to drink or road to walk on are perhaps trivial examples of this.[3] Even beyond these there is a 'core' entitlement component available to a person even when his or her endowments do not fetch any exchange value. Unwaged household work for example ensures a set of 'core' entitlements (Kabeer 1991). These 'core' entitlements could also flow through nature, society or a safety network provided by the state.

The entitlements vector can, therefore, be represented as:

$$x_i = x_{0,i} + x_i\{b_i(d.v)\} \qquad\qquad 6.2b$$

$x_{0,i}$ represents the core component, and b_i the distortion parameter. Both can be considered components of the E-mapping.

Within a household

For a household, the entitlement and endowment vectors for different members can be combined into an entitlement matrix and an endowment matrix. E-mapping will still be possible (Sen, 1990: 143) though complicated, since it will involve a matrix-matrix mapping. Such complication can be avoided, however, by using a stylised two-member household

---

[3] In some societies, even these could get monetised. In some others (Basu, 1992) the macro conditions may not permit access to free public goods, like tap water or the street.

with a male and a female member and taking the ratio of different components of the entitlement vector and the endowment vector. One can then retain the vector form of the entitlement-endowment mapping. The undistorted situation for any given element of the entitlement will be represented by:

$$x_{i,2}/x_{i,1} = d_2/d_1 \qquad\qquad 6.3a$$

The first distortion can be introduced through the elements of value vector. A lower wage can be given to the female workers for an identical item of work (Moore, H. 1988: 101). This represents the first 'discounting' of the female endowments through the macro level factors which operate upon the labour market (Blumberg, 1991). The entitlements ratio is accordingly modified to:

$$x_{i,2}/x_{i,1} = (d.v)_2/(d.v)_1 \qquad\qquad 6.3b$$

Another distortion parameter b_i can again be envisaged for the ith element representing an explicit or implicit discount on the contribution made be the female member.[4] Its value will differ for different elements of the entitlement vector, like cheaper food, costly proteins or access to formal health care.

The ratios of different elements of the e-vectors of the two members can themselves be expressed as a vector. Its elements will be dimensionless numbers, being ratios of identical variables. If the ratio vector for entitlements is expressed as N_i, and the contribution ratio as C, we get:

$$N_i = N_{0,i} + N_i \{B_i{}^* C\} \qquad\qquad 6.4$$

with $N_{0,i}$ representing the 'core' entitlement ratio vector.

Certain important implications related to gender disparities immediately follow from this rather abstract representation of entitlement-endowment relationship. One important result relates to the role of female labour participation (FLP). In the context of this study, FLP is the most important component of $(d.v)_2$. If it is high, $N_j \{b_j{}^* C\}$ will be high. Therefore N_j

---

[4] It represents the 'discount' at the household level corresponding to a woman not getting 'a dollar's worth for every dollar that she brings in' (Blumberg, 1991), the working woman in northern India who has to hand over her wages to her mother-in-law (Sharma, 1993) or unmarried Japanese girls who have to hand over their wages to their parents (Johansson, 1996).

will be high even if $N_{0,j}$ is low. In other words, high FLP is a sufficient condition for lesser inequality,[5] a result on which the literature is unanimous (Murthi et al., 1995).

It is also possible on the other hand that $N_{0,j} \rightarrow 1$. In such a case N_j is high even if b_j or C is zero. In other words, where the exchange-independent entitlements ensure high core ratios, FLP is not even a necessary condition for relative entitlements equality. This is a point often made while emphasising the role of cultural factors and is substantiated quantitatively in Chapter 7 while examining the association between FMR and FLP. Transfers, through society or state or a common property regime, can also achieve high $N_{0,j}$.

A stylised anti-female policy

Another insight is obtained by taking elements of the endowment vector in order or importance, i.e., unskilled labour, skilled labour, capital and land. This yields the design of a stylised 'anti-women policy' in a straight-forward manner (Agnihotri, 1992). Such a policy would aim at keeping the exchange-dependent component of entitlements to a minimum and consist of the following elements in order of severity:

- Preventing women's access to land ownership/use.
- Creating institutional difficulties in her ability to be productive with the given parcel of land.
- Preventing access to surplus investable capital.
- Creating institutional difficulties for her entrepreneurship using the capital.
- Preventing access to acquisition of skills.
- Curtailing use opportunity or reduce wages for that skill.
- Preventing access to unskilled labour (not feasible).
- Curtailing wages and employment opportunity.

These elements have been identified in a number of analyses in literature on gender disparities.[6] These have been based on a 'discursive'

[5] Lesser entitlement inequality and therefore lesser survival inequality. This assumption needs to be qualified with a 'ceteris paribus' condition which will include personal factors in particular.

[6] See, for example, Ram (1991) on acquisition of skills of fishing; Agarwal (1985, 1988, 1994) on land ownership, access to land use facilities including credit; Moore (1988: 101) on low wages for identical skilled job and Lessinger (1989) on the constraints on entrepreneurship.

style[7] and are often pursued independently if not in isolation. But the formal elaboration of the entitlement-endowment relationship done here puts these different elements of gender disparities in one coherent framework.[8]

The 'exchange intensity' of different components

The third useful insight is obtained by arranging different elements of the entitlement ratio vector in a descending order of the core component. The more exchange-intensive the concerned entitlement, the lower will be the 'core' component. One can think of air, water, cheap food, costly food, informal health care, formal costly health care, in the given order of exchange intensity. N_0 component for air or water will almost always be unity.[9] But inequality in respect of access to cheaper food and costlier food may differ within the same household. Even with respect to cheaper food, seasonal fluctuations in access and equality cannot be ruled out (Babu et al. 1993; Behrman, 1988, Behrman and Deolalikar, 1990). Similarly, the inequality in respect of access to professional health care can be higher compared to that in calorie intake (Basu 1989: 207). A concrete illustration of this is given by Mitra (1978) who cites the inequalities in respect of access to health care in four villages in Maharashtra (Mitra, 1978: 19–21). The inequalities are the least for free and traditional medical care, less for the traditional low cost health care and the highest for the formal high cost health care.

The differences in the N_0 components and the functional form of N_i {B_i* C} for different elements of the entitlement vectors has, as will be seen, important consequences. Before analysing this aspect it is necessary to look at the allocational process within a household.

---

[7] Kabeer (in p.c.) uses this term to distinguish it from more 'formal' and technical style of analysis. There appears to be some tension between these two styles although my experience which is borne out in both parts of this chapter is that the two together have a synergy which has often been overlooked.

[8] The search for a 'general theory of gender stratification' has much to gain from this approach and vice versa. Various elements of the 'anti-women policy' listed here find considerable parallels (Blumberg 1991 Chapter 4). But pursuing this issue is out of the scope of the present study.

[9] Except in the case of 'singularities' like denial of oxygen to the new born child (also known as infanticide).

III

Bargaining and conflict

In its simpler form,[10] the bargaining problem between two members of a stylised household uses the notion of status quo or a breakdown solution which will depend upon the fall-back position of the two individuals. The fall-back position decides their bargaining strength. Bargaining involves transition to a new state. There will be a variety of different possible new states from which one has to be selected. The states in which both members are worse off, called the 'dominated collusive solutions', will be rejected as bargaining will not be worthwhile. The status quo will prevail. The undominated collusive solutions will differ in terms of how much better these are for one member or the other. Most often these will be more beneficial to one member than the other . The decision to select one of these is the one that introduces the element of conflict.

Different alternatives have been suggested for resolution of this conflict and selection of one of the undominated collusive solutions. Kanbur and Haddad (1994) analyse one possible solution in their stylised two-member household. The two members agree to increase the size of the cake from S to X. S is the size of the cake if they do not cooperate and each is left with a share of s_1 and s_2 which represent the fall-back position in the event of non-cooperation. But now $X > S$, bargaining is worthwhile and the issue at hand is how to distribute the cake.

One representation of the Nash bargaining outcome is the solution to the following problem:

$$\text{Max } (x_1 - s_1)(x_2 - s_2) \qquad \qquad 6.5a$$
$$\text{s.t. } x_1 + x_2 = X \qquad \qquad 6.5b$$

where the allocation of each person is given by x_1 and x_2.
The solution to this problem turns out to be:

$$x_1 = (s_1 - s_2)/2 + X/2 \qquad \qquad 6.6a$$
$$x_2 = (s_2 - s_1)/2 + X/2 \qquad \qquad 6.6b$$

---

[10] Introduced originally by Nash and extended among others by Sen (1987), and Kanbur and Haddad (1994). Also see Dasgupta (1993: Chapter 11) for more detailed discussion of these models.

A rearrangement of 2.1 and 2.2 reveals that:

$$(x_1 - s_1) = (x_2 - s_2) = (X - S)/2 \qquad\qquad 6.6c$$

In other words the increment in the size of the cake will be shared by the two members equally. Such a distribution will rarely take place in real life. It tacitly assumes that both members make equal contribution to the increment in the size of the cake.[11] This will often not be the case. Intuitively, a distribution of this increment is more likely to take place in the ratio of s_1/s_2 rather than in equal proportions. Another likely possibility is that the increment X–S is distributed in the ratio of c_1/c_2 where c_1 and c_2 are the contributions made by the two members. In that case:

$$(x_1 - s_1)/(x_2 - s_2) = c_1/c_2 \qquad\qquad 6.6d$$

While this may appear quite an appealing possibility, it is beset with measurement and perception problems. How is the contribution made by the women to be valued and by whom?

The cooperative conflict

Sen (1987a) brings in the role of perceptions about the contributions made and the importance attached by different members to their wellbeing. These perceptions affect the allocative behaviour in an important way. Three propostitions are made about the outcome of the bargaining (Sen, 1987: 24–25):

- Breakdown wellbeing response. Given other things, if the breakdown position of one person were worse in terms of wellbeing, then the collusive solution, if different, would be less favourable to his or her wellbeing.
- Perceived interest response. Given other things, if the self-interest perception of one of the persons were to attach less value to his or her own wellbeing, then the collusive solution, if different, will be less favourable to that person, in terms of wellbeing.

---

[11] This is the result of one of the assumptions of Nash bargaining which is unduly restrictive. Dasgupta (1993: 339) suggests that the maximisation problem in 6.5a can be more generally and appropriately be stated as: Max $(x_1-s_1)^a (x_2-s_2)^b$ where a and b are positive constants and b/a is a measure of relative 'bargaining strength'.

- Perceived contribution response: Given other things, if in the accounting of the respective outcomes, a person was perceived as making a larger contribution to the overall opulence of the group, then the collusive solution, if different, will be more favourable to that person.

These 'directional features' (Sen 1990: 134) open up the possibility of considering the role of perceptions and more importantly power which shapes these perceptions (Kabeer 1995: 5). The earlier formulations of the bargaining games treat the fall-back position as determined by wealth or income of the concerned members, like s_1 and s_2, representing the fall-back position in the example given earlier. The breakdown wellbeing response, recognises the role of threats and exercise of physical violence. It is important to make the distinction between 'physical security' and 'exchange security' (Agnihotri, 1992: Chapter 2) in terms of wellbeing. The latter provides a necessary condition for stronger fall-back position while the latter provides only a weak sufficiency condition. A woman factory worker may be 'exchange secure' and yet get beaten by her drunken husband, i.e., be physically insecure. This will result in a weaker bargaining position not commensurate with her 'perceived contributions'. It is not that such a physical security is 'biologically' determined; social practices and patterns contribute strongly to it (Dasgupta 1993; Kabeer, 1995).

Shaping perceptions

This brings one to the process of socialisation (Folbre, 1986: 252). Socialisation can create conditions where the 'underdog comes to accept the legitimacy of the unequal order and becomes an implicit accomplice' (Sen, 1987b: 7). It shapes the perceptions of different individuals from early childhood (Johansson, 1996; Papanek 1990). Even in simulation exercises (game theory) differential response of members on the basis of gender has been recorded (Eckel and Grossman, 1994). This point is of crucial importance when considering the effect of cultural factors on entitlement asymmetries.

Perceptions remain crucial even when it comes to the contributions. Differentiation made by Agarwal between reproductive labour and direct productive labour is relevant here (Agarwal, 1985: 70–73). Collecting fuel wood for use in the household can be perceived to be of little significance no matter how much time and energy is spent on it. The same fuel when sold in the market is considered to be a significant activity. Such differences in perception are not confined to the households alone, they can significantly affect policies. Changes in the definition of working females in the Indian census operations between 1961 and 1981 illustrate this.[12]

Sen attaches considerable importance to the process of visibility in the evaluation of contributions. Gainful employment outside the house is an important part of such 'visibility' for him. These give women '(*a*) a better breakdown position (*b*) possibly a clearer perception of her individuality and wellbeing and (*c*) a higher 'perceived contribution' to the family's economic position' (1990: 144).

The importance of the perceived contribution or 'women's relative economic power' has also been highlighted by Blumberg in her 'general theory of gender stratification' (1991: 100–101). But she also highlights the ability of the 'macro level' controlled mostly by men, 'to act as a kind of discount rate on the exercise of women's relative power at the 'macro level'. This aspect is present in Kabeer (1991) who criticises Sen for emphasising on the visible contributions and ignoring the role of 'invisible' contributions. Recognition of exchange-independent components of entitlements satisfactorily incorporates the view points of both Blumberg and Kabeer.

Elements of e-mapping, i.e., the 'core entitlements ratios', the distortion parameter, and the value vectors relate to the power dimension of the allocational process. These are formed on the basis of long term processes. These elements and through these the perceptions, are formed by a process of repeated bargaining and feedback. It is necessary to look at this aspect of the entitlements issue in some details.

IV

Bargaining and inequality

The links between entitlements ratios and the inequality within the household can be explored further following the analysis by Kanbur and Haddad. Within the stylised two-member household one can assume,

---

[12] These changes have been discussed by Vannemann and Barnes (1992) in the Indian Development District Database (Appendix V-6, Economic Activities).

without any loss of generality that $s_1 > s_2$. The inequality within the household can then be measured by the deviation from half of the better-off individual's share of the cake. In other words:

$$I = (x_1/x) - 1/2 = (x_1 - x_2)/2x = (s_1 - s_2)/2x \qquad 6.7a$$

Three observations are made by Kanbur and Haddad from the above equation:

- The inequality between s_1 and s_2 is always greater than that between x_1 and x_2 (as $X > S$).
- When the inequality between s_1 and s_2 increases then, *ceteris paribus*, the inequality between x_1 and x_2 increases.
- When X increases, *ceteris paribus*, the inequality between x_1 and x_2 decreases.

Kanbur and Haddad consider the last point as particularly important which says that 'an increase in total household resources will, other things being equal, lead to a fall in inequality'. They call it a basic point, 'the intuition being that since it is the surplus above the threat point that is divided equally in the symmetric Nash bargaining solution, as this surplus grows, the allocation approaches equal shares' (Kanbur and Haddad, 1994: 449). This intuitive understanding is clear as $(x_1 - s_1)$ and $(x_2 - s_2)$ both are equal to $(X-S)/2$. It can also be seen that the absolute difference between the pieces of the cake will remain same in both the cases as $(x_1 - x_2) = (s_1 - s_2)$.

The other possible solution considered earlier where $x_1/x_2 = s_1/s_2$ leaves the inequality intact as:

$$I = (x_1/X) - 1/2 = (x_1 - x_2)/2X = (s_1 - s_2)/2S \qquad 6.7b$$

This distribution may benefit the dominated member in absolute terms and yet keep the inequality intact.

The more likely case that the increment X–S is distributed in the ratio of c_1/c_2, the contributions made by the two members gives:

$$(x_1 - s_1)/x_2 - s_2) = c_1/c_2 \qquad 6.8a$$

If the contribution made by the woman is w and that by the man is 1–w, we get:

$$(x_1 - s_1)/x_2 - s_2) = (1 - w)/w \qquad\qquad \text{6.8bi}$$

Two results immediately follow:

i) $$(x_1 - s_1) - (x_2 - s_2) = (1 - 2w)(X - S) \qquad\qquad \text{6.8bii}$$

This means that the gap between the shares $(x_1 - s_1)$ and $(x_2 - s_2)$ increases if $w < 1/2$ as long the woman's contribution is less than half.

ii) The inequality $I' = (x_1 - x_2)/2X$ is less than the inequality $I = (s_1 - s_2/2S$ if $w > s_2/s$, i.e., the inequality will reduce only if the contribution made by the woman to the increment X–S exceeds her fall-back share.

This representation can be used further to analyse the repeated bargaining process. Bargaining within the household is rarely a one-off situation. One can have a simple model of non-consumptive accumulation of the cake which increases from a size S_0 to a size S_n at the end of nth round of bargaining. For simplicity, the contribution made by the woman or w can be held constant across these rounds. In that case, x_1 and x_2 will provide the fall-back position for the next round of bargaining and so on. The two results shown here will continue to hold.

The representation of allocation is more realistic compared to either of the two cases mentioned earlier, that is one where the increment is equally divided (Kanbur and Haddad, 1994) or the one where it is always divided in the ratio of s_1/s_2 leaving no chance of changing the inequality. The role of contribution becomes important here and the change in inequality depends upon the contributions made.[13]

The inequality vector

For a single entitlement, N_i is same as the ratio x_2/x_1. In reality, however, the inequality I will be a vector with I components corresponding to the I components of the entitlement vector. The N_0 values will be different for

---

[13] If the wife feels that the gains from the joint utility maximisation will not benefit her proportionate to her contribution, she may refuse to participate in increasing the size of the cake even when $x > s$. This is precisely the case reported by Jones (1983) in Cameroon where the wives refused to work on their husbands' irrigated rice fields when they felt that they would not be adequately compensated for their efforts!

different components as also the functional form of $N_i\{b*C\}$. Where the core entitlement ratio is high the inequality will be less. The core ratio, however, is likely to reduce as exchange intensity of a given element increases. It will then depend more and more upon the effective exchange component.

In a repeated bargaining process, described earlier, the distribution of the increment will take place in accordance with the equation 6.4, that is:

$$N_i = N_{0,i} + N_i\{B_i * C\} \qquad 6.4$$

rather than its special case: $(x_1 - s_1)/(x_2 - s_2) = c_1/c_2$ where c_1/c_2 is nothing but the equivalent of $(d.v)_2/(d.v)_1$. The perceived contribution by the woman can get further 'devalued' through the distortion parameter b_j.

The scalar expression for the inequality I can be extended to its vector counterpart by expressing:

$$I = (x_1/x) - 1/2 = (x_1 - x_2)/2x \qquad 6.9a$$
$$\text{or, } I = (x_1/2x)(1 - x_2/x_1) \qquad 6.9b$$

x_1/X is the male share of the concerned entitlement and x_2/x_1 is the female to male ratio of that entitlement. If x_1/X is expressed as M then the expression for I_j, the jth component of the inequality vector can be expressed as:

$$I_j = M_j(1 - N_j)/2 = M_j(1 - N_{0,j} - N_j\{b_j * C\})/2 \qquad 6.10$$

The maximum inequality will be $I = 1/2$ when the male share of the entitlement is 100 per cent and the female share zero.[14] When both have equal share, $I = 0$.

V

Beyond entitlements

Extension of the scalar expression for inequality within the household into its vector form is an important step forward. First, it recognises that

---

[14] It is possible to normalise I_{max} to unity. But that is not of much relevance here.

inequalities in respect of different components of entitlements in the commodity space will be different. Relative equality in calorie consumption can co-exist with an inequality in protein consumption or access to health care or the other way round. These inequalities can combine in many different ways to produce a similar outcome in terms of longevity.

Interdependence of inequalities

Another important point that emerges relates to the sex differentials in mortality. For these, it is the inequality in a given component that is more crucial than the equality in others. In fact, critical inequality in any of the components of entitlement can negate the relative equality in all other components. This interdependence is like that of different links in a chain. *The chain of survival snaps at its weakest link and not at the strongest link.*[15]

A considerable amount of debate has taken place, however, about the primacy of one inequality over the other, for example, the debate on the relative importance of inequality in consumption of calories vis-à-vis that in health care (e.g., Basu, 1992 or the review in Harriss, 1989). Such debate overlooks the fact that either of the inequality can create higher mortality. Substantiating the links between, say, inequality in access to health care and sex differentials in mortality in one sub-sample would not negate the links between inequality in calorie consumption and mortality differentials in another sub-sample.

Use of the inequality vector in the space of entitlements informs a third issue; that of absolute and relative levels of entitlements. It is argued that an increase in overall prosperity of the household, could benefit the dominated member in absolute terms even if the relative inequality increases. What needs to be recognised here is that the extent of the gains made by the two members will differ from component to component. Further, as indicated earlier, the gains made by the dominant member will be higher in respect of exchange-intensive commodities. *The inequality in, say, access to modern health care, can create far greater sex differentials in mortality than relative equality in, say, calorie consumption can compensate* for. This would aggravate the relative survival inequality while conferring gains on both the groups *in absolute terms.*

---

[15] Such an interdependence can be crudely captured through the function:

$E_R = \pi E_j$ for $j = 1$ to j.

E_R, the resultant equality will tend to zero if any of the equality goes to zero. Summation functions do not capture this interdependence. (Sen accepts this suggestion in the context of aggregating the entitlement inequalities: personal discussions, 1996).

Choice of a suitable space

This distinction between different components of the inequality vector raises a new issue: the appropriateness of the space in which the inequality is examined. Should it be the space of commodities or the space of wellbeing? Haddad and Kanbur (1992) focus on calorie consumption inequality and examine changes in it as the overall prosperity within the household increases. But one should not assume on this basis that the rest of the inequalities behave similarly and simultaneously. At a given level of prosperity, inequalities in respect of different elements of entitlements will differ in nature and the outcome inequalities will be quite different from any one of these inequalities. In the present context, where the sex differentials in mortality is the issue under consideration, focus on any one of the input inequalities is clearly a misspecification of the problem. One needs to look at the inequality in the space of outcomes for that is what ultimately matters. Sen (1992) makes out a detailed and convincing case for selecting the inequality in the space of functionings as the relevant focal variable. Dasgupta (1993) too favours the study of the outcome variables.

The capabilities approach (Sen 1985) looks at outcomes in what is formally termed as the space of functionings. It links this space to the space of entitlements. This approach not only recognises the one to many relationship between the two spaces, it also introduces a very important consideration: that of human diversity. Entitlements tell us only a part of the story. How people convert these entitlements into wellbeing depends upon their personal features and circumstances.

This aspect is discussed by Johansson (1991) in an interesting way. She considers how relative welfare is transformed into relative mortality. She highlights the complex and context-dependent influence of biological, environmental and social factors on sex differentials in mortality. Two points become clear: (*a*) The proximate determinants of mortality differentials can be numerous and their relationship complex and historical and (*b*) mortality outcome depends on both welfare levels and personal circumstances. Viewing sex ratio patterns as expressions of asymmetry in the space of functionings, incorporates both welfare levels and personal features in the analysis.

But functionings or a person's actual achievement are only a subset of what the person is capable of achieving. The larger set or the ability to achieve represents the capability set or simply the capabilities of a person. This is elaborated formally.

In order to get a more complete understanding of inequalities in the space of functionings, it is necessary to link the spaces of functionings, commodities and endowments. This is done using the entitlement-endowment relationship developed in the previous sections. This links an outcome in the space of functionings to personal features, the core component of entitlement, exchange-dependent components of entitlements and endowments of a person.

This bridges an important gap in the literature between the capabilities approach and the entitlements framework. These two approaches have surprisingly been pursued independent of each other in the past even though the commodity space provides a common link between the two. The linkage elaborated here offers new insights into the process of feedback between endowments, entitlements and functionings. This is important not only from the analytical point of view but also has relevance for policy-making.

To do so, however, the capabilities approach needs certain modifications. One of these relate to the issue of evaluation of a person's capabilities, whether such evaluation is done in relative terms or absolute terms. This is of critical relevance to the present analysis as it forms the basis of disaggregation of sex ratio data.

Outcomes in the space of functionings are probabilistic. As such, the range of feasible functionings can only be inferred through a larger population sample. However, such a range and the distribution within it can significantly differ between different sub-samples drawn up on the basis of different identities like gender, age, caste, or location. This makes the evaluation of the functionings or the capabilities both sample specific and context specific. This aspect is elaborated formally by introducing a new concept of 'range' in the space of functioning.

Context dependent nature of distribution in the space of functionings provides a satisfactory basis for disaggregation of a larger sample along different identities. A two way exchange of information appears feasible. Known identities can be used to locate different patterns in the space of functionings. Conversely, patterns in the space of functionings can be used to infer relevant identities. A formal recognition of this two-way flow of information has important methodological implications.

Inequalities in the space of functionings depend upon *asymmetries in personal features, exchange-independent components* of entitlements and *exchange-related components* of entitlements. In the mortality context, these broadly correspond to the *biological, socio-cultural and economic factors*. Their explicit recognition leads to the disaggregation of sex ratio data based on these factors. Empirical investigation at these levels of disaggregation, carried out in previous chapters, have already provided new and useful insights about the sex ratio problem. But their basis did not have an analytical sanction. Analysis presented here provides such a sanction.

Organisation of the discussion

Section VI reviews Johansson's framework for context specific and historical nature of sex differentials in mortality. Section VII elaborates upon the concept of capabilities and the link between the space of functionings and the space of entitlements. Integration of the entitlements framework and the capabilities approach is discussed in Section VIII as also the process of feedback. The context-dependent nature of the capabilities is discussed next (section IX) paving the way for disaggregation of sex ratio data along useful criterion discussed in the final section.

VI

Welfare to longevity

In a thought provoking review of changing explanations of sex differentials in mortality over three centuries, Johansson raises two important questions: how is relative welfare transformed into relative longevity (1991: 135) and whether the relationship between biology, welfare and longevity is simple and timeless or complex and historical (1991: 140). Both these questions are pertinent to this study for sex differentials in mortality determine the sex ratio of a population.

Using a simple framework, Johansson (1991: 138–39) establishes the context-dependent nature of sex differentials in mortality. From a very basic biological standpoint, mortality is influenced by two broad factors: exposure patterns and resistance levels. Exposure refers to any of the factors resulting in biological damage while resistance refers to a person's innate or acquired capacity to resist such exposure. Both factors can vary by gender: Patterns and levels of exposure could depend upon gendered roles performed by men and women: resistance could depend upon access to suitable resources to acquire and enhance such resistance.

Exposure levels between two groups can be compared through three simple categories: greater than, similar to and less than. The same holds for the resistance levels. These three logical possibilities combine to give nine biological possibilities for sex differentials in mortality (Table 6.2). These can range from high excess female mortality to high excess male mortality to, equality of mortality.[16] Similar mortality levels can themselves arise in three different sets of conditions. Different societies can display, at different times, any of these combinations depending upon sex differentials in exposure levels and in resistance to exposure.

Table 6.2
Sex differentials in exposure, resistance and mortality

Resistance differentials (female–male)	Exposure differentials (female–male)		
	Higher	Equal	Lower
Higher	Mortality equality	Moderate excess male mortality	High excess male mortality
Equal	Moderate excess female mortality	Mortality equality	Moderate excess male mortality
Lower	High excess female mortality	Moderate excess female mortality	Mortality equality

Both exposure and resistance depend upon a complex interaction between various biological, environmental and socio-economic factors. Two illustrative representations of these factors and interactions are shown in Figures 6.1 (Johansson, 1987: 213) and 6.2 (Pacey and Payne, 1985: 103). Figure 6.1 describes various factors which influence levels of exposure and resistance to these. Figure 6.2 illustrates different factors and their interactions in shaping the health of a child. These clearly suggest that any understanding of sex differentials in mortality or sex ratio patterns for that matter, must be context specific and historical and not context neutral and ahistorical.

---

[16] Mortality equality is defined as male to female mortality ratio within 10 per cent of each other, moderate excess when they are within 20 per cent of each other and high excess when they differ beyond 20 per cent (Johansson, 1991: 139).

Protection From Exposure = Natural protection + Protection achieved through investment at:		
Ecological level	**Community level**	**Household level**
Density	PUBLIC HEALTH	Personal cleanliness
Isolation	Water quality	Food preparation and storage
Altitude	Food quality	–
Climate	Human waste removal	Human waste disposal
Insects	Garbage/dirt removal	Household cleanliness
Snakes, etc	Pest control/eradication	–
Micro flora	Air quality	–
Micro fauna	Working conditions	–
	Immunisation campaigns	Cooperation with health
	Quarantines	measures
	HEALTH INFORMATION	Receptivity to new information
	PREVENTIVE MEDICINE	Regular health check-ups
	Control of toxic substances	Avoidance of toxic substances
Resistance to/recovery from exposure = Natural resistance + Resistance achieved through investment at:		
Biological level	**Community level**	**Household level**
Genetically determined characteristics of the immune system and cell mediated resistance	Hospital care sanatoria etc. antibiotics/vaccination medical care/information	Home nursing care Purchase of medicines Receptivity to information
	Welfare measures	Living standards
Virulence of pathogens	Financial aid, social support	Nutrition
	for victims of episodic or	Housing/space and warmth
	chronic 'stress', deprivation	Clothing
	disasters (famine, war, etc.)	Leisure, emotional support
		Security

Figure 6.1: Illustrative determinants of protection from exposure and resistance to diseases. **Source**: Johansson, 1987: 213.

It is also clear from the two figures that access to material resources alone does not determine mortality. Personal factors and circumstances have an important role to play in it. Absorption of nutrients between two children can, for example, differ by as much as 9 per cent on account of intestinal dysfunction (Harriss, 1990: 371). Clearly an identical

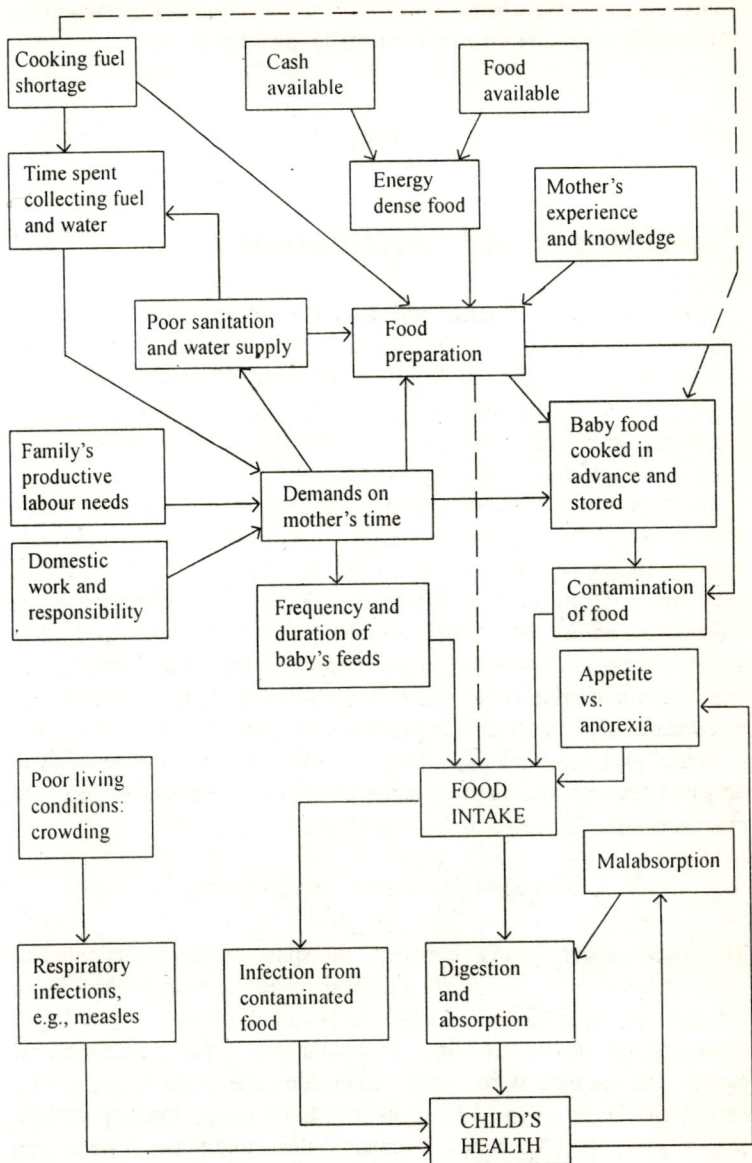

Figure 6.2: Illustrative complexity of factors affecting health outcome.
Source: Payne and Pacey (1985: 103).

consumption of nutrients will not produce the same outcome for them. Human diversity has to be taken into account therefore, to see how welfare differentials are transformed into mortality differentials.

VII

Capabilities and functionings

Human diversity is a fact of life; a fact which impinges upon many outcomes, not just mortality. The outcome of an identical command over a given resource bundle can differ for differently situated individuals or the same individual at different points of time. An identical diet can produce quite different results for, say, a farm labourer, a nursing mother, a school teacher and a company executive.

The capabilities approach (Sen, 1985) takes human diversity into account explicitly. It recognises that different persons perform differently even if their 'entitlements' are similar. An outcome, for example mortality, in the space of 'functionings', is influenced by the personal features which affect one's ability to convert entitlements into certain outcomes. Any systematic asymmetry in such an outcome between two sub-samples of a population can arise either due to asymmetry in their command over resources or asymmetry in their personal circumstances. Sex differentials in mortality is one such asymmetry. It could arise from differences in personal features, like the resistance levels, or differences in access to resources affecting survival, like health care.

Capabilities and functioning

The space of functioning represents the space of accomplishment of different individuals. Longevity is a basic dimension in this space. There are other important dimensions like the health of a person, her ability to attain a given standard of education, communicate, participate in social events, and the like. With n such dimensions, the 'state of being' of a person can be represented by a point in the n-dimensional space or a 'being' vector b_i for person I. It indicates the actual position I occupies along different dimensions: the level of education, the state of health, extent of participation in social events and so on.

Functionings only indicates what the person has actually done. But that does not tell the entire story. The possible range of such points in the space of functioning which the person could have occupied, gives more complete information about his state of being. This set of 'being' vectors b_i is called the 'capability' of an individual. In other words, while functioning represents the actual achievement, capability refers to the ability or the freedom to achieve.

The capability set (From Sen, 1985)

Formally let
x_i = the vector of commodities controlled by 'I',
$c(.)$ = a function that converts the commodity vector into a vector of characteristics of those commodities,
$f_i(.)$ = a personal 'utilisation function' of 'I' reflecting one pattern of use of x_i that 'I' can actually make out of a set F_i of all f_i.
The achieved functions of 'I' will be given by the 'being' vector:

$$b_i = f_i \{c(x_i)\} \qquad\qquad 6.11a$$

The set of all b_is for a given commodity vector x_i is given by:

$$P_i(x_i) = [b_i 1 b_i = f_i (c(x_i)) \text{ for some } f_i | F_i] \qquad\qquad 6.11b$$

If the choice of commodity vector is enlarged to $x_i | X_i$ which represents the person's entitlements, then the set of all b_is for 'I', given his personal features F_i and entitlements X_i will be given by:

$$Q_i (X_i) = [b_i 1 b_i = f_i (c(x_i)) \text{ for some } f_i | F_i, \text{ and, some } x_i | X_i \qquad 6.11c$$

Q_i the 'capability' of I represents his freedom to achieve certain being b_i out of the overall 'feasible' set of b_is.[17]

---

[17] The notion of freedom is important. It is quite likely that a person's being may remain the same in two different circumstances in which the freedom of choice may substantially differ. Let the 'wellbeing' be defined by certain maximal element, say, $b(*)$ for a given capability $Q_i (F_i, X_i)$. It is quite possible that the wellbeing defined above may remain the same in a different situation (F_i', X_i') where the capability Q_i' still contains the maximal element $b(*)$ but the set of b_i s is sharply reduced. The ability or freedom to achieve can get reduced without affecting the wellbeing.

It is easy to note the correspondence between X_i in the commodity space and Q_i in the space of functioning. There is an element of choice in selecting $x(I) \mid X(I)$. This is also true for $b(I) \mid Q(I)$. Once again if we envisage an n-dimensional space of functionings, b_i will be represented by a point in that space and Q_i will be represented by the set of all such possible points that I could have occupied.[18]

For a given $x(I)$ there is a set of b_i I $P_i(x_i)$ to choose from, given one's personal circumstances. $P_i(.)$ is remarkable similar to $E(.)$ and although literature does not invoke a P-mapping, it appears plausible to use such a term which represents the mapping from the space of commodities to the space of functionings. In other words $Q_i(X_i)$ can be expressed as:

$$Q_i(X_i) = [f_i 1 f_i = P_i (c(x_i)) \text{ for some } f_i \mid F_i, \text{ and, some } x_i \mid X_i \qquad 6.12$$

The function $P(.)$ transforms a given commodity vector into a vector of being. One can use as broad a definition for $P(.)$ as the one used for $E(.)$. However, this and some of the other issues discussed elsewhere[19] are not germane to the immediate next task; that of linking the three spaces of functionings, commodities and entitlements. This is discussed next.

VIII

Linking the two approaches

As seen above, the capabilities approach deals with the issue of distribution in the space of functionings, given certain entitlements. It links the space of functionings with that of commodities through P-mapping. Similarly, entitlements framework deals with the issue of distribution in the space of commodities linking it to the space of endowments through E-mapping.

It appears quite logical that the two approaches can be brought together for connecting the space of functionings, commodities and endowments.

---

[18] This set will correspond to the volume bound by an n-1 dimensional surface representing the maximum values of individual functionings subject to conditions of correaliasability. The trouble, however, is what equivalent of 'budget constraint' to chose from. This methodological and philosophical point is well beyond the scope of the present discussion. The close similarity between X_i in the commodity space and Q_i in the space of functioning is, however, intuitively clear, once stated.

[19] Sen, in p.c. (1996).

But such a possibility has somehow been overlooked so far. The entitlements framework has been used to discuss problems of resource distribution in specific contexts while the capabilities approach has been used to discuss issues of wellbeing, freedom and equality.[20]

The linkage between these three spaces is warranted in its own right analytically but it also has considerable practical utility. It is basically a person's endowments that translate into entitlements resulting in certain outcomes in the space of functionings. This sequence can be represented in a simple manner as:

$$\text{Functionings} \leftarrow P(.) \ \{\text{Entitlements}\} \leftarrow E(.) \ \{\text{Endowments}\}$$

An interesting link emerges immediately. What shapes the endowments of a person? The functionings. A person's ability to work depends upon her ability to be adequately nourished. But it is her ability to work that entitles her to nourishment! The sequence shown above is not open ended. There is a feedback operating here. Functionings of today are decided by endowments of yesterday but they in turn determine the endowments of tomorrow. This feedback is not apparent until the three spaces are linked together but is obvious the moment these are linked. This is illustrated in Figure 6.3. Elements of the endowment vector transform into those of entitlements through E-mapping. The elements of commodity vector transform into those of functionings through P-mapping and feedback into the person's endowment. The elements of functionings aggregate into wellbeing but that is a separate issue; discussed elsewhere (Footnote 4).

Dynamic aspects of wellbeing

The importance of this link, although obvious by hindsight, cannot be emphasised enough. Entitlements approach and the cooperative–conflict models have looked at the temporal aspects of the bargaining process and the inequality within the household for quite some time. But none of these discussions have proceeded with the formalism of the framework. Even if the technical aspect of the matrix-matrix mapping mentioned by

---

[20] For entitlements see Gasper (1993) for an exhaustive review, Kabeer (1991, 1995) in the gender context and Sen (1981) in the context of hunger. For capabilities see Sen (1985) in general, Sen (1987c, 1992) for discussions on wellbeing and freedom and Periera, J. 1993 in the context of health.

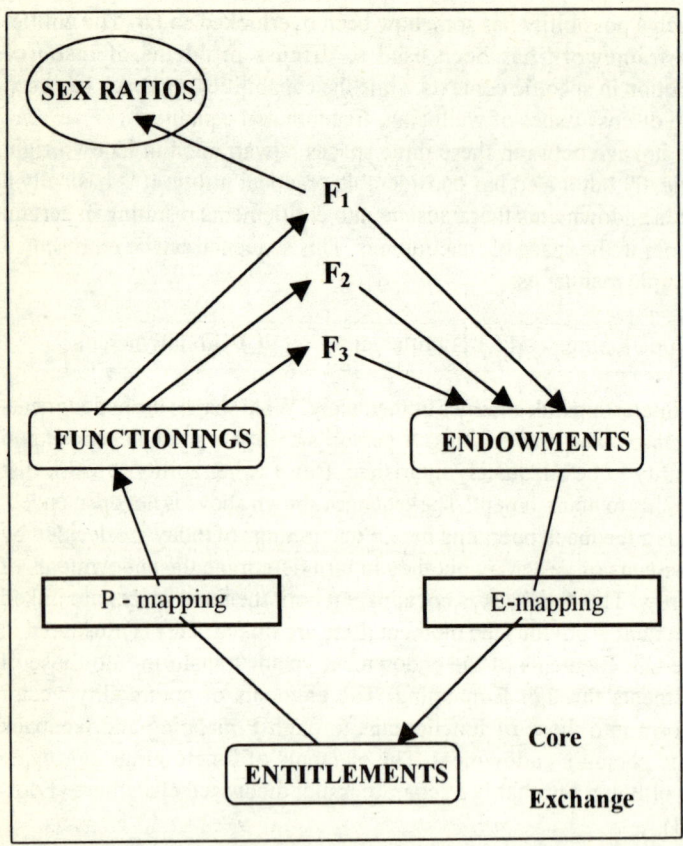

Figure 6.3: Functionings, entitlements and endowments— links in a chain.

Sen (1990: 143) were solved, the entitlement-endowment relationship could not be dynamised, for, it is not the entitlements of a person that directly feedback into the endowments of that person. Such feedback comes through the space of functionings. Any analysis of the feedback process had to, therefore, link these three processes. It is astonishing that this had not been done so far. Jettisoning formalism in favour of qualitative discussions, is in my opinion, one major reason for this 'omission'.[21]

[21] In p.c., both Sugden, who has thoroughly reviewed 'Inequality Re-examined' (Sen, 1992) and Sen himself, agreed that linking the three spaces appears quite straightforward (almost trivial), of course by hindsight, and wondered why it was not done so far. I wonder to what extent my having a background in Physics (and not 'Economics') helped in this process. Also see discussion in Chapter 9 section II).

Linking inequalities in the three spaces

Be that as it may, the link elaborated here provides one possible way of linking the inequalities in the three spaces. The entitlement inequality in resource allocation depends upon the 'core' entitlement ratios, endowment ratios and different distortions which are part of E-mapping. Further, the components of the commodity vector can be arranged in increasing order of their exchange intensity where 'core' portion will gradually decline and the exchange intensive component will become more and more dominant. As such one can express it as:

$$I(f_1) = I \{I[P(.)], I(x_1), I(x_2), \dots I(x_n)\}$$
$$= I\{I[P(.), I\{x_i 0, x_i \{b(D.V)\}\} \quad 6.13$$

This expression enables one to identify different sources of asymmetry in the space of functionings viz., personal features, 'core' entitlements, endowments, E-mapping and P-mapping. *In the specific context of mortality, these correspond to the biological [P(.)], socio-cultural [x_i 0] and the economic [x_i{b(D.V)] aspects* representing various 'slips between the cup and the lip' that is, the 'cup' of equality in the space of functionings and the 'lips' of 'I'.

A given asymmetry in the space of endowments may get corrected through the $x_{i,0}$ components in the space of entitlements. Conversely an equality in endowments may get aggravated through E(.), undervaluation of female labour being a clear example. Likewise the entitlement asymmetries in the space of commodities may get modified through P(.) into the space of functionings.[22]

But this also offers scope of plurality of interventions to bring about changes in the pattern of inequality in the space of functionings. Endowments asymmetry can, for example, be corrected through higher $x_{i,0}$ components, for example, through transfers. But the interventions will also have their limitations. Some of the functionings may change very slowly with time, like physical growth, some may change rapidly while others may need technological or social intervention.

---

[22] Kabeer (1991) differentiates, for example, between biological wellbeing and economic wellbeing. The relative economic inequality and biological inequality need not be the same.

IX

Capability and its context

Evaluation of the capabilities can, however, not be context-independent. It is human diversity once again, that makes evaluation of capabilities context specific. While the freedom to achieve certain functionings is relevant, it is equally relevant to consider what this freedom is being compared to. In isolation the concept of capability will not mean much; it is to be evaluated against a 'norm'. A life span of 52 years will have completely different meaning depending upon the 'norm' of average life expectancy in the society one is living in. Such 'norms' will be context-specific and not context-independent. Most discussion in literature tacitly presumes that the identity of I, is the same for all I's concerned. In reality, however human beings have different and multiple identities which is indeed one of the basic themes of the capabilities approach. It is necessary to take this into account.

Range—The missing link

Given the personal features, there is a choice of functionings $f_i | F_i$ and $x_i | X_i$. But it is not possible to put the same person through all the counterfactuals $f_i | F_i$ and $x_i | X_i$. An idea of feasible functionings will, therefore, have to be obtained by looking at a larger sample. Assuming for a moment that all persons in this sample had identical personal features, one will obtain a range, say, F_0–F, with certain distribution. This distribution will correspond to the probability of any 'I' occupying a given position between F_0–F in respect of that functioning. Taking the example of longevity again, it would be distributed within, say 0–80 years for all I's with similar personal factors.[23]

This distribution and range takes care of the stochastic and choice variations in the space of functionings keeping the personal factors constant. If this condition is relaxed, that is, variations in personal factors

---

[23] The terms, features, factors and circumstances have all been used to describe the person-specific aspects. In the literature on capabilities the use of any specific term has not crystallised yet as the issue of P-mapping has not been raised so far. Till this happens some vagueness will persist in terms of using any of the three terms interchangeably.

are taken into account, then the range F_0–F will be part of a larger range R_0–R such that $F \mid R$. This wider range of outcome arises in a sample covering a wider range of personal features. One can evaluate f_i or Q_i either with respect to the range F_0–F, or, with respect to the range R_0–R.

The example of longevity can again help concretise this point. It is possible to evaluate the longevity of a woman against a sample of all women from, say, Uttar Pradesh or, Kerala. One could also enlarge the sample to women from north India or India as a whole or Asia for that matter. The age distribution and range would differ and evaluation of the life span will depend upon the choice of the sample. Unlike inanimate particles, like electrons, human beings have multiple identities and their distribution in the space of functionings will depend upon these identities.[24] Identity invariance of the distribution will be a special and infrequent case. Further, even for similar individuals, this distribution will differ between different functionings, like mortality and levels of education.

In formal terms, for an individual 'I' and a given functioning 'j'; $f_{ij} \mid F_{ij}$ $\mid R_{ij} \mid R$, where $R_{ij} \mid R$ represents the sample $s_j \mid S$; the larger sample from which number of sub-samples s_j are drawn. Such sub-samples can be selected through a number of 'identities', like class, gender, caste, location and so on. S could, for example, represent the total Indian population while s_j can represent the tribal or the non-tribal population.

Relativism versus absolutism

This brings up the debate between absolutism and relativism in the space of functionings. The value of different functionings is time and culture specific. The ability of a girl to play the piano is viewed quite differently in England and in China. Again, in England today it does not mean the same thing as it did in the Victorian era. But Sen argues against such relativism or total relativism at least. To him, certain basic functionings are of absolute importance even if the deprived person does not recognise these as such. Coming to terms with certain deprivations is a coping strategy for many a people and one cannot justify their perpetuation merely because these are culturally acceptable, like foot binding practices in China (Papanek, 1990) or bride burning in India.

---

[24] In the case of electrons, any sub-sample of say one million electrons out of a larger sample of ten million electrons will display identical statistical behaviour, but that will not be the case for a sub-sample of one million people with specific identities, drawn from a larger sample of ten million people.

The absolute versus relative debate is context specific. When Sen argues against total relativism, he is essentially locating I, for example, a parrot in a cage in a larger sub-sample that includes free parrots. Such counter-factual could well be beyond the perceptions of the 'victim' or the intentions of the 'absolutist'. There are two questions involved here, 'inequality among whom' and 'inequality of what'?

Even the question of 'inequality of what?', is sample or context specific; whether the sample consists only of caged parrots or includes free parrots is important. The wellbeing of caged parrots can still be compared, but freedom will not come into the calculation. The space of functionings will now be a n-1 dimensional space with freedom = 0 held constant. The material of the cage, that is whether it is gold or steel, its size or the diet available will remain relevant. Freedom will not be relevant unless the counterfactual of 'being free' is invoked and compared against being caged.

It is also possible to put the parrots outside the cage. But if some of them do want to come back to the cage, Sen may not have grounds to complain unless he demonstrates that the choice was not 'free'. Such 'tainted' choices are indeed made in real life by the victims. An upper middle class north Indian woman shown in the documentary 'Let her die' (BBC Television, Channel 2) is a case in point. She argues that just as she has the freedom, as a consumer, to chose the colour of her dress, she also has a right to chose the sex of her foetus. While she uses the choice language quite effectively, she is in fact articulating the choice imposed on her by the family into which she has married.

A two-way information exchange

To recapitulate then, evaluation of capabilities is range specific. The range and the distribution within it are, in turn, sample specific. The samples can be selected on the basis of different identities. In some cases, the range and the distribution within it may be identity invariant. In that case, the concerned identity will not be relevant for that functioning. Infant mortality, may for example, show the same range and distribution among, say, the tribal and the non-tribal segments of the population. In that case the identity of the infant, whether tribal or non-tribal is not of consequence. But if the IMR differs significantly between the two groups, the identity becomes important for evaluation and scrutiny.

This enables a two-way exchange of information between the space of functionings and the identities of I. Distribution within the space of functionings can provide useful information about identities that are relevant. Alternatively, if certain identities are known to be distinct, one can look for significant differences in patterns in the space of functionings. In terms of sex ratio patterns, either significant differences can be stipulated on the basis of distinct identities, like caste, class and location or relevant identities can be inferred from the differences revealed by data, like age, as indeed has been done in Chapter 3. The underlying identities and the mechanism through which these affect sex ratios provide suitable areas of inquiry.

Roots of the identities

Identities by themselves will not explain why the range and distributions differ among different sub-samples. But these provide important clues about the processes concerned. Functionings, as seen earlier, depend upon elements of P-mapping or of entitlements which in turn depend upon E-mapping and endowments of a person. Identities mentioned above may be affecting the distribution in some or all of these elements and it is important to know which components they affect. Gender identity is, for example, associated with different wage rates. Similarly poverty is associated with different infant mortality rates. The association between an identity and an outcome in the space of functioning can be understood only through the linkage between the three spaces: functionings, commodities and endowments.

X

Basis of disaggregated analysis

As seen in the foregoing analysis, inequality in the space of functionings can arise due to asymmetries of personal features, core or exchange-independent components of entitlement and the exchange-dependent component of entitlements. In the case of mortality, these broadly correspond to biological, socio-cultural and economic factors. It is worth examining some of the identities associated with variations in sex ratios and the elements these correspond to.

Personal features

With regards to the differences in personal features, the biological vulnerability of the male infant vis-à-vis his female counterpart is universally recognised and well documented. This vulnerability, if significant, should reflect in the sex ratio pattern among children. This forms the basis, and a crucial one, of disaggregation of sex ratio data into different age groups. This has been examined in Chapter 3 and has provided extremely interesting and new insights.

Core entitlements

As seen in the review of literature, the status of women has a significant bearing on their access to resources. Such status affects their core entitlements and, consequently, their survival. Culture plays a significant role in determining the status of women. Available literature points out two specific factors: ethnic identities and kinship practices. Among ethnic groups, tribals are known to be more equitable towards their womenfolk compared to non-tribals. This forms the basis of the suggestion that the sex ratio data be analysed separately for the tribal and non-tribal population. Similarly, kinship practices are known to affect the status of women, a fact recognised in the debate on the north–south divide. Kinship therefore forms another basis of disaggregation of sex ratio data. Analyses in Chapters 4 and 5 bear this out.

Exchange entitlements

As seen previously, the exchange component of entitlements become more and more important as the core component diminishes or the commodity gets more exchange-intensive. As far as the net exchange value D.V is concerned, labour participation is the most significant component for the vast majority of people. A number of studies have highlighted the role played by female labour participation in ensuring better survival of women. The effects of FLP are studied in Chapter 7.

In conclusion

The list of indicative disaggregations suggested here has been shown to be useful in Chapter 3, 4 and 5 and later in Chapter 7. It is possible to stipulate these bases of disaggregation in an ad hoc manner as indeed done in certain cases in the literature and by myself. At a less ad hoc level, some of these differences can be stipulated through a framework like Johansson's. But it is also possible to use the theoretical framework developed here. It may at times appear abstract, but it has been useful both in terms of completeness and in terms of other insights obtained through this formalism. It is useful to reiterate these. First and foremost, the elaboration of E-mapping made in Chapter 2, permits one to put different aspects of gender disparities into one coherent framework. The 'anti-women' strategy outlined there is one illustration of it. Coming to the specific inequality of concern presented here, for example, in survival, the recognition of exchange-independent components of entitlements is important both analytically and from the policy point of view.

Survival-as-functionings view provides further useful insights. The many-to-one dependence of survival on different components of entitlements and the importance of focussing on the weak links in the chain are two examples of it. Without going beyond entitlements, the issue of P-mapping and the role of personal features in survival asymmetries could not have been anticipated easily. Similarly, without linking the spaces of endowments, commodities and functionings, the feedback process could not be easily made explicit.

On a more general, methodological and abstract level, important modifications have been made to the entitlements framework as well as the capabilities approach. These will be relevance to a much larger field of analysis. Exchange-independent components, concept of range, identity specific range and distribution in the space of functionings, aggregation of components of entitlement vector into elements of functionings and that of elements of functioning vector into wellbeing and the repeated bargaining process provide rich areas for further research. Most of these are outside the scope of the present analysis, even though it was necessary to develop these in the above context. These areas of research must be left aside for the present and this analysis must move to more immediate concerns, that is, the analysis of the correlates of sex ratios.

The Chapter 7 begins this exercise by looking at the effect of female labour participation on sex ratios. Previous analyses of this topic have not disaggregated the juvenile sex ratio data either by age or social groups or by the kinship variable. When this is done, new light is thrown on the FMR-FLP relationship and the relative importance of economic and non-economic parameters is highlighted. The results and insights provide further justification for the disaggregated approach as each of the bases of disaggregation turns out to be a fruitful one.

Chapter 7

Female labour participation and sex ratios

I

An outline

In first part of this analysis, the sex ratio data are disaggregated by age, social groups and kinship groups. The analytical framework that follows examines the two components of female entitlements compared to male entitlements: the exchange-dependent and the exchange-independent components. Female labour participation (FLP) in economic activities is an important determinant of the exchange-dependent components and has been recognised as an important correlate of FMRs in the literature (from Bardhan, 1974; Miller, 1981; to Murthi et al. 1995). However, these analyses do not use the disaggregated FMR data nor take into account the possibility of and need to disaggregate the FLP data. The analysis attempts to fill this gap. It introduces three new elements: (*a*) separate analysis of FMR-FLP relationship for the 0–4 and 5–9 age groups; (*b*) separate analysis for the three social groups and (*c*) use of the kinship variable. Each of these provides new insights into the effect of FLP on FMRs.

The fact that FMR59 is a better indicator of discrimination against the girl child than juvenile FMR was highlighted in Chapters 3 and 4. As the effect of FLP on FMRs is linked to the perceived future economic value of the female child and through it to the discrimination against her, such effect should be more pronounced in the 5–9 age group FMRs than in FMRs in 0–9 age group. This is tested here.

Female-friendly kinship systems permit a higher participation of women in productive activities. These also ensure better 'core' entitlements for them. As such, FLP is less likely to be critical for female survival in the regions where the kinship system is female-friendly. This is tested using the dichotomous kinship variable developed in Chapter 5.

Ethnicity is another cultural variable that affects both FMRs and FLP. The Scheduled Tribe groups have different kinship systems and patterns of female labour participation. The Scheduled Castes too differ in these respects from the 'general' category. It is useful, therefore, to analyse if the FMR-FLP relationship differs among these groups significantly. This is done using the 1981 Census data for the three groups.

The analysis indicate that FLP coupled with kinship explains a substantial part of the sex ratio variation at the district level. High FLP provides a sufficient but not necessary condition for high FMRs. Where the kinship system ensures means of survival, FLP becomes less critical, even insignificant.

As hypothesised, FMR in the 5–9 age group captures the effect of FLP much more sharply than FMR in the juvenile age group. The relationship between FMRs in 0–4 age group and FLP is weak. Where it is not so, it signifies survival disadvantages for the female child and infant.

The relationship between FMR and FLP in the three social groups differ significantly. The survival conditions in respect of Scheduled Caste female children in the north is found to be the most adverse.

Use of FLP for the overall district population has certain limitations. It is highly weighed in favour of the poor.[1] The FMR values also reflect the patterns among the poor who account for a large proportion of the population. As such, the data for the overall population at the district level masks the 'prosperity effect'. To study this effect it is necessary to analyse the FMR-FLP relationship separately for different income levels. This aspect is discussed briefly along with the possible approach to analyse the 'prosperity effect' which forms the subject matter of the next chapter.

Organisation of the discussion

Section II analyses the JFMR-FLP relation (with and without the kinship variable) using the 1961 and 1981 Census data. Section III examines the FMR-FLP relation separately for the 0–4 and 5–9 age groups. The next

---

[1] The proportion of working women among the poor and the landless is much higher (Chen. M., 1989). Most ST and SC population fall under this category (Dunn, 1993).

section examines differences in FLP among the three social groups followed by separate FMR-FLP regression for each of these groups and a discussion of the results. Section V examines the influence of kinship on FLP using the analysis of variance. The limitations of FLP and the scope for further research are discussed in the concluding section.

II

Work, worth and culture

Miller (1981: Chapter 6) hypothesises a link between female work and female worth. According to her, higher participation in economic activities enhances the status of women ensuring them more equitable access to basic survival inputs. This is reflected in a balanced sex ratio. Low participation affects this access adversely resulting in more masculine sex ratios than usual.

Her analysis of the 1961 Census data for 323 rural districts yields a correlation of 0.43 between JSR and FLP (ibid.: 118–23). JSR is defined as the number of male children per 1,000 female children in the 0–9 age group while FLP is measured by the ratio of working women to total women in the 15–34 age group (ibid.: 118). To account for the overall levels of male employment, a disparity index is introduced (ibid.: 120). The correlation between the JSR and this disparity index does not improve significantly. From the plot of standardized residuals, Miller confirms the existence of a north–south divide (ibid.: 122). JSRs in the north are more masculine than predicted and those in the south are less masculine than predicted.

An analytical approximation

If high FLP is associated with high FMRs, and low FMRs with low FLP, one can, as a first approximation envisage a linear relationship of the type:

$$FMR = FMR_0 + S * FLP \qquad\qquad 7.1$$

FMR_0, the constant term, represents the surviving number of women per 1,000 men if FLP were, hypothetically, zero. The slope, S, of the line indicates the extent of increase (decrease) in FMR for a given increase (decrease) in FLP. *A higher intercept and a flatter slope represents favourable survival conditions for women while a lower intercept and a steep slope indicates adverse survival conditions.* This is helpful in comparing the survival conditions among different groups.

Analysis of the 1961 Census data

Table 7.1a provides the regression results for the 1961 data[2] with FMR for the 0–9 age group as the dependent variable and FLP as the independent variable. The definition of FLP used here differs to some extent from the one used by Miller.[3] The data pertains to 337 districts examined during the 1961 Census. The FMR-FLP relation is significant but weak (Adj. R. Sq. = 0.24):

Table 7.1a
Regression results: JFMR on FLP (1961 Census data)

Term	Value	Std. Err.	T-value	Adj. R. Sq.
Regression without kinship dummy				
FMR_0	931	4.4	212.8***	0.24
Slope	0.13	0.01	10.2***	
Regression with kinship dummy for the constant term				
FMR_0	975	4.4	223.4***	0.56
Kin. FMR_0	−53	3.4	−15.5***	
Slope	0.06	0.01	5.7***	
Regression with kinship dummy for the constant and the slope				
FMR_0	988	5.1	195***	0.58
Slope	0.03	0.01	2 ns	
$KinFMR_0$	−81	6.8	−11.7***	
Kinslope	0.1	0.02	4.6***	

[2] Data taken from the Indian Districts Development Data Base (Vannemann and Barnes, 1992).

[3] Here the ratio of working women to total female population for the all-age group instead of the 15–34 age group has been used. Miller's definition may be more useful to fine tune the explanatory power of FLP. The main interest here is to examine the increase in the strength of regression brought about by using FMR59 together with kinship variable. This increase is considerable and the definition used by me would suffice.

$$JFMR = 931 + 0.13\ FLP \qquad\qquad 7.1a$$

The association becomes stronger when one uses the kinship dummy (Adj. R. Sq. = 0.56). Equation 7.1a now becomes:

$JFMR = 922 + 0.06\ FLP$	K = 1, 'core' north	7.1b
$JFMR = 972 + 0.06\ FLP$	K = 0, 'rest'	7.1c

The intercept, FMR_0, is much lower (922) in the 'core' north, compared to the other regions or the 'rest' (972). The low value of the slope, 0.06, indicates that increasing FLP by 100 women per 1,000 female population will increase the FMR by about 6 female children per 1,000 male children.

A more interesting result follows, however, when the kinship dummy is used for the slope as well. FLP becomes much less significant (T = 2.01*) in the 'rest' of the regions while remaining highly significant (T = 4.6**) in the 'core' north. The overall slope of 0.06 in the equations 7.1b and 7.1c splits into a steep slope (0.13) for the 'core' north and a flat slope (0.025) for the 'rest' of the regions (Figure 7.1a). One gets:

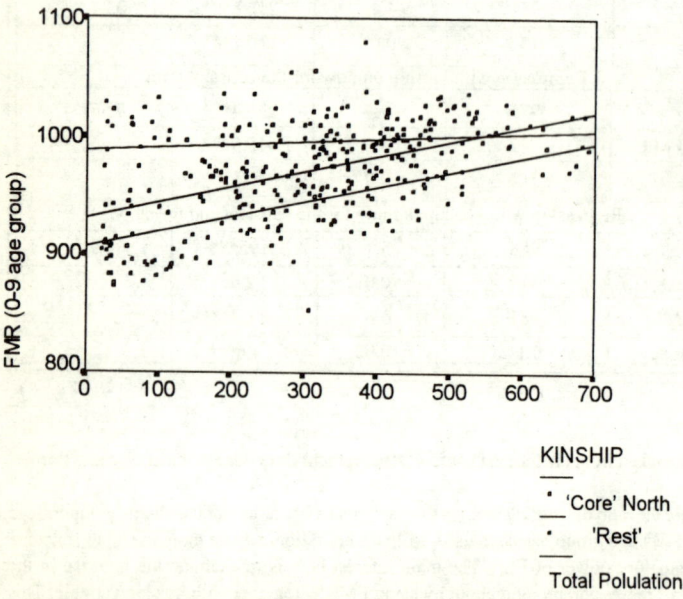

KINSHIP

' 'Core' North

' 'Rest'

Total Polulation

Figure 7.1a: JFMR-FLP by kinship: 1961 Census data.

$$JFMR = 907 + 0.13 \ FLP \qquad (K = 1, \text{'core' north), and,} \qquad 7.2b$$
$$JFMR = 988 + 0.025 \ FLP \qquad (K = 0, \text{'rest'}) \qquad 7.2c$$

A decrease in FLP by 100 reduces JFMR in the 'core' north by about 13 females per 1,000 males compared to only 3 per 1,000 males in the rest of the regions. Another implication of the above equations is that the base FMR of 988 in the 'rest' of the country will be attained in the 'core' north when FLP is as high as 650.[4]

JFMRs from the 1981 Census data

How does the situation in 1981 compare with that in 1961? Table 7.1b presents the regression results. The definition of women's work has undergone changes between the two census enumerations.[5] However the 'total workers' category used in the 1981 Census is comparable with the 1961 definition of workers and has been used in calculating the FLP. One gets the following FMR-FLP relation for 1981:

$$JFMR = 919 + 0.18* \ FLP \qquad 7.3a$$

The FMR_0 term, 919 is significantly lower compared to the 1961 value of 931. The slope has become comparatively steeper. It is worth examining whether the situation has changed uniformly in the two kinship regions. Using the kinship dummy for both the intercept and the slope one gets:

$$JFMR = 901 + 0.18* \ FLP \qquad (K = 1, \text{'core' north}) \qquad 7.3a$$
$$JFMR = 978 + 0.024* \ FLP \qquad (K = 0, \text{'rest'}) \qquad 7.3b$$

---

[4] This is only a hypothetical calculation. In reality FMR will increase non-linearly with FLP through the feedback effect.

[5] The definition of 'working' women has undergone a lot of change from the 'liberal' enumeration of the 1961 Census to the increasingly 'strident' definitions in subsequent censuses. This 'stridency' relates to the non-recognition of the female work which does not 'directly' contribute to family income. This led to highly restrictive definition of work and a drastic reduction in enumeration of females in the workforce in the 1971 Census. Later, in 1981, this was remedied by introducing two categories, main workers and marginal workers. The 'main workers' category corresponds to the 1971 definition of workers while the 'total workers (main + marginal)' category in 1981 is comparable with the 1961 definition. A detailed discussion of this issue is not within the scope of this paper. For this see Vannemann and Barnes (1992).

The constant term has declined in both the regions but in the 'rest' category it is above the FMR at birth. The slope has become steeper only in the northern region. In the other regions, FLP is, in fact, insignificant (Figure 7.1b).

Table 7.1b
Regression results: JFMR on FLP (1981 Census data)

Term	Value	Std. Err.	T-value	Adj. R. Sq.
Regression without kinship dummy				
FMR_0	919	3.3	276***	0.34
Slope	0.18	0.01	13.8***	
Regression with kinship dummy for the constant and the slope				
FMR_0	978	4.7	209***	0.61
Slope	0.02	0.01	1.6	
$KinFMR_0$	−77	5.9	−13***	
Kinslope	0.16	0.03	5.8***	

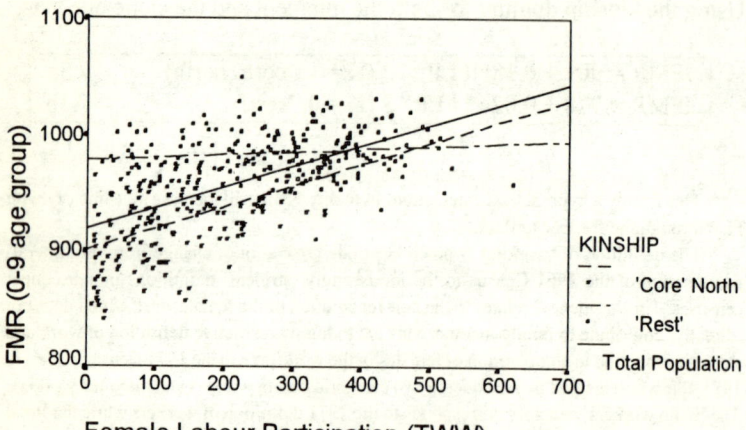

Figure 7.1b: JFMR-FLP by kinship: 1981 Census data.

III

Disaggregating the juvenile age group FMRs

Before discussing these results further, it is useful to disaggregate the juvenile age group FMR data into the 0–4 and 5–9 age groups. As seen in chapters 3 and 4, FMR59 is a more appropriate variable than JFMRs to study the effects of discrimination against the girl child. The effect of FLP should accordingly be sharper in the 5–9 age group FMRs. Further, the effect of FLP on FMRs in the 0–4 age group should be much weaker since excess male infant mortality or the FMR at birth are not affected by this discrimination.[6] It is, therefore, necessary to disaggregate the JFMR data.

Table 7.2a provides the results of regression of FMR04 and FMR59 on FLP for 1961 and 1981. As anticipated, the *FMR59-FLP association is stronger compared to FMR04 and FLP*. For 1961, one gets:

FMR04 = 963 + 0.09 FLP	7.4a
FMR59 = 900 + 0.17 FLP	7.4b

Low FMR_0 and a steep slope characterise FMR59 while for FMR04 the slope is very flat and FMR0 is close to FMR at birth.

The 1981 data (Table 7.2b) indicate worsening FMR in the 5–9 age group. The change is only marginal in the case of FMR04:

FMR04 = 958 + 0.08 FLP	7.5a
FMR59 = 885 + 0.26 FLP	7.5b

Incorporation of the kinship dummy reveals that the *worsening condition in FMR59 can be attributed to the northern region*. The equations, based on the 1961 Census data elaborate this:

FMR04 = 999 + 0.02 FLP	(Kinship = 0)	7.6a
FMR04 = 948 + 0.08 FLP	(Kinship = 1)	7.6b

[6] This will of course not hold once sex-selective abortion, female infanticide or female infant mortality on account of discrimination become significant. These will result in FMR04 figures much below the FMR at birth, i.e., 950–970.

Table 7.2a
Regression results: FMR04 and FMR59 on FLP (1961 Census data)

FMR04:

Term	Value	Std. Err.	T-value	Adj. R. Sq.
		Without kinship dummy		
FMR_0	963	4.2	226***	0.13
Slope	0.09	0.01	7.03***	
		Kinship dummy for both the constant and the slope		
FMR_0	998	6	167***	0.30
Slope	0.02	0.01	1.4 ns	
$KinFMR_0$	−50	8	−6.2***	
Kinslope	0.06	0.02	2.28**	

FMR59:

Term	Value	Std. Err.	T-value	Adj. R. Sq.
		Without kinship dummy		
FMR_0	900	5.5	163***	0.25
Slope	0.17	0.01	10.8***	
		Kinship dummy for both the constant and the slope		
FMR_0	977	5.9	165***	0.65
Slope	0.03	0.01	1.98 ns	
$KinFMR_0$	−110	8	−13.8***	
Kinslope	0.14	0.02	5.4***	

FMR59 = 977 + 0.03 FLP	(Kinship = 0)		7.6c
FMR59 = 867 + 0.17 FLP	(Kinship = 1)		7.6d

A weak relationship for FMR04, even after the use of the kinship dummy (Adj. R. Sq. = 0.29), and quite a strong association for FMR59 (Adj. R. Sq = 0.65) are clearly seen. For the 5–9 age group FMRs, FLP is quite significant (T = 5.4**) in the 'core' north and much less so (T = 1.98*) in the rest of the regions. For the 0–4 age group, FLP is much less significant in the 'core' north (T = 2.3*) and *insignificant elsewhere*.

The corresponding equations for the 1981 data are:

Table 7.2b
Regression results: FMR04 and FMR59 on FLP (1981 Census data)

FMR04:

Term	Value	Std. Err.	T-value	Adj. R. Sq.
		Without kinship dummy		
FMR_0	958	3	314***	0.12
Slope	0.08	0.01	7***	
		Kinship dummy for both the constant and the slope		
FMR_0	984	5	187***	0.20
Slope	0.02	0.02	0.93 ns	
$KinFMR_0$	−33	6.7	−5***	
Kinslope	0.06	0.03	1.85**	

FMR59:

Term	Value	Std. Err.	T-value	Adj. R. Sq.
		Without kinship dummy		
FMR_0	885	4.3	205***	0.39
Slope	0.26	0.02	15.4***	
		Kinship dummy for both the constant and the slope		
FMR_0	973	5.5	178***	0.71
Slope	0.03	0.02	1.75*	
$KinFMR_0$	−114	7	−16.5***	
Kinslope	0.24	0.03	7.5***	

$FMR04 = 984 + 0.02\ FLP$	(Kinship = 0)	7.7a
$FMR04 = 951 + 0.07\ FLP$	(Kinship = 1)	7.7b
$FMR59 = 973 + 0.03\ FLP$	(Kinship = 0)	7.7c
$FMR59 = 859 + 0.27\ FLP$	(Kinship = 1)	7.7d

The only noteworthy and significant change is that the slope for the FMR59-FLP has become steeper. If FMRs in the northern region are to catch up with the FMR_0 level of the 'rest' of the regions, FLP as high as 400 women per 1,000 female population is required. While this may be less than the corresponding value of 650 in 1961, it should be seen against the backdrop of a decline in the mean FLP value in this region. In 164 districts covered by the 'core' north, *the mean FLP has dropped to 131 in 1981 from 231 in 1961.*

The low value of FMR_0 and the steep slope for the FMR59 in the 'core' north indicate the *relative survival adversities* faced by female children in the region. Another matter of concern is the sharp drop in the constant term: from 948 for FMR04 to 867 for FMR59 in the 'core' northern region. The drop is much less sharp and well above the FMR values at birth, (from 999 to 977), in the 'rest' of the regions. This drop, as indicated earlier, indicates the *extent* of excess girl child mortality in the age group 1–4.

While a combined disaggregation of the FMR-FLP relationship by age group and kinship provides valuable insights, an additional cultural factor, ethnicity, needs to be taken into account. This is examined next.

IV

The three social groups

Differences in the kinship practices and sex ratio patterns among the Scheduled Tribes, the Scheduled Castes and the rest of the population have been adequately elaborated upon earlier (Chapters 2, 4, and 5). Differences in FLP among these three groups have been mentioned in the literature. But this has mostly been done *en passant* and the differences have not been analysed seriously even though the FLP data has been available in earlier censuses. A brief analysis of the 1981 FLP data presented here brings out significant differences in FLPs among these three groups.[7]

The descriptive statistics presented here cover two separate aspects. Table 7.3a relates to the differences between the mean FLP on an all-India basis. Mean FLP values are presented for the overall population of the district, and for the population of each of the three groups. Both categories, total workers (TW) and main workers (MW), are analysed.

Differences in FLP among the three groups are self-evident. FLP is low among the general category, high among the Scheduled Tribes. FLP

---

[7] A discussion of FLP patterns and changes in these over the decades is in order. This is not attempted for limitation of space and because the issues that follow from the present analysis do not critically depend upon these details.

Table 7.3a
Descriptive statistics for FLP:[8] *(1981 Census data)*

Category	Total Workers		Main Workers		Number of Districts
	Mean FLP	Std. Err.	Mean FLP	Std. Err.	
All	219	7	147	5.8	366
ST	374	7.5	275	7.9	243
SC	274	7.8	199	7	349
Gen.	186	6.5	121	5.3	366

(All = Total population, ST = Scheduled Tribes, SC = Scheduled Castes, Gen. = Non-ST/SC).

among the Scheduled Castes occupies an intermediate position. This pattern holds for both total workers and main workers.

As the SC and the ST population is not uniformly distributed throughout the country, the analysis is repeated for four set of districts with four different ranges of SC and ST population percentages: *negligible* (less than 1 per cent), *low* (1–10 per cent), *significant* (10–20 per cent) and *high* (above 20 per cent). This enables one to compare FLP values within comparable sets of districts. Within each concentration range, the two kinship regions are analysed separately.

Table 7.3.2a presents the results for paired T-test for districts with different ranges of Scheduled Tribe concentration. The following pattern clearly emerges:

(*a*) FLP among the Scheduled Tribe groups are significantly higher for each of the four ranges and in both kinship regions.

(*b*) FLP in the 'core' northern region is significantly low among the non-Scheduled Tribe in each of the four range. For the Scheduled Tribe population, FLP is low only in districts with negligible or low concentration of Scheduled Tribes. Where their concentration is significant or high, FLP is high in both kinship regions.

(*c*) FLP initially rises among both Scheduled Tribe and non-Scheduled Tribe segments as Scheduled Tribe population percentage increases. The rise tapers off as the Scheduled Tribe tribal concentration goes above 20 per cent.

[8] The mean FLP reported above is *the mean of the value of FLP* in respect of districts shown in column 6. For ST and SC population only in those districts where their population exceeds 1 per cent of the district population have not been included in calculating the mean FLP.

Table 7.3.2a
Results of paired T-tests among Scheduled Tribe and non-Scheduled Tribe groups
(Descriptive statistics for FLP)

Total Workers: (1981 Census data)

ST Conc.	Kinship = 1			Kinship = 0		
	Mean FLP (Std. Err.)		Number of districts	Mean FLP (Std. Err.)		Number of districts
	ST	Non-ST		ST	Non-ST	
Negl.	212 (33)	127 (23)	16	286 (23)	196 (23)	21
Low	309 (17)	183 (12)	34	409 (11)	267 (14)	75
Sign.	386 (22)	206 (14)	13	409 (17)	259 (20)	26
High	398 (34)	179 (22)	9	432 (14)	264 (16)	49

Main Workers: (1981 Census data)

ST Conc.	Kinship = 1			Kinship = 0		
	Mean FLP (Std. Err.)		Number of districts	Mean FLP (Std. Err.)		Number of districts
	ST	Non-ST		ST	Non-ST	
Negl.	157 (30)	75 (13)	16	234 (22)	153 (20)	21
Low	198 (17)	105 (9)	34	328 (12)	206 (12)	75
Sign.	260 (32)	130 (12)	13	305 (22)	192 (20)	26
High	263 (41)	121 (22)	9	293 (18)	181 (16)	49

The pattern described here holds for both the TW and the MW categories.

Table 7.3.2b presents the results of paired T-tests for FLPs at the district level among districts with different SC population percentage ranges. The 'negligible' and 'low' categories have been merged together as there are very few districts in the 'low' category. Here the FLP values of the

Table 7.3.2b
Results of paired T-tests among SC, ST and general groups
(Descriptive statistics for FLP)

Total Workers: (1981 Census Data)

SC Percentage	Kinship = 1			Kinship = 0		
	Mean FLP (Std. Err.)		*Number of districts*	*Mean FLP (Std. Err.)*		*Number of districts*
	SC	Non-SC/ST		SC	Non-SC/ST	
Low	267	185	19	350	259	50
	(17)	(17)		(15)	(16)	
Sign.	190	107	80	368	247	104
	(12)	(8)		(13)	(11)	
High	170	88	50	279	211	30
	(14)	(8)		(28)	(27)	

Main Workers: (1981 Census Data)

SC Percentage	Kinship = 1			Kinship = 0		
	Mean FLP (Std. Err.)		*Number of districts*	*Mean FLP (Std. Err.)*		*Number of districts*
	SC	Non-SC/ST		SC	Non-SC/ST	
Low	196	116	19	256	182	50
	(15)	(14)		(17)	(15)	
Sign.	133	62	80	286	179	104
	(10)	(4)		(12)	(9)	
High	106	47	50	192	136	30
	(11)	(4)		(25)	(20)	

Districts with both SC and ST population percentage > 1%
Total Workers:

Mean FLP (Std. Err.)		*Number of districts*	*Mean FLP (Std. Err.)*		*Number of districts*
SC	ST		SC	ST	
263	312	72	349	400	163
(11)	(14)		(10)	(8)	

Main Workers:

181	208	72	270	303	163
(11)	(13)		(10)	(9)	

general and the SC category have been compared. Separate comparison of FLP among the SC and the ST population is made in those districts where the percentage of both SC and ST population is above 1 per cent. The pattern that emerges here is more complex and intriguing:

(a) FLP among the Scheduled Castes is significantly higher compared to FLP in the general category in all groups and all regions. Similarly, FLP among the Scheduled Tribes is significantly higher than that among the SCs.

(b) SC concentration and FLP are negatively correlated among both SC and general categories. The effect is significant and pronounced in the main worker category and in the 'core' northern region.

(c) FLP in the kinship region 'rest' is significantly high for all the three ranges of SC population percentage.

These patterns are significant in the context of the dynamics of assimilation of the Scheduled group in the mainstream population. For the purpose of the present discussion, it provides adequate justification for a separate analysis of the FMR-FLP relation by social group.

Separate regression results

Results presented here compare the FMR-FLP relationship among the three groups separately. The analysis is, however, based on a different variable from the 'total workers' category used earlier to facilitate a comparison between the 1961 and 1981 figures. The new independent variable, LGMWW, is the log of 'main' women workers per 1,000 female population.[9]

Table 7.4.1 provides a summary of the regression results between FMR and LGMWW for the ST and non-ST population. The equations for the JFMR-LGMWW relation are:

Scheduled Tribe population

JFMR = 1,040 – 18.4* LGMWW	Kinship = 0	7.8.1a
JFMR = 899 + 73.4* LGMWW	Kinship = 1	7.8.1b

[9] Use of Log (MWW) gives a better fit between FMR59 and FLP compared to the other three choices of Main women workers (MWW), Total women workers (TWW) or Log (TWW). Significance of this observation is discussed in Chapter 8 in the context of seclusion which can become effective only below a threshold level of FLP.

Table 7.4.1
Regression results: FMR04 and FMR59 on FLP* (1981 data)
(Scheduled Tribe and non-Scheduled Tribe population)

FMR04:

Term	Value	Std. Err.	T-value	Adj. R. Sq.
FMR_0	992	16	61.5***	0.17 [Non-Scheduled Tribe]
Slope	−2.3	7.4	2.8***	
$KinFMR_0$	−79	21	−3.8***	
Kinslope	28.9	10.2	−0.3 ns	
FMR_0	1,037	36	28.9***	0.02 [Scheduled Tribe]
Slope	−11.3	14.5	−0.78 ns	
$KinFMR_0$	−125	57.9	−2.2**	
Kinslope	49.2	24.5	2**	

FMR59:

Term	Value	Std. Err.	T-value	Adj. R. Sq.
FMR_0	942	13.5	70***	0.62 [non-Scheduled Tribe]
Slope	17	6.2	2.7***	
$KinFMR_0$	−175	17.2	−10***	
Kinslope	54.9	8.6	6.4***	
FMR_0	1,038	35.8	29***	0.30 [Scheduled Tribe]
Slope	−23.1	14.5	−1.6 ns	
$KinFMR_0$	−334	57.8	−5.8***	
Kinslope	125	24.5	5.1**	

Note: * LGMWW = Log of Women Main Workers per 1,000 female population is used as the FLP variable.

Non-Scheduled Tribe population

JFMR = 965 + 8.1* LGMWW	Kinship = 0	7.8.2a
JFMR = 833 + 51.8* LGMWW	Kinship = 1	7.8.2b

The association is considerably weak for the Scheduled Tribe population with Adj. R. Sq. value of 0.22 compared to 0.62 for the non-Scheduled Tribe population. In fact, for the Scheduled Tribe population the Adj. R. Sq. value for the FMR04-LGMWW relation is 0.02, *revealing no association at all.*

For the non-Scheduled Tribe population, FLP is insignificant in the non-northern region for the JFMRs. But this is mainly on account of the

0–4 age group. For the FMR59, FLP is significant in both the kinship regions. The equations for FMR04 and FMR59 respectively are:

FMR04 = 992 − 2.3* LGMWW	Kinship = 0	7.8.3a
FMR04 = 913 + 26.5* LGMWW	Kinship = 1	7.8.3b

and

FMR59 = 943 + 17.0* LGMWW	Kinship = 0	7.8.4a
FMR59 = 768 + 71.8* LGMWW	Kinship = 1	7.8.4b

Low values of FMR_0, steep slopes and sharp drop in the FMR_0 value for 0–4 and 5–9 age group in the 'core' northern region stand in sharp contrast with the pattern in the rest of the regions.

General and Scheduled Castes categories

Table 7.4.2 provides the summary of results for the general and the SC population. For the general as well as the SC groups, the familiar pattern of weak association between FLP and FMR04 (Adj. R. Sq. < 0.2) and much stronger association between FMR59 and FLP (Adj. R. Sq. > 0.65) can be seen. Interestingly, *among the Scheduled Castes, FLP is insignificant for FMR04 in both the kinship regions* while for the general category it remains significant in both the regions. As far as FMR59 is considered, FLP is significant only in the northern region and insignificant in the rest. We get the following equations:

For the general category:

FMR04 = 1,012 − 12.4* LGMWW	Kinship = 0	7.9.1a
FMR04 = 923 + 21.5* LGMWW	Kinship = 1	7.9.1b

and

FMR59 = 966 + 6.2* LGMWW	Kinship = 0	7.9.1c
FMR59 = 788 + 63.1* LGMWW	Kinship = 1	7.9.1d

For the SC category:

FMR04 = 964 + 12.5* LGMWW	Kinship = 0	7.9.2a
FMR04 = 907 + 27.3* LGMWW	Kinship = 1	7.9.2b

FMR59 = 946 + 14.4* LGMWW	Kinship = 0	7.9.2c
FMR59 = 736 + 67.7* LGMWW	Kinship = 1	7.9.2d

Table 7.4.2
*Regression results: FMR04 and FMR59 on FLP**
(1981 Census data)
(SC and general population)

FMR04:

Term	Value	Std. Err.	T-value	Adj. R. Sq.
FMR_0	1,012	16	63***	0.14 [Non-ST/SC]
Slope	−22.4	7.4	−1.67*	
$KinFMR_0$	−89	21	−4.3***	
Kinslope	34	10.7	3.2***	
FMR_0	964	23	42***	0.18 [SC]
Slope	12.5	9.8	1.28 ns	
$KinFMR_0$	−58	28	−2.03**	
Kinslope	14.8	12.7	0.2 ns	

FMR59:

Term	Value	Std. Err.	T-value	Adj. R. Sq.
FMR_0	966	13.7	70***	0.67 [Non-ST/SC]
Slope	6.2	6.4	0.98 ns	
$KinFMR_0$	−178	17.6	−10***	
Kinslope	60.9	9.1	6.7***	
FMR_0	946	21	45***	0.73 [SC]
Slope	14	9	−1.56 ns	
$KinFMR_0$	−210	26	−8.1***	
Kinslope	53.7	11.6	4.6**	

* LGMWW = Log of women main workers per 1,000 female population is used as the FLP variable.

Very low values of FMR_0 in the equations for FMR59 and high slopes in equation 7.9.1d and 7.9.2d should raise serious concern. There is a likelihood of faster deterioration in the survival condition of SC female children, an apprehension voiced in my earlier analysis done at the macro level and some studies in this region done at the micro level (Adithi, 1995: in p.c; Wadley, 1993). An additional point of concern is the low value of FMR_0 in the 0–4 age group which indicates excess female mortality well within infancy. FMR_0 for the general category is low, 923, while for SC category it is 907, well below the usual FMR at birth.

It is thus clear that the effects of FLP on female survival are dependent upon the cultural context. This brings one to the question of the influence of cultural factors on economic variables like FLP. The next section addresses this issue.

V

Kinship and FLP

The question of how economic and cultural factors are related or influence each other has often been raised in the literature. However, the analysis of economic factors in isolation creates an impression of their insulation from the cultural factors. The fact that the cultural factors are not easily measurable or quantifiable, unlike economic factors, has also widened the chasm between the two sets of analysis.[10] However, as the results show, the two can be integrated (see also Basu, 1992; Kishor, 1993). Such integration is warranted since an economic variable like FLP is influenced by several non-economic factors like kinship, ecology, class or group ideology (Bardhan, 1974; Chen, 1982; Desai and Jain, 1994; Miller, 1981). Further, these factors may combine. Ecology may shape the labour demand: the labour demand for a wheat growing region will be different from that of a rice growing one. But within the same ecological regions different social groups will have different attitudes towards the participation of their female folk in the labour market. Tables 7.3.1 and 7.3.2a, b demonstrate this quite adequately. Within the social groups again, level of prosperity as well as the strategy to build up such prosperity may affect FLP (Desai and Jain, 1994; Papanek, 1989).

Available literature rarely goes beyond the qualitative aspects of this discussion. Given the availability of FLP data at the district level for the three social groups, it should be possible to estimate the influence of cultural factors on FLP. This is attempted next by examining the extent to which kinship affects FLP and whether this effect differs among the three social groups.

---

[10] See Kabeer (1991) for an interesting discussion on this point.

The first step is straightforward: to see if FLP differs significantly between the two kinship regions and among the three groups. Tables 7.3.1 and 7.3.2a, b show that it does. The second step is to regress FLP on the dichotomous kinship variable. This is the same as performing an analysis of variance test. But one would also like to know the extent to which FLP and kinship covary and the extent to which kinship picks up the effect of FLP[11] when used together with FLP in explaining the variations in FMR.

Analysis of covariance

This can be done using analysis of covariance through the sequential sum of squares method. Kinship is used as a dichotomous factor with value 0 and 1 and FLP as a covariate. The sequential sum of squares method indicates the extent to which different factors, taken in a particular sequence explain the observed overall variance. In the first sequence, effects of FLP are estimated first, followed by those of kinship and then the interaction term between the two. In the next sequence the order is reversed; effect of kinship are estimated first followed by the effect of FLP and the interaction term. Where kinship picks up a substantial part of the variation explained by FLP, one should expect a high correlation between the two. This can be verified by regressing FLP on kinship.

Table 7.5.1 and the corresponding pie chart present the result of such an analysis. Covariance between TWW and kinship for overall population is examined first. It is clear that kinship picks up substantial part of the explanation provided by the FLP. When used first in the sequence, FLP explains about 40 per cent of the variation and kinship another 27 per cent (R. Sq. of 0.71). The interaction term contributes marginally. *But when kinship is used first in the sequence it explains 62 per cent of the variance while FLP explains only 4 per cent.* Not surprisingly, *association between kinship and FLP is strong* as shown by the R. Sq. value 0.35 for the regression of FLP on kinship.

The pattern is similar for the non-ST, general, and SC categories (Table 7.5.2). Among tribals, association between kinship and FLP is weak (R. Sq. = 0.11), and FLP contributes very little to the explanation in either of the sequences. This is not surprising as most of the tribal groups have kinships which come under the 'female-friendly' category.

---

[11] Since one expects kinship to affect FLP and not the other way round.

Table 7.5.1
Analysis of variance of FMR59 with kinship and FLP
(Total population)
(Sequential sum of squares method)

	Sequence-1 FLP first		Sequence-2 kinship first		Adj. R. Sq.	Adj. R. Sq. between FLP-kinship
Variance Explained	SS	%	SS	%		
FLP	4,36,961	40	42,540	4		
Kinship	2,96,304	27	6,90,726	62		
Interaction	50,020	5	50,020	5		
Unexplained	3,22,478	29	3,22,478	29		
TOTAL	11,05,764	100	11,05,764	100	0.71	0.35

Variance Explained

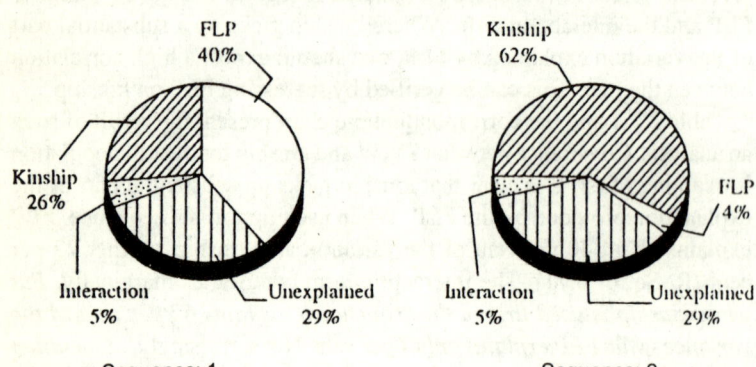

Sequence: 1   Sequence: 2

Extending the kinship classification

It could be argued that the twofold classification of kinship categories may be inadequate and as simplistic as the north-south classification. This is not so since the difference here is not just regional but based upon two different social systems; what have been termed as male-centred

Table 7.5.2
Analysis of variance of FMR59 with kinship and FLP
(by social groups)
(Sequential sum of squares method)

ST and non-ST population:

Variance Explained by	Non-Tribal		Tribal	
	Sequence-1 FLP first	*Sequence-1 kinship first*	*Sequence-1 FLP first*	*Sequence-1 kinship first*
	Percentage	Percentage	Percentage	Percentage
FLP	36	6	6	1
Kinship	27	57	16	21
Interaction	4	4	9	9
Unexplained	33	33	69	69
Total	100	100	100	100
R. Sq.		0.66		0.30
R. Sq. for FLP on Kinship		0.27		0.11

SC and Non-SC/ST (General) population:

Variance Explained by	Non-SC/ST		SC	
	Sequence-1 FLP first	*Sequence-1 kinship first*	*Sequence-1 FLP first*	*Sequence-1 kinship first*
	Percentage	Percentage	Percentage	Percentage
FLP	33	5	38	6
Kinship	24	53	25	57
Interaction	4	4	4	4
Unexplained	39	39	33	33
Total	100	100	100	100
R. Sq.		0.61		0.67
R. Sq. for FLP on Kinship		0.29		0.29

Notes: i) LGMWW = Log of Main Women Workers per 1,000 female population used as FLP.

ii) F values highly significant in each case except for ST category in sequence 2.

versus female-friendly. The geographical 'north' has sizeable areas which do not share the kinship system of the classificatory north. Such regions can be found not just in Himachal Pradesh but in UP, Rajasthan and south Bihar (Annexure 3A). The geographical 'south' also has districts, though very few, categorised under the 'core' north. These includes the Jalgaon, Dhule and Nasik belt of Maharashtra. In fact, in non-ST central India, different segments of the population follow different kinship systems within the same locality (e.g., Goody, 1990; Karve 1966). But in the present analysis, such 'fine tuning' has been ignored.

I have nevertheless examined a threefold kinship classification. The 'rest' was further split into the Dravidian kinship system comprising of the four southern states and the 'rest' of the districts. The difference between these two categories turned out to be insignificant as far as the FMR-FLP relationship is concerned (results not presented).

VI

Limitations and scope for further work

Some of the new insights gained in the analysis of the FMR-FLP relation warrant further research. These are outlined next. There are some limitations to the analysis as well. One of these relates to the issue of prosperity.

The prosperity effect

FMR and FLP data for the overall population at the district level is weighed in favour of the poorer groups and masks the prosperity effect. FMRs are weighed in favour of the poor because they are numerous. As far as FLP is concerned, there is preponderance of women from the landless, tribal and the SC households in the overall work force as seen earlier. Separate analysis for the SC, ST and the general category reduces some of the 'masking'. The 'poverty effect' can be further controlled if FMR and FLP data is available by prosperity levels. This is discussed in detail in Chapter 8.

Is FLP the only important economic variable of consequence? That is certainly not the case. Overall prosperity of the household is another important variable. The links between these two and their effect on female survival is discussed in the next chapter. It throws light on the dynamic aspects of the sex ratio imbalances, especially on the decline of the FMRs in the wake of prosperity in situations of low FLP.

Kinship and FLP—Further analysis

The undisputed finding that high FLP provides a sufficient condition for better survival among females (Chapter 2) is supported by the results given earlier. However, high FLP is not a necessary condition for better survival if the kinship system is female-friendly. Improvement in the FMR-FLP association upon inclusion of the kinship variable supports Kishor's (1993) assertion that the economic and the non-economic factors should be analysed together. Results in Section VI and Tables 7.5.1 and 7.5.2 provide some quantitative dimensions of the interaction between these two at a macro level. It is necessary to analyse the covariation further once the 1991 Census data on FMR04 and FMR59 becomes available for different social groups. Time trends in different FMR-FLP relationship in different regions and among different social groups will have important policy implications.

Different social groups

Differences in the FMR-FLP relation among different social groups have important policy implications. Such differences also need to be separately analysed for the two kinship groups. Most analyses including Kishor, 1993 and Murthi et al., 1995, use the SC and ST population percentage as a suitable variable to take into account the effect of their presence. In my view, these groups require separate analysis of their own.

Such analysis would throw light on the dynamics of assimilation of the SC and ST population in to mainstream society and the nature and extent of the process or 'Sanskritisation' and its consequences on gender disparities. Decline in FLP among Scheduled Castes in districts where their concentration is high merits further scrutiny in this regard.

There have been some suggestions that increasing FLP afffects child mortality adversely (Basu, 1992; Desai and Jain, 1994; Kishor, 1993). The main argument is that increased female participation in the labour force is at the cost of child care. This debate can be fruitfully informed by examining the effect of FLP on FMR04 and comparing these with the effects on FMR59. We have indeed encountered negative slopes in the kinship = 0 region for the general population and also for the ST population (equations 7.5.1a and 7.5.3a). This is discussed in the concluding chapter and requires further analysis.

Plurality of policy interventions

Policy implications of these results perhaps have immediate relevance. One point that clearly stands out is the *need for plurality in design of policy interventions*. Policies for the Scheduled Caste population in the north will differ from those for the Scheduled Tribe groups in, say, the north-east. Further, such intervention will need the coordination of efforts between different agencies and have to be region and group specific. The need for plurality and specific aspects of intervention are discussed in the last chapter.

Conclusion

The disaggregated approach has significantly advanced the analysis of the association between FMR and FLP. The role of cultural factors in facilitating higher FLP has been quantitatively analysed in a new way. More important, however, is the issue raised about separating the 'poverty effect' and the 'prosperity effect'. Intuitively, higher prosperity levels are expected to improve the lot of both the sexes and one can expect balanced FMR patterns and an FMR-FLP relationship favourable to women.

The analysis in Chapter 8 shakes this 'intuitive optimism and indicates worsening FMRs in the wake of prosperity, especially where FLP is low among the non-poor. This raises important and disturbing questions about the spread of the ethos of female subordination among the non-poor and through them among the poor. This discussion focuses upon the dynamic aspects of the sex ratio imbalance much more than the present chapter does.

Interestingly, as one moves to the process dynamics of sex ratio imbalances, the available data becomes less satisfactory. Yet through an indirect use of two data sets important advances are made concerning the association of prosperity, FLP and the FMR, generating an urgent agenda for future research. It is to this aspect to which we turn now.

Chapter 8

The prosperity effect

I

An outline

Is there an association between FMR patterns and prosperity levels? Literature and the data analysed here show that the FMRs among the poor are significantly higher than those among the non-poor. Why this should be so is intuitively not clear.

Analysis of the association between FMRs and prosperity at the household level is necessary given two contradictory arguments in literature. One is concerned about the increasing gender gap in survival in the wake of prosperity. The other is optimistic about the eventual gender equality at higher levels of prosperity. The two have quite different implications for policy.

Lower FMRs among higher income groups have mainly been attributed to increasing discrimination against the female members or, more charitably, have been described as the case of men gaining more in the wake of prosperity rather than females being discriminated against (Bhatia quoted in Caldwell and Caldwell, 1990; Clark, 1989; Kishor, 1993; Mendelbaum, 1988: 65; Murthi et al. 1995). The reasons cited for this are both economic and cultural. In cultural terms, prosperity goes together with 'high culture' (Goody, 1990) and the female subordination associated with it. Emulation of this aspect by the upwardly mobile groups (Goody, 1990; Berreman, 1993) and emergence of an 'anti-female bias' among these groups has been reported in both south India (Heyer, 1992; Kapadia,

1994) and north India (Parry, 1979; Wadley, 1993). In economic terms, higher prosperity is associated with lower FLP and higher incidences of dowry (Chapter 2: Section VIII) both reinforcing the perception of the female child as a liability.[1]

But some economic literature is optimistic about the eventual gender equality at higher levels of prosperity. Possible existence of a Kuznets curve between gender inequality and prosperity at the household level (Kanbur and Haddad, 1994) or at the societal level (Lentican et al., 1996) comes in this category. Similarly, non-discriminatory resource allocation during times of plenty and discrimination against female children during times of scarcity has been reported within the same households (Behrman 1988). Krishnaji (1987) also refers to a U-shaped relation between FMRs and landholding size at the state level.

Certain demographic literature is also hopeful that the decline in FMRs will stabilise at a certain point in time. It is argued that as female children becomes more scarce they will be valued more and have better survival chances (Pissani and Zaba, forthcoming). In reality, such reversal of fortunes does not seem to be happening (Billing, 1991).

The tension between the hypothesised turning point in the lot of women and the observation driven analyses of the worsening FMRs needs to be resolved. This is important for both policy and social action since the two have quite different implications.

Is there a turning point?

A closer look at the idea of the turning point reveals that the allocational behaviour in the household is crucially determined by female contribution to prosperity and not by prosperity per se. Once this is recognised the tension described earlier diminishes considerably. Based on the framework developed in Chapter 6, three points are made. First, the search for a Kuznets curve is more appropriately done in the space of functionings than in the space of entitlements. Second, the shape of the Kuznets curve is important. Two parameters are introduced to elaborate this: the 'severity' of the curve, that is, the inequality at the turning point (lowness of FMRs in this case) and its 'attainability', that is, the prosperity levels at the turning point. Both are, it is argued, affected by the female contribution

---

[1] Such perception existed even among the aristocratic groups in Victorian England (Johansson, 1996).

to prosperity. Finally, it is possible that a turning point may not occur at all and the inequality may continue to increase with prosperity.

Two issues are addressed here: (*a*) to verify if a Kuznets curve exists and (*b*) to see whether female contribution to prosperity affects its shape. These tasks are constrained by the absence of suitable data on FMRs by income levels. However, it is possible to use two available data sets which provide indirect evidence on prosperity levels and FMRs. The first set, from the 1961 Census, provides data on household composition by landholding size groups. The second set, available from the NSSO surveys, provides data on FMRs by per capita expenditure (PCE) class. These data are analysed in some details taking both landholding size and the PCE as reasonable indicators of household prosperity.

The FMR data by landholding size are analysed separately for the two kinship regions. The trend of a U-shaped relationship between FMRs and landholding size is noticed in both the north and the south but the attainability and the severity differ substantially. In the northern region, the FMRs at the turning point are quite low (below 900). In the southern states, FMRs are high. The effect of FLP on FMRs is positive and significant in the north while in the south it is insignificant.

The NSSO data from the 43rd (1987–88) and the 50th (1992–93) rounds are analysed. These do not reveal any U-shaped relation between FMRs and PCE. The association between the two turns out to be negative and significant even in the southern states. Very low FMRs among the high PCE brackets in the south is a matter of some concern. It goes counter to Miller's observation that FMRs among the 'propertied class' in the south are not low (Miller 1981: Chapter 7). FMR levels in the southern states among the rural non-poor in the nineties are considerably lower than those seen from the 1961 landholding data.

These low FMRs support the concern about the emerging 'anti-female bias' among the propertied classes in the south. These also throw light on the social locus of the spreading 'northern pattern' across the south (Chapter 5). Geographically, such spread follows the route of cultural circulation between the two regions. Socially it appears to take the 'prosperity route' in that the groups attaining prosperity tend to show increasing female subordination.

Prosperity and reduced infant mortality

One caveat is in order here. A higher level of prosperity will by and large by negatively associated with infant mortality rates and sex differentials in these rates.[2] These will result in lower FMRs among the non-poor, particularly in the 0–4 age group. Similarly, if prosperity creates more optimum conditions for childbearing, foetal wastage will decline reducing FMRs at birth, even if marginally.

The two effects namely, reduced male infant mortality, mainly a biological phenomenon and increased female child mortality, mainly a behavioural phenomenon may thus operate together in the wake of prosperity. One is associated with development and affects the mortality levels and sex differentials in infant mortality. The other relates to discrimination and the consequent sex differentials in childhood and post-neonatal mortality. Both will lower FMRs. The first process is desirable as it prevents avoidable male deaths. The second process is not as it perpetuates and increases avoidable female deaths. This distinction, made throughout this analysis, is re-emphasised here. It is difficult however, to estimate this effect of prosperity in the absence of appropriate data. Data on sex ratios at birth, IMR and 0–4 age group FMRs are not available by prosperity levels. Nevertheless where sex ratios go well below 960, it is plausible to infer discrimination against female children.

The spreading ethos of female subordination

Coming back to the significant decline in FMRs among the non-poor in the south, it is argued that a rapid diffusion of the ethos of female subordination in the social superstrata needs to be taken seriously. If such a diffusion also spreads rapidly within the social substrata, the process could rapidly multiply given the increasing irrelevance of physical barriers to circulation between the south and the north. This has important policy implications. First, the spread of the ethos of female subordination must be halted through intervention at the state and societal level. Second, focussing on the non-poor groups in the south will be an important part

---

[2] Though this not necessarily the case. For a fascinating historical account of four different stages of development and mortality patterns in Japan (1900–60) see Mosk and Johansson (1986).

of such an intervention. The intervention strategy for them will be quite different from the one among the poor.

Organisation of the discussion

The next section examines the issue of intra-household inequality and suggests departures from the framework of Kanbur and Haddad (1994). Sections III and IV, analyse the data from the 1961 Census and the NSSO survey rounds. Section V briefly reviews the literature on the effects of prosperity on FMRs and on discrimination against females. Implications of the results are discussed in the concluding section.

II

Inequality within the household

Resource allocation within the household is not equal among its members and the use of average resource consumption figures at the household level can give quite a misleading picture of welfare within and between households (Haddad and Kanbur, 1990).

The choice of a suitable space and the focal variable is important while measuring inequality within the household. As discussed earlier, the space of functionings is a more appropriate space for measuring the inequality and within it mortality is an appropriate variable for the present purpose. However, even if the space or the focal variable is agreed upon, there could be different approaches to measuring inequality (Woolley and Marshall, 1994). Here the measure of inequality adopted by Kanbur and Haddad (1994; KH henceforth) will be followed.

KH define inequality in resource allocation within the household as the deviation from half of the dominant member's share. Using this measure they stipulate the existence of an inverse-U relationship between inequality and the prosperity at the household level under certain conditions. They find evidence for such a curve in respect of calorie adequacy of different members within the household in the Philippines (1992).[3]

---

[3] Lentican et al. (1996) report a Kuznets curve in respect of elementary education in some Asian countries. The analysis is of course not at the household level.

The choice of the focal variable is criticised here on practical and analytical grounds. Analytically it is considered incomplete if not a misspecification. On the practical side, certain implications which can follow from the unqualified application of the results need to be critically examined.

First, the shape of Kuznets curve will differ for different elements of the commodity vector, like calorie, protein or health care.[4] Unless this is made explicit, it could be wrongly assumed that the shape of the Kuznets curve is similar for all the elements of the commodity vector. Even if this were so by chance, the shape of the curve in the space of outcomes will be altogether different.

Another erroneous impression that can prevail is that the shape of the curve depends only on the overall prosperity level of the household independent of the female contribution to prosperity. This stems from the solution in the Nash bargaining problem in which the increment in the size of the cake is always distributed equally between the two members leaving the gap, i.e., $x_1 - x_2$, unchanged at the end of every round while the size of the cake X continues to increase (Chapter 6). This is unrealistic.

These two impressions taken together can translate into a convenient 'tickle down optimism' in the realm of the household. It could be argued that the lot of the female members within the household will improve as the overall prosperity of the household increases. As such, policy efforts should be geared towards making the households more prosperous rather than investing in social services and welfare measures like primary education, preventive health care, sanitation or housing.[5] Such an argument will have many enthusiastic takers and their ideology-driven keenness in withdrawing from social sector investment would appear to have found a spurious 'objective' justification.

It is not being suggested that KH make the above arguments. These consequences may be farthest from their intensions. But that does not prevent these arguments from being made and it is necessary to pre-empt these. This is especially so in view of the decline in social sector investment in India in real terms (Seeta Prabhu, 1994).

On analytical grounds too, the Kuznets curve assertions need to be qualified in respect of its shape. Two parameters are crucial: prosperity

---

[4] This has been discussed in Chapter 6. Further, Lentican et al. (1996: 256) report that the inverted U-shape is not exhibited in respect of secondary education or agricultural employment while it is observed in respect of primary education.

[5] Presumed to be more beneficial towards the female members in general by increasing their core entitlements.

level at the 'turning point' and the extent of inequality at this turning point. Figure 8,1 illustrates this. At zero prosperity level there will be no inequality for there is nothing to share. It could increase as prosperity increases. In some cases, the turning point is reached faster and the inequality at this point is low. In other cases it can be reached only at a very high level of prosperity and the inequality may be quite high, even one.[6] There are other intermediate variants possible as shown in the figure. If the turning point prosperity level is too high, the inequality will rise linearly with prosperity.

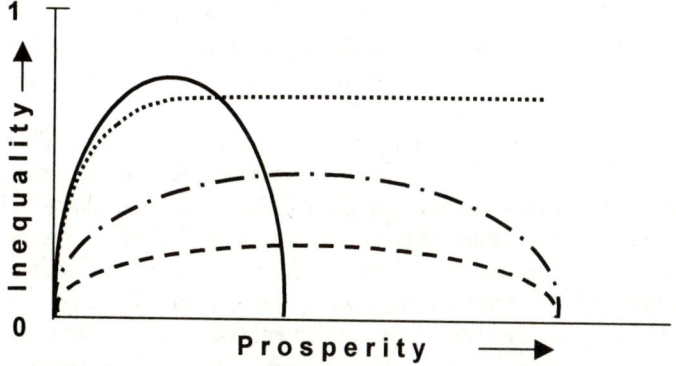

Figure 8.1: 'Severity' and 'attainability' of different Kuznets curves.

The 'height of inequality' or the 'severity' of the Kuznets curve and the turning point prosperity or its 'attainability' are important. At a very basic level, these can give rise to four possible combinations.

The combinations are self-explanatory. If the severity is low, the attainability is not of critical consequence. If it is high but the attainability is early, for example, schooling opportunity for the girl child, it can be

---

[6] Non-hypothetically, this would correspond to a dowry death (bride-burning) in a rich household.

Table 8.1
Severity and attainability of Kuznets curves:
Four possible combinations

Attainability of the 'turning point'	Inequality at the 'turning point'	
	Low	High
Early	Not critical	Mixed
Late	Less critical	Unacceptable

remedied through state intervention or social action. But when the inequality is severe and attainability is late, prosperity is of little consequence especially if the question of survival is involved. Awaiting the turning point will be like 'Waiting for Godot' for the women concerned.

While the attainability may be constrained by the prosperity or the size of the cake, the severity of the curve for a given level of prosperity will be negatively correlated with the female contribution to it. In other words it is not prosperity alone that will decide the inequality, female contribution to the prosperity will also be important.

In terms of the entitlement-endowment relation, the 'severity' will be negatively correlated with the exchange component d.v, the distortion parameter b and the core component of entitlements N_0. Given that b and N_0 vary for different commodities or elements of the entitlement vector, the shape of the Kuznets curve will vary for these elements. Different curves depicted in Figure 8.1 can correspond to inequality-prosperity curves for different elements of the entitlement vector. The effect in the space of outcomes will be a combined one affected by the sharpest inequality (assuming that the personal features are constant). It is therefore more appropriate to search for the Kuznets curve in the space of functionings rather than in the space of entitlements. Without engaging in a debate on the superiority of one over the other, reasons why a search in the space of functionings is useful and legitimate are indicated here:

(a) Inequalities in different elements of the E-vector have a combined effect on the inequality in respect of a specific outcome in the space of functionings. As already noted, reduction of inequality in one element may be a necessary but not sufficient condition for reducing the inequality in the space of functionings. Different levels of inequality for different elements of the E-vector can co-exist at a given resource level with different outcomes in the space of functioning.

(*b*) Increasing levels of prosperity may modify the E-mapping. Women may be withdrawn from labour as the household becomes more prosperous. This could affect their entitlement ratios through the b(d.v) component. In such a situation, core entitlements becomes critical. Whether these deteriorate or are maintained at a high level through culture, mobilisation or collective action, or through social sector investment by the state will depend upon specific circumstances.

(*c*) Finally, the measurement problems associated with a summary outcome like sex ratio are less compared to those related to the individual entitlements.[7]

It is worth examining, therefore, how an increase in the prosperity of the household, affects the sex ratios at the larger societal level. This is done in the next two sections.

III

Prosperity and FMRs-I

The data source

The 1961 Indian Census data provide the composition of households in different landholding groups at the district level (Government of India, 1964). Ten landholding sizes are defined starting with households with less than 1 acre of land to the households with more than 50 acres of land.[8] The survey is based upon 20 per cent of the sample and the number

---

[7] KH have themselves indicated the methodological problems that exist with calorie adequacy concept used in examining the inequality. Then there is the issue of the measure used. For a recent discussion on different measures of inequality see Woolley and Marshall (1994). Another issue is of seasonal fluctuations that has been dealt by Babu et al. (1993) and Behrman (1998). Behrman discusses the issue of inequality aversion at different times: the lean season versus the season where surplus is available. Differences in inequality also exist with respect to different intakes, e.g., calories, protein, vitamins etc. Sex ratios provide a measure integrated over these various factors and fluctuations.

[8] These households are engaged in cultivation only. Data for two other groups, households engaged in household industry only and those engaged neither in cultivation nor in household industry is also available. But these are not relevant for our purpose. (Census of India, 1961 Part III (i) and (ii): Tables XI to XVII).

of households covered in absolute numbers is quite large. As most of the Scheduled Class and Scheduled Tribe farmers have small landholding groups,[9] the larger landholding households would essentially represent the non-poor in the 'general' category. It is reasonable to assume that the landholding size was a good indicator of the prosperity for the rural cultivating households in 1961.

The 1961 data also provide information about the female labour participation among these rural households. The figures of family labour and the hired labour are provided separately. The break-up of family workers is given by gender; such a break-up is not provided for the hired workers. For the purpose of this analysis the former is adequate. The family female labour participation (FFLP) varies by regions and different landholding classes within a given region.

The NSSO (National Sample Survey Organisation) survey rounds provide data on household composition in different expenditure classes in rural and urban areas. There are 12 PCE (per capita expenditure in Indian rupees) classes. It is again reasonable to assume that the PCE is a good indicator of the prosperity of the households.

Grouping of the 1961 census data

The 1961 Census data are available at the district level. However, at this level, the sample size for the larger landholding size groups are rather small. This introduces the problem of large variability in the FMR values. To avoid this difficulty, state-level data was used in an earlier analysis (Agnihotri, 1995b). But this creates the problem of over-aggregation of regional variation in both FMR and FFLP patterns. The FLP patterns in the Uttarakhand region of UP, for example, are closer to those in Himachal Pradesh than to western UP.[10] One can, however, combine data for a cluster of contiguous districts which will provide an adequately large sample size. Such grouping is used in this analysis. The clusters are selected from the two kinship stereotypes regions: the 'core' north and the 'core' south. The mixed kinship regions are not included in the analysis.

From the north-western region, 7 groups of districts from Punjab,[11] 6

---

[9] Tables SCT-V Part (A) and Part (B): summary figures for SC/ST farmers.

[10] As a result, the state-level data can often give a high FMR value in the less than 1 acre category which will affect the shape of the U-curve disproportionately.

[11] Present Haryana and parts of Himachal Pradesh (not included in the analysis here) formed parts of Punjab then.

divisions from UP, the Gwalior division[12] of MP and the Alwar, Bharatpur and Sawai Madhopur regions of Rajasthan have been included in the analysis. From the south, 11 groups of districts from the four southern states have been included. These two sets of groups correspond to the two 'core' kinship types.

Figure 8.2a shows the box plots for the FMRs by landholding groups for the two kinship regions. Notwithstanding the variability in the FMRs, a U-shaped relationship can be noticed. But low FMRs (well below 900) in the 'north' for the landholding groups owning 7.5 acres or more, are also evident. This is quite low by the 1961 standards. On the other hand, the curve is much shallower in the south with the FMRs staying above 950 for most of the groups.

The box plots for FLP for the two kinship groups (Figure 8.2b) provide some clues about these differences. In the south, FLP is high and nearly the same across most of the landholding groups. It is relatively low in the landholding groups owning 30 acres of land or more. In the north, FLP is low and declines steadily as the landholding size goes up. These values are quite low even though the 1961 enumeration of FLP has been considered as very 'liberal' (Vannemann and Barnes, 1992). This 'inverted saucer' shape in the south and saucer shape in the north is perhaps what distinguishes the 'female-friendly' kinship from the 'male-centred' kinship. This is in agreement with observations made by Desai and Jain (1994: 127) about rural Karnataka. They find an increased workload among women from larger land owning household, 'but much of it is concentrated on the family farm instead of in wage labour'.

Kuznets curve and the north–south divide

A U-shaped relationship can be described by:

$$y = a - bx + cx^2 \qquad\qquad 8.1$$

The turning point will be given by setting the first differential of y to zero, i.e., $-b + 2cx = 0$, or $x = b/2c$. If b is much larger than 2c the relationship will be nearly linear.

Equation 8.2 gives the results of regression of FMRs on FLP and the log of landholding size. For calculating the logarithm of the landholding

---

[12] In some states, some districts are grouped into 'revenue divisions' or simply division for administrative purposes. In those cases the data at the 'divisional level' has been used.

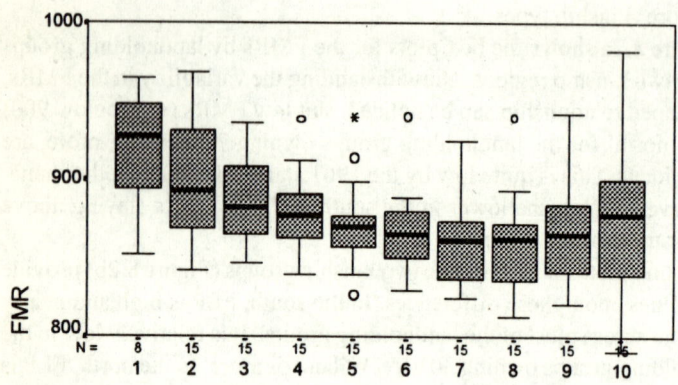

Groups by Landholding size

15 Divisions in the north (K=1)

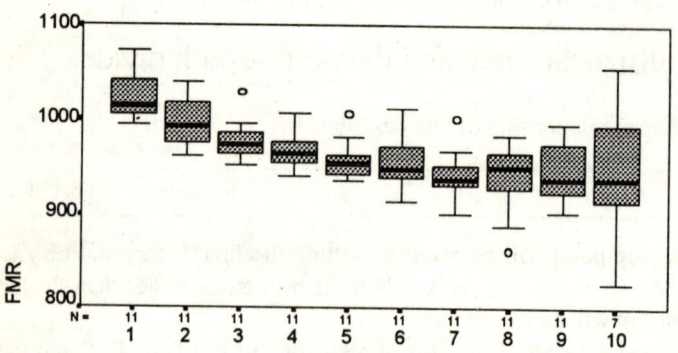

Groups by Landholding size

11 Divisions in the South (K=0)

Figure 8.2a: Box plot of FMRs by landholding size (1961 Census data).
Source: 1961 Census, Household Economic Tables, Part III: Tables B-X to B-XVII FMRs for all-age group for households engaged only in cultivation.

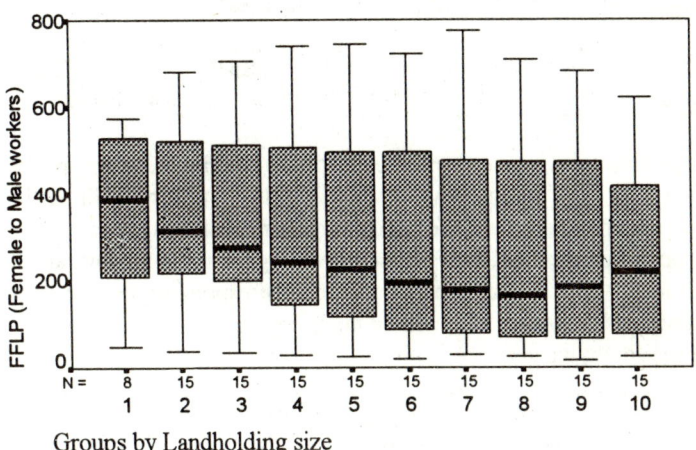

Groups by Landholding size

15 Divisions in the North (K=1)

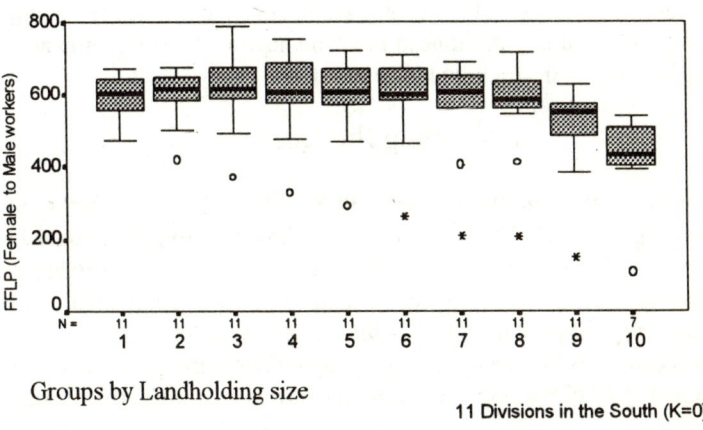

Groups by Landholding size

11 Divisions in the South (K=0)

Figure 8.2b: Box plot of FFLP by landholding size (1961 Census data).

size, the mean of the size range is used. This measure is crude since the mean of the range does not represent the mean landholding size in that group. Further, the class of the land is not taken into account, that is, whether irrigated or unirrigated. Given this, the results have to be interpreted cautiously. For the north, the regression results give:

FMR = 879 + .09* FLP –55* Logland + 21* Logland²	8.2a
T-value 139** 8.9*** 5.1*** 3.7*** R. Sq. = 0.47, F = 42***	

The turning point is given by Logland = 55/42 = 1.31 which corresponds to about a 20 acre landholding. Two points are noteworthy. First, the turning point prosperity is quite large or unattainable for a majority of the rural population. Second, the FMR at the turning point is quite low, about 870 (at FLP = 200). So the prosperity levels corresponding to a 'reasonable' level of FMR, say, 940, will be much higher.

For the south, we get:

FMR = 1052 – .06 FLP –57* Logland +6.5* Logland²	8.2b
T-value 38*** 1.5 2.8***0.5 R. Sq. = 0.22, F = 9***	

FLP is negatively correlated with FMR, but not significantly (Significance of T = 0.11). 'Logland' is negatively correlated and significant. The term Logland² is insignificant (Significance of T =0.6). The constant term is quite high compared to the one for the northern region indicating a much stronger effect of the cultural term compared to the economic ones like FLP and landholdings. These results are in agreement with the findings of Chapter 7, that is, variations in FFLP do not affect FMR significantly in regions of female-friendly kinship systems.

Probing the 'core'

It is possible to study the effects of FLP in the 'core' north further by examining the FMR-FLP relation by landholding groups. It could be argued that the strong association between FMR and FLP seen in Chapter 7 essentially reflected the pattern among the poorer population and a similar effect may not hold among the higher landholding class.

This can be examined by taking the landholding groups of 12.5–14.9 acres and 15.0–29.9 acres which represent the richer farming households.[13]

[13] The Number of households in these size groups is quite large and does not present any problem of variability in FMRs on account of small sample size. Such problem presents itself in the landholding groups of 30.0 acres and above.

In this landholding size, the number of Scheduled Caste farmers is insignificant. The Scheduled Tribe population in these divisions is negligible. As such, the effect variables like the percentage of the SC and ST population, kinship, occupation[14] and prosperity have been controlled. The FMR-FLP regression line is given by:

FMR = 837 + 0.08* FLP			8.3a
T-value	128***	4.6***	Adj. R. Sq. 0.41; F = 21***

This confirms a positive and significant association between FMR and FLP among the richer farming households in the northern kinship region.

Culture or kinship is important but not the sole determinant of FLP. The labour market is affected by ecology, technology, infrastructure and similar other factors (Chen, 1989: Basu, 1992; Mathur 1996). It could also be affected by policy interventions. Given the positive association between FMR and FLP, it is likely that policies leading to improved FLP may improve the survival chances of women. It is worth examining this association further.

The number of farm families in the two landholding groups discussed here is large enough to permit a similar analysis to be done at the district level. Scatter diagram of FMR versus FLP for the districts of Punjab (which include present-day Haryana but exclude areas now in Himachal Pradesh) and western-central UP (Figure 8.3a) reveal, however, three distinct clusters. There is a large cluster with very low FMR and very low FLP. It consists of most districts of present-day Punjab, districts of the Doab region[15] and districts north of the Doab in the upper Gangetic plains.[16] There is another cluster of four districts from present-day Haryana viz., Rohtak, Hissar, Gurgaon and Mahendragarh with high FLP and moderate FMRs (875–900). The third cluster consists of the Zansi Uplands and districts towards the east upto Allahabad. It has moderate FLP and high FMRs. The cluster formation notwithstanding, the association between very low FMRs and very low FLPs is clear.

A more homogenous set of districts can be selected from among the wheat growing districts of western UP within the Doab and Zansi Uplands. If one excludes the landholdings of 1 acre and less, which represent poor farmers group, and the landholdings of 50 acres and above on sample size considerations, scatter plot of FMR and FLP shows a strong association (Figure 8.3b). The regression results are given:

[14] These households are engaged only in cultivation.
[15] Districts between the Doab (literally, two waters) of Ganga and Yamuna.
[16] FLP has been plotted on a logarithmic scale to spread this cluster more clearly.

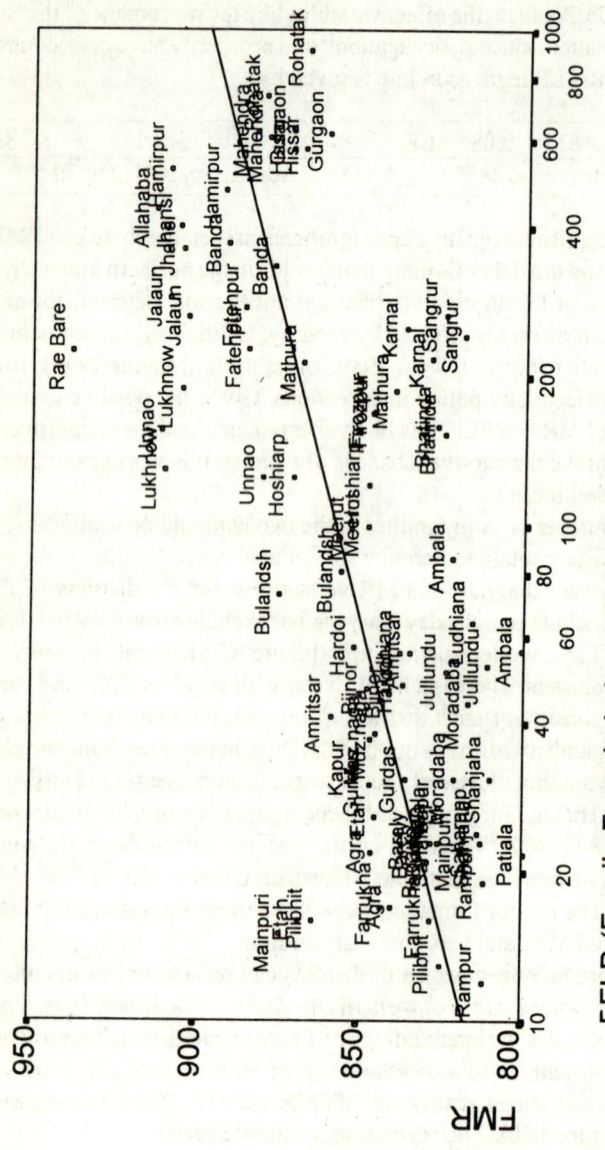

Figure 8.3a: Scatter plot of FMR by FFLP among large farmers (Punjab and western UP).

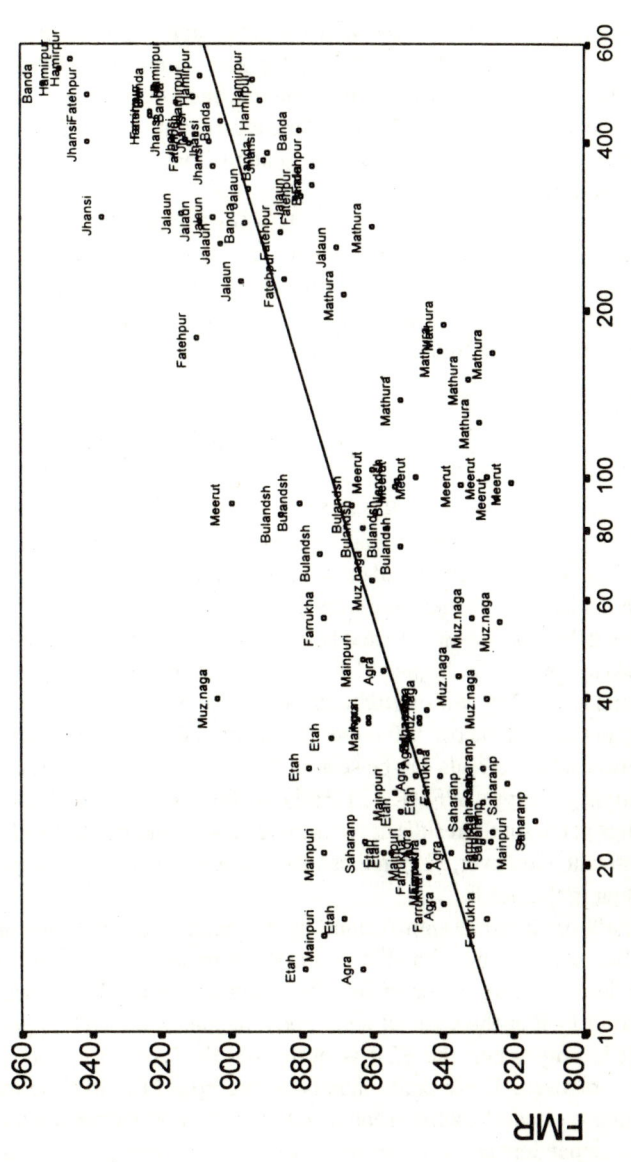

FFLP (Family Female Labour Participation)

Figure 8.3b: Scatter plot of FMR by FFLP (wheat growing districts: Doab and Zansi Uplands).

FMR = 867 + 0.17* FLP −72* Logland +38* Logland²	8.3b
T-value 101*** 14*** 4.3*** 4.9*** Adj. R. Sq. = 0.65; F = 78***	

If FMR is regressed on Logland and Logland² and the standardised residuals are plotted against the FLP, a strong association emerges again (Figure 8.3c). Once again two clusters emerge, the Doab districts with low FMR and low FLP and the Zansi Upland cluster with higher FLP and FMRs. Fatehpur is an exception from the general Doab pattern in having high FMR and FLP.

The wheat and rice growing districts of UP, north of the Doab, provide another homogenous agro-ecological cluster (Government of India, 1980: Plate 6). Starting from Bijnor in the north-west it extends to Allahabad in the south-east. For these 12 districts and landholdings with a size between 1–30 acres, one gets the following relation:

FMR = 836 + 0.25* FLP	8.3c
T-value 240*** 15.3*** Adj. R. Sq. = 0.74; F = 233***	

The steep slope (0.25) and high R. Sq. (0.7) are worth noting. The FMR-Log(FLP) map once again shows a dense cluster in the lower left quadrant (Figure 8.3d). This feature can also be seen in the three earlier maps. These is discernible cluster with very low FMR and FLP below 100 followed by rather sparsely distributed points for FLP upto 200. Thereafter FMRs pick up sharply at higher FLP values. This indicates that more gains are made in FMR with initial increase in the FLP. Conversely, it could be said that FLP below 100 represents a rather high level of female subordination whose effects can be seen in the very low values of FMR.

A preliminary analysis of FMR-FFLP relation for households with large landholdings in the south (results not presented), shows the effect of FFLP to be significant. However, FLP in these groups never go to levels as low as those seen in the north.

These patterns assume significance in the context of seclusion of females. Seclusion is not feasible when the female members in the household have routine opportunities for interaction with the external domain. High FLP at the societal level goes together with such opportunities. It is only when the FLP is quite low that seclusion can be effectively practised. There could thus be a threshold FLP level below which seclusion effects become pronounced. Blumberg's observation that decline in independent control over income reduces the power within the household much more rapidly (Blumberg 1991) is relevant here. This

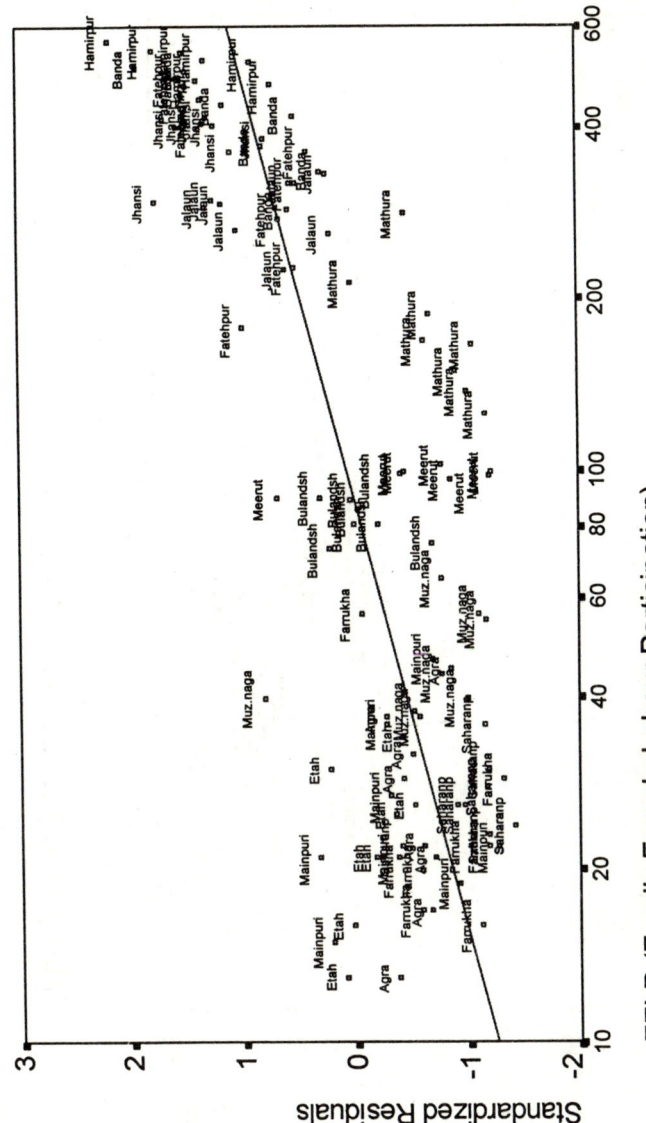

Figure 8.3c: Scatter plot of standardised residuals of FMR by FFLP (wheat growing districts: Doab and Zansi Uplands).

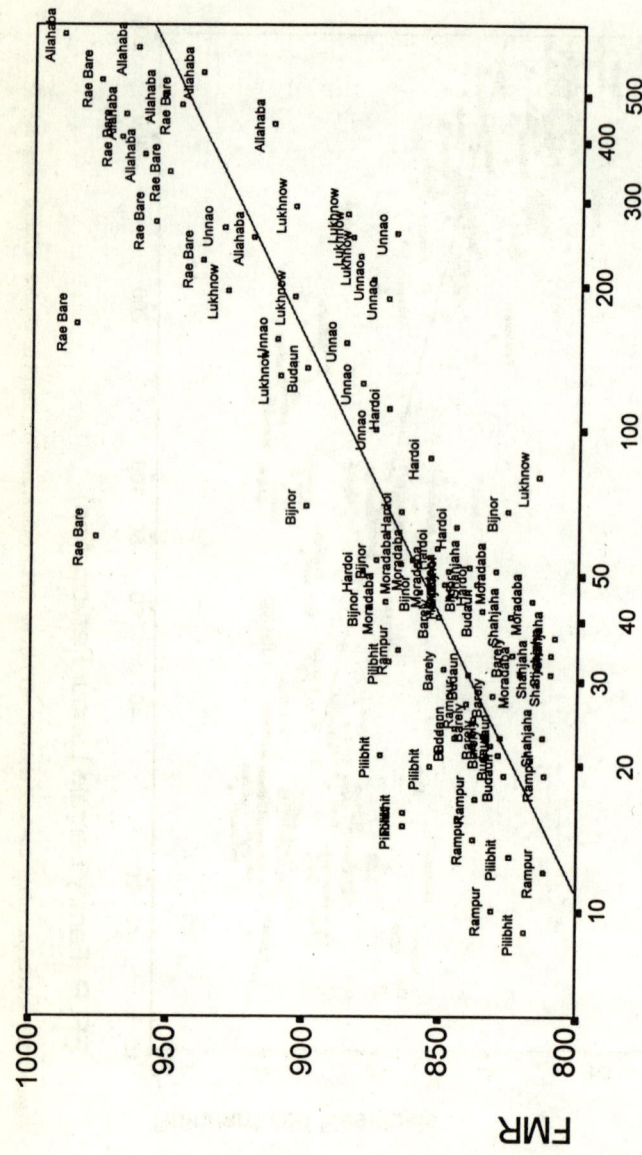

Figure 8.3d: Scatter plot of FMR by log (FFLP) (wheat and rice growing districts: North of the Doab).

issue calls for a more detailed analysis of the FLP patterns and the effectiveness with which seclusion is practised.

These findings have important policy implications. These show that low FMRs and FLPs are strongly associated with regions where basic entitlements are not taken care of by the kinship regime. Within the northern kinship region, relatively higher levels of FLP do occur within different crop regions, for example, wheat versus wheat-rice or rice. Within the same crop region FLP can vary depending upon the availability of irrigation as can be seen in the case of the Doab versus Zansi Upland.[17] In all these instances wherever FLP is high, FMRs are invariably high. In other words, high FLP provides a sufficient condition for better survival chances for females even among the non-poor in the 'core' northern region.

These results chime with Kishor's analysis (1993: 254–55) of the relative girl child mortality and exogamy[18] at different levels of FLP. Her analysis indicates that:

(*a*) Higher FLP weakens the impact of exogamy on female child mortality.

(*b*) The association between the two is weak in low exogamy region.

(*c*) Low FLP and high exogamy produce especially high levels of female child mortality.

(*d*) A given increase in FLP brings about a greater reduction in girl child mortality when exogamy is high rather than when it is low.

IV

Prosperity and FMRs-II

NSSO data

While data from the 1961 Census pertain to the rural agricultural context, the NSSO data provides FMR figures for the overall rural and non-agricultural urban context. There are 12 classes based on average monthly per capita expenditure. Separate data are available for adult and children

---

[17] Chen, (1989) on labour demand variations by crop region and irrigation facility.

[18] Taken as a measure of female subordination or 'lower cultural worth' of the female.

in the population. *However, NSSO's definition of children covers the 0–14 age group.*

A major limitation of the NSSO data is the sample size which is rather small, especially among the higher PCE brackets. For this reason, even state-level FMRs would suffer from large variability. In the analysis presented here, data at the all-India level are used first followed by data for the three southern states of Tamil Nadu, Andhra Pradesh and Karnataka. Data for Kerala are not used in view of pronounced male out-migration from the state. The data pertain to the 43rd (1987–88) and 50th round (1992–93) which are large sample size survey rounds.

At the all-India level, FMR-prosperity relationship shows no signs of a Kuznets curve. FMR and the log of the average monthly per capita expenditure (AMPCE) have a linear and negative association for the rural as well as the urban population, among both adults and children and for both the 43rd and 50th rounds. The results of regression of the type:

$$FMR = FMR_0 - k* \log(AMPCE) \hspace{3cm} 8.4c$$

are given in Table 8.2a (figures for the 50th round are in brackets).

Table 8.2

Regression results: FMR on log (AMPCE): All-India

All-India level, Rural and Urban (Adults and Children separately)**

Category	Constant*	Coefficient*	R. Sq	F-Value*
Adults (R*)	1,518	−246	0.97	346
	(1,540)	(−234)	(0.94)	(158)
Adults (U*)	1,725	−342	0.88	73
	(1,628)	(−273)	(0.92)	(112)
Children (R)	1,156	−126	0.85	55
	(1,256)	(−152)	(0.71)	(24)
Children (U)	1,326	−178	0.63	15
	(1,499)	(−235)	(0.93)	(137)

Notes: (* all terms are highly significant at 1 per cent level; R= Rural, U= Urban)
(** **Source**: NSSO Data Division: in p.c.)

Figures 8.4a and 8.4b present the results graphically for the rural and the urban areas separately. The constant term FMR_0 is very high in all these expressions but then Log(AMPCE) hardly goes below 1, corresponding to an average monthly per capita expenditure of Rs 10.

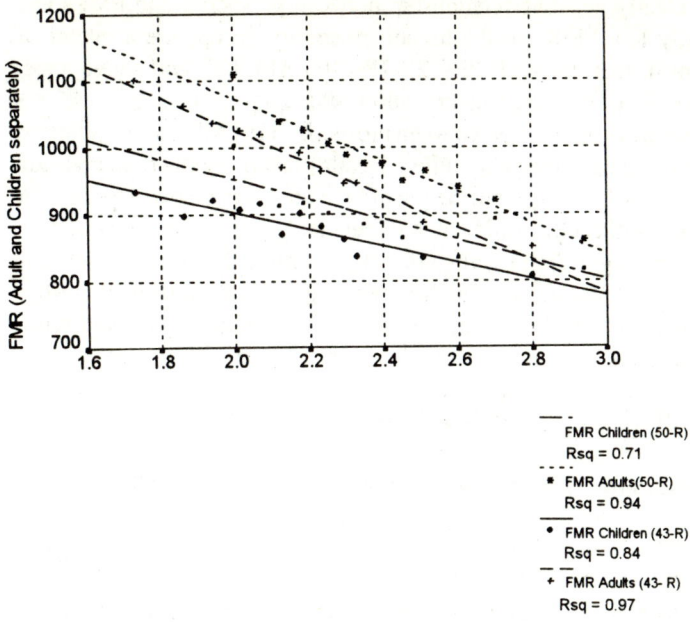

Figure 8.4a: FMR-log (AMPCE) plots—All-India (NSSO 43rd round).

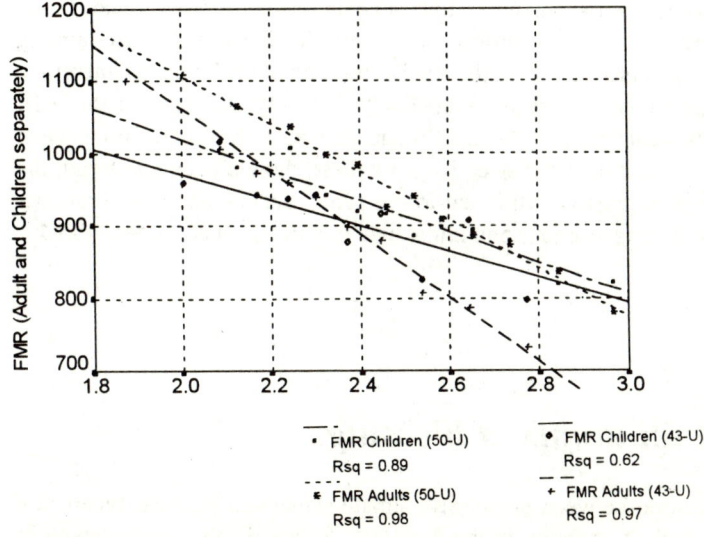

Figure 8.4b: FMR-log (AMPCE) plots—All-India (NSSO 50th round).

The clearly negative relationship between prosperity and FMRs and unusually low FMRs in the higher prosperity groups are a matter of concern. In fact, for logPCE = 2.6 (Rs 400 AMPCE) and above, most FMRs in the 0–14 age group are below 900.

The negative association between prosperity and FMRs is also reflected for the southern states (excluding Kerala) taken together. Regression results for FMR (adults) and the log of PCE are given below. The data for children is subject to considerable fluctuations due to the smaller sample size, hence regression results are not presented. The rural–urban differences are insignificant. The following equation adequately describes the relation for the 50th round (R. Sq. = 0.93) with the constant term, coefficient and F values being highly significant at a 1 per cent level.

$$FMR = 1,695 - 280* \, Log(PCE) \hspace{3cm} 8.5a$$

For the 43rd round the equation is quite similar (R. Sq. = 0.81):

$$FMR = 1,617 - 286* \, Log(PCE) \hspace{3cm} 8.5b$$

Low FMR values in the higher PCE brackets is a matter of concern. Even making allowance for the fluctuations, the FMRs are quite low. Among the adults these often go below 900; a very low value by the southern standards (Figures 8.5a–d).

This calls for an analysis of NSSO data across different rounds to see if there is a trend of uniform and sharp decline in the FMRs among prosperous groups. Given the level of training of the NSSO enumerators, enumeration errors are much less likely. The only uncertainty in the FMR figures would relate to the sample size. However, these could fluctuate in either direction. But if over 30 years these show a declining trend, the low FMRs must be attributed to the actual decline and not to random errors. This is a serious and immediate research agenda for the NSSO.

V

Not an unmixed blessing

Association between prosperity, female status and FLP has received a good deal of attention in the literature. Some of this was reviewed in

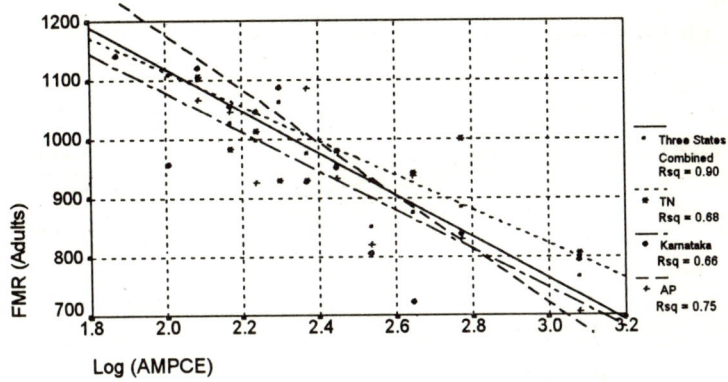

Figure 8.5a: FMR-log (AMPCE) plots—South (NSSO 43rd round, Urban).

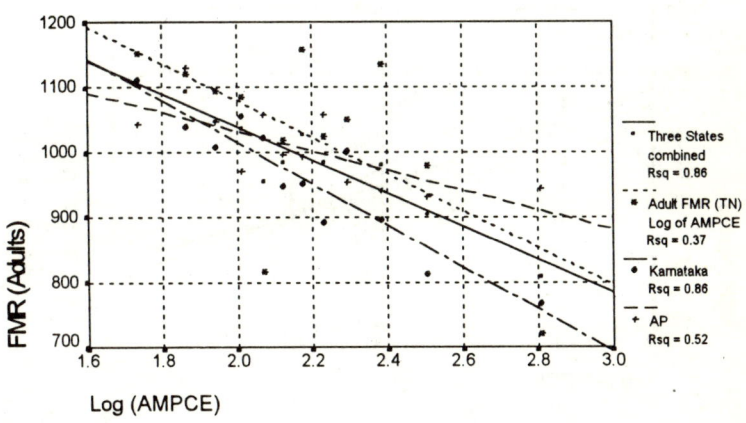

Figure 8.5b: FMR-log (AMPCE) plots—South (NSSO 43rd round, Rural).

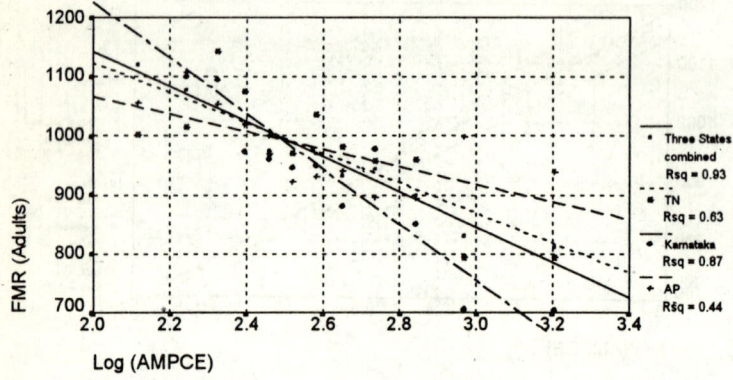

Figure 8.5c: FMR-log (AMPCE) plots—South (NSSO 50th round, Urban).

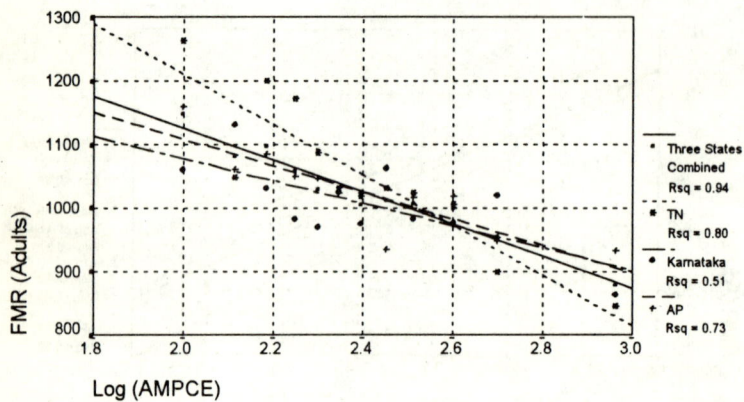

Figure 8.5d: FMR-log (AMPCE) plots—South (NSSO 50th round, Rural).

Chapter 2 (Sections VIII and IX). The pattern of low FLP among the non-poor is particularly sharp in the north, Within the same region and among similar castes the rich follow the 'high culture' norm and the poor the 'low culture' norms (Goody, 1990: Chapter 7). Similarly, communities which become prosperous begin to adopt the 'high culture' norms (Berreman, 1993; Goody, 1990; Parry, 1979 among others).

The withdrawal of women from 'external' wage earning activities has been a feature in the south too. The frequently cited observation reported by Gulati, 'In the neighbourhood where these (poor) working women live, the households which can afford not to send their women to work, specially manual work, gain in social esteem' (1978: 167) pertains to Kerala and is echoed in many micro level studies of the south. Vera-Sanso (1995) in her study of the labour market in Madras finds that the 'intermediate social contexts of wider kingroup and community' affect the FLP quite significantly. One of the important guiding concepts that affects this participation is the 'maanam' or the status of the family. Upward mobility or the quest for such mobility results in the withdrawal of women from participation in the external labour market. While the 'south' may manifest imperfect assimilation of the written orthodox Brahminical culture, there are instances of communities practising forms of seclusion similar to the 'north' (Ganesh, 1989) and an emerging 'anti-female bias' among some of the agriculturally prosperous communities (Heyer, 1992 and Kapadia, 1994). In practical terms this includes the introduction of dowry, low FLP, a move away from cross-cousin marriages and the like. Caldwell and Caldwell (1990) have reported similar trends of 'northernisation' while Miller (1989) talks of its consequences in terms of sex ratio patterns.

Status production

Papanek's emphasis on the context of withdrawal of women from external labour market needs some elaboration here. Such withdrawal in the wake of prosperity is often done for the purpose of status production. For a family there is a tension between the need for income and the need for status. Participation in external labour market, especially low paid labour, could entail a loss of status whereas withdrawal could result in loss of income but enhancement of status. The trade-offs made by the families depend upon the social milieu or the 'intermediate social contexts of wider kingroup and community'. A wider acceptance of higher wage and modern sector employment for the female members of the family can be understood in this context. These opportunities, for example, garment factory jobs, have a chance of being interpreted afresh unlike traditional sector jobs. Studies of such sectors indicate their favourable acceptance at the community level in terms of the participation of the female members (Kabeer, 1995).

Papanek (1989: 100–105) identifies four components of family status production work. These are:

(*a*) Indirect support activities for the paid work of other members.
(*b*) Support for the future paid work and the status aspiration of children.
(*c*) Politics of status maintenance.
(*d*) Performance of religious acts and rituals.

These activities become relevant with the onset of prosperity. In fact, these are part of strategies for social mobility and class differentiation. To quote Papanek (1989: 112):

> In other words, households with a small advantage that have achieved some degree of social differentiation withdraw women from paid employment not only because this is considered a mark of status attainment. They do so because status production tasks are seen as an effective methods for further social mobility.

A dilemma

Desai and Jain (1994) bring in another perspective by viewing women's withdrawal from wage work to family farm work as an income stabilisation strategy. While the family as a whole decides to diversify the labour use portfolio, the labour market dictates that men go in for wage earning activities. Women stay behind to do the unpaid farm and other work. But this leads to an ironical situation where the 'women's unpaid family labour may reduce their direct control over resources, while it may increase access to resources by raising total family income' (1994: 119). In formal terms this dilemma is summed up by the expression:

$$I = (x1 - x2)/(x1 + x2)$$

This means that the gap (x1 - x2) may increase faster than (x1 + x2), increasing the inequality within the household. The relative inequality will increase if the N_0 component of the female entitlements does not go up in 'recognition' of her cooperation in withdrawing from the wage market.

While seclusion may be infrequent in the south, it is quite commonplace in the north-west. In some of the Indo-Aryan literature, the ideal woman is described by the term 'Asuryampashyaa' (literally, not seen by the sun)—one upon whom even the Sun-god has not been able to cast his eyes. Mendelbaum's authoritative discussion of the practice of seclusion makes two salient points. The first is the extremely limited participation of women in the external sphere. The second is the emulation of this 'ideal' by those who prosper. It is quite likely that such seclusion is getting entrenched in the agriculturally 'prosperous' northern districts. Association between very low FMRs and very low FLP, examined here suggest the existence of a threshold level of FLP below which the seclusion effect is highly pronounced.

A 'burden' on prosperity

Literature concerned with the work participation of women focusses on one economic aspect: labour. In recent years, the effects of the other important variable, capital, has attracted attention in terms of dowry. Subramaniam (1996) looks upon the birth of a daughter as a 'negative income shock' in life-cycle terms. The perceptions of this shock depend upon the trends in the dowry market. Such a shock, that is the birth of a girl child, results in reduced household expenditure by as much as 15 per cent in anticipation of the future expenditure to be incurred. While Subramaniam suggests that a separate investigation will be required to determine who bears the burden of this reduced household expenditure (1996: 288), the findings of such an 'investigation' are intuitively clear from the significantly higher mortality rates among higher parity female children reported in the literature (Dasgupta and Bhat, 1995; Chen et al., 1981; Khan, 1993). The effect analysed by Subramaniam pertains to (ICRISAT) International Centre for Research in Semi Arid Tropic data for villages in the south and it is plausible to expect this effect and the perception of 'daughter as a liability' to be far sharper in the north.

The optimism expressed by Pissani and Zaba (forthcoming) needs to be questioned against this backdrop. The expectation that the 'scarcer the female children, more valued they will be' betrays a mechanical appli-cation of the demand and supply theory. It assumes that grooms and brides are undifferentiated products and an unsegmented market. It also implicitly assumes a 'closed' system within which the supply of brides takes place. In reality the system is open and the brides can be 'imported' (Parry, 1979: 218). The self-equilibrating pattern of sex ratios that Pisani and Zaba hope for has not been seen in the north-west over the last five to six decades which is a large time span indeed. Female children have continued to become more and more scarce and their devaluation continues.

There is thus a considerable literature expressing concern about the reduced autonomy of females in richer household. This loss of autonomy is a result of their withdrawal from 'visible' economic activity which plays an important role in improving the status and future mobility of the household in the long-term. But in immediate terms it costs women their autonomy by reducing the exchange-dependent component of their entitlements. If the exchange-independent component does not remain high either through culture or mobilisation, the women have worst of both the worlds. Prosperity does not come for them as an unmixed blessing.

VI

The elimination round

Low FMRs in the south

Very low FMR values in the southern states in the top three PCE brackets also assume importance in this context. Unlike the 1961 data, these FMR values are well below 900, which is quite low by southern standards. If these values are not a result of enumeration errors, random errors due to small sample size or migration, they are disquieting. In Section V, the issue of an emerging anti-female bias among the more prosperous groups in the south has been discussed. While some authors like Goody (1990), Heyer (1992), Rao (1993) and Kapadia (1994) talk of this in an exclusively southern context, Miller (1989) and Caldwell and Caldwell (1990) have raised this issue in the context of increasing 'northernisation'. In Chapter 5 it was suggested that this trend would spatially spread along the route of cultural circulation. Socio-culturally, however, it could spread among the economic superstrata which is already showing the symptoms of increasing demands for dowry and preference for 'stranger' marriages over cross-cousin marriages (Kapadia, 1994) and lower FLP.

A positive feedback spiral

It is possible to schematically depict the process as follows. We have two broad geographical regions; the north-west and the south-east. In both the regions, there is a social superstratum and social substratum. The social superstratum in the north-west represents the 'dominant Hindu ethos' in which strong female subordination is a distinguishing feature. This ethos influences the social substratum through the proximity effect or the emulation effect by the status-seeking segments (castes) within the substratum. The social superstratum in the south-east follows many aspects of the high culture but has 'attenuated adherence' to the ethos and 'suspect' kinship practices while the social substratum adheres to the 'low-culture'.

In the past, the geophysical barriers and inadequate development of communication restricted social circulation between the two regions. Even within a given region, the process of economic development being relatively slow, social mobility was not very rapid or frequent.

Development, however, has brought about rapid changes notably in communication and mobility, both physical and social. These changes have accelerated the process of increasing female subordination in the social substratum within the north-west through 'emulation'. It has also accelerated the process of diffusion of this ethos into the south-east within the social superstratum through the process of Sanskritisation or northern-isation. It is slowly seeping into its social substratum. In the near future, this ethos is likely to spread faster into the social substratum in the south-east among the upwardly mobile groups and gradually the poor. With physical barriers between the north-west and the south-east becoming more and more irrelevant, the spread of this ethos would link up geo-graphically across the social substrata. To use an analogy this would 'close the circuit'. As the anti-female ethos in the social superstratum in the north-west goes on deepening, the spread of the ethos of female subordination will go through a positive feedback loop, spiralling at an unprecedented scale in the south-east.

This apprehension is not imaginary. 1991 Census data on the 5-year age group sex ratios for Haryana[19] shows a sharp deterioration in FMR04 values between 1981 and 1991 (Table 8.3).

These FMRs strongly suggest the possibility of excess female infant mortality or high rates of sex-selective abortion. The rates of sex-selective abortions in India today are nowhere near the South Korean rates.[20] But

---

[19] In p.c. with the office of the Registrar General (India).

[20] Sex-selective abortions account for less than 0.5 per cent of the total births in India where as in South Korea this is about 5 per cent (Dasgupta and Bhat, 1995).

Table 8.3

Decline in FMR04 in the districts of Haryana: 1981–91

Year	Amb.	Kuru.	Karn.	Jind	Sone.	Roh.	Farida.	Gur.	Mah.	Bhi.	Hiss.	Sirsa
1981	934	880	931	879	890	938	921	956	947	933	913	938
1991	888	868	915	868	883	860	895	928	893	902	866	896

Notes:
1) Amb. = Ambala, Kuru. = Kurukshetra, Karn. = Karnal, Soni. = Sonepat, Roh. = Rohtak, Farida = Faridabad, Gur. = Gurgaon, Mah. = Mahendragarh, Bhi. = Bhiwani, Hiss. = Hissar

2) Newly formed districts of Yamunanagar (883), Kaithal (856), Panipat (900), and Rewari (908) all have low FMR04 values (1991 Census).

data on these rates are not disaggregated by prosperity and region. Given reports from micro studies, the incidence of sex-selective abortion among the non-poor is likely to be much higher than among the poor. Further, the elements that constitute the perception of the 'female child as a liability' operate among the non-poor in north India more strongly. The process of declining FMRs among the social and economic elites does not seem to be self-equilibrating and it is quite likely that the social superstratum in India will follow the Korean path in terms of prenatal sex selection.

The process of increased female subordination described here quite closely conforms to the developments among the Pramalai Kallars, a community which has come under sharp focus for the practice of female infanticide in recent years (Mazumdar, 1994: Section II). This brings one to the issue of excess female mortality at or before birth.

Sex-selective abortions and female infanticide

The rise in sex-selective abortions and emergence of female infanticide in various parts of the country are two serious aspects of excess female child mortality. Incidence of prenatal selection have rapidly increased in the last decade or so in India (Mazumdar, 1994). Work on female infanticide in Tamil Nadu and in Bihar (Mazumdar, 1994; Srinivasan, 1994; Venkatachalam and Srinivasan, 1993) shows that this practice has reappeared among certain communities and emerged among some others who did not practice it before. Why is this happening? One can plausibly apprehend that another positive feedback loop is likely to operate in linking prenatal selection and female infanticide.

Medical anthropologists (like McKee, 1984) note that parents prefer to put a distance between their action and the death of the offspring. That is why mothers or fathers very rarely kill the baby themselves. The task is assigned to village midwives or elderly women. Prenatal selection is a new technological tool which has gained acceptability as something scientific, neutral and performed by the 'professionals' concerned. It has accorded legitimacy to the elimination of a child on the basis of its sex. Where money and facility are available, it is resorted to by the social superstratum. Those who do not have the access to this facility look for 'affordable' alternatives since the process has been 'sanctified' anyway.[21] This 'affordable'[22] alternative is infanticide. As the incidence of infanticide spreads, those who practice prenatal selection occupy of 'holier' pedestal. After all, they are not resorting to the 'barbaric' or the 'cruel' practice of killing a new born infant. So the doctor who goes around the countryside with this 'mobile facility' in his new luxury car can claim to be doing social service.[23] The verdict is now passed not on whether the elimination on the basis of sex is acceptable or otherwise but on which method is more acceptable; sex-selective abortion or infanticide. The technological alternative gets legitimised in comparison with infanticide while sanctifying the idea of elimination of the child on the basis sex. This in turn spreads the practice of infanticide further among those who do not have access to the facility, e.g., high castes in rural Bihar, or those who can not afford it, e.g., rural poor in Salem district of Tamil Nadu. Notwithstanding the spread in the facility of the 'facilities' for prenatal selection, it will continue to remain beyond the reach of a large number of people in foreseeable future. The two processes will therefore, feed on each other.

It is pertinent to quote the results of a simulation exercise here. It examines th impact of biased sex selection technologies, i.e., those which enhance the chances of bearing a son but not of a daughter. It shows that even if the population has unbiased sex preference or preference towards daughters, the availability of the biased technology results in highly masculine population sex ratio. Where the technological bias and son preference converge, the sex ratios are very highly masculine indeed. The predicted sex ratios are indicated in Table 8.4,

[21] Well to do people go for family planning methods. We limit our families in our own indigenous way. What is the difference? If it is legal to kill a baby in the womb ... why should it be wrong killing a new born baby?'-Response of many Kallar women on the question of female infanticide (Mazumdar, 1994: 14).

[22] Coasting about Rs 50 (Srinivasan, 1994; Venkatachalam and Srinivasan, 1993) as against the cost of sex determination which cost over Rs 500 (Mazumdar, 1994).

[23] 'Let her die' BBC 2. Similarly, one of the clinics offering sex selection facilities actually described the girl child as a 'liability' to the family and a 'threat to the nation' (Mazumdar, 1994: 3) in their 'promotional' leaflet.

Table 8.4
Sex selection technologies, son preference and estimated sex ratios

Country, Year	Mean ideal number of children	Mean ideal number of sons	Predicted sex ratio male/female
Belgium, 1966	2.82	1.16	1.24
USA, 1970	2.86	1.46	1.40
Korea, 1971	3.65	2.20	1.68
India, 1970	3.58	2.15	1.86

Source: Mason and Bennett, 1977.

This clearly shows that unregulated access to biased prenatal selection can vitiate the sex ratios *even in societies without a gender bias*! Further, this model assumes that the son preference may remain static. One sees no reason why it would not aggravate the sex ratio further.[24] Given the liabilities associated with the rearing of the girl child everybody will want that a girl be born but in the neighbour's household!

VII

Implications

These findings have important implications. First, it reveals the inadequacy of prosperity alone in ensuring equitable survival chances for the female members of the society. Second, it indicates the need for different types of measures to enhance survival chances of the girl children among the non-poor groups. Increase in women's employment among the non-poor cannot be brought about, for example, through public works programmes. Similarly the traditional sector, especially agriculture, does not offer much hope for enhancement of such a participation. It is also necessary to recognise that the more prosperous families will have higher threshold level of wages and 'modernity' of the job concerned in which their women-folk could participate. Johansson's observations (1984, 1991, 1996) in the historical context are relevant here. The excess female mortality in

---

[24] Dr Ronald Ericsson, who has invented one of the sex selection techniques, has been quoted by Mazumdar (1994: 1) as having said that 94 per cent of the couples seeking his services, from about 46 clinics all over the world, wanted a male child!

the cultures reviewed by her declined only with industrialisation and not during the phase of modernisation of agriculture. It will be a risky proposition to expect the modernising agricultural sector to create large-scale female labour employment.

Acquisition of skills and their use in the non-traditional sector has shown some promise in this regard. But within such sector too the distinction between women as housewives and women working outside the domestic confines is important. Outside earnings has two advantages, explicit earnings and social interaction which act as an effective antidote to seclusion and all its adverse consequences.[25] Earnings within the confines of the household could co-exist with higher 'discount rates'. This has been documented in the case of 'Lace workers' in Andhra Pradesh (Mies, 1982) and female participation in the dairy sector in Rajasthan (Sharma and Vanjani, 1993).

It will be necessary to have, to use a cliché, a package of policies in place for the non-poor. This will consist of four elements: providing physical security, skill acquisition, avenues for their utilisation and FLP levels well above seclusion threshold. Specific policy details are discussed in the next chapter.

To conclude

Prosperity by itself cannot ensure reduction in relative gender inequality in survival. But it is important to recognise the significantly distinct processes that operate as prosperity increases. There is need to collect further data on this aspect. Some of the possibilities have been outlined above. The available evidence, however, shows a strong negative association between prosperity and FMRs especially where FLP is very low. The trend among the more prosperous groups is disturbing even in south. This is subject to the caveats about sample size. The preponderance of available evidence suggests, however, that social and policy interventions should begin straight away.

The concluding chapter outlines some of these solutions in more details in the background of the overall findings. It recapitulates the diversities

[25] It is worth referring to Nag's (1989) comparative study of Kerala and West Bengal both outside the 'core' Indo-Aryan kinship regions and with low FLP. In Kerala, the mobilisation being strong, low FLP does not stand in the way of women's access of social and health infrastructure.

in the FMR patterns which had not been noticed or focussed upon so far. It then discusses the findings about the economic and cultural correlates. This takes the discussion of the sex ratio problem beyond some of the prevalent 'stereotypes'. A strong plea is then made in favour of plurality in design of policy intervention, a more focussed collection and analysis of data and a simultaneous action for partial solutions. This realistic advocacy of partial solutions recognises the size and the complexity of the problem. But it also recognises that the problem is diverse and not monolithic. This recognition provides the optimism to work at solutions which are partial and workable though neither complete or conclusive. But then any prudent policy has to ensure that the best does not become the enemy of the better. It is useful to see, however, the trends which are revealed by the 1991 data. This is the subject matter of the next chapter.

Chapter 9

What do the 1991 Census data reveal?

I

An outline

The preceding analysis has mainly relied on the data from the 1981 and the 1961 Population Censuses. As India prepares herself for the 2001 Population Census, an obvious question arises as to what trends do the 1991 Census data show. As mentioned earlier, many details from the 1991 Census are yet to become available. The 5-year age group data break-up for the Scheduled Caste and Scheduled Tribe population is one such case. It is unlikely to become available any time soon.

While this places some limitation on our ability to use the 1991 Census data, certain useful analysis can still be done. At present, the 5-year age group data for the overall district-level population are available and so are the FLP figures. In addition, the child mortality estimates at the district level based on the 1991 data have also become available. It is, therefore, possible to have district-level maps of the 0–4 and 5–9 age group FMRs and examine the changes that have occurred between 1981 and 1991. It is also possible to verify the extent to which the 1991 data corroborate the findings in respect of the male–female mortality relation (Chapter 3) and the FMR-FLP relation for the 0–4, 5–9 and the 0–9 age groups (Chapter 7). While making these comparisons, some of the differences between the 1981 and 1991 data have to be taken note of, for example, the creation of a number of new districts between 1981 and 1991.

The analysis presented here is organised as follows. Section II briefly discusses the differences between the 1981 and the 1991 FMR data followed by an analysis of the sixteenfold combination of the districts in the 1991 Census, the distribution of FMRs in the 0–4 and 5–9 age groups in these districts and the FMR maps. These are compared with the 1981 patterns. This is followed by an analysis of the 1991 infant and child mortality figures at the district level. Finally, the FMR-FLP relation is examined on the lines of the analysis in Chapter 7 and the results are discussed.

The analysis of the 1991 data reveals a growing masculinisation of the sex ratios even in the 0–4 age group. While there is a perceptible decline in the number of districts where the FMR04 was unusually high, the number of districts where FMR04 has gone below 960 is quite large. This masculinisation is quite strong in the region of Indo-Aryan kinship as revealed by the data on sex differentials in child mortality.

Analysis of female and male mortality based on the Q1, Q2, Q3 and the Q5 values provides an exciting possibility of inferring gender bias from the mortality data. It reveals the gradual shift from excess male mortality during infancy to excess female child mortality in the subsequent years of childhood. This has important implications both methodological terms and for future research.

The FMR-FLP relation confirms the patterns observed in the earlier analysis. The significant differences between FMR04 and FMR59 and the ability of the latter to capture the discrimination effect are demonstrated once again. A convergence of the FMR04-FLP and FMR59-FLP relationship is also seen in the non-Indo-Aryan kinship regions while in the Indo-Aryan kinship region, a sharper deterioration in the survival of the girl child is seen.

II

FMRs by 5-year age group

The 1991 Census data used here (Office of the Registrar General of India: in p.c) cover nearly 450 district units. These are not quite comparable with the 1981 data on an overall basis for a number of reasons. First, a number of new districts have been created between 1981 and 1991. Second, the 1981 Census could not be conducted in the state of Assam while in 1991 the census operations could not be conducted in the state of Jammu and Kashmir. Third, the 1991 data used here include a large number of districts in the north-east. In the IDDD database, these districts have been merged together. Finally, the 1991 data on the 5-year age group are provisional and not yet available separately for the three social groups. These differences notwithstanding, a number of important trends can still be identified.

Difference between FMR04 and FMR59

T-tests for paired samples confirm the significant difference between FMR04 and FMR59 on an all-India basis. FMR04 values are higher than the FMR59 values in most districts. The difference persists even if we select the low FMR04 districts, that is, districts where FMR04 is below 960.

Table 9.1
T-tests for paired samples

Number of Variable	2-tail Pairs Corr.	Sig.	SE of Mean	SD	Mean	Paired Differences Mean	SD	SE of Mean	T-value	df	2-tail sig.
FMR04			957.21	34.8	1.65	13.78	42.69	2.019	6.83	446	.000
	447 .491	.000				95%CI (9.813, 17.753)					
FMR59			943.42	47.16	2.23						

Distribution of FMR04 and FMR59 support this pattern further (Figure 9.1). Once again the mean of the FMR04 values is higher than the mean of FMR59 and FMR04 values are less dispersed, closer to normal distribution and rarely fall below 850. FMR59 values, on the other hand, are more dispersed, more skewed and assume quite low values.

It is useful to examine the sixteenfold combination of FMR04 and FMR59 for the 1991 FMR data. The distribution of districts falling in different FMR ranges is given in Table 9.2. To facilitate comparison with the 1981 data the number of districts in the 1981 Census are given in parentheses.

Two trends are unmistakable. Both lead to a decline in FMRs but one is desirable and the other is not. A desirable decline has taken place in the number of districts where the FMR values have been unusually high. The very high FMR04 category districts have reduced from 82 in 1981 to 30 in 1991. Of these, 15 districts in the north-east were not included in the 1981 IDDD database as separate units. Thus the decline is effectively from 82 units in 1981 to 15 units in 1991, signifying a reduction in the infant mortality rates and the concerned agencies can take justifiable pride in it. It remains to be seen, however, if the decline in the infant mortality that has occurred among the ST and SC population is of comparable magnitude.

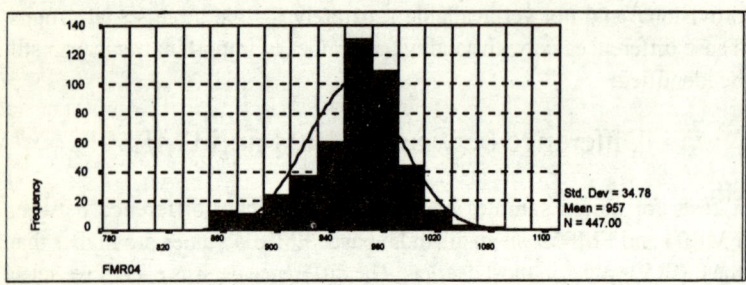

Female - male Ratio in the 0-4 age group

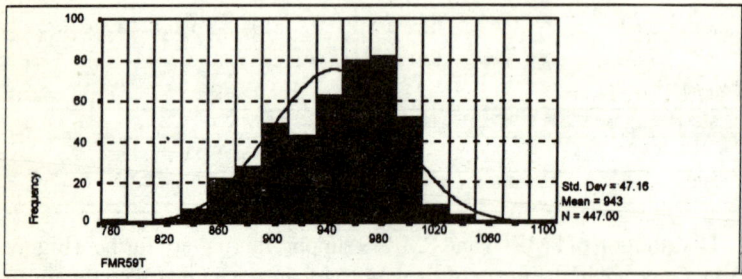

Female - male Ratio in the 5-9 age group

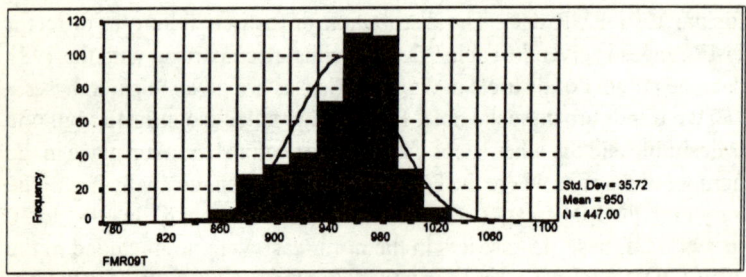

Female - male Ratio in the 0-9 age group

Figure 9.1: Distribution of FMRs: 1991 Census data (447 districts).

Table 9.2

Distribution of districts by levels of FMR04 and FMR59

FMR59 Range	FMR04 Range			
	Low	Moderate	High	Very High
Low	41 (10)	45 (54)	25 (27)	1 (6)
Moderate	4 (1)	62 (26)	67 (55)	15 (18)
High		46 (12)	91 (83)	12 (28)
Very High	2	8 (1)	20 (15)	2 (30)

The number of districts in which the FMR04 has deteriorated to low levels (< 910) has increased from 13 in 1981 to 47 in 1991. Most of these districts are in the north-western region of the country except Salem and Dharmapuri in Tamil Nadu, Kottayam in Kerala, and Sangli in Maharashtra. Similarly, the number of districts where FMR04 is below 960 has increased from 106 in 1981 to 208 in 1991, pushing further and deeper into the southern states. This trend is disturbing and indicative of increasing girl child mortality in the post-neonatal period and the 1–4 age group. The 47 districts with low FMR04 could signify high rates of sex-selective abortions or even female infanticide. Given that this is the region where FMR values among the SC population are significantly lower than those for the overall district population, *an analysis of the 5-year age group FMR figures for the SC population in the 1991 Census assumes priority.*

These changes in FMR levels can be seen more clearly through the district-level maps. Maps 9.1a, b and 9.2a, b provide the FMR04 and the FMR59 maps for the 1981 and the 1991 Census. The increase in area with FMR04 < 960 is quite conspicuous and so is the shrinkage of area where FMR04 and FMR59 values were very high in the 1981 Census.

Interestingly, the number of districts with alarmingly low values of FMR59 i.e., below 850 has, in fact, reduced from 27 in 1981 to 12 in 1991. In certain parts of eastern UP and Bihar, FMR59 values have marginally improved, while in some of the regions, notably northern Rajasthan, these have deteriorated. Given the decline in the FMR04 values, the overall FMRs in the juvenile age group are bound to be lower. In fact, the number of districts where the FMR09 is below 910 has increased from 49 in 1981 to 71 in 1991.

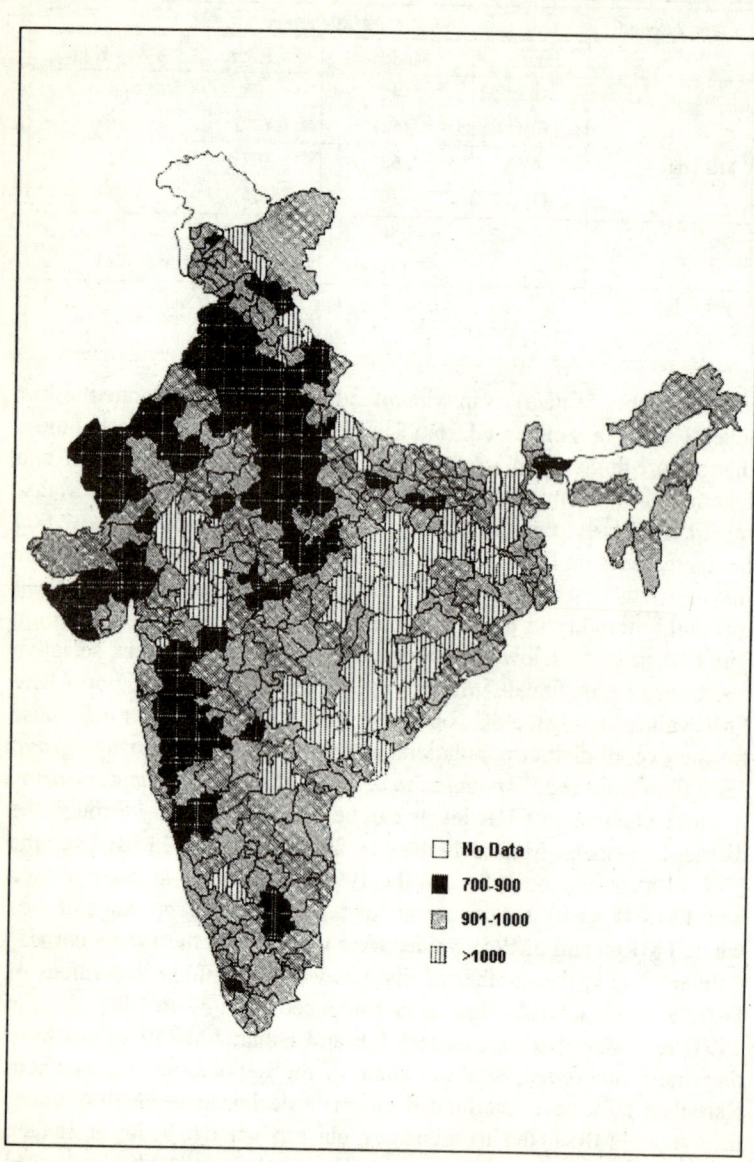

Map 9.1a: FMR04: 1981 (total population).

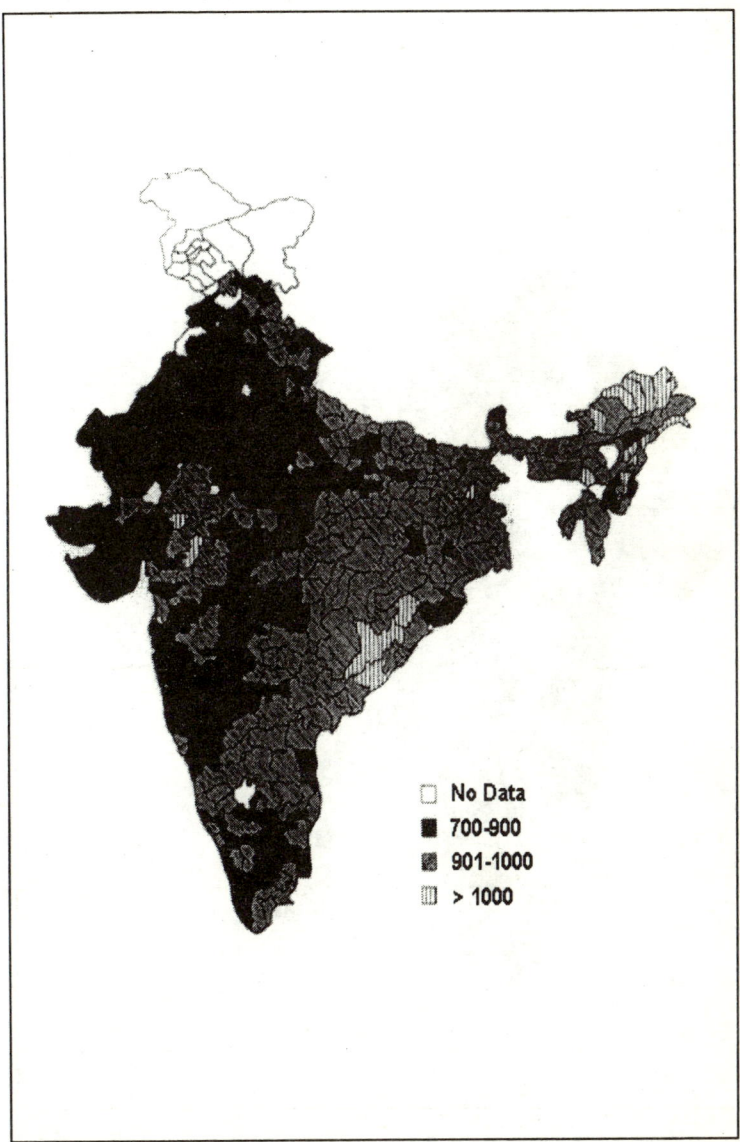

Map 9.1b: FMR04: 1991 (total population).

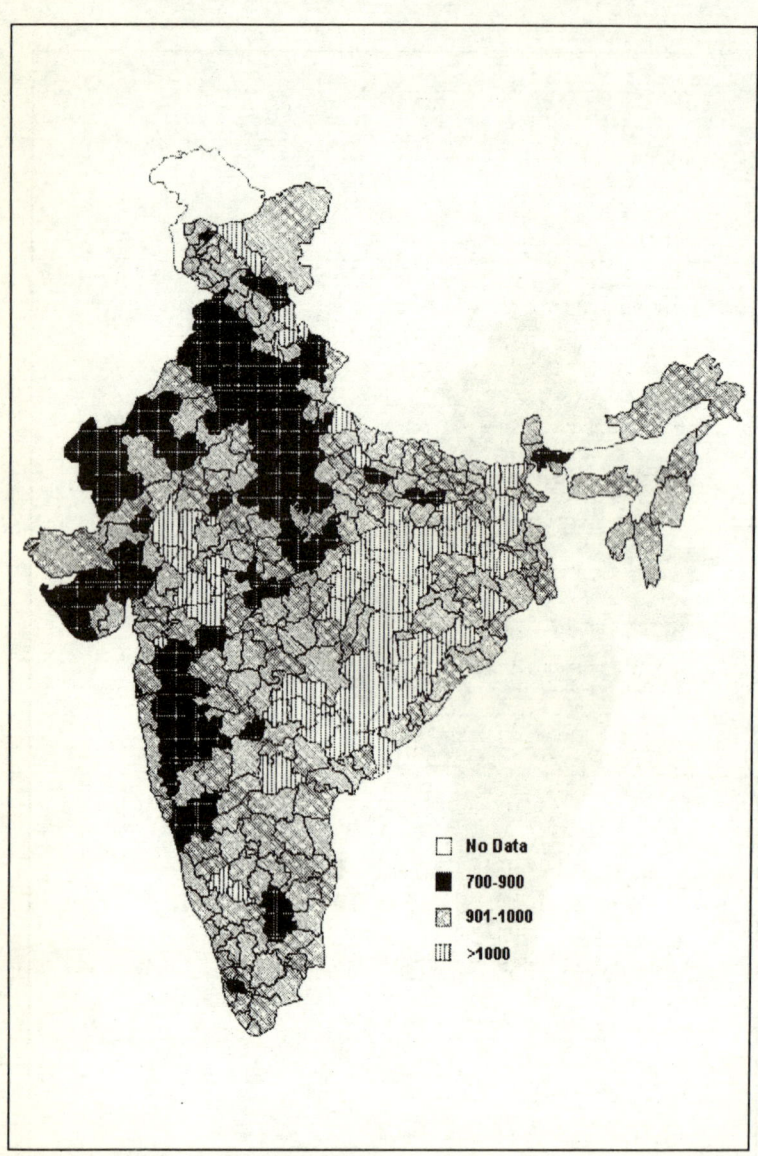

Map 9.2a: FMR59: 1981 (total population).

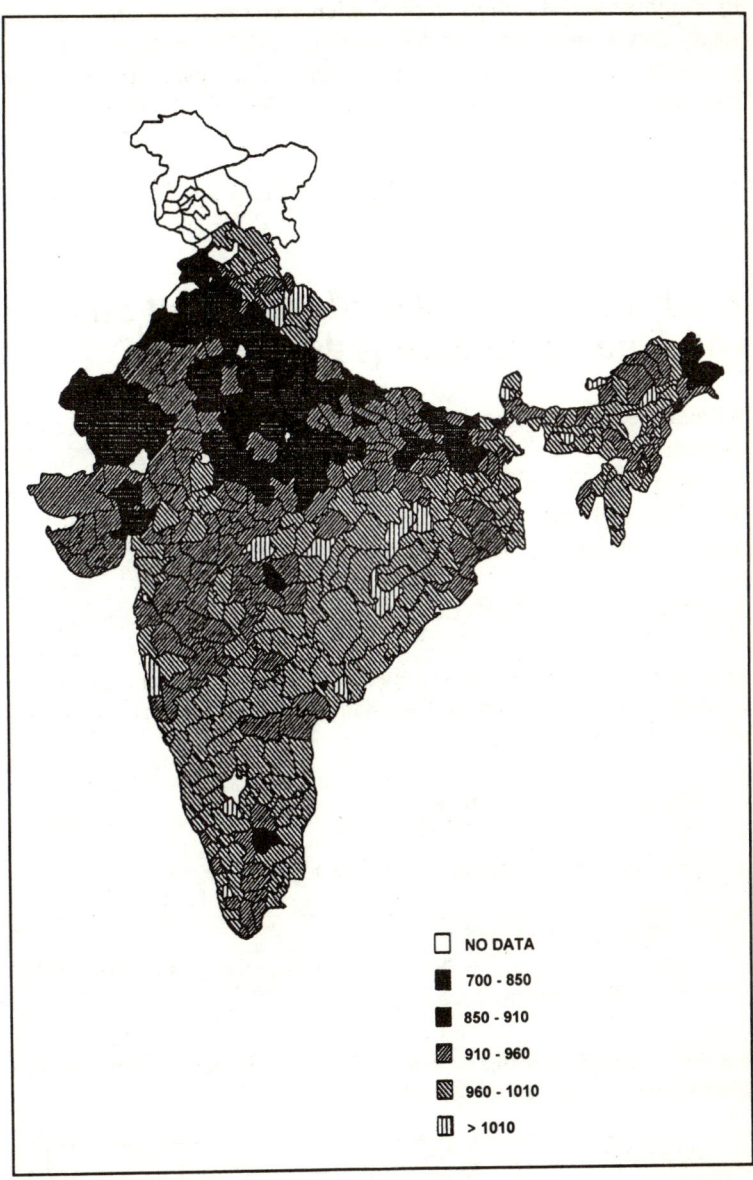

Map 9.2b: FMR59: 1991 (total population).

Since the 1991 Census data on the 5-year age group are not yet available by the three social groups, further inferences cannot be drawn at this stage. This is proposed to be done at a later date when the data become available. For the present we can turn to the district-level infant and child mortality data which have become available for the 1991 Census.

III

Analysis of the district-level infant and child mortality data (1991 Census)

As indicated in Chapter 3, the 1981 Census data provided for the first time estimates of infant and child mortality at the district level. Similar estimates have become available in respect of the 1991 Census data recently. It is useful to analyse the relation between the male and female mortality rates and compare the results with the 1981 data.

Relationship between female and male mortality

In Chapter 3, the female–male mortality relation was examined on the basis of the 1981 Census data. The infant mortality rates between the two sexes is related linearly as:

$$IMRf = 9.9 + 0.86 \ IMRm$$

This relationship holds for the 1991 data as well. We get:

$$IMRf = 11 + 0.85 \ IMRm$$

(Adj. R. Sq. = 0.69, F = 991***, T-value for the constant is 4.85***, and 31.4*** for the slope.)

Similarly, the relationship between the under-5 mortality data from the 1981 Census was given by:

$$U5MRf = -4.7 + 1.1 \ U5MRm$$

The corresponding equation based on the 1991 data is given by:

U5MRf = –0.08 + 1.04 U5MRm

(Adj. R. Sq. = 0.85, F = 2,605****, T-value for the constant is –0.04, and 51*** for the slope.)

It was hypothesised in Chapter 3 that the constant and the slope value of the female–male mortality relationship reveals the story of gender bias. It was further seen that in the case of infant mortality, the slope is less than unity (around 0.85) and signifies excess male mortality. In contrast to this, the slope value for the under-5 mortality is above unity, signifying excess female child mortality.

Since the sex differentials in mortality change from an excess of male mortality during infancy to an excess of female child mortality between the age of 1–4, it is plausible to expect this gradual change in the female–male mortality relationship to be revealed through mortality data under the age of 2, 3 and 4 years of age or the Q_i values which give the probability by the ith birthday. The 1991 data do provide the Q2 and Q3 values. It will be instructive, therefore, to examine the male–female mortality relation for the Q2 and Q3 values.

The district level female and male mortality data for the 2nd and 3rd birthday are related as follows:

U2MRf = 6.9 + .94 U2MRm

(Adj. R. Sq. = 0.80, F = 1,817***, T-value for the constant is 3.29***, and 42.6*** for the slope.)

and

U3MRf = 2.68 + 1.00 U3MRm

(Adj. R. Sq. = 0.86, F = 2,741***, T-value for the constant is 1.38, and 52.3*** for the slope.)

The slope values differ significantly from each other and gradually change from 0.85 to 1.01. The other noteworthy feature is the gradual decline in the value and significance of the constant term. It shows that there will be no 'residual' mortality for the females if the mortality levels for the Q3 and Q5 levels approach zero. But this does not seem to be the case during infancy or the under-2 mortality data where the gains in mortality reduction appear to be flowing faster to male children and the reduction in male mortality will still leave a residual, even though small, mortality for the female children.

The gradual change in the linear relationship between IMR and U5MR opens up an exciting methodological possibility of examining gender bias using mortality data. Before dwelling on this, it is useful to examine the role played, if any, by the cultural variable, that is, kinship.

The kinship variable

In the previous analysis of the mortality data, the kinship variable had not been explicitly used. It will be instructive to see if the male–female mortality rates are related differently in different kinship regimes. Given the difference in the nature and the extent of the gender bias across the 'core Indo-Aryan' and the 'rest' of the regions, it is plausible to expect differences.

An analysis of the Q1 values for the female and male children, based on the 1991 data, and using the kinship variable for both the slope and the constant term yields the following relationship:

$$IMRf = 7.6 + 12.6* K + (0.82 + 0.006* K)\ IMRm$$

(Adj. R. Sq. = 0.73, F = 407***, T-value for the constant is 2.92*** and 26.1*** for the slope.)

The kinship dummy for the constant is significant (T-value = 2.86***) but it is not so for the slope (T-value = 0.123).

The situation changes for the under-5 mortality where we get:

$$U5MRf = 1.2 + 3.7* K + (0.96 + 0.1* K)\ U5MRm$$

(Adj. R. Sq. = 0.89, F = 1,181***, T-value for the constant is 0.61 and 42.1*** for the slope.)

The kinship dummy for the constant is insignificant (T-value = 0.5) but is significant for the slope (T-value = 2.92***). In other words, the slope values are quite steep in the kinship = 1 region or the region where the 'core Indo-Aryan' kinship practice prevails.

These patterns are separately corroborated by looking at the distribution of the sex differentials in mortality directly. Table 9.3 gives the descriptive statistics for the sex differences in mortality for Q1–Q5 values.

The excess female infant mortality in the core Indo-Aryan kinship region is conspicuous. This excess steadily increases in the next four years of life. In the 'rest' of the regions, there is an excess of male mortality

Table 9.3

Sex differentials in mortality across the two kinship regions

SDM	K = 0		K = 1	
	Mean	95% CI	Mean	95% CI
Q1m–Q1f	6.06	4.14, 7.98	−6.08	−8.64, −3.52
Q2m–Q2f	3.76	2.11, 5.40	−9.03	−11.32, −6.73
Q3m–Q3f	2.62	1.32, 3.91	−11.19	−13.19, −9.19
Q5m–Q5f	1.84	.37, 3.30	−13.47	−15.74, −11.21

during infancy which gradually declines to a marginal value of 1.8 in the under-5 mortality.

The importance of the kinship variable can also be gauged by examining the relationship between FMR values and sex differentials in mortality. Using the kinship dummy for both the constant term and the slope, we get:

$$FMR59T = 971.4 - 56.7* K + (0.2 + 0.67* K)* (Q5m - Q5f)$$

(Adj. R. Sq. = 0.55, F = 182***, T-value for the constant is 492*** and 1.25 for the slope.)

The kinship dummy is significant both for the constant (T-value = −15.5***) and the slope (T-value = 3.06***).

The equation for FMR04 involving the sex differentials in the infant and under-5 mortality gives the following result:

$$FMR04T = 971.9 - 35.8* K - 0.04* (Q5m - Q5f) - 0.1* (Q1m - Q1f)$$

Adj. R. Sq. = 0.23, F = 45***, T-value is significant for the constant term [497***) but is insignificant for both the sex differentials in the under-5 mortality (−0.38) and infant mortality (−1.07) but significant for the kinship dummy for the constant term (−10.6***].

One can infer the value of FMRs at birth indirectly by setting the sex differentials in mortality to zero. For the kinship = 0 region, the value turns out to be close to 971 while in the Indo-Aryan kinship region it is between 914 and 930 which still belies the argument that the masculine sex ratios in this region can be explained away by invoking the low FMR at birth.

IV

The FMR-FLP relationship

Examining this relationship for the 1991 district-level data is the next logical step. Such analysis is possible only in respect of the overall district-level population. Yet it provides useful information about the relationship between female workforce participation and female survival in 1991.

The JFMR-FLP relationship for all the districts in 1991 is significant:

FMR09T = 954 – 44* K +0.05* TWW

[Adj. R. Sq. = 0.55, F = 270*** and highly significant constant term · (T = 279***), slope value (T = 5.5***) and the kinship dummy for the constant (T = –16.3***)].

The results are nearly identical if we use MWW (main female workers per 1,000 female population).

For FMR in the 0–4and 5–9 age groups we get:

FMR04T = 957 – 27* K +0.05* TWW

[Adj. R. Sq. = 0.25, F = 76*** and highly significant constant term (T = 233***), slope value (T = 3.8***) and the kinship dummy for the constant (T = –7.9***)].

FMR59T = 952 – 60* K +0.06* TWW

[Adj. R. Sq. = 0.54, = 0.54, F = 261*** and highly significant constant term (T = 209***), slope value (T = 4.7***) and the kinship dummy for the constant (T = –16.4***)].

The results are nearly identical if we use MWW instead of TWW.

When the kinship dummy is used for both the slope and the constant, the following results are obtained. For the kinship = 0 region, all three FMRs can be described more or less with one equation:

FMR = 964 + 0.02* TWW

The constant term is highly significant for all three variables while the slope is significant at a 10 per cent level.

This convergence between the three sex ratios does not hold for the kinship = 1 regions. Both the slopes and the constant terms differ significantly.

$$FMR09 = 899 + 0.12* \text{TWW}$$
$$FMR59 = 877 + 0.15* \text{TWW}$$
$$FMR04 = 924 + 0.07* \text{TWW}$$

Once again the Adj. R. Sq. values are high in the case of FMR59 and FMR09 but lower in the case of FMR04. The significantly low value of the constant term for FMR59, i.e., 877, compared to 924 for FMR04 is noteworthy and underlines the role of behavioural factors in shaping FMRs in the 5–9 age group. The steeper slope in the case of the FMR59 further confirms this.

If we compare with the 1981 data, the constant term for FMR04 in the kinship = 0 region has come down from 984 to 964. But it is close to FMR at birth. In the kinship = 1 region, however, it has come down from 951 to 924, well below FMR values at birth. The slope values have remained more or less the same.

It is instructive to look at the relationship between FMR and FLP using the female workforce participation for 'main workers'. In the kinship = 0 region, the relationship can again be given by one equation:

$$FMR = 964 + 0.02* \text{MWW}$$

For the kinship = 1 region, however, we get:

$$FMR09 = 895 + 0.24* \text{MWW}$$
$$FMR59 = 874 + 0.31* \text{MWW}$$
$$FMR04 = 920 + 0.17* \text{MWW}$$

While the constant terms are similar to those obtained when TWW is used as the independent variable, the slopes are considerably steeper, even in the case of FMR04. The extent to which the lower constant term and the steep slope for FMR04 should be treated as an 'early warning system' is a matter of further investigation. While the extent of the effect may be a matter of debate, the effect itself is not.

In the analysis of the 1981 data, the FMR-FLP regression was carried out with log of MWW as the independent variable. Such an exercise can be done here. However, in the absence of disaggregated FMR data for the ST and SC population, such 'fine-tuning' is not attempted and is deferred until such a break-up is available.

While the FMR-TWW slopes have become steeper in the 1991 data, the female workforce participation itself has come down compared to the 1981 figures. The 1991 and the 1981 figures are comparable in methodological terms.

Table 9.4
Mean female workforce participation–1991 district data

Variable	Kinship = 0 (Number of Districts = 263)		Kinship = 1 (Number of Districts = 184)	
	Mean	95% CI	Mean	95% CI
MWW	239	(225, 253)	99	(90, 109)
TWW	312	(297, 328)	166	(152, 181)

Compared to the 1981 figures, the female workforce participation has declined significantly. Their withdrawal from the workforce and their increasingly adverse survival conditions are a matter of serious concern for policy-makers.

V

Conclusions

1991 Census data confirms the trend of further decline in FMRs. While the decline in FMR04 from unusually high values to values below 1,000 is to be welcomed, the decline below the balanced range of 950–980 is to be viewed with concern. The adverse survival conditions of female children vis-á-vis male children is sharp in the Indo-Aryan kinship region. This is corroborated by the mortality data as well as the FMR-FLP relation.

The significant increase in the number of districts where the FMR04 values are low but the FMR59 values are high is puzzling. There are 51 districts where the difference FMR59-FMR04 > 20. It indicates that the two 5-year cohorts have behaved differently. In the older cohort, born between 1981 and 1985, the survival of the girl child may not have been affected by sex-selective intervention, a trend which may have accelerated in the later half of the eighties. Any definite conclusion on such a trend can be made only after the 2001 Census data become available.

Excess girl child mortality in the Indo-Aryan kinship region is revealed through the direct mortality data (Q1–Q5 values). As seen earlier, the 'rest' of the regions, comprising over 260 districts, show a mean excess male child mortality even at the Q5 level. But in the Indo-Aryan kinship region, excess female mortality reigns from infancy itself and increases further in the next four years. This pattern is further corroborated by the FMR -FLP analysis.

An exciting possibility of inferring gender bias from mortality data emerges from the analysis of the 1991 data. It is possible to group various regions and social groups on the basis of the slope values in the female and male mortality relationship. It is necessary to work out child mortality estimates at the district level for the Scheduled Castes and Scheduled Tribe population separately as previously suggested. It is also possible to analyse the long-term mortality data from different states to see the differential distribution of gains made in mortality reduction.

Results from the 1991 data only confirm the need for a more focussed and gender-sensitive data collection and tabulation in the 2001 Census. Briefly, the data by the 5-year age group should be made available by social groups on a high priority basis; data to analyse the prosperity effect should be collected and mortality estimates should be made available by social groups. These and other related issues are discussed in the concluding chapter 'Bringing it all together' to which we turn now.

Chapter 10

Bringing it all together

I

An outline

The analysis pauses at this stage, looks at different aspects of the issue that have been highlighted and brings them all together. This is done at three levels: connecting different insights; considering patterns of change over different time scales; elaborating the scope for further research and, discussing the policy implications. This puts the problem of sex ratio imbalances in a coherent perspective and reveals different policy and research issues that emerge.

The insights gained

There are several directions in which the study can claim to have made advances and improved the understanding of the patterns of sex ratio imbalances. These are briefly listed below.

- First, the issue of discrimination against female children. This is neither new nor unique to India, or, South Asia for that matter. It existed in pre-industrial Europe, the United States and Meiji-era Japan. However, the distinguishing feature of this discrimination in contemporary South Asia is the *incidence of excess female mortality under the age of 5 years*.

- Given high levels of mortality in earlier years, this pattern results in very low FMRs in India compared to the societies mentioned above. This feature of sex differentials in under-5 mortality provides a strong justification for studying the sex ratio patterns in the juvenile age group. So far the primary justification for analysing juvenile age group FMRs was to eliminate the effects of sex-selective migration.
- The third main feature of the study is the explicit recognition of the *'fault line' in the under-5 mortality*, that is, reversal of sex differentials in mortality beyond infancy, and an analysis of its demographic consequences. This necessitates the disaggregation of the 0–9 age group data into the 0–4 and 5–9 age group data. FMR59 emerges as the most effective variable to capture the effects of excess girl child mortality in the 1–4 age group. Similarly, unusually high FMR04 is an effective indicator of excess male infant mortality while its unusually low values indicate excess female mortality in infancy itself or, worse still, female infanticide and sex-selective abortion.
- The use of FMR data for 0–4 and 5–9 age groups closes some of the common escape hatches used in explaining away the pattern of low FMRs. Second, it enables us to distinguish between *high* FMRs and *balanced* FMRs. Third, it identifies situations where seemingly 'balanced' FMRs in the juvenile age group may arise due to an excess of both male mortality during infancy and female mortality in the 1–4 age group. Finally, it highlights the incidence of excess male infant mortality through unusually high FMRs: an aspect which no analysis of the sex ratio patterns has highlighted in the past. This is surprising since the JSR maps presented by Sopher (1980), Miller (1981, 1984) have had significant currency. Yet, regions with unusually high FMRs never attracted the attention of scholars or policy-makers. Just as the preoccupation with denying the unpleasant reality of low FMRs has resulted in adherence to different escape hatches described earlier, the preoccupation with excess female mortality and low FMRs has resulted in non-recognition of the problem of excess male infant mortality in regions of unusually high FMRs. In my own work over past four years, the description has slowly shifted from sex ratio (female to male) *decline* to sex ratio *imbalance*: a fine but important distinction. Highlighting the importance of sex differentials in infant mortality is thus the fourth major feature of this study.
- The absence of a separate analysis of FMRs among the Scheduled Castes and Scheduled Tribes has been another significant omission

in the study of the sex ratio problem. This omission has been made not only by policy-makers and academics but also by institutions exclusively concerned with the welfare of these groups. The analysis presented here has highlighted the adverse survival condition of female children among the Scheduled Castes in the north-western region of the country, the problem of unusually high FMRs among the Scheduled Tribes in certain districts, and the worsening FMRs among the Scheduled Tribes in some districts of Rajasthan and Madhya Pradesh. These aspects have never been highlighted in the literature. A separate analysis of FMR patterns for these two groups is, therefore, the fifth major feature of this study.

- District-level FMR maps are not new to the analysis of sex ratio. However, separate maps for FMR04 and FMR59 have highlighted two completely new aspects. The emphasis on exploring the spatial contiguity of these FMRs resulted in revealing the importance of geophysical regions. The entire field of regional studies in India has somehow passed the study of sex ratios by. The emphasis on the importance of geophysical regions as suitable spatial units for studying sex ratio patterns opens up an exciting field of analysis.

The second important aspect which these maps highlighted was the kinship system. The tentative formulation of the male-centred and female-friendly kinship regions has provided crucial insights into infant and child mortality patterns, FMR-FLP relations and contexts of prosperity. It has also helped pose a serious challenge to the *uncritical import of the 'core-periphery' description in the analysis of FMRs* and, more generally, in the analysis of gender inequality. Highlighting the regional aspects of FMR patterns and the new kinship categorisation represent the sixth major feature of this study.

The use of FMR59 and the kinship variable has enabled one to make important advances in the analysis of the FMR-FLP relation. Separate analysis for the Scheduled Caste, Scheduled Tribe and general population has sharpened this analysis further. The ability of these three factors in explaining the variations in FMR is comparable to what has been achieved in the multivariate analyses pursued by other scholars. Without belittling the importance of the multivariate analyses, it must be pointed out that these relatively sophisticated and elaborate techniques should *follow* the dis-aggregated analysis, not *precede* it or overlook it.

- Female labour participation is an important determinant of the exchange-dependent component of female entitlements. However, it represents only a subset of the overall entitlements. Chapter 6 has provided a coherent framework for the analysis of gender inequalities in general and survival inequalities in particular using the entitlements framework and the capabilities approach. Their application in the field of gender relations is still nascent. The present analysis significantly enhances the scope of this application. More exciting, however, is the advance made in linking the three spaces of functionings, commodity and endowments and dynamising the analysis of wellbeing. This is the seventh major feature of this study which has implications far beyond the immediate problem of the sex ratio imbalances in India.

- Finally, separate analysis of FMRs by prosperity perhaps represents the most crucial, even if tentative, advance. While the other disaggregations elaborate the diversity of the sex ratio patterns and the seriousness of the imbalances in different regions and groups, analysis of the prosperity effect raises crucial questions about the processes behind these patterns and their future shape. From the policy point of view, this is a vital aspect. This is admittedly an area where data availability is not satisfactory but the concerns raised are crucial and spell out certain urgent agenda both for research and intervention.

A *purdah of scholarship*

Having listed out the areas in which the study can claim some modest advances, it is appropriate to pause once more and reflect on why some of these advances were not made earlier. Is it merely a happenstance, for example, that the demographic consequences of the patterns of infant and child mortaliy were not examined, that the data was not analysed for the Scheduled Caste and Scheduled Tribe populations separately, that the NSSO data were never seriously analysed from the sex ratio angle or that the inadequacy of the state-level averages was not realised by different scholars?

Three likely reasons that can be advanced for the oversights are: (*a*) non-availability of data, (*b*) lack of explicit emphasis and (*c*) the dominance of certain discourses.

Non-availability of data is not a tenable excuse. Some of the insights obtained in this analysis have used the data from the 1961 Census, available for over 30 years now! Data from the 1981 Census have also been available for over a decade now and the NSSO data are currently in their 50th round.[1] It could be argued that my focus on the 0–4 and 5–9 age group sex ratios was fortuitous (which it was), and therefore all subsequent development based on it was a matter of chance. Interestingly, however, separate 5-year age group data by provinces were available right from the time of the 1891 Census. More interestingly, Natarajan (1972: 32–33) does provide these data in a table, providing the sex ratio figures for the 0–4 and 5–9 age groups for the total population by provinces. These values are compared with figures from 5 countries in Europe and the UK.[2] The drop between FMR04 and FMR59 values is quite sharp in many provinces. It was the observation of similar drops in my analysis which led to the inquiry into the fault line in the under-5 mortality. It is difficult to believe that Natarajan's census centenary monograph on 'The changes in sex ratio' did not enjoy adequate circulation or serious readership.

Absence of an explicit focus is also a weak excuse. Excess female mortality in the 1–4 age group has been highlighted by Harriss (1989), Chen (1982), and Chatterjee (1990). Emphasis placed by Harriss (1989: 49, 61) on separate age group-wise analysis of sex ratios and Chatterjee's (1990) recognition of the gender gap being the largest (in age groups) where mortality rates were the highest (1990: 4), could not have been more explicit. Similarly, the effects of prosperity on female status has been highlighted in a number of studies and in specific demographic contexts by Krishnaji (1987) and Bardhan (1974). High FMRs among the Scheduled Tribes has been highlighted in the literature even if *en passant* (Dange, 1972; Miller, 1981). If scholars from North America overlook the significance of the separate data for the Scheduled Castes or Scheduled Tribes it is understandable. When scholars from India, well aware of these social categories, choose to overlook the data, it is altogether a different matter. As pointed out in Chapter 3, some of these scholars

---

[1] Two observations are relevant here even though they are on a personal note. After my presentation of the sex ratio analysis by mother tongues based on the 1961 and 1981 data (IASP 1996), the ex-Registrar General of India (Mr P. Padmanabha) repeated his lament that there is a wealth of census data lying unanalysed. Second remark came from the Jt. Director (Data) of the NSSO during personal discussion. He observed that except Krishnaji there has hardly been any analysis of the NSSO data in the sex ratio context that he was aware of.

[2] England and Wales, Ireland, Italy, Sweden, Austria and Hungary.

were working in same institutional set-up and were aware of research in both relevant streams of inquiry, that is infant and child mortality patterns and sex ratio patterns. Yet they failed to see the connection between the two. This study has specifically benefited from the observations of Krishnaji about the role of prosperity and the U-shaped relation between FMRs and landholding groups, from Miller's observation about distinct FMRs among Scheduled Tribes (quoting Dange, 1972), from the Caldwells (1990) observation about excess male infant mortality apart from Harriss (1989) and Chatterjee (1990) mentioned earlier. It is again difficult to believe that these studies did not enjoy adequate circulation or serious readership.

The dominance of certain discourses, the persistent stereotypes and fragmentation of knowledge within rigid disciplinary boundaries appear to be three main reasons for some of these oversights. The sharpest indication of this comes in the denial of high female mortality rates using convenient 'escape hatches' described earlier. Another indication comes through the prevailing notions about the Scheduled Caste and Scheduled Tribe population. The first wrong notion about the Scheduled Tribes is that they are tucked away in the north-eastern region of the country. The second implicit assumption is that since they constitute 'only' 8 per cent of the population, demographically they do not form a significant category. The low priority given to the publication of data on the Scheduled Caste and Scheduled Tribe population[3] is matched by an absence of analysis even when the data becomes available.

The dominance of the 'core–periphery' description and its uncritical import into the sex ratio debate can also be understood in this context. Any suggestion to reverse the dominant discourse is immediately confronted with the repeating of the stereotypes, defence of the status quo, invoking the need to do much more research and putting the entire burden of such research and proof on the shoulder of one who 'dissents'.[4]

---

[3] These are always published towards the end in census publications. Even the Indian Districts Development Database, which is a result of a joint collaboration between the ICSSR (Indian Council of Social Science Research) and the University of Maryland, has not yet entered the 5-year age group data for the SC and ST population in its database. The variable exists, the columns are blank!

[4] It was suggested, for example, in a seminar at the London School of Hygiene and Tropical-Medicine (November 1996), that the lowness of FMR59 compared to FMR04 may after all be on account of over-reporting the age of young boys in the 0–4 age group! Even if there is no sociological justification for or evidence of such age misstatement, the implication was that it should be checked out as it was after all an arithmetical possibility and that it was incumbent upon me to disprove this proposition.

The offence of 'dissent', no more than a suggestion to examine alternative possibilities, gets compounded if it comes from outside the discipline, especially through an interdisciplinary analysis. One cannot but help recall the observation made by Johnston and Clark (1982) that in development policy discourse, different schools of thought give little impression of building upon the foundations laid by each other. 'Their attitude is more one of dancing on an enemy's grave' (1982: 19).

Be that as it may, this is a worthwhile topic of inquiry from the point of view of the 'sociology of knowledge' and whether, when and why an 'outsider' in a disciplinary context is able to see the emperor without his clothes more easily.

Another important issue of interdisciplinarity needs a brief mention. While this analysis focusses on a demographic outcome, it also begins to get to the root of the process dynamics of such outcome. This outcome, that is, the sex ratio patterns, come within the purview of demography, but the processes fall within the domain of anthropology, sociology and economics. The experience throughout this study has been that the qualitative, anthropological studies provide valuable insights which need then be validated at the meso or the micro level using suitable data. As one goes from the patterns to the processes, the current availability of data becomes less than satisfactory. But that provides a justification for the generation of suitable data rather than retaining a false dichotomy between the two approaches. That a fruitful dialogue between the two approaches can come about quite quickly has been demonstrated in the field of the intra-household allocational behaviour. Here the data intensity of the 'diverging preference' model was once regarded as a big obstacle, if not an embarrassment. The situation has rapidly changed within a decade itself and the diverging preference models are now well accepted and data validating these continue to be available and generated. Close to home, Basu's (1992) attempt to look at the cultural determinants of demographic outcomes using a suitable and large sample is a good example of such an approach. There is no reason why such an approach cannot be adopted for sex ratio analysis. Concrete illustrative suggestions are made in this regard in Sections IV and V.

The next two sections speculate on two specific links with the past. The first concerns the high FMR patterns in the recent past and the second concerns the role of culture. FMRs in India have been high in the earlier decades of this century while the cultural aspects of discrimination against female children have existed for centuries. Second, the culture of female subordination has been quite strong in the northern kinship region. It is necessary to understand why it might have been so.

II

High FMR levels in the past

Very high levels of infant mortality in the past (Chandrasekhar, 1959; Dyson, 1992) coupled with the skewed pattern of juvenile mortality provide the clue to the first puzzle. These result in very high FMR levels in early childhood. The subsequent excess of female child mortality was not able to 'overcome' the effect of excess male infant deaths (see the simulated values in Table 3.6) and FMRs remained high.

The 3-year age group FMR data from the 1931 Census illustrates this (Table 10.1). Very high values of FMRs in the 0–3 age group can be clearly seen. FMRs in the 4–6 age group are, on the other hand, low in the north-western region. Yet, the combined FMRs in the 0–6 age group remain quite high.

It is only when the infant mortality rates have declined significantly that the effects of excess female mortality become more pronounced. It is instructive to compare the district-level maps for the 5-year age group FMR for the 1961 and 1981 Census data. In the 0–4 age group (Maps 10.1a, b), the expansion of the region with FMR < 960 and the shrinkage of the number of districts with FMR04 > 1,010 is unmistakable. In the 5–9 age group (Maps 10.2a, b), the increase in the number of districts with FMR59 < 850 is quite dramatic. Part of it would be due to reduced infant mortality rates even if a substantial part of it may be due to increase in excess female child mortality. Decline in the number of districts with FMR59 > 1,010 is not very significant. In the absence of separate 5-year age group data for the SC and ST population, more cannot be said about the changes. One has to await the 1991 Census data to compare the changes between 1981 and 1991.

Table 10.1
FMRs in 1931: 0–6 age group (**provinces and princely states**)

Region	FMR03	FMR46	FMR06
India	1,040	976	1,010
Ajmer-Merwara	1,031	965	1,002
Assam	1,034	996	1,017
Bihar & Orissa	1,078	992	1,035
Bombay	1,032	956	996
Bengal	1,048	969	1,011
CP & Berar	1,058	996	1,030
Coorg	1,037	970	1,008
Delhi	990	925	962
NWFP	998	930	965
Madras	1,044	1,009	1,028
Punjab	977	916	949
UP	1,040	931	989
Baroda	1,002	918	965
Bihar & Orissa S*	1,061	1,010	1,038
Bengal S*	1,049	1,008	1,029
Bombay S*	1,049	1,003	1,026
Central India Ag*	1,077	985	1,034
CP S*	975	1,096	1,030
Gwalior	1,012	943	980
Hyderabad	1,079	1,082	1,080
J & K S*	992	949	973
Mysore S*	1,050	1,018	1,035
Madras S*	1,045	1,370	1,208
Cochin S*	997	979	990
Travancore S*	993	979	988
Punjab S*	1,042	1,009	1,027
Punjab states Ag*	986	920	957
Rajputana Ag*	1,035	950	996
Sikkim S*	1,012	1,009	1,011
UP S*	1,063	1,014	1,040
W. India S* Ag*	1,048	992	1,022

Note: Constructed from corrected unsmoothed figures.

S* = Princely States

Ag* = Agency

Source: Agarwala S.N. (1967).

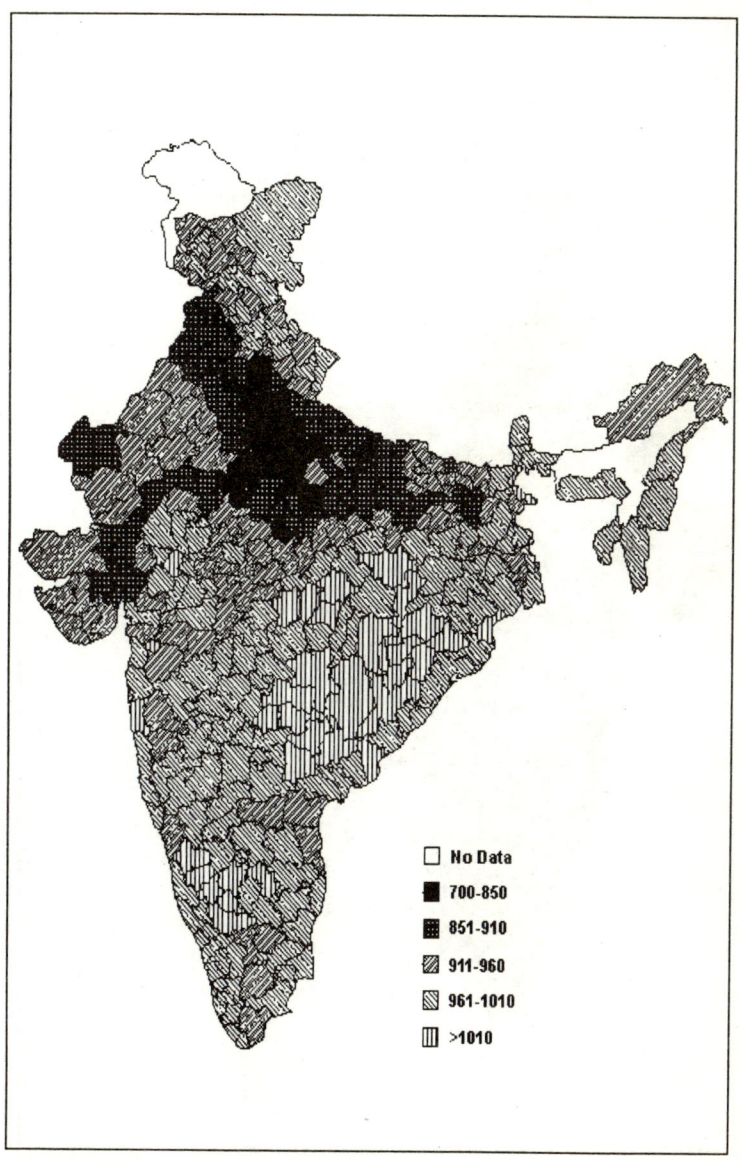

Map 10.1a: District-level map of FMR04: 1981 Census (total population).

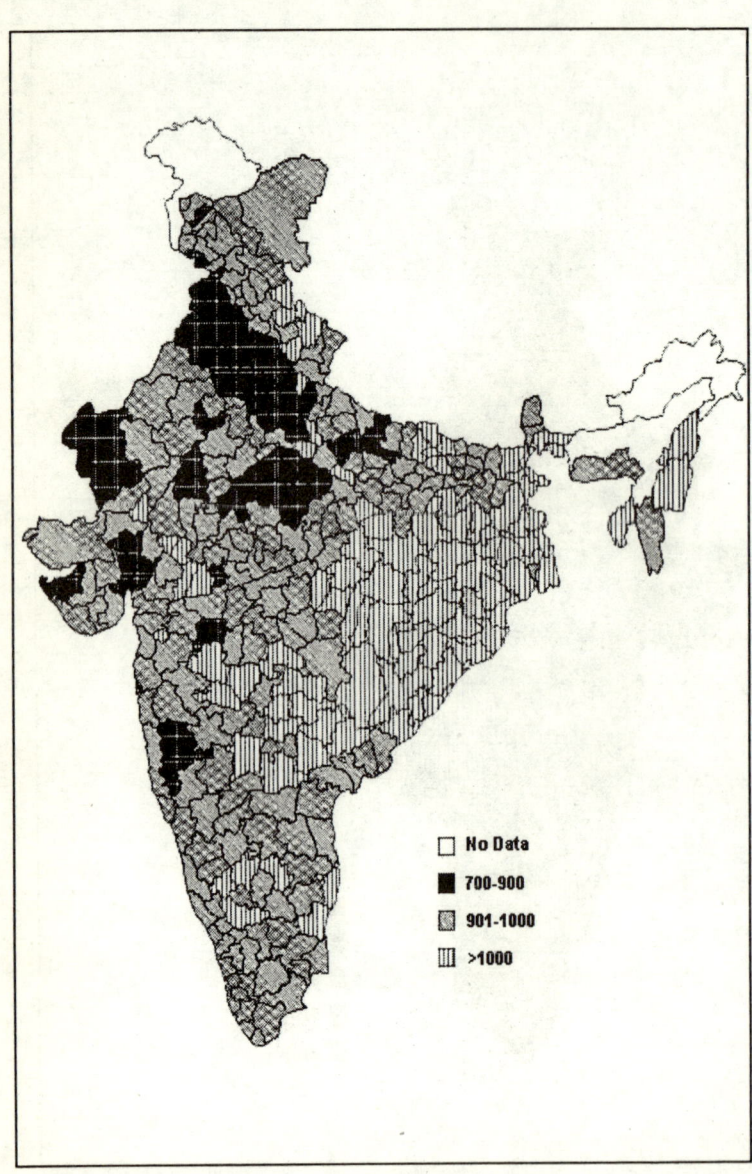

Map 10.1b: District-level map of FMR04: 1961 Census (total population).

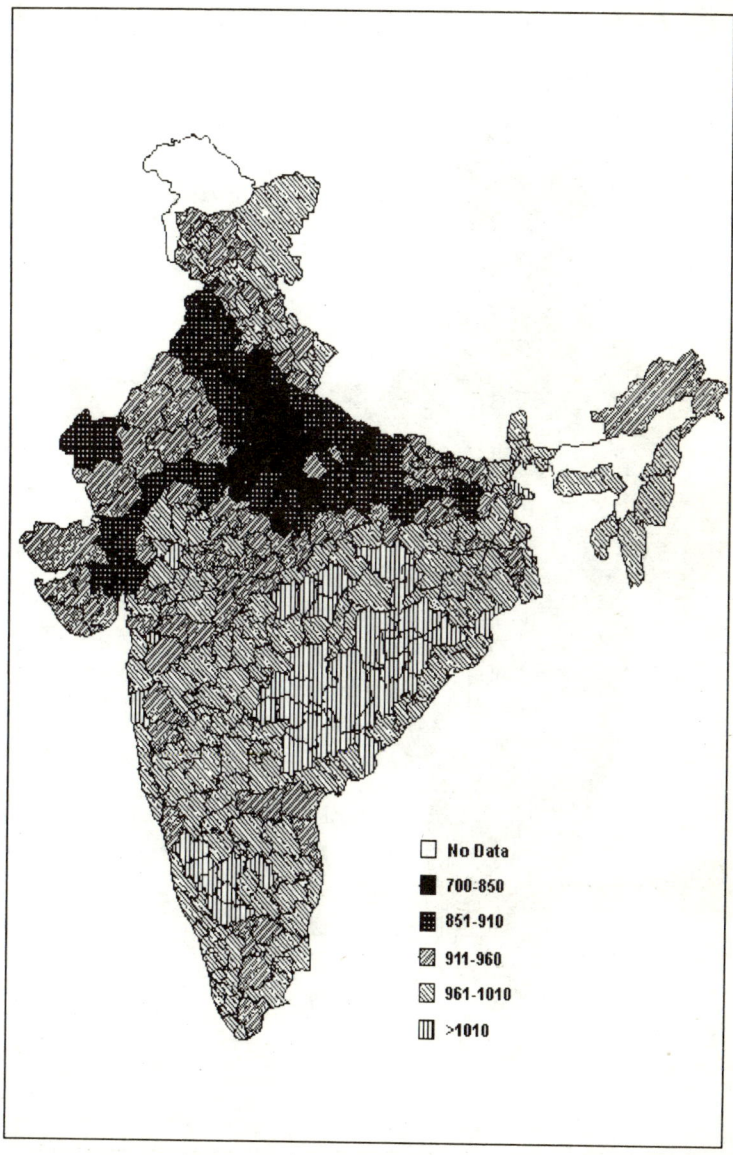

Map 10.2a: District-level map of FMR59: 1981 Census (total population).

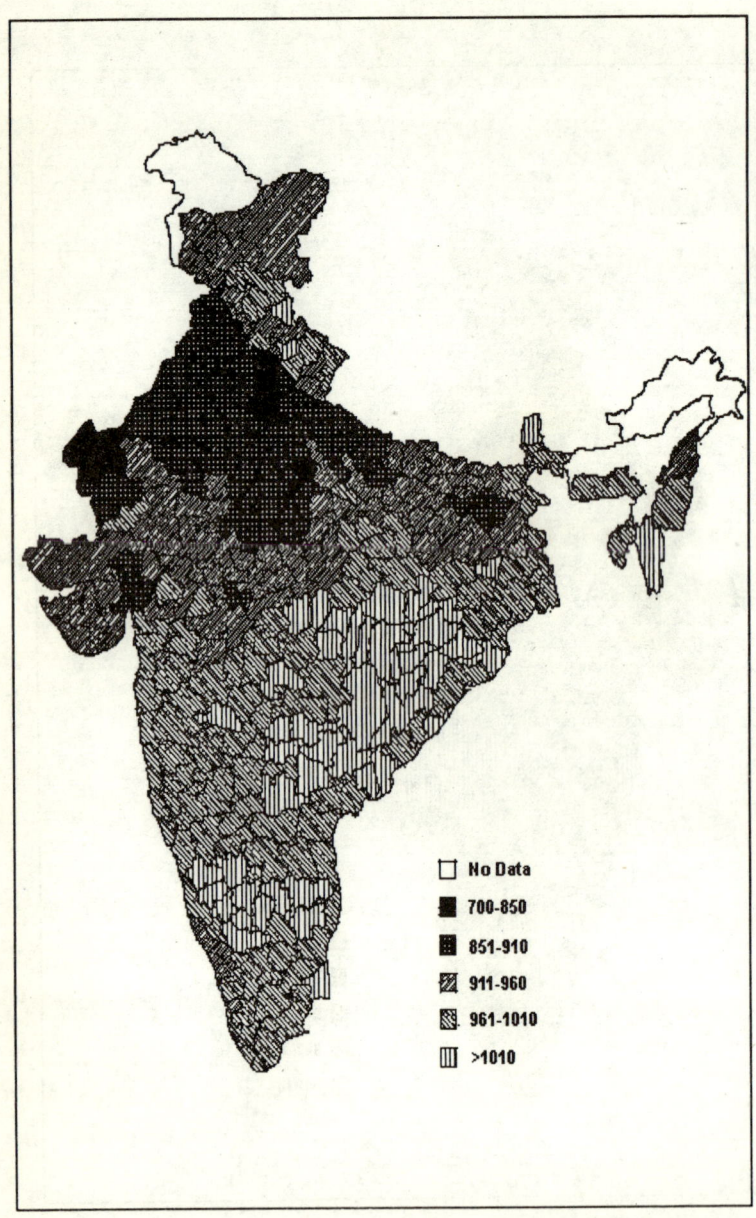

Map 10.2b: District-level map of FMR59: 1961 Census (total population).

Some declines are more unequal than others

This brings us to another important distinction. FMRs can decline both through reduction in the infant mortality levels and increase in excess female mortality rates. These two components of the decline in FMRs need to be differentiated. The former is desirable while the latter is not. The decline in FMR04 and FMR59 from unusually high levels to a balanced range of 950–980 is to be welcomed. But it will also mean that the districts with FMR > 980 will no longer be available to compensate for the 'rogue' districts with FMR04 below 950 and FMR59 below 900! The all-India level FMR figure will decline as a consequence. But the debate on the FMR decline must decisively move beyond the all-India average or the state-level average to the district and even sub-district level.

A decline in FMR04 below 950 needs to be viewed with caution and those below 900 with alarm. Similarly a decline in FMR59 below 850 and sharp drops between FMR04 and FMR59 need to be viewed with alarm. Reduction of infant mortality will have to be the priority in districts with unusually high FMR04 and FMR59. Prevention of female child mortality will be a priority in districts where FMR04 is moderate or high but FMR59 is low. Districts where FMR04 themselves are very low need steps for ascertaining the causes for and reducing the incidences of excess female mortality during infancy itself. Worse still, in some of these districts, the possibility of very high sex-selective abortion and female infanticide rates will have to be investigated.

A rethink

The demographic consequences of the sex differentials in infant mortality force us to rethink some of the traditional explanations of high FMRs among the poor. The relative contribution of high infant mortality vis-à-vis absence of discrimination needs to be weighed. Once again the differences in the FMR04 and FMR59 provide a useful guide: the effects of infant mortality will be reflected in the FMR04 while the effects of discrimination will be seen in the drop between FMR04 and FMR59 and the lowness of FMR59. Where the 5-year age group data is not available, the 'balanced' juvenile sex ratios among the poor should be viewed with suspicion given higher infant mortality among them. This will hold for any other groups with high infant mortality rates, like for instance groups among which lower age of marriage prevail. Similar care has to be exercised while examining the 'lower' FMRs among the non-poor. As mentioned before, however, prosperity can not be given this benefit of doubt when FMRs go well below 950.

Development and discrimination

The distinction made indicates a correspondence between development, infant mortality and FMR04 on one hand and discrimination, high female mortality and FMR59 on the other. Schematically, the four different combinations of these can be shown as follows:

High development	Balanced FMRs	Very low FMRs
Low development	Very high FMRs	Balanced (?) FMRs
LEVEL	Low discrimination	High discrimination

It can be plausibly argued that infant mortality levels are a suitable indicator of development while excess female child mortality is a suitable indicator of gender bias. The aim of social action or state intervention should be towards creating conditions for development without discrimination.

III

A burden of the past

The second puzzle worth speculating over relates to the intensity of female subordination in the 'core' Indo-Aryan kinship region. It is not enough to state the fact of subordination through its various indicators. Why did this level of subordination come about in this particular region?

The spread of the Indo-Aryan system has not been uniform in the north. It had preferred routes along fertile river basins viz., Sapta-Sindhu (seven waters) to the Punjab (five waters) and finally to the Doab (the region bound between the two waters of Ganga and Yamuna rivers). Spate et al. (1967) has identified three routes of perennial significance concerning waves of incoming invasion into the subcontinent; the Kabul-Peshawar-Delhi axis, Delhi-Mathura-Patna fork towards the east and the Agra-Ujjain-Kathiawad route towards the west.

Features of the Indo-Aryan people relevant to the present discussion are (*a*) their use of iron for both plough and sword,[5] (*b*) cultivation of wheat, and (*c*) expertise in warfare involving horse-riding and chariotry (Agarwal, 1985; Fairservice, 1987; Wolpert, 1993: 37). Each of these may have contributed to the relative devaluation of women. Wheat requires much less participation of women in agriculture. Use of iron plough gives men a decisive advantage in cultivation besides providing a quantum jump in accumulation of agricultural surplus. The scale of these surpluses would be far higher than the one available to growers of rice and millet cultivars with copper–bronze technology. Finally, the constant warlike conditions faced by the region could put women at a disadvantage, increasing the perception of women as liability required to be protected from the adversaries.[6]

Ecologically, however, the winter grasses: wheat and barley, could not spread everywhere (Possehl 1987). These did spread in the Doab and Malwa and along the limited plain tract of the Mathura–Dwarka route. In the rest of the western region the summer grasses of *ragi, bajra* and *jowar* (millets) remained cultivars of choice. Towards the east, rice held sway beyond an ecological transition zone (Libbee, 1980). South of the Narmada, wheat did not spread much except in the Khandesh region of Maharashtra.

Politically, the spread of the Aryans was mainly confined to the Punjab Doab 'core' during the legendary Mahabharata time. Its spread eastwards was weak where the spread of fire and iron was slow: Magadh (Patna) was a clear challenger to Delhi and Bihar (Anga); Bengal (Wanga) and northern Orissa (Kalinga) were considered inferior and outside the pale of the Aryan domain (Aryawarta) (Karve, 1965). The westward influence was limited to some pockets along the Mathura, Dwarka axis.

[5] Major tribes traced back to the time of the writing of the *Mahabharata* have been linked archaeologically to the use of iron through PGW (painted grey ware) pottery. The core region where the Aryan groups established themselves through their skills in warfare coincides with the spread of PGW (Thapar, 1985).

[6] There is a body of literature (e.g., Divale and Harris, 1976; Harris, 1993) relating to the relative devaluation of women in clans and societies facing constant warlike situation. The preoccupation with 'protecting' women of ones clan intensifies among the warrior groups in such an environment. Quite logically abducting those of the rival clan would get suitably glorified. Abduction of women for the purpose of marriage was sanctified among the warrior clans in the Mahabharata period.

The southward spread of the Aryan influence was neither characterised by wheat nor sword. In fact, the south has never experienced any invasion or warfare comparable to those experienced in Indo-Aryan region. From the time of the legendary Rama to that of Aurangzeb (Schwartzberg, 1992), the south could be occasionally invaded, temporarily subjugated but could never be held on a long-term basis (Wolpert, 1993). The in-migrating priestly class was the one which mainly diffused different aspects of the Indo-Aryan culture.[7] But they have been assimilated quite substantially within the folds of an 'advanced' civilisation practising sedentary agriculture even though not on the scale of agriculture practiced in the Ganga–Yamuna Doab.[8]

The dividing belt between the north and the south, a belt of tribal population (Raza and Ahmad, 1990) is considered a buffer between the two regions by some scholars (e.g., Roy Burman, 1972). The tribals have inhabited a continuous terrain from east to west unsuited for agricultural expansion (Raza and Ahmad, 1990). This belt has one breach along the Malwa–Khandesh axis through the geologically known Burhanpur pass (Spate et al., 1967). West of this pass, the tribal population is essentially Dravidian while on its east they are Austro-Asiatic, primarily Munda (Parkin, 1992).

Even in the north, marginal areas especially the hilly ones were never very attractive for long-term occupation. Clear cultural differences mark the Pahari (hill dweller) Hindus and those dwelling in the plains (Goody, 1990). The latter are characterised by 'incomplete assimilation within the dominant Hindu ethos' (Berreman, 1993).

Historically, the 'core' Indo-Aryan region always remained in some kind of ferment or another until the establishment of the Mughal empire. The Hindu kingdoms in the north gave way by 1192 AD. The Turko-Afghan incursions began with Mehmood of Gazni whose almost annual raids along the Mathura–Kathiawad route also saw large scale killing of people and violation of women (Wolpert, 1993: 107–108). This was bound to bring about a qualitative difference in the psyche of the invaded people who were so far used to incoming groups who either got absorbed into

---

[7] Interestingly, the Caldwells (1990) refer to the absence of any caste equivalent to the Rajputs or Jats in the south. It will be interesting to distinguish between the 'brahminisation' of the south vis-à-vis the absence of its 'Kshatriyaisation' (or warriorisation). But that is quite outside the scope of to this discussion.

[8] In fact, the Pancha-Dravida brahmins (five Dravida Brahmin clans), who support and practice the southern kinship are considered equals, even superior to the Pancha-Gauda clans of the north (Sopher, 1980).

society or confined their activities to fights on the battlefield (e.g., Alexander of Macedonia) without taking recourse to the destruction of temples or the abduction of the womenfolk.

It is worth noting that the major brunt of these wars was borne by the Rajput in the north-west. They continued to resist the Mughals until the time of Akbar. Some of their chiefs were forced to give their women in marriage to Muslim kings. Some successfully resisted it, some could not. The practice of mass self-immolation or 'Johar' by women of the princely clans when the defeat of their menfolk at the hands of the Muslim chieftain was imminent, became popular among the Rajputs. Theirs is a group which had a high rate of female infanticide and very low FMR even in 1931 (Miller, 1981).

It is plausible to speculate, therefore, that ecological, technological and historical factors reinforced each other in the north-western plains to create a strong ethos of female subordination,[9] the effects of which are still being felt. However, these links between Indo-Aryan expansion and the ethos of female subordination warrant much deeper inquiry than is possible here and the analysis must move now from the past to the present where the problem of low FMRs is serious and to the future where it is threatening to worsen.

IV

Issues for further research and policy formulation

A number of research and policy issues emerge from the analysis done in this study. These relate to different features of this analysis listed in Section I. These are elaborated here in some detail. Some of these details relate to

---

[9] Many may argue about the equitable position of women in the Vedic period when they could compose religious hymns, engage in debate on scriptures with their husbands and so on. This is not disputed and need not be. The simple point is that such 'Vedic period' was decisively overshadowed, Ramayana onwards and has never staged a comeback. The subordination of women in the subsequent period is well documented within the mythical literature, legends and historical accounts. This subordination again is not a mandatory part of Hinduism as the south clearly shows. It is merely imposed by one orthodoxy within Hinduism and needs to be questioned as such.

the nuts and bolts of policy and the research themes which could be pursued while others are more general.

Research issues

Empirically, the research issues broadly relate to the use of 5-year age group data, sex differentials in infant and child mortality, separate analysis of the data for the Scheduled Castes and the Scheduled Tribes, analysis by regions and by prosperity levels. Analytically, important questions are raised regarding the spreading ethos of female subordination, inequality within the household and the larger framework of gender inequalities. An illustrative list of issues that require further policy and research focus is given here:

Mortality:

- Separate mortality estimates for the Scheduled Castes and Scheduled Tribes.
- Separate mortality estimates by prosperity levels.
- A more realistic modelling of FMRs in terms of infant and child mortality rates.
- Inferring gender bias in mortality through longitudinal mortality data.
- Inferring sex differentials in mortality from FMR04 and FMR59 patterns and identifying regions and groups likely to be affected by excess male and excess female mortality in infancy and by excess female mortality in the 1–4 age group.

These ideas have applicability well beyond the Indian context. Modelling of FMR04 and FMR59 and inferring gender bias through longitudinal data are useful analytically and can be used where good quality data are available. Inferring sex differentials in mortality from FMR data, on the other hand, can be useful in cases where good quality mortality data are not available at disaggregated levels.

FMRs:

- Inferring patterns of sex-selective migration especially among the Scheduled Caste and Scheduled Tribe group by comparing the all-age group and the juvenile age group data.
- Fine-tuning the regional analysis of the spatial distribution of sex ratios and identifying regions with unusually low or high FMRs.

- Separate analysis of the sex ratio patterns for the Scheduled Castes and Scheduled Tribes.
- Separate analysis of the sex ratio patterns by prosperity levels.

Each of these have remained neglected areas of scholarship but each has a potential to generate a wide range of agenda for focussed micro research. Inferring sex-selective migration patterns among different communities is useful given the absense of any break-up of the migrating population by social groups. This can be of considerable use in the context of regional studies.

The other important contribution to regional studies can come from the fine-tuning of the spatial patterns of FMR04 and FMR59. While the district-level maps have provided new insights in this analysis, districts could also hide considerable diversities. The FMR04 and FMR59 maps should be drawn at the sub-district level, subject to Visaria's caveat about the sample size (Chapter 2). This will considerably sharpen the 'contour mapping' of the FMRs and throw important light on the spatial dynamics of masculinisation of FMRs and regions with persistently high infant mortality, especially if such maps are compared across 1961 and 1991.

The importance of a separate analysis of the sex ratio patterns for the Scheduled Castes and Scheduled Tribes cannot be emphasised more. The seriousness of the situation among the Scheduled Castes in the northern regions, the unusually high levels of infant mortality in tribal pockets and low FMRs among Scheduled Tribes in Rajasthan and northern MP, provide strong reasons for such study. There is a considerable amount of FMR and FLP data available by individual castes and tribes even in the 1961 and 1971 Censuses. It is imperative that these studies get initiated. Not doing so will be inexcusable.

FLP:

- Study of long-term trends in FLP patterns and the FMR-FLP relationship and a separate analysis of this relationship by social groups regions and income groups.
- Possible existence of a 'seclusion threshold' and its policy implications.
- Study of the apparent conflict between FLP and child survival among the poor. The scope of drudgery reduction and its role in resolving the conflict.

- Trends of declining FLP among the non-poor and the possibility of arresting such trend.
- Focus on the unwaged productive work and its gender consequences.

These nuances have emerged from the analysis done in Chapters 7 and 8. Until now, the role of FLP has been analysed in an aggregated manner in most literature. From the policy point of view as well as academically, FLP data also need disaggregation. While in some of the cases, e.g., FLP by regions or social groups, disaggregated data are available, in many other cases these need to be generated.

The analytical framework

Elaboration of the entitlements framework and its integration with the capabilities approach generates another exciting agenda for research. First, the dynamic aspects of wellbeing and the process of continuous bargaining, formally elaborated, need to be connected with the 'general theory of gender stratification' attempted by Blumberg (1991). In concrete terms, each partner's net share of the cake (net of expenditure) has to be linked with the bargaining strength for the next round given the observation that 'control over surplus gives more leverage than control over subsistence' and given that more of women's earning is spent on the nutrition of children and subsistence activities. Second, the scalar, one-dimensional bargaining process has to be extended to its vector counterpart and dynamised. Third, the entitlement-endowment relation has to be empirically examined for different earning levels. This will verify the tentative and intuitive assertion that the more exchange intensive the given element of entitlement vector, the less will be its 'core' component.

The ability of this framework to cover the issue of overall gender inequalities, through the space of functionings, represents another major advance. Given the information on the entitlement-endowment relation for different elements of entitlements, the inequalities in different functionings can be mapped. One can, for example, study various sex ratios in education, in level of skill acquired, in terms of utilisation of these skills, access to capital and property. It is also possible to examine the Kuznets curve between these different inequalities and prosperity.

The expression for inequality in two-person bargaining can be extended to the process of repeated N-person bargaining. Linking this with Gini coefficient measure of inequality will be an intellectually challenging and worthwhile exercise.

The issue of P-mapping, aggregation of elements of entitlement vector into elements of functioning vector and the aggregation of elements of a functioning vector into an index of wellbeing, interdependence of the elements in the process of aggregation are other exciting areas of inquiry for the future.

Policy issues

A number of policy issues are linked to these research issues. Some are related to providing suitable inputs for research while the others are related to using the insights generated from the research. Adverse survival conditions among Scheduled Caste female children in the northern plains provides a suitable instance of this. On one hand, policy has to take note of the seriousness of the situation brought out in Chapters 4 and 7, while on the other hand, separate child mortality estimates have to be computed for this group and the 5-year age group data for the 1991 Census released on a priority basis to facilitate further research.

The second set of issues are connected to policy intervention and social action. The immediate or short-term objective of these interventions will be to ensure survival of the children concerned. The medium and the long-term objective will be to improve the status of women, at least to a level where the gender bias in survival disparities disappear. The status enhancement strategies will involve aspects of *economic worth, cultural worth, visibility* and *power*.

The two spiralling feedback loops described in Chapter 8 become relevant here. One relates to the spread of the ethos of female subordination in the wake of prosperity and the other relates to the likelihood of sex-selective abortions and infanticide reinforcing each other. Both these trends will have to be countered through the interventions discussed next.

Plurality in the design of policy intervention

Disaggregation of FMR data and the analysis of the FMR-FLP relationship has clearly brought out the need for plurality in the design of policy or social interventions. The nature of the sex ratio imbalances and their causes vary across regions, age groups, social groups and economic groups. The policy will have to be sensitive to these variations. The nature of interventions, for example, in a region marked with excess female child mortality will differ from those in the regions where there is excess male infant mortality. While the focus of policy in the former set of districts will be on ensuring the survival of female children, the focus in the latter set of districts will be on reducing infant mortality in general. Similarly, in regions or among groups where kinship is female-friendly, enhancing FLP need not be a priority. But in regions where FLP is low, enhancing FLP will need to be a priority. Even within a region with a female-friendly kinship system, the creation of employment avenues among the non-poor may require some priority.

The realm of the possible

What follows is a brief discussion of these three aspects of policy. Some of the suggestions relating to the generation of data, use of available data and further research may not appear 'analytical' enough. But these are listed on purpose. Often the 'analytical' is dismissed as 'impractical' while the 'practical' is looked down upon as not being 'analytical' or 'academic' enough. A real life problem like sex ratio imbalances needs, however, both analytical insights and practical solutions. The possibilities listed here deal with the 'doability' of some of the solutions which require following up, some at least on an urgent basis. Listing these explicitly pre-empts some of the escape hatches likely to be encountered against such follow up. Further, listing some of the linkages that I have fortuitously explored would save the time and effort of those interested in pursuing the themes but who may be unaware of their 'doability'.

Data availability and generation

The issues requiring attention in the census organisation are:

- Early release of the 5-year age group data by social groups for the 1991 Census and such release on a priority basis in all subsequent census operations.
- *Separate estimation of mortality rates for the Scheduled Caste and Scheduled Tribe population* based on the 1981 data followed by estimations based on the 1991 data. Where population size is small, estimation can be made at the regional or state level by individual caste or the tribe since the relevant population data are available.
- A special population census in some of the very low FMR districts should be conducted to settle once and for all the issue of under-enumeration. This is crucial if the inquiries about demographic

outcomes have to go beyond the domain of demography. The other alternative is to ignore the under-enumeration issue and live with the hiatus between demography and other disciplines on this matter.

- Incorporating the 1961 tabulation schedule on *FMR by landholding size for the 2001 Census* with the minimal modifications suggested in Chapter 8.
- Initiating separate study of the sex ratio patterns among the Scheduled Caste and Scheduled Tribe populations through the Census 1991 monograph series. Similar studies can be taken up in respect of few major Scheduled Castes and Tribes, especially those among whom sharp deterioration in FMRs is prima facie noticed.
- The sample registration survey (SRS) estimates of infant and child mortality should be separately made by prosperity levels and for the Scheduled Caste and Scheduled Tribe population.
- Identification of districts and groups which reveal prima facie evidence of high levels of sex-selective abortions or female infanticide and initiating micro studies in these districts. In fact, based on the identification of very low FMRs in the 0–6 age group for the overall population at the district level, a number of studies (about 12) has been launched to look at the likelihood of female infanticide. It will be necessary to separately identify the low FMR areas for the three groups and initiate more such studies. However, the quality of these studies leaves much scope for improvement.[10] Even at the risk of being immodest, it can be suggested that many of the nuances highlighted in this study need to be brought to the notice of the investigating groups before these studies are launched.

NSSO data

There is a wealth of NSSO data on family composition and FLP by prosperity levels. As mentioned in Chapter 8, these have not been put to any use in the sex ratio context. These data need analysis. Further, NSSO data for the 50th and subsequent rounds will become available at the regional level. This should be of considerable interest to regional studies on gender inequalities. There are three limitations to the NSSO data: the

---

[10] This is based on my reading of three to four of the reports which were available. It is perhaps unfair to make the observation above without giving the agencies a chance to defend themselves. But the spirit in which this observation is made does not indict these agencies out of such future exercises; it only suggests an augmentation of their capabilities.

sample sizes are small; the data are not corrected for migration; and data on children is presented for the 0–14 age group.

Ensuring survival

A scheme aimed at ensuring the survival of female children in the 18 districts in the north-western region where FMR59 for the Scheduled Caste population is below 800, needs the topmost priority. This scheme has to be a centrally sponsored given that the districts are spread over a number of states.

Next in priority come the districts where the FMR59 for the Scheduled Caste population is below 910. In these districts, the FMRs for the Scheduled Caste and the general population are more or less similar. Both the groups should be covered under the concerned schemes.

At the other end of the spectrum are districts with unusually high value of FMR04 and FMR59. Reduction of infant mortality has to be the topmost priority in these districts along with universal midday meal programme. High FMR59 indicates continuation of excess male child mortality beyond infancy arising from harsh health environment. Elimination of malnutrition through a midday meal programme will give the children a fighting chance against the harshness of the health environment. Simultaneously, a detailed study of the 'causes of death' should be launched in all these districts where FMR59 continues to be comparable with or higher than FMR04. The same argument applies even more strongly to the individual Scheduled Tribe or Scheduled Tribe where 5-year age group FMRs show these features.

Districts facing both high infant mortality and high excess female child mortality need to be targeted next. In these districts, a combination of both measures, that is, those aimed at reducing infant mortality and those aimed at ensuring the survival of the girl child, will be required.

One possibility which can work towards reducing infant mortality level and incidentally prevent female infanticide is to provide attractive incentive to the health worker for covering every case of pregnant mother with anti-tetanus injection. It should be mandatory for the health worker to report the outcome of the delivery to the nearest health centre within a short stipulated time. An unusually large number of female infant deaths can then be made a subject of a detailed probe. This may have a non-marginal impact on female infanticide, especially if the post-neonatal survival package is available and is effective.

Finally, the child mortality patterns in a region should form an important criteria for transfer of funds from the Central government to the state governments and within the states from the State governments to the districts and other local self governments. After all, infant mortality is a good indicator of development and excess female mortality a good indicator of discrimination against half (very nearly!) the population. Together these are effective indicators of how a government performs and the financial rewards and disincentives should take this into account.

Worth through work

The survival enhancing strategies indicated above are in the nature of enhancing the core entitlements component. It is equally important to enhance the exchange-dependent component, or direct control over earnings. This is especially important in regions and among groups where the kinship is not female-friendly.

Aspects of FLP

The diversity of the sex ratio patterns has been elaborately spelt out in earlier chapters. However, certain nuances of FLP also merit an explicit mention. These are listed here:

(*a*) First, the role of FLP is not very critical in the female-friendly kinship region in ensuring high FMRs. Hence the emphasis on enhancing the levels of FLP in these regions need not be strong. However, these regions do require a selective emphasis on sustaining a high level of FLP among the non-poor. This will mean the creation of employment opportunities in high skill and high wage work and introducing positive discrimination if necessary. It will also require creation of an enabling environment that facilitaties easier childrearing and reduced drudgery in the status production activity which women will have to do anyway.

(*b*) In regions of male-centred kinship, raising FLP will require strong emphasis. There are three distinct issues: breaking the 'seclusion threshold' of FLP if there is one; the creation of a large number of unskilled and low skilled jobs for the women among the poor; and the creation of skilled employment opportunity for the women among the non-poor groups and the necessary means for making these operational.

(*c*) In creating employment opportunity among the non-poor, the aspect of external wage work or at least explicitly accounted earnings needs emphasis. Such opportunities can range from explicit factory-based employment on one hand to the domestic, unaccounted work in the dairy sector on the other and intermediate forms of home-based, weak bargaining position productive work like lace making (Mies, 1982). The domestic unaccounted work is unlikely to be of much help as exemplified by the activity in the dairy sector (Sharma and Vanjani, 1993; Upadhyaya, 1994).

In districts with very low FMRs (identified earlier) and abysmally low FLP, crossing the seclusion level FLP has to be the first priority. While the use of public works programme could be an important strategy towards increasing FLP, especially among the poor, a variety of other methods can be explored. These could include:

- Higher incentive to cultivation of crops, especially non-wheat crops (and perhaps non-irrigated crops), where women's involvement in labour is high.
- Encouraging sectors where women's work force participation is high, for example, food processing.
- A graded level of positive discrimination in the organised sector, both private and public. The lower the overall FLP in the district or region, the higher should be the component of positive discrimination in these sectors. Since incentives are provided to industries for going into underdeveloped regions, there is no reason why these cannot be provided to industries which employ certain percentage of women.[11] The level of incentive can also be linked with the level of FLP, that is, higher incentives can be given for regions with very low FLP.
- Certain public sector jobs, for example primary school teachers, carry symbolic prestige value. The low FMR and low FLP districts should be made to have at least 50 per cent of these posts manned by female staff. If this creates resentment among the male aspirants for the job, it is up to the polity to make efforts to raise the level of FMRs and FLP.

[11] I recall with certain sense of regret a wasted opportunity in this context. The Lijjat group, run by women and which employs women for preparation of ready to eat snacks wanted to expand their operations in Orissa where both I and my wife, Anita, happened to work. The group was requesting only a five year sales tax holiday from the State Government. They wanted no other concessions. Anita, who was looking after the women's welfare portfolio, failed to convince the decision makers in the Industries Department to accept this proposal. Later, when I became the Director of Industries in the State Government, I did not pursue the matter. It would not have been very difficult for me to push this concession through. Perhaps if I had this benefit of hindsight, I would have done so.

- A major constraint on skilled women entering the organised sector job market is the task of childrearing. There is no opportunity for them today, especially in the public sector, to enter the job market at, say, the age of 35, when they have discharged their 'reproductive responsibilities'. Such opportunities should be created.

In regions where FLP values are already high, emphasis needs to be given to aspects like education, skill acquisition, diversification of women's engagement in the labour market, provision of credit for such diversification and so on. Sector-wise watch has to be kept, however, for signs of any systematic decline in FLP. Expansion of the tertiary sector, where FLP is normally high, is also one alternative.

More crucial is the problem of the withdrawal of women from external work participation among the non-poor. This is a trend which has to be countered. The specific details of this will, however, depend on the context and will not be gone into here. But it must be emphasised that creation of high and visible FLP among the non-poor will be an important component of the strategy of halting the trends of female subordination and the consequent decline of FMRs among both the poor and the non-poor.

Drudgery reduction

The aspect of drudgery reduction, highlighted by Desai and Jain (1994), provides another important policy issue. This is important for two reasons, the mother's health and the children's survival. If, as some studies point out, there is a conflict between childrearing and entering the labour market, the solution will lie in the realm of reducing the drudgery of reproductive work. Here we are talking mainly of the poor. Among them, high FLP is a matter of necessity rather than choice. In this group, the burden of both time and energy spent on basic necessities like fuel or water can be quite high. Reduction in this burden can reduce the tension between childrearing and earning a wage. Again, innovative methods need to be introduced for this purpose. It is not enough, for example, to make fuel available easily, incentive for sale of pressure cookers, a fuel efficient device, can achieve similar results among the urban poor to start with.

The drudgery reduction tasks can also be combined innovatively with increasing visibility of women in the public sphere. Incentive for sale of women's bicycles, can for example, be one such idea. This may sound rather strange to an audience which takes women's visibility in the external sphere for granted. But it is very real to someone familiar with the stark contrast between, say, Pune and Patna, in terms of women using bicycles on the streets.

Power and visibility

This brings us to the question of visibility and participation of women in the 'external' sphere, an important aspect of women's status (Basu, 1992). A crucial element of this participation relates to the question of safety. There is a growing perception about sexual vulnerability of young females in the north which is surprisingly echoed even in Tamil Nadu (Venkata-chalam, 1993; Vera-Sanso, 1995). In fact, some of the persons who eliminated their daughters gave their likely future sexual vulnerability as one of the excuses for the elimination. This trend is deeply disturbing. Oldenburg's conjecture (1992) on the role of violence, son preference and daughter's vulnerability needs to be taken more seriously than it has been so far. While he has been derided for pursuing 'spurious correlations' (Mitra, 1993) it cannot be denied that women are likely to feel more unsafe in a violence prone region, statistics or no statistics. As Dasgupta (1993: 321) points out, 'The idea that men should be protectors of women may sound grand, but it does not do much for the female autonomy under the best of circumstances; it can in the worst of circumstances be devastating'[12] This link between 'Women's seclusion and men's honour' (Mendelbaum 1988), requires, therefore, to be studied in greater depth.

Another aspect of physical vulnerability leading to the devaluation of a girl child is a women's vulnerability as a newly married bride on account of dowry transactions. The 'pernicious aspects' (Goody, 1990) of dowry need serious attention. The available social legislation such as the Dowry Prevention Act has turned out to be ineffective (Malhotra et al., 1995; Subramaniam, 1996) but the solution lies in making it more effective rather than lamenting its non-enforceability. It needs to be realised that it is the constant threat to the life and wellbeing of the daughter which deepens the perception of daughter as a liability, not dowry per se. Hence the legislation need not aim at eliminating dowry but at eliminating dowry related deaths and physical harassment.[13]

[12] The recent conflict in Bosnia is a relevant example of this.

[13] The ineffectiveness of legislation, e.g., Anti-dowry Act, to ban dowry in the past does not really represent the failure of legislation per se, but of its design and the loopholes left in it. At the risk of some digression it is worthwhile suggesting a measure I have in mind. This would simply ban any person from marrying for a period of 5 years if his wife dies within 7 years of marriage *from any cause whatsoever*. The obsession with not letting one innocent

Finally, there is the role of power which provides macrostructures with the ability to strongly affect women's entitlements at the micro level (Blumberg, 1991). Recent legislative initiatives in India on positive discrimination in favour of women's representation in formal political fora, holds out certain promise in this regard. Already, the provision of one-third representation to women on lower levels of self-government have been put in place. Currently a tussle is going on about extending this to the state assemblies and the Parliament. Much can be argued for or against such move, but the fact remains that the participation of women in the political process will have a non marginal impact on their status as a whole. The other plain fact is that these women are more likely to appreciate women's problems at the ground level. The point about promoting the sale of women's bicycles made earlier, will have much weaker support in a Parliament where only 5 per cent of MPs are women.

V

Limitations of the present study

While this analysis has considerably advanced the understanding of the sex ratio problem in India it suffers from certain limitations. These limitations have to be addressed in future studies on this subject.

Further disaggregation

The first limitation relates to the disaggregation of the data by urban and rural location of the population. With growing urbanisation of the Indian population, its effects on sex ratios in different regions require detailed study. Urbanisation has an impact on infant mortality, female participation

---

person suffer must be curtailed in favour of the numerous 'innocent' victims of kitchen fire. The society today hides behind the excuses of inadequacy of law and 'social character' of people and pleads helplessness before the growing menace of 'dowry deaths'. The measure described above will have a salutary effect on the dowry deaths and, more importantly, on apprehensions that the perpetrators of such deaths remain unaffected. A system of substantial reward for providing information about attempts to violate this law can also be in place. Such rewards, incidentally, have been used in the campaign against eradication of small pox.

in wage earning, education levels, age of marriage and the like which in turn affect the mortality levels and sex differentials among these. Given the amount of ground that was required to be covered in the disaggregations suggested here, urban–rural differential could not be taken up for analysis except in passing through the NSSO data on FMRs by prosperity levels. At that level of aggregation, rural–urban differences were not very significant. Murthi et al. (1995: 25) find that 'urbanisation is associated with higher levels of female disadvantage in child survival' even though it has a negative and significant impact on overall child mortality. Clearly boys gain more compared to girls. Kynch and Sen (1983) have also noted similar asymmetry in terms of access to health service in metropolitan India.

The second limitation in the study relates to the non-SC/ST or the 'general' category. As culture is an important variable, it is perhaps useful to break up the 'general' category further. Religion is one important cultural factor. However, limited analyses of the impact of religion, especially Islam, on sex ratios (Sopher, 1980 and my own quick analysis not reported here) show that region is more decisive than religion in shaping sex ratios. In any case this contentious issue would have required a much more detailed analysis than the space within this study could permit. As such this aspect has not been pursued.

The third limitation concerns the parity effect. Higher the parity lower the sex ratio at birth. As the number of children per household declines, the sex ratios at birth and hence the overall sex ratios are likely to get more and more masculine. As disaggregated data on births by parity is not available at the level of this study, this effect has not been studied. It must be mentioned, however, that the parity effect can still not explain either the drops between FMR04 and FMR59 or the high female mortality directly estimated.

Analysis of other correlates

Another set of limitation relates to the study of other correlates of FMR. However, as this analysis has shown, the first objective was to get the 'tuning' right before moving on to analysis of other correlates using techniques of multivariate analysis. Such analysis can be separately done for different layers that have been disentangled here but this is an issue for future research.

It is appropriate to discuss the question of spatial autocorrelation even if briefly. It is possible that the FMR patterns at the district level are affected by FMRs patterns in the adjoining districts. Kishor (1993: 253–54) explicitly takes this effect into account and finds it to be significant. However, she admits that 'there is no theoretical justification for assuming that gender differences in mortality in one district are causally related to those in neighbouring districts. However, similar unmeasured factors may influence gender differences in mortality among neighbouring districts leading to an assumption of spatial autocorrelation of disturbances'.

Taking spatial autocorrelation into account at the level of analysis done in this study was not considered warranted. The emphasis in this study has mostly been on segregating the effect of different variables, like separating FMRs by age groups, the FMR-FLP patterns among the Scheduled Caste, Scheduled Tribe and the others or separately analysing the FMR-FLP relation by prosperity within the 'general' category.

The second reason why analysis of spatial autocorrelation were not taken into account was the possibility that the geophysical regions could be capturing the effects of the 'unmeasured factors' (Kishor, 1993). The relative homogeneity of FMRs within geophysical regions and sharp discontinuities across these regions suggests that factors other than spatial autocorrelation could be involved. Kishor's analysis implicitly assumes spatial autocorrelation to be isotropic, i.e., same in all directions. But the analysis here has shown that there could be sharp discontinuities across topographical discontinuities, for example, a river or sharply rising mountain range and even sharply different crop pattern. The spatial autocorrelation may, therefore, not be isotropic. Handling the level of complexity introduced by the anisotropy was much beyond the level of analysis pursued here.

Female education

The importance of education as a correlate of FMR must be mentioned here. However, the effects of education on the female disadvantage is mixed. There are different aspects of education: formal versus informal, and, within the formal primary versus higher education. Gender bias among highly educated mothers has been reported by Dasgupta (1987) while Murthi et al. (1995: 24) indicate favourable impact of female literacy on relative female child survival but thier analysis does not differentiate between different levels of education. Bourne and Walker's analysis (1991) of the district-level mortality estimates by educational levels of the mothers shows high rates of reduction in mortality rates up to middle-level education, but the results in the case of higher education are mixed.

356 • *Sex ratio patterns in the Indian population*

Tinkering on the margins

One of the important schools of thought on gender relations relates to the role of property relations. As indicated earlier, a strong case has been made by Agarwal about 'getting the property relations right'. She places particular emphasis on the inheritance of land and land ownership by women. Johansson (1997, in p.c.) also considers the property relations to be of crucial importance. This study has not analysed this aspect in any detail and the range of policy initiatives does not touch the inheritance aspects. Is one then merely tinkering on the margins?

The answer is yes and no. Two submissions are made in this regard. First, this study is concerned with a very basic aspect of gender inequality, survival. It recognises that the overall pattern of gender inequalities impinges on the survival inequality. It does not dispute that getting the inheritance right (de facto, not merely de jure) represents a sufficient condition for having survival equality, for, this would have reduced overall inequalities. While it is quite easy to debunk other possible solutions and say that unless we get the property inheritance right nothing else would work, such a solution represents a far cry as Agarwal's account itself indicates.

My focus here is on the survival first and a belief that it can happen even without going for the more radical solution of inheritance equality. The first dent that needs to be made in ensuring survival, is in the 0–5 age group itself. Other societies which did practice discrimination against female children could still let them survive till the age of five without much ado. Let Indian society achieve that first.

The issue of strategy becomes important here. The stylised 'anti-female' policy clearly shows, and Agarwal admits, that it is very difficult to make a dent on land right patterns. It is far easier to achieve universal immunisation, bring about transfer of nutrition, impart skills and provide employment opportunity for unskilled and skilled work to women. These steps may be adequate for ensuring relative equality in survival. It is prudent to attempt this first and that has been the thrust of the policy interventions suggested here. Anyone who follows the analysis will recognise that the problem of excess female child mortality has to be first rescued from various escape hatches and veils of averaging and from a tendency to deny the existence of the problem. Then it has to be broken into 'manageable' segments from the policy point of view. This has been done here and is followed by a number of suggestions which converge towards two rather limited objectives: ensuring survival in the under-5 age group and reducing the 'devaluation' of the female child. The case has been rested at this stage. That the solutions suggested are not radical enough is accepted if that is a charge still sought to be levelled.

The second charge of tinkering on the margins relates to the silence about the ban on sex-selective abortions. This has not been discussed. I really have no answer to this question. Should sex-selective abortions be banned? In principle yes. In practice, I do not know how. Should the prenatal selection be banned? One hundred per cent. But I do not know how. Ashish Bose had once asked me, 'What can you do when the parents are hellbent on killing their daughter right at birth?" (in p.c., 1995) My answer then was, 'Our inability to prevent this is no justification for not saving those girl children who have survived the first month of their life.' My position remains the same. I still do not know any short-term solution to this issue except the idea about coverage of pregnant mothers with anti-tetanus injection and indirectly monitoring the result of the pregnancy.

VI

For whom the bells toll?

Finally, an ethical question. I am often asked what is wrong if we have high rates of sex-selective abortion or a low FMR for that matter. Is it not better that the female foetuses are aborted rather than have female infants being killed at birth or being allowed to die due to neglect? Will the smaller number of surviving female children not be looked after better? I do not accept this for a number of reasons. First, evidence from the female deficit regions has not shown signs of 'surviving' females getting treated better, yet. Second, the 'surviving' female children could still continue to spend their life in an atmosphere of 'devaluation'. They may be socialised into accepting their lot but that is a different matter altogether. Third, the 'dowry market' catches up with the wealth levels (Rao, 1993) and the well-treated 'surviving daughters' become 'ill-treated' daughters-in-law. Fourth, the sex ratio distortion will be alarming when son preference and biased sex selections converge (Table 8.4) and there is no reason why the effect will not spiral out of hand. Those who wish to have a proof of the adverse sociological consequences of such imbalance display a naive or spurious objectivity. If we invoke society's ability to cope with the imbalance, as Pisani and Zaba (forthcoming) do, by suggesting that two brothers can share one wife, one needs to ask what are the limits to such coping capacity? Five brothers sharing one wife, taking a cue from the *Mahabharata*? And why should the five should be brothers anyway? If this spurious objectivity is stretched further, what is the harm in maintaining two classes of women, one for biological reproduction and the rest for recreational purposes? And once suitable technological advances have been made, for instance if babies can be grown outside the womb, why not do away with former category altogether?

The issue is ultimately ethical: should a portion of population be considered expendable on the basis of gender. If the answer is yes, what prevents such notions of expendability being extended to other factors like the colour of eyes, hair and skin? Acceptance of sex-selective abortions is another thin end of the wedge and needs be opposed as such. For those who may not wish to oppose it, the following reminder from a not too distant past could be useful:

When they attacked the jews, I was not a Jew, therefore I was not concerned. And when they attacked the Catholics, I was not a Catholic, and therefore, I was not concerned. And when they attacked the unions and Industrialists, I was not a member of unions and I was not concerned. Then they attacked me and the Protestant Church—and there was nobody to be concerned.

(Martin Niemoller, 1892–1984)

Annexure 3A

Estimating FMRs from mortality levels and differentials[1]

We begin with a sex ratio at birth of F0 females per 1,000 male population. Following notation is used for analysis:

FMR(i, j)	= females per 1,000 males in i–j age group
Fi	= FMR at ith birth day
F(i, j)	= number of females in the age group i–j
M(i, j)	= number of males in the age group i–j
q(n, x)	= probability of death between the age x and x + n
p(n, x)	= survival probability between the age x and x + n
IMRf	= female infant mortality rate per 1,000 live female births
IMRm	= male infant mortality rate per 1,000 live male births
dIMRmf	= IMRm-IMRf
CMRf	= female child mortality rate = q(4, 1, f)
CMRm	= male child mortality rate = q(4, 1, m)
dCMRmf	= CMRm-CMRf

Different simplifying assumptions will be made here. But these 'err on the safer side', that is, the more realistic ones will result in even higher FMR values, for example, skewed nature of the under-5 mortality towards younger ages. As such the overall argument is not vitiated by making these assumptions. Further, given the magnitude of differences involved, the complexities associated with the 'realistic' assumptions need not be pursued in the present context but can be a part of a worthwhile future research agenda.

Sex ratio for the 0–1 age group can be approximated as:

[1] I am thankful to Basia Zaba of the Population Research Group of the London School of Hygiene and Tropical Medicine for her help and useful comments on this 'model'.

$$FMR(0, 1) = 1,000* F(0, 1)/M(0, 1); \qquad \text{1.1a where,}$$
$$F(0, 1) = [F0 + F0* p(0, f)]/2 = F0* [1 + (1 - IMRf/1,000)]/2$$
$$= F0* (2 - IMRf/1,000)/2 \qquad \text{1.1b and,}$$
$$M(0, 1) = M0* (2 - IMRm/1,000)/2 \qquad \text{1.1c}$$
$$\text{or } FMR(0, 1) = F0* (2,000 - IMRf)/(2,000 - IMRm)$$
$$= F0* [1 + (IMRm - IMRf/2,000 - IMRm)] \quad \text{or,}$$

$$[FMR(0, 1) - F0]/F0 = dIMRm/(2,000 - IMRm) \qquad \text{1.2}$$

This expresses proportionate increase in $FMR(0, 1)$ over F0. This increase or decrease is much more sensitive to change in the male female infant mortality gap rather than the levels of male mortality, that is, IMRm.

We can similarly calculate $FMR(1, 4)$ which will be determined by CMR levels and differentials. We will assume that the mortality in the 1, 4 age group is uniformly spread across all the four years. A more 'realistic' pattern of deaths in the four years would be 4:2:1:1, but that will not change the picture much. We can therefore approximate,

$$FMR(1, 4) = 1,000* F(1, 4)/M(1, 4) \qquad \text{2.3a where,}$$
$$F(1, 4) = (F1 + F5)/2 = [F1 + F1* (1 - CMRf/1,000)]/2$$
$$= F1* (2 - CMRf/1,000)/2 \qquad \text{2.3b and,}$$
$$M(1, 4) = M1* (2 - CMRm/1,000)/2 \qquad \text{2.3c and,}$$
$$FMR(1, 4) = 1,000* (F1/M1)* (2,000 - CMRf)/(2,000 - CMRm) \text{ or,}$$

$$FMR(1, 4) = 1,000* (F1/M1)* [(1 + dCMRmf)/(2,000 - CMRm)] \text{ 2.4a}$$

But F1/M1 itself can be expressed as:

$$F1/M1 = (F0/M0)* (1 - IMRf/1,000)/(1 - IMRm/1,000)$$
$$= F0* [1 + dIMRmf/(1,000 - IMRm)]/1,000$$

This allows us to express change in $FMR(1, 4)$ over F0 as:

$$[FMR(1, 4) - F0)]/F0 = dIMRmf/(1,000 - IMRm)$$
$$+ dCMRmf/(2,000 - CMRm)$$
$$+ dIMRm* dCMRm/(1,000 - IMRm)* (2,000 - CMRm) \qquad \text{`2.4b}$$

The first term and hence IMR gap will dominate the expression and FMR (1, 4) will be higher than F0 if there is excess male infant mortality. The second term will tend to reduce this effect through excess female child mortality, that is, dCMRmf will be negative. Given the denominator (2,000–CMRm) in the second term, excess female child mortality has to be nearly twice as large as excess male infant mortality to compensate its effect on FMR. The interaction term will be quite small.

We can also express F5/M5 ratio similarly and approximate it as FMR (5, 9) under a simplifying assumption that no deaths take place in 5–9 age. We have:

$$F5/M5 = [F1*(1 - CMRf/1,000)]/[M1*(1 - CMRm/1,000)]$$
$$= (F1/M1)*(1,000 - CMRf)/(1,000 - CMRm) \qquad 3.1$$

Using the value of F1/M1 above, we can express FMR(5, 9) as

$$FMR(5, 9) = F0*[1 + dIMRmf/(1,000 - IMRm)]*[1 + dCMRmf/(1,000 - CMRm)] \text{ or,}$$

$$[FMR(5, 9) - F0]/F0 = dIMRmf/(1,000 - IMRm)$$
$$+ dCMRmf/(1,000 - CMRm)$$
$$+ dIMRmf* dCMRmf/(1,000 - IMRm)*(1,000 - CMRm) \qquad 3.2$$

The first and the second terms are equally dominant and if excess female child mortality exceeds excess male infant mortality or -dCMRmf > dIMRmf, the FMRs in 5–9 age group will go below F0. The interaction term will be small again.

While this expression above gives an idea of the relative impact of IMR and CMR on the FMR(5, 9), we can also express it in terms of under-5 mortality q(5, 0) or simply Q5. We have:

$$F5 = F0*(1 - Q5f/1,000) \text{ and } M5 = 1,000*(1 - Q5m/1,000)$$

If we have q(5, 5, f) and q(5, 5, m) as the deaths during the 5–9 age group then,

$$FMR(5, 9) = 1,000*(F5 + F10)/(M5 + M10)$$
$$= 1,000*(F5/M5)*[2 - q(5, 5, f)/1,000]/[2 - q(5, 5, m)/1,000]$$
$$= 1,000*(F5/M5)*(2,000 - q(5, 5, f)/(2,000 - q(5, 5, m)) \qquad 4.1a$$

The value of q(5, 5) are typically below 10. As such it is quite acceptable to express FMR(5, 9) as:

$$FMR(5, 9) = 1,000*(F5/M5) = F0*(1,000 - Q5f)/(1,000 - Q5m)$$
$$= F0*(1 + dQ5mf/(1,000 - Q5m) \qquad 4.1b$$

or,

$$[FMR(5, 9) - F0]/F0 = dQ5mf/(1,000 - Q5m) \qquad 4.1c$$

clearly the excess female mortality under-5 will determine the sex ratios in the 5–9 age group.

We thus see that FMR59 is a much more effective indicator of the discrimination against female children compared to FMR04 which represents a complex interplay of IMR levels, gap and the CMR levels and the gap. This is reflected in juvenile FMR figures which are a composite of FMRs in the 0–4 and 5–9 age groups.

While the algebra given here is cumbersome and not expressed in standard demographic terms, it brings out the relative importance of IMR levels and differentials compared to the CMR levels and differentials. It also establishes the need to analyse the JFMR data into separate age groups of 0–4 and 5–9.

Annexure 5A

Regions with homogenous sex ratio patterns

Region 1   All districts of Himachal Pradesh, Jammu and Kashmir and hilly districts of UP viz., Chamoli, Pithoragarh, Uttarkashi, Dehradun, Garhwal, Tehri Garhwal, Almora and Nainital. These form part of the northern Himalayas.

Region 2   Part of the 'Great Plains': All districts of Punjab and Haryana. (Although a few districts in Haryana could be part of region 3).

Region 3   Districts of western UP in the upper Gangetic plain: Saharanpur, Muzaffarnagar, Bijnor, Meerut, Ghaziabad, Bulandshahar, Moradabad, Rampur, Budaun, Bareilly, Pilibhit, Shahjahanpur, Aligarh, Mathura, Agra, Etah, Mainpuri, Farrukhabad, Etawah, Jalaun, Jhansi, Lalitpur, Hamirpur, Banda and Kheri; Bharatpur and Sawai Madhopur which constitute the sub-region of Banas Chambal basin and Alwar. (Alwar defies the sub-regional classification. It has been included here although it belongs to the sub-region of Aravalli range and associated uplands of semi-arid Rajasthan.); Chambal ravines of Bundelkhand in MP which include the districts of Bhind, Morena, Gwalior and Datia (The 1981 classification includes Guna and Shivpuri. We have used the 1961 classification quoted in Bose [1994: 44–48]. These classify Guna and Shivpuri under northern Malwa uplands).

Region 4   Middle Gangetic plain consisting of the remaining districts of UP.

Region 5   Districts of Bihar in the lower Gangetic plain: All districts of Bihar, except Katihar and Purnia which are clubbed with region 7 and the districts in region 6.

Region 6   South Bihar hills and plateau: Districts of Palamau, Ranchi, Hazaribagh, Singhbhum, Dhanbad, Santhal Parganas.

Region 7   Katihar and Purnia of Bihar, all districts of West Bengal and Cuttack, Puri and Balasore districts of Orissa. (Although Purulia could be clubbed with region 6, and the hilly districts could form a separate group.)

Region 8   Semi-arid Rajasthan and the plains of Gujarat: All districts of Rajasthan except those in region 10 (hilly region) and all districts of Gujarat except Valsad and Dang clubbed in region 11, covering districts on the West coast.

Region 10   Hilly districts of Rajasthan (Bose, 1994: 45), viz., Bhilwara, Udaipur, Chittaurgarh, Dungarpur, Banswara and Jhalawar, Malwa plateau and Narmada valley (Bose, 1994: 46) in MP, the districts of Mandsaur, Ratlam, Ujjain, Shajapur, Dewas, Jhabua, Dhar, Indore, West Nimar, Rajgarh, Hoshangabad, Jabalpur, Narsimhapur. (West and East Nimar show a sharp divide which may be worth analysing at the block level).

Region 11   Western coastal districts: Starting from districts of Valsad and Dang at its northern end, going down through Thane, Raigarh and Ratnagiri in Maharashtra, Goa, Uttar and Dakshin Kannada in Karnataka to all districts of Kerala.

Region 12   North Malwa uplands, that is, Guna and Shivpuri, north central MP, that is, Chhatrapur, Tikamgarh, the Vindhya range and Rewa plateau, Vidisha, Raisen, Sagar, Damoh, Bhopal, Panna, Rewa, Satna, East Nimar and, Jalgaon, Dhule and Nasik districts of Maharashtra. (This grouping draws on the 1961 regions [Bose, 1994].)

Region 13   Remaining districts of MP covering Satpuras, Bagherkhand, Chhattisgarh, Bastar and all districts of Orissa except three coastal districts (region 7) and Ganjam which is clubbed with region 19.

Region 14   Western Ghats in Maharashtra: Ahmednagar, Pune, Satara, Sangli, Solapur and Kolhapur; inland Karnataka, that is, Belgaum and Dharwar; North Maidan, that is, Bidar, Gulbarga and Bijapur; and the central Maidan, that is, Bellary and Raichur (1961 Census classification [Bose, 1994: 47]).

Region 15   Marathwada, Vidarbha and Mahakosal regions of Maharashtra covering the rest of its districts.

Region 16   Rest of the districts of Karnataka covering south Maidan, and Malnad and Chittoor of Andhra which shows different characteristics from Rayalaseema where it is included in the census classification.

Region 17   Eastern coastal region I: all districts of Tamil Nadu and Pondicherry.

Region 18   Telangana region of Andhra Pradesh: Mahboobnagar, Rangareddy, Hyderabad, Medak, Nizamabad, Adilabad, Karimnagar, Warangal, Khammam and Nalgonda.

Region 19   East coastal Andhra Pradesh and south Orissa: The Ganjam district of Orissa and rest of the districts of Andhra Pradesh except those in region 20.

Region 20   Anantpur, Cudappah and Kurnool of Rayalaseema and the two southern coastal districts of Prakasam and Nellore classified as a separate sub-region.

Remarks

(a) Delhi, Chandigarh and Mumbai are not included in the regional analysis.

(b) The central zone which represents the north–south transition is difficult to classify and indicates tracks which further cut across these regions. These could be analysed at a more detailed level with smaller regions.

Districts classified by kinship system[1]

The 164 districts (1981 Census) in the 'core' northern region include:

- All districts of Punjab and Haryana.
- All districts of Uttar Pradesh except the hilly districts viz., Uttarkashi, Chamoli, Tehri Garhwal, Dehradun, Garhwal, Pithoragarh, Almora and Nainital.
- All districts of Rajasthan excluding the hilly districts of Udaipur, Bhilwara, Chittaurgarh, Dungarpur, Banswara and Jhalawar.
- All districts of Bihar except those in the south Bihar hills and plateau; Palamau, Ranchi, Hazaribagh, Singhbhum, Dhanbad and Santhal Pargana.
- All districts of Gujarat except Panch Mahals, Valsad and the Dangs.
- Chambal ravines and north Malwa uplands of Madhya Pradesh. These cover districts of Bhind, Morena, Gwalior, Datia, Guna, Shivpuri, Tikamgarh, Chhatrapur, Panna, Sagar, Damoh, Satna, Rewa, Ujjain, Shajapur, East Nimar, Rajgarh, Vidisha, Bhopal, Sehore, Raisen, Hoshangabad and Narsimhapur.
- Jalgaon, Dhule and Nasik districts of Maharashtra which form part of the northern Malwa uplands and Pune and Satara.

The region 'rest' includes all districts of the four southern states, West Bengal, Orissa and the north-eastern states and districts not included above.

It will be incorrect to think that this classification is static. In fact, within this century itself many a socio-cultural practices have undergone change. Many districts especially those on the border of two different regions are difficult to classify, for example, Purnia and Katihar in Bihar, or the district of Dehradun in UP or Pune and Satara in Maharashtra. Moreover different social strata within the same district follow different kinship practices. However the classification here has not been 'fine-tuned'. This could follow once the usefulness of the broad classification is established which was the main purpose of this analysis.

[1] Agnihotri, 1997.

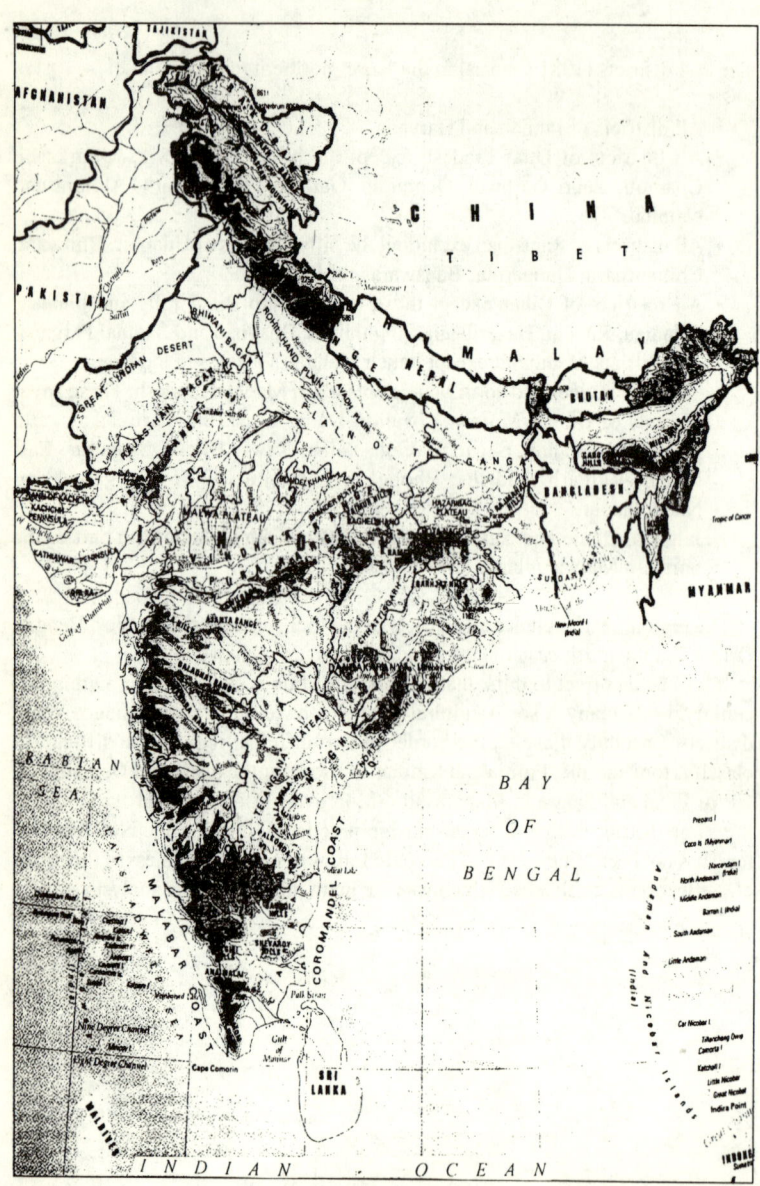

Physical map of India

Bibliography

Agarwal, B. 1985. 'Women and technological change', in Ahmed I. (ed), *Technology and rural women*. London: George Allen and Unwin.

———. 1988. 'Who sows? Who reaps? Women and land rights in India', *Journal of Peasant Studies*, 15(4): 531–81.

———. 1994. *A field of one's own: Gender and land rights in South Asia*. Cambridge: Cambridge University Press.

Agarwala, S.N. 1967. *Corrected age data of the 1931 Indian Census*. London: Asia Publishing House.

Agnihotri, S.B. 1992. *Intrahousehold dynamics and its social dimensions*. Published MA thesis. Norwich: School of Development Studies, University of East Anglia.

———. 1995a. 'Missing females: a disaggregated analysis', *Economic and Political Weekly*, 30(19): 2074–84.

———. 1995b. 'Sex ratios and the search for an intrahousehold Kuznets curve'. Paper presented at the 11th World Congress of the International Economic Association, December, 1995, Tunis.

———. 1996a. 'Sex ratio variations in India: What do languages tell us?'. Paper presented at the annual conference of the IASP (Indian Association for the Studies of Population) 1996, Vadodara, India.

———. 1996b. 'Juvenile sex ratios in India: A disaggregated analysis', *Economic and Political Weekly*, December 28: 3369–82.

———. 1997. 'Workforce participation, kinship, and sex ratio variations in India', *Gender, Technology and Development*, 1(1): 75–112.

Ananthram, S. 1989. *Declining sex ratio in India: 1901–81*. Ph. D. Thesis JNU, New Delhi.

Aslanbeigui, N. and **Summerfield, G.** 1993. 'Impact of the responsibility system on rural women in China: An application of Sen's theory of entitlements', *World Development*, 17(3): 343–50.

Babu, S.C., Thirumaran, S. and **Mohanam, T.C.** 1993. 'Agricultural productivity, seasonality and gender bias in rural nutrition: Empirical evidence from south India', *Social Science and Medicine*, 37(11): 1293–1301.

Bardhan, P.K. 1974. 'On life and death questions', *Economic and Political Weekly*, special issue number 9: 1293–1304.

———. 1982. 'Little girls and death in India', *Economic and Political Weekly*, September 4, 17(36): 1448–50.

———. 1986. 'On the economic geography of sex disparity in child survival in India: A note'. Proceedings of SSRC on Sex Differentials in Mortality and Health Care in South Asia, Dhaka, January 1986. Mimeo.

Basu, A.M. 1989. 'Is discrimination in food really necessary for explaining sex differentials in childhood mortality?', *Population Studies*, 48: 193–210.

Basu, A.M. 1992. *Culture, the status of women, and demographic behaviour.* Oxford: Clarendon Press.

Becker, G. 1981. *A treatise on the family.* Cambridge: Harvard University Press.

Behrman, J. 1988. 'Nutrition, health, birth order and seasonality: Intra-household allocation among children in rural India', *Journal of Development Economics*, 28.

Behrman, J. and **Deolalikar, A.B.** 1990. 'The intrahousehold demand for nutrients in rural south India—Individual estimates, fixed effects and permanent income', *The Journal of Human Resources*, 25(4): 665–96.

Beliappa, J. and **Rama, S.** 1994. *Declining sex ratio and the problems of female infanticide— A study in Salem district of Tamil Nadu.* New Delhi: Department of women and child development, Government of India (mimeo).

Bennet, L. 1991. *Gender and poverty in India.* Washington, D.C.: The World Bank.

Berreman, G.D. 1993. 'Sanskritization as female oppression in India', in Miller, B.D. (ed.), *Sex and Gender Hierarchies*, pp. 366–92. Cambridge: Cambridge University Press.

Bharadwaj, S.M. 1973. *Hindu places of pilgrimage in India.* London: University of California Press.

Billing, M.S. 1991. 'The marriage squeeze on high caste Rajasthani women', *The Journal of Asian Studies*, 50(2): 341–60.

Blumberg, R.L. 1991. *Gender, family and economy: The triple overlap.* Newbury Park: Sage.

Bose, A. 1991. *Population of India—1991 Census results and methodology.* New Delhi: B.R. Publishers.

——. 1994. *Demographic zones in India.* Delhi: B.R. Publishers.

Boserup, E. 1970. *Women's role in economic development.* London: Allen and Unwin.

Bourne, K. and **Walker, G.M.** 1991. 'The differential effects of mother's education on mortality of boys and girls in India', *Population Studies*, 45: 203–219.

Caldwell, J.C. and **Caldwell, P.** 1990. *Gender implications for survival in South Asia.* Health transition working paper number 7, Canberra: NCEPH, Australian National University.

Caplan, L. 1993. 'Bridegroom price in Urban India: Caste, class and "dowry evil" among Christians in Madras', in Uberoi (ed.), pp. 357–82.

Chandrasekhar, S. 1959. *Infant mortality in India—1901–55,* London: George Allen and Unwin.

——. 1972. *Infant mortality, population growth and family planning in India.* London: George Allen and Unwin.

Chatterjee, M. 1990. *Indian women: Their health and economic productivity.* Washington: The World Bank.

Chen, L.C. 1982. 'Where have the women gone', *Economic and Political Weekly*, March 6: 364–72.

Chen, M. 1989. 'Women's work in Indian agriculture by agro-ecologic zones', *Economic and Political Weekly*, October 28: 43 WS-79–89.

Chhabra, R. 1981. 'India's sobering Census', *People*, 8(3).

Chowdhry, P. 1993. 'High participation, low evaluation: Women and work in rural Haryana', *Economic and Political Weekly*, December 25: A135–A146.

Clark, A.W. 1987. 'Social demography of excess female mortality in India, new directions', *Economic and Political Weekly*, 22(17): WS12–21.

——. 1989. 'Mortality, fertility and the status of women in India, 1881–1931', in Dyson T. and Crook, N. (eds.), pp. 119–49.

Collins R. 1991. 'Women and men in the class structure', in Blumberg (ed.), pp. 52–73.

Dange, A.S. 1972. 'An analysis of sex ratio differentials by regions in Madhya Pradesh', *Arth Vijnana*, 14: 273–86.

Dasgupta, M. 1987. 'Selective discrimination against female children in rural Punjab, India', *Population and Development Review*, 13(1): 77–100.

———. 1995. 'Life course perspectives on women's autonomy and health outcomes', *American Anthropologist*, 97(3): 481–91.

Dasgupta, M. and **Bhat, P.N.M.** 1995. *Intensified gender bias in India: A consequence of fertility decline*. Working paper number 2, Center for Population and Development Studies, Harvard University.

Dasgupta, P. 1993. *An inquiry into wellbeing and destitution*. Oxford: Oxford University Press.

Desai, P.B. 1969. *Size and sex composition of population in India, 1901–1961*. London: Asia Publishing House.

Desai, S. and **Jain, D.** 1994. 'Maternal employment and changes in family dynamics: The social context of women's work in rural south India', *Population and Development Review*, 20(1): 115–36.

Divale, W.T. and **Harris, M.** 1976. 'Population, warfare and the male supremacist complex', *American Anthropologist*, 78: 521–37.

Doss, C.R. 1996. 'Testing among models of intrahousehold resource allocation', *World Development*, 24(10): 1597–1609.

Drèze, J. 1991. 'Famine prevention in India', in Sen, A.K. and Drèze, J. (eds.), *The political economy of hunger*. Dhaka: University Press.

Drèze, J., Guio, A. and **Murthi, M.** 1996. 'Demographic outcomes, economic development and women's agency', *Economic and Political Weekly*, 31(27): 1739–42.

Drèze, J. and **Sen, A.K.** 1991. 'Public action for social security', in Ahmed, E. et al. (eds.), *Social security in developing countries*. Oxford: Clarendon.

———. 1995. *India: Economic development and social opportunity*. Delhi: Oxford University Press.

Dunn, D. 1993. 'Gender inequality in education and employment among the Scheduled Castes and the Scheduled Tribes in India', *Population Research and Policy Review*, 12(1): 53–70.

Dyson, T. 1975. *India's population: An analysis of its size, age-structure, fertility and mortality*. IDS discussion paper number 72. Brighton: IDS.

———. 1981. 'Preliminary demography of the 1981 census', *Economic and Political Weekly*, August 15: 1349–56.

———. 1984. 'Excess male mortality in India', *Economic and Political Weekly*, March 10: 422–26.

———. 1992. *Infant and child mortality in India*, London School of Economics (mimeo).

———. 1994. 'On the demography of the 1991 census', *Economic and Political Weekly*, December: 3235–39.

Dyson, T. and **Crook, N.** 1989. *India's Historical demography*. Collected papers on South Asia number 8. Richmond: Curzon Press.

Dyson, T. and **Moore, M.** 1983. On kinship structure, female autonomy and aemographic balance, *Population and Development Review*, 9: 35–60.

Eckel, C. and **Grossman, P.** 1994. 'The relative price of fairness: Gender differences in a punishment game', University of Arizona, Tuscon (mimeo).

Fairservice, W.A. 1987. 'A review of the archaeological evidence in connection with the identity of the language of the Harrappan script', in Jackobson (ed.), pp. 175–93.

Folbre, N. 1986. 'Hearts and spades: Paradigms of household economics', *World Development*, 14(2): 245–55.

Fruzzetti, L. 1990. *Ritual in a Bengali Society*. Delhi: Oxford University Press.

Ganesh, K. 1989. 'Seclusion of women and the structure of the caste', in Krishnaraj, M. and Chanana, K. (eds.), *Gender and the Household Domain*, pp. 75–96. New Delhi: Sage.

Gasper, D. 1993. 'Entitlement analysis: Relating concepts and contexts', *Development and Change* 24: 679–718.

Gbenyon, K. and **Locoh, T.** 1992. 'Mortality differences in childhood by sex in sub-Saharan Africa', in Van de Walle E, Pison, G and Sala-Diakenda, M. (eds.), *Mortality and Society in Sub-Saharan Africa*, pp. 231–51. Oxford: Clarendon.

George, S., Abel. R. and **Miller, B.D.** 1992. 'Female infanticide in rural south India', *Economic and Political Weekly*, 27(22): 1154–56.

Ginsberg, C.A. and **Swedlund, A.C.** 1986. 'Sex-specific mortality and economic opportunities: Massachusetts, 1860–1899', *Continuity and Change*, 1(3): 415–45.

Goody, J. 1976. *Production and reproduction*. Cambridge: Cambridge University Press.

*——. 1990. *The oriental, the ancient and the primitive*. Cambridge: Cambridge University Press.

Gosal, G.S. and **Mukherji, A.B.** 1972. 'Distribution and relative concentration of Scheduled Caste population in India' in Government of India, pp. 473–82.

Government of India. 1964. 'Household Economic Tables-BX to B-XVII', *Census of India 1961, Part-III-(i) and (ii)*. Delhi: Office of the Registrar General, India.

——. 1972. *Economic and socio-cultural dimensions of regionalisation*, Census centenary monograph No. 7. New Delhi: Office of the Registrar General, India.

——. 1980. *Agricultural Atlas of India*. Calcutta: National Atlas and Thematic Mapping Organisation, Department of Science and Technology.

——. 1983. 'Population by Language/Mother-tongue Table C-7', *Census of India 1981, Part-IV-B(i)*. New Delhi: Office of the Registrar General and Census Commissioner, India.

——. 1988. *Child mortality estimates of India*. Occasional paper number 5 of 1988 (1981 Census). New Delhi: Office of the Registrar General, India.

——. 1989. *Social and cultural tables: Part IV, A(iv), Table: C-2 (Scheduled Tribes)*. New Delhi: Office of the Registrar General, India.

——. 1989. *Social and cultural tables: Part IV, A(i), Table: C-2 (Scheduled Castes)*. New Delhi: Office of the Registrar General, India.

——. 1991. *Survey of the causes of death—Annual report 1991*. New Delhi: Office of the Registrar General and Census Commissioner, India.

Gulati, L. 1978. 'Profile of a female agricultural labourer', *Economic and Political Weekly*, 13(12): PA 27–35.

Haddad, L. and **Kanbur, R.** 1990. 'How serious is the neglect of intra-household inequality', *The Economic Journal*, 100: 866–88.

——. 1992. 'Is there an intra-household Kuznets curve? Some evidence from the Philippines', *Public Finances*, 47: 77–93.

Harris, M. 1993. 'The evolution of human gender hierarchies: A trial formulation', in Miller, B.D. (ed.), pp. 57–79.

Harriss, B. 1989. 'Differential child mortality and health care in South Asia', *Journal of Social Studies*, 44: 2–123.

——. 1990. 'The intrafamily distribution of hunger in South Asia', in Drèze, J. And Sen, A.K. (eds.), *The political economy of hunger*, Volume-I, pp. 351–424. Oxford: Clarendon Press.

Heyer, J. 1992. 'The role of dowries and daughters' marriages in the accumulation and distribution of capital in a south Indian community', *Journal of International Development*, 4(4): 419–36.

Hill, J. and **Pebley, L.**1989. 'Child mortality in the developing world', *Population and Development Review*, 15(4): 419–36.

Hill, J. and **Upchurch P.** 1995. 'Gender differences in child health: Evidence from the demographic and health surveys', *Population and Development Review*, 21(1): 127–51.

Huber, J. 1991. 'A theory of family, economy and gender' in Blumberg (ed.) pp. 35–51.

International Institute for Population Sciences (IIPS). 1995. *National Family Health Survey, India 1992–93.* Mumbai: IIPS.

Jacobson, J. (ed.). 1987. *Studies in the archaeology of India and Pakistan.* Warminster: AMIS (American Institute of Indian Studies).

Jain, A.K. and **Visaria, P.** (eds.). 1988. *Infant mortality in India: Differentials and determinants.* New Delhi: Sage.

Johansson, S.R. 1984. 'Deferred infanticide: Excess female mortality during childhood', in Hausfater, G. And Hardy, S.B. (eds.), *Infanticide* pp. 463–86. New York: Aldine

——. 1991. 'Welfare, mortality, and gender. Continuity and change in explanations for male/female mortality differences over three centuries', *Continuity and Change*, 6(2): 135–77.

——. 1996. 'Excess female mortality', in Digby, A. and Stewart, J. (eds.), *Gender, Health and Welfare*, pp. 32–66. London: Routledge.

Johansson, S.R. and **Mosk, C.** 1987. 'Exposure, resistance and life expectancy: Disease and death during the economic development of Japan, 1900–1960', *Population Studies*, V41: 207–235.

Johnston, B.F. and **Clark W.C** 1982. *Redesigning rural development.* London: John Hopkins.

Jones, C. 1983. 'Mobilisation of women's labour for cash crop production: A game theoretic approach', *American Journal of Agricultural Economics*, 65.

Kabeer, N. 1991. *Gender, production and wellbeing: Rethinking the household economy.* IDS discussion paper number 288. Sussex: IDS.

——. 1995. *Necessary, sufficient or inrelevant? Women, wages and intra-household power relations in urban Bangladesh.* IDS working paper number 25, Sussex: IDS.

Kanbur, R. and **Haddad, L.** 1994. 'Are better off households more unequal or less unequal?', *Oxford Economic Papers*, 46: 445–58.

Kanitkar, T. 1991. 'The sex ratio in India: A topic for speculation and research', *Journal of Family Welfare*, 37(3): 18–22.

Kapadia, K. 1994. 'Bonded by blood: Matrilateral kin in Tamil kinship', *Economic and Political Weekly*, April 9: 855–61.

Karkal, M. 1987. 'Differentials in mortality by sex', *Economic and Political Weekly*, August 8: 1343-47.

Karve, I. 1965. *Kinship organisation in India.* Bombay: Asia Publishing House.

Kennedy, R.E.. 1973. *The Irish: Emigration, marriage and fertility.* Berkeley: University of California Press.

Khan, M.E. 1993. 'Cultural determinants of infant mortality in India', *The Journal of Family Welfare*, 39(2): 3–13.

Kishor, S. 1993.'"May God give sons to all": Gender and child mortality in India', *American Sociological Review*, 54(April): 247–65.

Klasen, S. 1994. 'Missing Women Reconsidered', *World Development*, 22(7): 1061–71.

Kulkarni, P.M. 1978. *Homogenity in sex ratio at birth*,. Bangalore: Institute for Social and Economic Change (mimeo).

Kundu, A. and Sahu, M.K. 1991. 'Variation in sex ratio: Development implications', *Economic and Political Weekly*, 26(41): 2341–42.

Krishnaji, N. 1987. 'Poverty and sex ratio—some data and some speculations?' *Economic and Political Weekly*, 22(23): 892–97.

Kynch, J. and Sen, A.K. 1983. 'Indian women: Wellbeing and survival', *Cambridge Journal of Economics*, 82(7): 363–80.

Lentican, C.P, Gladwin, C.H. and Searle J.L. (Jr.) 1996. 'Income and gender inequalities in Asia: Testing alternative theories of development', *Economic Development and Cultural Change*, 44(2): 235–63.

Lessinger, J. 1989. 'Petty trading and gender segregation in urban South India', in Afshar, H. and Agarwal, B. (eds.), *Women, poverty and ideology in Asia*. London: Macmillan.

Libbee, M. 1980. 'Territorial endogamy and the spatial structure of marriage', in Sopher D.E. (ed.), pp. 65–104. London: Longman.

Madan, T.N. 1993. 'Structural implications of marriage alliance in north India: Wife-givers and wife-takers among the Pandits of Kashmir', in Uberoi, P. (ed.), pp. 287–306.

Mason, A. and Bennett, N.G. 1977. 'Sex selection with biased technologies and its effect on the population sex ratio', *Demography*, 14(3): 285–96.

Mathur, A. 1994. 'Work participation, gender and economic development: A quantitative anatomy of the Indian scenario', *Journal of Development Studies*, 30(2): 466–504.

Maharatna, A. 1996. 'Infant and child mortality during famines in late 19th and early 20th century India', *Economic and Political Weekly*, 31(27): 1774–83.

Malhotra, A., Venneman, R. and Kishor, S. 1995. 'Fertility, dimensions of patriarchy and development in India', *Population and Development Review*, 21(2): 281–305.

Mazumdar, V. 1994. 'Amniocentesis and sex selection'. Occasional paper number 21. New Delhi: CWDS (mimeo).

McElroy, M. 1990. 'The empirical content of Nash-bargained households', *The Journal of Human Resources*, 25(4): 559–83.

McKee, L. 1984. 'Sex differentials in survivorship and the customary treatment of the infants and children', *Medical Anthropology*, 8(2): 91–108.

Meillassoux, C. 1981. *Maidens, meal and money: Capitalism and the domestic economy*. Cambridge: Cambridge University Press.

Mendelbaum, D.G. 1988. *Women's seclusion and men's honour*. Tuscon: University Of Arizona Press.

Mies, M. 1982. *The Lace-makers of Nasrapur: Indian housewives produce for the world market*. London: Zed Books.

——. 1988. *Women: The last colony*. London: Zed Books.

*Miller, B.D. 1981. *The endangered sex*. Ithaca, N.Y.: Cornell University Press.

——. 1984. 'Daughter neglect, women's work and marriage', *Medical Anthropology*, 8(2): 109–25.

——. 1989. 'Changing patterns of juvenile sex ratios in rural India, 1961 to 1971', *Economic and Political Weekly*, 24(22): 1229-35.

——. 1993. *Sex and Gender Hierarchies*. Cambridge: Cambridge University Press.

Mitra, A. 1978. *Implications of Declining Sex Ratio in India's Population*. New Delhi: ICSSR.

Mitra, A. 1993. 'Sex ratio and violence—Spurious results', *Economic and Political Weekly*, 28(1): 67.

Moore, H. 1988. *Feminism and anthropology*. Cambridge, Polity Press.

Mosk, C. and **Johansson, S.R.** 1986. 'Income and mortality: Evidence from modern Japan', *Population and Development Review*, 12: 416–37.

Murthi, M., Guio, A. and **Drèze, J.** 1995. *Mortality, fertility and gender bias in India: A district level analysis*. DERC discussion paper number 61, London School of Economics.

Nag, M. 1989. 'Political awareness as a factor in accessibility of health services', *Economic and Political Weekly*, 24(8): 1229–35.

Nanda, A.R. 1993. *Union primary abstracts for Scheduled Castes and Scheduled Tribes*. Census of India, Paper 1 of 1993. New Delhi: Office of the Registrar General and Census Commissioner, India.

Natarajan, D. 1972. *The changes in sex ratio*, Census centenary monograph number 6, Census of India. New Delhi: Office of the Registrar General and Census Commissioner, India.

Nath, V. 1991. 'Official paper on 1991 Census', *Economic and Political Weekly*, 24: 1229-36.

Nathanson, C. 1984. 'Sex differences in mortality', *Annual Review of Sociology*, 10: 191–213.

Nayar, U.S. and **Anilkumar, K.** 1994. *Declining sex ratio and the problems of female infanticide—A study in Gujarat*. New Delhi: Department of Women and Child Development, Government of India (mimeo).

Nigam, R.C. 1964. *Language Tables, Census of India 1961, Vol. -I, Part II-C (ii)*. New Delhi: Office of the Registrar General and Census Commissioner, India.

NSSO 1991. *Sarvekshana*, July–September 1991: S-4–S34.

———. 1994. *Sarvekshana*, April–June, 1994: 1–80.

Oldenberg, P. 1992. 'Sex ratio, son preference and violence in India', *Economic and Political Weekly*, 27(49): 2657–62.

Padmanabha. P. 1981. 'The decisive decade: A note on the provisional results of the 1981 Census of India', *Yojana*, 25(9).

Pakrasi, K. and **Halder, A.** 1973. 'The sex ratio in India by parity and region', *Acta Med. Auxol*, 42–55.

Papanek, H. 1984. 'False specialization and the Purdah of scholarship—A review article', *Journal of Asian Studies*, 44(1): 127–47.

———. 1989. 'Family status production work: Women's contribution to social mobility and class differentiation', in Krishnaraj, M. and Chanana, K. (eds.), *Gender and the Household Domain*, pp. 96–116. New Delhi: Sage.

———. 1990. 'To each less than she needs, from each more than she can do: Allocations, entitlements and value', in Tinker (ed.), pp. 162–81. Oxford: Oxford University Press.

Parkin, R. 1992. *The Munda of central India: An account of their social organisation*. Delhi: Oxford University Press.

Parry, J.P. 1979. *Caste and kinship in Kangra*. London: Routledge and Kegan Paul.

Pereira, J. 1993. 'What does equity in health mean?', *Journal of Social Policy*, 22(1): 19–48.

Pisani E. and **Zaba B.** (Forthcoming) Son preference, sex selection and the marriage market.

Possehl, G.L. 1987, 'African millets in South-Asian pre history', in Jacobson (ed.).

Preston, S.H, Keyfitz, N. and **Schoen, R.** 1972. *Causes of death: Life tables for national populations*, London: Seminar Press.

Preston, S.H. and **Haines, M.R.** 1991. *Fatal Years: Child mortality in late nineteenth century America*. Princeton: Princeton University Press.

Raju, S. 1991. 'Gender and deprivation: A theme revisited with geographical perspectives', *Economic and Political Weekly*, December 7: 2877–39.

Ram, K. 1991. 'The ideology of feminity and women's work in a fishing community in south India', in Afsher, H. and Agarwal, B. (eds.), *Women, poverty and ideology in Asia*. London: Macmillan.

Ramchandran, K.V. and **Deshpande, V.A.** 1964. 'The sex ratio at birth in India by region', *Milbank Memorial Fund Quarterly*, 84–94.

Rao, V. 1993. 'The rising price of husbands: A hedonic analysis of dowry increases in India', *Journal of Political Economy*, 101(4): 666–77.

Raza, M. and **Ahmad, A.** 1990. *An Atlas of Tribal India*. New Delhi: Concept/ICSSR.

Rosenzweig, M. and **Schultz, T.P.** 1982. 'Market opportunities, genetic endowment and intra-family resource distribution: Child survival in rural India', *American Economic Review*, 72: 803–15.

Roy, B.K. 1972. 'An approach to regionalisation of types of farming in India', in Government of India, pp. 227–52.

Roy Burman, B.K. 1972. 'Distribution of the Scheduled Tribes of India: An exploratory geo-cultural appraisal' in Govt. of India, pp. 483–538.

Saraswati, Pandita Ramabai. 1888. *The high caste Hindu women*, London: George Bell and Sons (Reprinted, 1976, West Port: Hyprian Press Inc.)

Sargent, J., Harriss-White, B. and **Janakranjan, S.** 1996. *Development, property and deteriorating life chances for girls in India: A preliminary discussion with special reference to Tamil Nadu*. Madras: MIDS (mimeo).

Schrimshaw, S. 1978. 'Infant mortality and behaviour in regulation of family size', *Population and Development Review*, 4(3): 383–403.

Schultz, T.P. 1990. 'Testing the neoclassical model of labour supply and fertility', *The Journal of Human Resources*, 25(4): 599–634.

Schwartzberg, J.E. (ed.). 1992. *A historical atlas of South Asia*. Oxford: Oxford University Press.

Seeta Prabhu, K. 1994. *Impact of structural adjustment on social sector expenditure: Evidence from Indian states*. Department of Economics, University of Bombay. (mimeo).

Sen, A.K. 1981. *Poverty and famines: An essay on entitlements and deprivations*. Oxford: Clarendon Press.

*——. 1985. *Commodities and capabilities*. Amsterdam: North-Holland

——. 1987a. *Gender and cooperative conflicts*. United Nations University, WIDER discussion paper number 18.

——. 1987b. *India and Africa: What do we have to learn from each other?* United Nations University, WIDER discussion paper number 19.

——. 1987c. *The standard of living*. Cambridge: Cambridge University Press.

——. 1990. '*Gender and cooperative conflicts*' in Tinker (ed.).

*——. 1992. *Inequality Re-examined*. Oxford: Clarendon Press.

Shapiro, S., Schlesinger, E.R. and **Nesbitt, R.E.L.**. 1968. *Infant, perinatal, maternal and childhood mortality in the United States*. Cambridge, MA.: Harvard University Press.

Sharma, M. and **Vanjani, U.** 1993. 'When more means less—Assessing the impact of dairy development in the lives and health of women in rural Rajasthan (India)', *Social Science and Medicine*, 37(11): 1377–89.

Sharma, U. 1993. 'Dowry in north India: Its consequences for women', in Uberoi, P. (ed.).

Simmons, G.B., Smucker, C., Bernstein, S. and **Jensen, E.** 1982. 'Post neonatal mortality in rural India: Implications of an economic model', *Demography*, 19(3): 371–89.

Smucker, C.M., Simmons, G.B., Bernstein, S., and **Misra, B.D.** 1980. 'Neonatal mortality in South Asia: The special role of Tetanus', *Population Studies* 34(2): 321–36.

*Sopher, D.E. (ed.) 1980. *An Exploration of India*. London: Longman.

Spate, O.H.K. and Learmonth, A.T.A. 1967. *India and Pakistan: Land, people and economy*. London; Methuen & Co.

Srinivasan, K. 1994. 'Sex ratios—what they hide and what they reveal', Economic and Political Weekly, 30(51): 3233–34

Srinivasan, V. 1994 *Female Infanticide in Bihar*. Patna: Adithi (mimeo).

Srivastava, 1979. *Migration in India*. Census of India, 1971, paper 2 of 1979, New Delhi: Office of the Registrar General and Census Commissioner, India.

Subramaniam, R. 1996. 'Gender bias in India: The importance of household fixed-effects', *Oxford Economics Papers*, 48(2): 280–99.

Thapar, M. 1985. *Recent archaeological discoveries of India*, Paris: UNESCO.

Thomas, D. 1990. 'Intra-household resource allocation: An inferential approach', The *Journal of Human Resources*, 25(4): 635–64.

Tinker A., 1996. *Improving women's health in India*. Washington D.C.: World Bank.

Trautmann, T.R. 1981. *Dravidian Kinship*. Cambridge: Cambridge University Press.

——. 1993. 'The study of Dravidian kinship', in Uberoi, P. (ed.), pp. 74–90.

United Nations. *Demographic yearbooks*—Different years.

Upadhyaya, C. 1994. 'Beyond gender', *Economic and Political Weekly*, 25(45): 2922–24.

Vannemann, R. and Barnes, D. 1992. 'Appendix V-6, Economic Activities', *Indian development district database*. Centre for Population, Gender and Social Inequality: University of Maryland.

Vera-Sanso, P. 1995. 'Community, seclusion and female labour force participation in Madras, India', *Third World Planning Review*, 17(2): 155–67.

Venkatachalam R. and Srinivasan V. 1993. *Female infanticide*, New Delhi: Har-Anand.

Visaria, L. 1988. 'Level, trends and determinants of infant mortality in India', in Jain, A. and Visaria, P. (eds.), pp. 67–126.

Visaria, P. 1971. *The sex ratio of the population of India*. Monograph number 10, Census of India 1961. New Delhi: Office of the Registrar General, India.

——. 1994. 'Rural non-farm employment in India: Trends and issues for research', *Indian Journal of Agricultural Economics*: 50(3): 399–409.

Visaria, P. and Visaria, L. 1981. 'Indian population scene after 1981 Census', *Economic and Political Weekly*, November (special issue): 1727–80.

Wadley, S. 1993. 'Family composition strategies in rural north India', *Social Science and Medicine*, 37(11): 1367–76.

Waldron, I. 1983. 'Sex differences in human mortality: The role of genetic factors', *Social Science and Medicine*, 17: 321–33.

Wolpert, S. 1993. *A new history of India*. Oxford: Oxford University Press.

Woolley, F.R. and Marshall, J. 1994. 'Measuring inequality within the household', *Review of Income and Wealth*, 40(4): 415–32.

Index

About the author

Satish Balram Agnihotri belongs to the Indian Administrative Service and is currently Secretary to the Government of Orissa in the Department of Women and Child Development. He obtained his Ph.D. from the School of Development Studies, University of East Anglia, UK, after doing an MA in Rural Development, preceded by an M.Tech. in Environmental Sciences and Engineering and a M.Sc. in Physics.

Dr Agnihotri is a Fellow of LEAD (Leadership in Environment and Development) International, New York. He has worked in the fields of renewable energy, environment, industry, rural development and general administration. His current research interests include gender inequality, policy innovations in government and promotion of appropriate technology. Dr Agnihotri has contributed several articles to journals such as *Gender, Technology and Development, Economic and Political Weekly* and *Journal of Development Studies*.